THE HOUSE OF MORGAN

THE
HOUSE
OF
MORGAN

——◆——

EDWIN P. HOYT, JR.

ILLUSTRATED

DODD, MEAD & COMPANY

NEW YORK

For my bankers

Library of Congress Catalog Card Number: 66-24266

*Printed in the United States of America
by The Cornwall Press, Inc., Cornwall, N. Y.*

FOREWORD

A book about any family whose roots can be traced back to the days of the *Mayflower* must depend heavily on library researches and this one is no exception. The author is under considerable obligation to librarians at the Connecticut State Historical Society, the Connecticut State Library, the Hartford Public Library, the Widener Library of Harvard University, the Sterling Library of Yale University, the New York Public Library, the Scoville Memorial Library of Salisbury, Connecticut, the Hotchkiss Library of Sharon, Connecticut, and the Kent Public Library of Kent, Connecticut, the Kent School Library, also of Kent, the Wisconsin State Historical Society of Madison, Wisconsin, and the Morgan Library of New York City for the loan of materials.

Since the purpose of this book was to examine the Morgan family within the framework of the development of America, the author has relied largely on the body of public information available, rather than seeking personal interviews with family, friends, and business associates. The exception here is in the author's seeking out of Henry S. Morgan. Mr. Morgan was kind enough to see the author and to steer him to what he called "reasonably accurate" sources of information, although he had no part in the book's planning or execution and made no attempt to interfere or even to discuss a point of view. This may not be readily apparent to the reader since the author has chosen to use only materials relating to the public lives of the Morgans, on the theory that for the purposes of the larger social study their private lives are their own.

In no way did Henry Morgan encourage the publication or writing of this book. No member of the Morgan family has approved or sponsored this book in any way, official or unofficial.

The House of Morgan has played an important part in the development of America, a role comparable only to that of the Rothschilds or Barings in England's growth of Empire. The Morgans directed the pattern of growth of American railroads, of the steel industry, and are as much responsible for the popularity of the combination as opposed to competition—sometimes called the trust—as any other bankers or industrialists. Of all these men in the many generations of American Morgans, Pierpont was the most illustrious and most celebrated, even to the partial misunderstanding of the importance of his father in the scheme of Morgan banking. In these pages the author has tried to tell, through the Morgans, something of the development of American banking, commerce, and industry, not in detail, but in the broad outlines. The bulk of the story has dealt with three men and their times: Junius Spencer Morgan, who might be called the founder of the House of Morgan as a banking house, although the roots go deeper; J. Pierpont Morgan; and J. P. Morgan, Jr., who, again, has been eclipsed by his father although he presided over the banking empire when it had reached its greatest strength, during and after World War I, until the Great Depression of the 1930's. This Morgan lived to face, which his father could have faced only with the greatest pain, the dessication of a baronial control of the American economy in the revolutionary social and political changes of the twentieth century. The later Morgans, Junius Spencer Morgan, Jr., and Henry Sturgis Morgan and their sons, are dealt with in this book only fragmentarily. Junius the younger became a corporation man. Henry S. Morgan's career is far more

like that of the earlier Morgans and receives more attention
because of it, and possibly not enough attention, when one
considers that he and his firm have financed huge corporate
expansions and government enterprises and even international
banking ventures; the difference, of course, is that financial management in the last half of the twentieth century had become a
very specialized business, and it does not offer the general control
or guidance of business management in general that were the
properties and responsibilities of earlier generations of Morgan
bankers. In the sense of control and manipulation the investment
banking business had changed completely by 1965 over a century,
for that business really became important in America just about a
century earlier, when the United States began to absorb the lessons of the industrial revolution and create an industrial economy.
Yet the change in method is not that complete: one day the
author asked Henry Sturgis Morgan if his grandfather, the great
Pierpont, would not be dumbfounded at the computerized and
complex investment banking procedure of the 1960's. Not at all,
he said. It was simply a matter of procedural differences, and
Pierpont Morgan would be quite at home in the banking world of
the last half of the twentieth century.

CONTENTS

PART THREE. The Making of the Financier

PART FOUR. The Maturity of Pierpont

PART FIVE. The New J. P. Morgan Company

ILLUSTRATIONS

Following page 140

xiii

INTRODUCTION

OF ALL THE GREAT American fortunes there is one which stands alone. Not because it is the greatest, although it has seemed to be so at times; not because it is the most spectacular, although it has sometimes seemed to be so; but because it was in its most important time the best-regulated and most responsible and in many ways the most useful fortune that was ever acquired in the United States. It is the fortune of the Morgan family of Massachusetts, Connecticut, London, and New York.

Many public misunderstandings have been encouraged about the Morgan fortune. One of the family, the best-known, is always numbered among the "robber barons" or the "malefactors of great wealth" or the "moguls," as those who created huge fortunes have been called at various times in American history. He is J. Pierpont Morgan. Others, the men who established the fortune and the men who now carry it on, are scarcely known at all. The Morgans have never sought publicity and have hidden from it when they might conveniently do so.

Yet, the Morgans are really not of the Robber Baron class. Those fortunes were more quickly earned usually by outright speculation. In the nineteenth century the Vanderbilt fortune was the most spectacular—in the manner of a Roman candle—achieving its zenith during the lifetime of the progenitor, crusty old Commodore Cornelius Vanderbilt, who began as a Staten Island farmer's boy and ended with holdings equal to the cash in the United States Treasury at the moment that he died. Others have amassed more money in terms of dollars even than the Commodore, and more power in what grew to be a far larger nation than his, but in his day he was the most wealthy man in the United States and the most powerful. Unlike the Morgans the Commodore *was* an industrial baron, and he was proud of the manner in which he acquired his wealth, staking his ability and imagination against those of all comers, on both sides of the Atlantic Ocean. Here it is useful, perhaps, to elucidate the figure of this greatest "robber baron" of them all. The Commodore always played a lone hand; by his own lights and those of his times he was neither dishonest nor dishonorable. His times were scarcely honorable times, in any arena. Politics, business, morality—all were at low ebb in the United States in his day. Vanderbilt's fortune was acquired by robbing speculators and by selling stock in his successful enterprises to those who wished to buy. Sometimes, if widows and orphans were so unwise as to invest in railroad securities when the Commodore was on a speculative rampage of his own, they would be wiped out; the Commodore was not considering them one way or the other. His natural enemies and prey were jackals—the Jay Goulds and the Daniel Drews and thousands of much smaller fry who did not toil to produce but earned their living by speculations in railroad stocks in Wall Street.

These were not the Morgan ways. The speculations of men like Vanderbilt and Harriman and the other railroad barons, however, were based on solid assets and accomplishments. The speculations would never have been possible or successful had they not been based on something of value. Someone was creating something. The commodore's skill was in the transportation industry. Others showed skills in other productive industries. For the Rockefellers it was oil. For the Carnegies it was steel. For the Guggenheims it was raw ores. For the Dukes it was tobacco. Almost all the great American fortunes were secured by exploitation, exploitation of a natural resource or a public demand (as with the Astors and New York City real estate), or both.

In the twentieth century it has become popular to be critical of all these exploiters and fortune makers because they showed so little of what we now call statesmanship or patriotism. Had any of these nineteenth-century fortune makers been forced to face these modern critics they would have been unable to understand why they were reviled. They did not consider themselves unpatriotic or scoundrels—they reserved these terms for the Goulds and Fisks and Daniel Drews. The respectable fortune makers considered these men to be scoundrels. They could tell you *why* they were scoundrels. Because they cheated everyone, even each other. They had no end in view save the acquisition of wealth, and when they were beloved at all it was by the unknowing public and not by their peers. The respectable American men of wealth considered themselves to be leaders in the American community, contributing to the national well-being, and they earnestly believed that the wealth they acquired through their exploits was no more than their due for what they contributed in steel products, cheap, fast transportation, new machines and new processes to speed the industrial revolution.

Few of these men of wealth lived to see the coming of the era in which they would be reviled. One did, and he was a Morgan— J. Pierpont Morgan—and when he saw for a moment, briefly at the last, how he was regarded by the American community it was enough to break his spirit. Like all the others of his family J. Pierpont Morgan had lived what seemed to him to be an honorable and upright life, the private life of a gentleman. He had accepted for many years the responsibilities that his position in the world of finance thrust upon him and his family, and he had discharged these in the only way that he understood. When he discovered in 1912 that there were important, decent people in America who truly believed him to be a scoundrel, he was shocked and dismayed. "So it has come to that," he said, and in saying it, this taciturn old man enunciated his despair. A few months after he made that statement he was dead.

The story of the Morgan family is very much the story of American business success, for one cannot say that the Morgans earned their huge fortune by exploiting natural resources or human beings. The growth of the Morgan fortune parallels the growth of America; the use of the Morgan fortune parallels social change in America. By friends, enemies, and the dispassionate, the Morgans are always regarded among the foremost of American business families. When he set out to expose the evils of the great American fortunes, Gustavus Myers put the Morgans high on his list. Another who exposed was Ferdinand Lundberg, who concerned himself with America's sixty greatest families, and showed how their interlocking directorates and marriages put Americans in a spider web. The Morgans were second on his list, and he did them the honor of estimating their fortunes somewhere between the two and a half billion dollars he attributed to the Rockefellers in 1937 and the single billion dollars he attributed to the Fords. John T. Flynn, once an admirer and then an adverse critic of great wealth, numbered the Morgans among a dozen men and women of fortune who represented to him the significant fortune-makers since the Renaissance. By any and all standards the Morgans always counted. One interesting matter is that most of the Morgan fortune was made conservatively and for the most part it paralleled the growth of what we now call America's gross national product. Another matter of interest is that among the men of fortune none regarded themselves as more responsible and more patriotic than the Morgans. No Morgan ever believed that he failed to serve his country in time of need, if he saw the need. Another interesting point unrecognized, except by such shrewd observers of wealth and social position as Cleveland Amory, is that the Morgan fortune predated J. Pierpont Morgan by two generations. Amory has referred to the Morgans as the aristocracy of American business. The Morgans of the last half of the twentieth century do not like that term, although secretly Pierpont might not have found it annoying. The Morgans regard themselves as responsible leaders in the American business community, and no one can gainsay them that, for there is no other American family which can claim quite so close a tie to the progress of America or even so great a force of influence on American history outside the political arena as the Morgans. No Morgan has ever engaged in elective politics at a level higher than that of town selectman. No Morgan has ever been an ambassador. Yet the Morgans have influenced the course of Congresses, of Presidents, of cabinets, and of embassies. More, they have, in three great financial crises in America and one abroad, influenced the course of history. Perhaps in England and in Europe the Rothschilds could be called so important a force in the affairs of government and men, but in the economic life of America there have been none to match the Morgans.

PART ONE

The Morgan Clan

I

MIGRATION

I N 1625 THE House of Stuart fell on evil days with the accession to the English throne of Charles I, for Charles faced a rebellious and willful group of lords in Parliament. After innumerable frustrations and difficulties in exercising his rights to the Crown, Charles dissolved Parliament four years later and began to rule as he saw fit, leaning heavily on William Laud, Bishop of London and later Archbishop of Canterbury of the established church.

Throughout the lands of the Stuarts the hard times and questionable devices of taxation brought hardship and misery and deep resentment to a half-formed nation that was struggling to bring unity and reason to its attitudes toward religion and political affairs. So far back does the story of the House of Morgan in America go, for the growth of that house has its roots in the dissatisfactions of the people of Wales in the first half of the seventeenth century.

Wales was never a rich land, and the branch of the Morgan family which was to send a son to New England was not wealthy. It was a land of squires and small freeholders for the most part. Wales had come completely under English rule only in the middle of the sixteenth century and not all the new ways had been absorbed. Welsh was still the language of the homes and churches, but the educated classes began to learn the English language, which they had to do in order to retain their lands and privileges. The peasants and the lower classes would be another two centuries in coming to speak English, but by the time of the accession of Charles I the lesser nobility were all bilingual.

The coming of English rule to Wales was not an unmixed blessing for the younger sons of the squires. Anglicism brought primogeniture and entail, two obligations of inheritance which effectively limited the opportunities of younger sons of daughters of all but the noblest houses.

So it was with the branch of the House of Morgan which sent a son to the colonies. It is said by some genealogists that the family had descended to trade by the time that Miles Morgan was born in Llandoff, Glamorgan County, but the family was of sufficient importance and lineage to be among the minority of English-speaking Welshmen. They were harness-makers but they were educated tradesmen. William Morgan, Miles's father, moved to Bristol, England, to conduct the business.

Miles Morgan saw little future for himself in a land torn by argument over taxes and royal practices, and when he was twenty years old he sailed for the Massachusetts colony, arriving in April 1636 with two brothers, John and James. He arrived in the middle of a frightening power struggle which involved the Puritan church. Sir Henry Vane, a young aristocrat who was elected governor of Massachusetts colony in 1636, came under the influence of Anne Hutchinson, Mrs. William Hutchinson, who espoused a milder form of Puritanism called Antinomianism. One important part of this offshoot of Puritanism was a reduction in the power of the clergy.

This rebellion was put down in the years 1636 and 1637. Sir Henry Vane returned to England in disgrace, and John Winthrop, who represented the old order, became governor. Anne Hutchinson was banished from Massachusetts colony and joined the Roger Williams colony on Narragansett Bay. The Archbishop of Canterbury, close advisor to His Majesty, King Charles, looked with considerable disfavor on the various heresies of New England and sought to have the Massachusetts colony charter revoked. So there was conflict aplenty among the towns of the eastern seaboard of Massachusetts when Miles Morgan arrived there and went to Roxbury. He saw opportunity and perhaps escape from the entrapments of religious feuding in the discussion of a new settlement to be located at Agawam, a fertile spot on the Connecticut River. This was meadow land, for the most part. It had been called Agawam by the Indians; the name Springfield was given in 1640 to the settlement by William Pynchon of Roxbury, because Springfield was the name of his family home near Chelmsford in Essex. Pynchon advanced the money to buy the land from the Indians and the colonists agreed to repay him in time.

Springfield was settled in 1636. Miles Morgan joined William Pynchon and a number of other men of Roxbury to go there and build a village. The settlement began with a dozen families and was limited to fifty, although that limitation soon was forgotten. Although Springfield was legally a part of Massachusetts colony, effectively it was bound to the other colonies along the Connecticut River, which made it part of Connecticut for tax purposes and the furnishing of troops. Along with Hartford and Windsor and Wethersfield, the Springfield men faced the common enemies of cold and famine and the unfriendly Pequot Indians.

These were the days of Uncas, the Mohican chieftain who befriended the English colonists against their fierce enemies. The name was familiar in every Massachusetts and Connecticut home. Young Miles Morgan knew it and Indian troubles well.

Miles paid taxes in Springfield in the beginning on 34¼ acres of land. His name is not often found in the records of Springfield at the first. But by 1644 Miles Morgan was settled on his land which ran between what is now Main Street and Ferry Lane, with buildings in the North Parish of West Springfield on the west side of the Connecticut River. Each settler had a house lot which was eight rods from the street to the river, a like width on the meadow in front of the house, and a wood lot perhaps eighty by one hundred rods, located as close as possible to his house lot.

Miles Morgan had met a young woman named Prudence Gilbert on the ship that brought him to Massachusetts or somewhere in the colony. The family story, then, is that he bought a horse on the coast and carried his bride and her belongings back to the new settlement, accompanied by an Indian guide and a white male companion for extra safety. Miles then appears in the town records as father of the first of his children, on the fourteenth of December, 1644. It was his daughter Mary, the first of eight children born to Miles and Prudence Morgan before she died in 1660. Although these children were Morgans they do not belong to the House of Morgan whose fortunes are traced in these pages, any more than did the descendants of John and James Morgan, the two brothers of Miles who came across the Atlantic either with him or at about the same time. James settled in New London and begot a race notable in the trades of the sea. John left Massachusetts for Virginia, to establish the southern branch of the family, which was to include several famous military men. All are collateral descendants of William Morgan of Wales and Bristol, England, but the particular heredity of the banking family of Morgans begins with the second marriage of Miles Morgan in the winter of 1669 to Elizabeth Bliss, the daughter of a Hartford settler.

Springfield was an unusual settlement in one way: unlike the older villages and towns of the Eastern seaboard this frontier community placed scant reliance on religion. Perhaps the reason for its founding was to escape the strictures of the religious. Whether or no, in 1636 in Springfield no man need belong to the church in order to enjoy the freedoms of citizenship or to hold office as was the requirement elsewhere.

Miles Morgan prospered in Springfield, buying more land with the profits from his farming. His cattle brand became well known in the community's common meadows where all pastured; it was two slits in the left ear, straight down. He was appointed surveyor of highways and was given a seat in the third row of the meeting house by the town selectmen, a sure sign of his respectability, for the poor and worthless were placed under the stairs and up in the gallery.

Each settlement organized its own militia. William Pynchon was colonel of the Springfield militia as the principal organizer of the town and it was his responsibility to lead it into battle against the Indians when the need arose. Miles Morgan soon became a sergeant in the militia. He was given other responsibilities by the community, too. He was for a time a "fence viewer," which meant that he walked the town's fences to see that they were kept in order, and also to make sure that no citizen placed a fence where it ought not to be. He was also a monitor for the church, keeping the unruly from disturbing the service on Sundays.

For forty years the little settlement lived in relative peace, expanding to embrace a tract about twenty-five miles square. Nearly all this land was purchased from the Indians, piecemeal, for the Springfield colonists were a law-abiding lot who seemed to respect the rights of all. There was trouble and excitement in those years, but much of the trouble was internal. William Pynchon made the mistake of publishing a tract on redemption in which he offered some views that were not acceptable to the religious authorities in Boston and Salem. Pynchon had been magistrate; he was relieved of this honor and responsibility and called to justify himself in court. Knowing the futility of argument, Pynchon retracted his views but was so chagrined with the course of events in Massachusetts that he returned to England. His son remained in Springfield, but slowly the settlement lost its individuality and succumbed to the old Puritan ways.

As Miles Morgan's children by his first wife grew up he gave them pieces of his land so they could start life for themselves, and this in itself is an indication of his prosperity, for of the eight children of his first marriage, seven grew to manhood and womanhood. Four boys and three girls, each had the right to demand a fair share.

Two years after his second marriage another child was born to Miles Morgan. This boy was Nathaniel Morgan. Four years later came disaster, threatening all the Morgans and all they owned.

The seeds of the disaster were sown in the year of little Nathaniel Morgan's birth. The troublesome Pequots had been wiped out thirty-five years earlier, but in 1671 five tribes which had always been more or less friendly to the whites began to feel restless in the surge of English expansion into their lands. The Wampanoags had been pushed to the eastern shores of Narragansett Bay from their east-coast homeland. The Narragansetts were just then facing a legal attempt, carried out in the white man's courts, to foreclose a mortgage on almost all their tribal lands which extended from the Thames River to Narragansett Bay. They neither understood nor accepted a white man's law that said men could take the lands for a piece of paper. The Mohegans lived in the hill country between the Connecticut and the Thames Rivers, and their settlements adjoined those of Miles Morgan's town. The Podunks and the Nipmucks were also unhappy with settler encroachments on their hunting grounds north of Springfield.

The sachem or chief of the Wampanoags was Philip, son of old Massassoit who had befriended the colonists in their early days of need. Old friendships could not survive the demands of the colony for land, however, and in 1675 open hostilities broke out following a number of incidents in which white civilization exploded against the Indians ways.

That summer the first Indian attack was made on Swansea. The colonists replied by sending a force of Plymouth and Boston militia against Mount Hope, the Wampanoag stronghold on the Taunton River. This attack rallied all the Indians to the cause of Philip, and the siege of the various towns along the frontier became general. Mendon was hit on July 14, then Brookfield on August 2, Lancaster on August 19, and Deerfield and Hadley simultaneously on September 1. The next day the Indians struck Northfield and did such damage, killed so many settlers, and frightened the rest so much that the settlement was abandoned as worthless and defenseless four days later.

From the east and the south the news of the attacks on other settlements reached Springfield early in the summer. There was little to be done but fortify several houses and wait. The men carried their muskets and powderhorns with them into the fields every day. Major Pynchon and Captain Appleton formed the men into platoons and squads under their sergeants, and Sergeant Morgan drilled his men and instructed them in the arts of defense.

All summer the colonists of Springfield waited. It seemed somehow unreal that anything could happen in this valley of rolling hills and meadows. The Springfield Indians were as friendly as ever, or seemed to be, and there were no incidents. The Indians lived in a settlement on Long Hill, south of the town. Although there were no incidents, Major Pynchon was taking no chances, so he put Sergeant Morgan and the others to work erecting palisades along the southern side of the settlement, facing Long Hill and the Indian fort atop it.

Quiet as they were, the Springfield Indians were allied to Philip and his warriors. On the night of October 3, three hundred of Philip's Wampanoag braves were taken secretly into the Indian fort and hidden there. They laid plans to burn the town below and massacre all the inhabitants.

In the Indian fort that night was a brave named Toto, a member of the Windsor tribe, and a friend of the white settlers in Windsor. He stole away and told the people of Windsor what was going to happen to the settlement at Springfield, and the men of Windsor sent a rider hastily to warn their fellow settlers of the danger.

The news aroused Springfield that night and all the settlers deserted their houses and rushed into the stockades. Nothing happened. The next day the Springfield Indians were as friendly and unconcerned as ever. The report must have been false, or so many of the settlers began to believe. The Reverend Mr. Glover set a brave example for the others. He had fled to the Pynchon House, which was fortified, taking his library with him so it might be saved. Now he brought out his library and went home, telling others that they must not be stampeded by the hysteria of the times.

On October 4 all was quiet in the town and on Long Hill above. The townspeople were becoming convinced that the story of an impending attack was not true. The Reverend Mr. Glover's bravery and disregard for rumor was an example for them all. Slowly they began to go back about their affairs.

Only the military men were suspicious. Major Pynchon and Captain Appleton were not in the town. With the news of the attack on Hadley they had taken some of the men and rushed to defend that place, leaving Lieutenant Thomas Cooper in charge of the defense of Springfield.

Despite the Reverend Glover's calm, Lieutenant Cooper was worried. On the morning of October 5 he decided that the only way to determine the truth was to investigate the Indian fort, and he and Thomas Miller set out for Long Hill, carrying their guns.

When they came within range, the Indian opened fire on them, knowing that they were certain to be discovered. Both men were struck by arrows and when they were down the Indians launched their attack on the town below the hill. Lieutenant Cooper tried to help his companion, but when he turned, Miller was dead. Mortally wounded, the lieutenant made his way back to the Pynchon blockhouse and died there, trying to direct the defense.

The Indians swarmed down the Long Hill and over the palisades into the town. A man and a woman who were slow in reaching the forts were killed, but all other settlers were saved. The Indians raged through the houses and barns, looting what they wanted and destroying and burning the rest. They set fire to thirty houses and twenty-five barns, while the settlers, in the blockhouses, could do nothing but watch and shoot at any movement. The Indians burned the grain mills and the jail, but they were afraid to come near the meetinghouse.

Springfield's siege ended quickly because the Indians knew that part of the band of trained soldiers had gone to the defense of Hadley and would be returning, perhaps at any hour. They took their plunder and vanished into the woods, leaving the people of Springfield to survey their misery. With winter coming on, the burning of houses and barns was no less than disaster.

Fortunately, that part of the settlement which stood on the west bank of the river had not been attacked or destroyed by the Indians in their haste. This was the area in which Miles Morgan's major holdings were located, so his property was saved.

The winter was a harsh one for the settlers. Grain and food were kept under armed guard and were shared out among all the unfortunate. There was some talk of abandoning the settlement, but those who held land on the west bank counseled against it. Half the settlement had been saved. To abandon Springfield would be to give comfort to the hated Indians, and this would never do.

The Indian war moved away from Springfield, but not far and not for long. The next year Miles's third son, twenty-six-year-old Pelatiah, was killed by the braves of Sachem Philip. It was two more years before the Indians were ready to give up the struggle, after having been virtually wiped out.

At the end of the war the Morgan holdings were increased, for the lands of the Springfield Indians were seized in reprisal for the raid. Miles received part of the swamp that abutted his meadows on the west side of the river. He continued to prosper. He was elected constable, later selectman, and as he grew older he was considered to be one of the elder statesmen of the community as well as one of its most substantial citizens in terms of property. He was chosen to be a member of the committee to grant land, which gave him grave importance in the community. In 1684, when he was sixty-eight years old, he was freed from the necessity of performing further military service. He continued then as a man of substance until his death in 1699 at the age of eighty-three. The Morgan family then was an established and prosperous part of the community of Massachusetts.

CHAPTER

II

THE MORGANS OF MASSACHUSETTS

WHEN OLD Miles Morgan died just before the beginning of the eighteenth century, he willed to his youngest son, Nathaniel, the property the young man had been using since his marriage in 1691. Nathaniel had married Hannah Bird, the daughter of a Farmington man, and she had borne four of their nine children. They were living on a farm of seven acres which was located on the House Meadow at Agawam, surrounded by other houses, and a farm of forty acres in Chicopee field. Nathaniel was renting this from his father at the nominal fee of six pounds each year. This was the old man's way of disposing of his property. For one reason, he did this to avoid taxes on the estate. More important, he was shrewd enough to know that after his death there might be a contest over his holdings if he tried to leave his property by will. So instead he disposed of all his property while still alive, renting it to the children until his death. Thus each had his inheritance and there was no quarreling. It was an astute means of avoiding difficulties, particularly those which might be involved since there were two different families.

There seemed to be no difficulty among the children of his two

marriages, however. Nathaniel and his three half brothers administered the estate.

Miles's personal property at the time of his death indicated the
degree of change, for he had come to the new world with only
his clothing and a tiny bit of money. On his death, to the daughters
went the old man's personal property, as was the custom in New
England. It consisted of his clothing, homespun, and his bedding;
a brass kettle, a small iron kettle, a frying pan, and an iron pot
for cooking; fire tongs and pot hooks for cooking in the big open
fireplace; a hatchet and two axes for cutting firewood and hewing
logs; a cooking fork with long handle and tines, ladles, platters,
knives, a stone jug, a quart glass, an old looking glass and a bone
comb; a musket and a cutlass, five or six barrels, a tub, two pails,
a chest and a truckle bed which could be wheeled under the big
bed, and the old bed and two chairs. Besides this, daughter Hannah received five pounds, eighteen shillings, and a good cow, and
daughter Lydia received five pounds, eighteen shillings, and perhaps the heifer that belonged to the cow.

These personal belongings told much about the spartan simplicity of life in the Springfield community, where Miles's most
important possessions were still his hatchet, axes, musket, and
cutlass for protection against the wilderness and the Indians. Still,
many changes had come to Massachusetts since the days when
Miles and the others had settled the plains of Agawam. There
were the Indian wars, but besides these, the colony had been
troubled by the difficulties in the homeland, where Charles I had
lost his throne and then his head. Under the Commonwealth, Massachusetts became restive and in 1652 declared herself independent, but the Puritans were largely sympathetic to the Commonwealth in England. In 1661, after Charles II was proclaimed king
and the monarchy rested secure again, Massachusetts came in for
more trouble. Commissioners were sent to Massachusetts to
investigate the government there, and to compel loyalty to the
Crown. They received only token submission. These difficulties
persisted until the beginning of the eighteenth century.

The Morgans took little part in political or religious arguments,
and none at all in such affairs outside the community of Spring-

field. Old Miles had been respected for his probity and hard work. So was Nathaniel respected by the people of Springfield. He was a grown man of twenty-six when his father died, himself father of a growing family. Soon he succeeded to some of his father's civic responsibilities. He became fence viewer, which was by that time a far more important post, corresponding in some ways to the post of official surveyor. Later he was hay warden, a post that continued in importance in the community as long as certain lands were held in common. He, too, was constable of the town for a time and surveyor of highways. He also served as town assessor.

Nathaniel and Hannah Morgan prospered with the colony. Springfield was yet purely a farming region; Nathaniel and his seven sons farmed the land and sold their produce by sending it down the river if there was a surplus. They bought their plow-shares and metal spoons and cooking pots from peddlers who came either by boat or across the grassy trails by foot. Their wives spun thread from the wool of their sheep and they wove it themselves, into cloth.

Each household was still largely self-sufficient at the beginning of the eighteenth century. The men hunted for venison and other game, the women grew garden crops, and occasionally a cow or a steer was killed to supply the family with meat. This was not done often because cattle were too valuable for the table, by and large, in even such a prosperous landhold as that of Nathaniel Morgan.

Most of his sons married late, in their thirties, which showed how great a sense of responsibility they had, to first create their own livelihood before establishing a family. Of the seven sons, fifth was Joseph Morgan, who learned the weaver's trade in this growing village, which by the end of the first quarter of the century could support a weaver. Joseph farmed on his father's land as well. And like the others he accepted his responsibilities to the community. In 1723, when he was twenty-one years old, he became a soldier, a private in the company of Captain Josiah Kellogg of Suffield. He was called out to help fight a rebellious tribe of Indians, and in the ten weeks that he served that year he was paid five English pounds for his effort. Two years later he served for four months, earning not quite ten pounds, and then his military service ended.

Joseph worked as farmer and weaver for the next twelve years. There was a change in the community by then; money had come to Springfield. With the increase in goods and lands available, money was found to be useful for the first time. Joseph did not have to depend on his father for his earnings and was thus the first truly independent son of the family since Miles. With the money he received for weaving cloth for others he began to purchase lands, not just in his own town but in Tattum, Block Bridge, Westfield Path, and several other small communities around Springfield.

Nathaniel, the father, lived until 1752. Like his father before him, he divided his holdings among his sons before he died. Joseph Morgan received a part of the Chicopee Field lot, but only a part of it. It was not a matter of great importance, because by the middle of the eighteenth century Joseph had prospered well enough himself, so well that in his thirty-third year in 1735 he married Mary Stebbins and began raising his own family, on a farm of two hundred acres, which he mortgaged for £180. Like the two generations of American Morgans before him, Joseph sired many children, eight in all. Such large families were common and necessary, for the hardiness and longevity of the Morgans was more the exception than the rule among American families of the eighteenth century. Disease and Indians were the usual menaces. The Morgans *were* unusual; only one of Joseph's children died young, his second son, Baby Titus, who lived less than two years. The name was used again; eleven months after the baby's death another son was born and he was also named Titus Morgan. One reason for the high survival rate of the Morgans was the family physique. The boys all tended to grow tall and burly and strong.

In this third generation, living a hundred years after Grandfather Miles Morgan had come to the American wilderness, there was still plenty of room for all seven of his grandsons to live and prosper in Springfield and West Springfield, where the family properties were located. Not so in the fourth generation. Two of Joseph's five sons moved away from Springfield, Judah to East-hampton and Jesse to Northampton. The colony was becoming more crowded.

By 1640, when the spate of emigration from England ended, 298 ships had come to Massachusetts colony since the beginning, bringing 21,200 passengers, or four thousand families, and these had spread out and multiplied in the course of the century.

Seven of Miles Morgan's nine children married and bore children of their own. Six of Nathaniel's children married and bore children. Seven of Joseph's children married and bore children. So, in a hundred years Miles already had far more than one hundred living descendants. And as the population of all Massachusetts increased thus, the mode of living changed.

Joseph's land purchases accounted in part for the movement of the boys. Everything was growing and spreading out.

The first son of this Joseph was Joseph Morgan, Jr., who was born in 1736. He grew up a typical Massachusetts farm boy, learning to handle the cattle and to make hay and grow crops. In 1755, when the French and Indian War was well begun, he enlisted in the Springfield company of Captain Benjamin Day to join William Johnson's expedition to Lake George where thirty-five hundred New England men and four hundred Indians went to build a fort in anticipation of a French attack on the region. The fort was called Fort William Henry. On the eighth of September the French, under Baron Dieskau, did attack the English colonials, with a mixed force of foot soldiers and Indian irregulars. The English colonists stood fast and defeated the French in what was to be called the Battle of Lake George. Their commanders wanted the men to move on against Crown Point, but the New Englanders objected. They had won their battle. Harvest time was fast approaching, and they were eager to be home to put up their crops for the coming winter. So home they went, and Joseph Morgan, Jr., was mustered out with the other colonials, collected his pay of £4 1s. 11d. and went back to work on his father's farm.

Two years later Joseph, Jr., was back in service, this time under Colonel Monro, and again he was at Fort William Henry on Lake George. This time the French were in earnest in their attack. They came heavily reinforced under the Marquis de Montcalm, and after taking Forts Oswego and George on August 9, 1757, they attacked Fort William Henry. Colonel Monro was outnumbered and surrounded, and he surrendered the fort, expecting the treatment of prisoners that was usual among Europeans. Instead, he and his nearly defenseless men were set upon by Indians who were with the French and they were forced to fight a rearguard action all the way to Fort Edward.

Young Joseph Morgan survived this massacre and came home again for the harvest, and the winter. The next summer once again he was in uniform, again in action against the French. This time it was the French who were defeated and reeling back, first from Niagara, Crown Point, and the attack up the St. Lawrence. He joined in the battle of Quebec that ended with the ascent of the Plains of Abraham and the fight that the British won, where both British General Wolfe and French General Montcalm were killed.

Lieutenant Morgan, one might say, had seen enough of war to last him all his life when he came home to return to farming in the winter of 1759–60. He did not go back to soldiering. There was no need. The French surrendered Canada that year and the danger was ended.

Five years passed on the farm, and then the twenty-nine-year-old Joseph married Experience Smith in 1765. Five daughters were born to them before the Revolution. His father died in 1773. Three years later, in the spring of 1776, after the battles of Lexington and Concord and the organization of the rebellion against the Crown, Joseph Morgan was elected Captain of the Eighth Company of the Third Regiment of Hampshire County, Colonel John Moseley's regiment. On October 21 he took a detachment of ten men from Springfield to Fort Ticonderoga. The fortress was in trouble and seemed in danger of imminent attack by forces led by Sir Guy Charleton, British commander in Canada. For several months General Benedict Arnold and General Carleton had been gathering fleets and troops on Lake Champlain. On October 11 Arnold moved his 83-gun fleet into the channel between Valcour island and the western shore of the lake. Carleton came with an 87-gun fleet of far better trained crews; he attacked and in a seven-hour battle crippled the Americans. That night Arnold was lucky to escape by slipping past the British in the darkness. Two days later another engagement was fought at Split Rock, and then the American flotilla was totally destroyed. Carleton occupied Crown Point, and it seemed certain that he would undertake a siege of the American fortress at Ticonderoga. That was the reason for the hurried call to Springfield and every other town that could spare men to send to defend the fortress. Captain Morgan and his men hurried to the defense, but by the time they arrived General Carleton had decided that the winter was too close to undertake a costly siege. The British kept watch at Crown Point until November 3, then withdrew back into Canada, and Captain Morgan came home to Springfield.

All during the revolutionary war he was on call, and often on active military duty. He was, however, in his forties and a responsible leader of the town of Springfield, so as the war continued he found himself less concerned with the military activities of the day and more with the problems of supplies and securing of political independence. He was a member of the Springfield Committee of Correspondence, which was charged with the responsibility of keeping in touch with other communities, and keeping the people informed of the progress of the war and the need for colonial union against the foe. He served on committees that provided the ragged colonial armies with guns, clothing, and blankets. He served his town as selectman and tithingman and in half a dozen other positions.

As the war drew to a close he was appointed to a special commission to consider the proposed form of government for Massachusetts and to draw up the state constitution.

Joseph's son, the third Joseph Morgan, was born in 1780 on the family farm of one hundred acres, located in West Springfield, still, but on the road that leads north to Northampton. Now, a hundred and fifty years after the first Morgan came to Massachusetts shores, times had improved remarkably. This boy was born during the war of the Revolution, but by the time he began going to school the peace treaty was signed.

Six years after the boy's birth, when his father could realize the importance of the affair but he could not, Springfield went

down in American history as the site of the beginning of the noto-
rious Shay's rebellion.

In the spring and summer of 1786 scores of western Massachu-
sets farmers had left their fields to go to Boston and petition the
legislature to do something to help them in their need. The hard
times that followed the sudden break of the flow of capital from
England hurt the farmers most of all. Nearly all the small land-
holders were in trouble, and mortgage after mortage was foreclosed. Joseph Morgan knew this trouble. He had lost the two-
hundred-acre farm on the Northampton road a few years earlier
when he could not make the payments on the mortgage; he had
lost it to a Boston capitalist. Now his condition was improved, but
that of his neighbors was not, and many of them had come to
adopt a rebellious mood.

The farmers milled about the legislative rooms in Boston all
spring, demanding either a bank issue of cheap paper money,
which they could then borrow freely to pay their pressing debts,
or legislative action to prohibit the foreclosure of farms in these
hard times. The legislature heard them but did not heed, and on
July 8 the Massachusetts lawmakers ended their sessions without
action on the plight of the farmers.

A town meeting of protest was called in Worcester on August
15, and then in Joseph Morgan's own Hampshire County a convention was called, to which some fifty towns sent delegates. The
convention was held at Hatfield. Delegates condemned the legislature, particularly the Senate, which had blocked their relief, the
court system for its high costs (which were borne by the near
bankrupt in these cases), and the system of taxation, which penal-
ized the farmer in favor of the merchant and man of wealth.

The convention showed the temper of western Massachusetts
but did nothing concrete. Then mob violence began to break out
in various towns. A mob prevented the sitting of the court at
Northampton on August 31, because several foreclosure cases had
been called. A mob broke up the session of the court in Worcester
on September 5 for the same reason. Mobs stopped court action
against farmers at Concord and Great Barrington, and then the
forces of property and those of law and order moved in to enforce

the laws. Governor James Bowdoin sent six hundred militiamen to Springfield under General William Shepherd. These were not Springfield or western Massachusetts men, for many of the militia were also members of the mobs.

The force was dispatched to Springfield because the state Supreme Court was sitting there. When General Shepherd arrived with his troops he was confronted by an armed band of angry men, led by Captain Daniel Shays, late of the Continental Army, a farmer who had lost everything in the depression of those years. Shays threatened violence, and the court wisely adjourned.

Springfield had become the site of a federal arsenal, an enterprise that had begun as a cartridge factory in the barn of old Ebenezer Stebbins, a relative of the Morgans by marriage. In the years after the revolution the factory had been moved and had grown and come under government ownership.

Since Springfield was an arsenal town, Congress came into the matter and began to assemble a federal force to put down the rebellion.

When the court adjourned in the fall, it announced its intention to sit again at Springfield on December 26. Daniel Shays then moved into the area with a force of about two thousand men, some of them in West Springfield, around the Morgan holdings, and the majority on the Boston road. On January 25 a pitched battle was held 250 yards from the arsenal, and General Shepherd routed the rebels with cannon fire, killing three and wounding one man who was left on the field. There might have been more fighting, for the Shays force retreated no farther than Chicopee, but General Benjamin Lincoln arrived a few hours later and began pursuit of the rebels.

The result of this uprising was positive. The Massachusetts legislature lowered taxes and court fees, and exempted clothing, household goods, and the tools of a man's trade from the debt processes, so times grew a little better.

Conditions of travel were still primitive, and the backwoods communities like Springfield still depended largely on traffic up and down the Connecticut River for their supplies, but there were teachers in the towns now, and education of a far higher caliber than even the second Joseph Morgan had enjoyed. The power of the church had disappeared and the separation of church and state were guaranteed by the new federal government, as well as by the people through the commonwealth's own constitution. Springfield had common schools, where the children were sent to learn to read and write. They were taught ciphering, or simple arithmetic, and geography.

This Joseph Morgan began keeping a journal when he was twelve years old, and off and on he kept it all during his life.

Joseph wrote about school and trips to other towns on his father's business. The elder Joseph was a successful farmer, able now to expand and make investments in land and animals. One day young Joseph went to Norwich after sheep with the family's hired man. When he was thirteen years old he took considerable interest in a transaction by which his father let out sheep to a Mr. Pomroy, who agreed to return three quarters of a pound of wool each year for each head of sheep he took. Pomroy was to keep the sheep for three years. The next year, 1794, young Joseph was working on the town road crew, giving his labor in lieu of his father's taxes for roads.

Having gone to school for several years, and exhibiting a facility with the written word, young Joseph was selected to spend part of the winter of 1795 teaching in a backwoods school "over the mountains." He taught the rudiments of reading, writing, and arithmetic to some twenty youngsters who lived in a community too far from Springfield to attend the common school.

In 1796, when he was sixteen years old, Joseph resumed his own formal education, going to South Hadley for a month to a grammar school. Then, in the fall of the year a Mr. Cutter came to Springfield to keep a school, and he went to that school instead. For a time the teacher boarded with the Morgans.

The next year Joseph began his military training, and also to take more responsibility on the farm. He had not considered any life but that of a farmer, and might never have thought of doing anything else or living anywhere but in Springfield, had he not made a trip with Josiah Cooper to Hartford by boat down the Connecticut River in the autumn of 1797.

After Christmas, in the dull time when there is little to be done about the farm save prepare the harnesses and equipment for the spring's work, Joseph left home to teach school at Amos Town. He boarded with several families, making the rounds in the manner of a frontier teacher, sharing out the cost of his living among the parents of his pupils, and earning a cash fee of $7.50 per month besides his keep. School this year lasted until March 1, when it was time to go home and make ready for the spring plowing.

The next year, Joseph began to take an interest in public affairs and went to many meetings. He commented in his journal about a petition from the Town Meeting of Springfield to Congress, against a declaration of war on France, which was then interfering with American shipping and whose rulers had refused to receive U. S. Minister Charles Cotesworth Pinckney when he arrived. On the Fourth of July he went to the town square to celebrate with all the other citizens the day of National Independence, and he listened as his Uncle Titus Morgan made the principal oration.

Joseph's military training was carried out under the supervision of Captain Russell Ely, his brother-in-law, husband of sister Eurydice. The Elys were his friends as well as his relatives, being at a proper age (in their thirties) to both awe and attract a youngster in his late teens, and he spent many happy evenings there at balls and dinner parties.

Farming in the summer, spring, and fall and teaching in the winter months was the routine of Joseph's teenage years. In that winter of 1798 he taught school at Chester, beginning on December 8, and he did not come home for two months, even for Christmas. The important family holiday of New England was not Christmas in any event, but Thanksgiving, the holiday devised by the colonists to celebrate their deliverance by their God from the cruel fates of the new world into which they had wandered.

The year 1799 marked the end of the diaries for eight years of the young man's life. These were busy years, too busy with activity for the keeping of a diary.

The family of Joseph Morgan was now one of the leading families in Springfield and while Joseph was a farmer, he was a gentleman farmer, as much of a squire as might exist in western

Massachusetts in the late eighteenth and early nineteenth centuries.

In 1807, when he was twenty-seven years old, this Joseph married Sally Spencer of Middletown, Connecticut. The wedding was held in Middletown, so on September 17 Joseph went there and was married two days later. Then he brought his bride back to his own house, which he had now established in West Springfield.

Times had changed and life had improved so much in western Massachusetts that road travel became relatively common. This was accomplished by the linking up of the roads of the towns and their maintenance and widening. The roads were still little more than ruts. They turned to sloshing mud in fall and spring rains and froze into immovable tracks in winter. They spat dust on the traveler all summer long. Even so, four-wheeled wagons and coaches could be driven on the roads now for long distances. Joseph Morgan traveled widely and often, buying and selling lands and merchandise. Usually he went by horseback or wagon. Three months after his marriage he traveled to Cooperstown, New York, a trip that took a week.

Times had changed in another way, and this Joseph Morgan deserted the ways of the past. Life was becoming too complicated for the raising of so large a family as the one into which he had been born, or his father and grandfather before him. Only three children were to be born to Sally Spencer Morgan, spaced about two years apart. These young Morgans had much else on their minds than the raising of a large crop of children to work the farms and kitchens.

By 1808 Joseph Morgan was well established as a man of many business affairs. He continued to farm on the family acres and he would farm all his life, but farming was no longer his way of life. That year he bought a small farm for $400, to rent out. In April 1809 he purchased a house and 18 acres of land from Asaph Miller, not for his own use or that of a relative, but as another real estate investment. He rented the furnished house and land to Oliver Sprague.

The baby Mary Morgan was born in 1808, the baby Lucy in 1811. Between those two important events Joseph Morgan had grown from a man of moderate means to a man of wealth; he hired a number of men, and he bought one property after another. In 1811 he sold the house he had bought for $750 from Asaph Miller for $450, but he kept 17½ acres of land and let only a half acre go with the house. The next year he bought a 38-acre lot from L. Pomroy for $370. In 1812 he joined the Washington Benevolence Society in Northampton, and set himself up as a money lender, or private banker. Here was the beginning of the great Morgan banking fortune.

CHAPTER

III

THE BASE OF FORTUNE

IN THE SPRING of 1812 while Joseph Morgan was entering the banking business the infant United States government was preparing to go to war against Great Britain. One of the first preparations was the enactment of a general embargo on foreign trade. Another was the passage of a law empowering the President to call up one hundred thousand militiamen from the states and territories for six months of service. Neither law had any effect on the fortunes of Joseph Morgan, which shows how insular life was in Springfield, since it was virtually unaffected at the beginning by the embargo (unlike Boston, which suffered immediately), and how much the status and attitude of Joseph Morgan had changed compared to the status and attitude of his father. The second Joseph Morgan was a man of action, a farmer-soldier who dropped his plow at a moment's notice to don his uniform, pick up his gun, and move out with his fellow townsmen to defend his country.

The war of 1812 was not popular in New England. In Massachusetts nearly everyone who dared speak in defense of the administration and the war was denounced, and there, as in Connecticut and Rhode Island, the state government flatly refused to send its quota of militiamen to fight for the common good. For a number of years Joseph Morgan had served in the local militia company under Captain Sylvester Day. Now, when war was declared and the militia suddenly began to mean something, no more was heard of his service. Joseph was thirty-two years old, on the youthful side of maturity, and age had nothing to do with the sudden distaste for things military. He was not alone. Very few men in Springfield cared for the war. Nearly three thousand people lived in the town; almost uniformly they determined to play as small a role in the war as possible, and numerous memorials and petitions were sent to Congress asking for a speedy end to the war.

Joseph's father-in-law, Samuel Spencer, came up from Middletown for a visit that year. Joseph went back with him as far as Hartford. On that trip he took a pair of hogs to market. On other trips that year he looked over property, and sold other goods.

On July 18, 1813, Joseph's only son, Junius Spencer Morgan, was born at the family home in West Springfield. He was the son of a very wealthy man. In 1813 Joseph was buying expensive parcels of real estate, requiring large amounts of money; he bought the farm of A. Morgan for two thousand dollars.

Five months after the birth of his grandson, Joseph's father died, leaving his son the 112-acre farm on the Northampton road and other property which was valued at about $11,000. Joseph's wealth was growing rapidly. All this represented surplus which could be invested, and the farm rented out.

With the coming of the War of 1812 Joseph Morgan began to inform himself on public affairs. He bought a copy of a life of Napoleon, to learn something about the man who was terrorizing half of Europe, and whose war efforts across the Atlantic kept the British from decimating the little United States.

He bought a copy of Oliver Goldsmith's *History of England*—perhaps an odd purchase at a time when the United States was at war with England, but a truthful representation of the orientation of New Englanders.

Now and again in his diaries he noted the progress of the war, but without comment, even when he wrote down the lamentable report that the city of Washington had been taken and the public buildings burned by the British.

With the attack on the national capital even New Englanders began to support the war with more heart, and in 1814 Springfield was called on to supply a detachment of soldiery to join the common cause of defense. This Joseph Morgan was not numbered in that group. He was too busy and too far removed from soldiering.

The war really made far less difference to his affairs than one might think, for his investments were in local property and local business. In January 1815 he undertook the largest business venture of his life, one which marked a complete break with the past of all the Morgans in America. He went to Westfield, and there purchased from Asa Goodenough a stage line with a tavern headquarters located on the west side of the village green. This was a usual combination in the business of the day. Nearly all stage line owners maintained taverns, usually several of them along the ways they traveled. The taverns were primarily used for the convenience of passengers, as places of refreshment and rest, but they also served wherever they were located as neighborhood centers.

Joseph Morgan paid $10,000 for the tavern and the line—which included $2,000 for stages, the horses, and the buildings, furniture, and stock of food and beverages on hand. The next month he sold some of the stages to Rufus Cotton for $900. He kept the remainder and apparently engaged in the stage line business as well as the business of innkeeping.

Now Joseph's time was divided between the homestead in West Springfield and Westfield. When war ended with the signing of the Treaty of Ghent in 1815 he made note of the news with one of the few adjectives he had ever used to describe public affairs. It was "joyful" news, he said, and he and Sally soon traveled to Middletown to visit her parents, where they joined in the "rejoicing" at the end of the unwanted conflict.

Over the years Joseph had traveled often to Hartford and other cities, and it was quite apparent that travel and life in a town larger than Springfield now attracted him. In November 1816 Joseph purchased the Hartford Exchange Coffee House on the north side of State Street from a Mr. Bulkley, and two months later, on January 12, 1817, he moved the family to Hartford and became an innkeeper in the largest town in the area. The house was a big brick structure, for which he paid $16,000, including the barns. Either the capital drain of two taverns was too heavy, or, more likely, the Westfield tavern had proved not to his taste, for in June, Joseph disposed of his holdings there to his cousin Archippus Morgan.

The Exchange Coffee House was the center of business and social activity in all Hartford, and for the next dozen years Joseph Morgan lived and worked at the hub of the town's life. A week after he took residence the *Connecticut Courant* announced that there would be a meeting of merchants, ship holders, and others interested in commerce at Morgan's Exchange Coffee House a few days later.

Two months after Joseph's arrival President Monroe came to Hartford and was entertained by the prominent citizens of the town at Morgan's. What a change for the son of a country farmer, even a wealthy one, to be suddenly thrust into city society and mingling with Presidents!

Joseph was a good host. When Commodore MacDonough was to be presented a ceremonial sword by the Mayor of Hartford for his heroism in the War of 1812, the town turned out for a parade which ended in the Exchange Coffee House assembly room, a long dining room decorated with evergreens and hung with patriotic pictures. The company of notables assembled gaily and drank twenty-eight different toasts during the evening.

The Federal Republicans met at Morgans. The Domestic Manufacturers Encouragement Society met there. The first inaugural ball in Hartford's history was held there to celebrate the election of a new mayor. The volunteer fire department held its dinner meetings at the coffee house. The ladies organized their cotillions and danced there. A reading room was put in for those who had an hour to waste in the afternoon. Morgan's, in other words, was the club of the respectable people of Hartford, the place where ladies and gentlemen could assemble, separately or together, where spirits could be drunk in the men's saloon, or coffee in the ladies' rooms. When minstrel shows or other entertainment came to Hartford they set up in Morgan's assembly room. It was also the theater of the community.

All the new problems of running a public house kept Joseph Morgan busy for a number of months, but by the spring of 1818 he was looking around for other investment opportunities. He bought two pieces of land on the north side of the road between Hartford and Farmington. The first piece of land ran between the highway that led past the asylum for the deaf and dumb and the Hartford-Farmington road.

The second piece of land, nearby but separated by what is now Sigourney Street, consisted of forty-six and a half acres. Joseph paid $6,000 for the two pieces of land. Not long afterward he purchased an adjoining ten acres of land, and at other times he bought other parcels, bringing his holdings finally to about one hundred and six acres within the city limits of modern Hartford.

Within three years Joseph Morgan had established himself as one of the wealthier and more respected citizens of Hartford. He was involved in the sale of Hartford Bridge Stock for a company organized to bridge the Connecticut River with a structure one thousand feet long. By uniting Hartford and East Hartford the businessmen assured the growth of their community, but it was an expensive undertaking; the bridge cost $100,000. Joseph was a stockholder in the Connecticut Steamboat Company. On June 17, 1819, he participated in a meeting at which the Aetna Insurance Company was formed by a group of businessmen who were dissatisfied with the manner in which the Hartford Fire Insurance Company was doing business. The meeting was held at his Exchange Coffee House and he was elected a director of the new corporation. Later that year the company opened an office in the coffee house to solicit business.

Joseph turned to farming again on his new acreage. He joined the Hartford County Agricultural Society and became active in its efforts to improve farming. He continued his banking, lending money and discounting notes. He invested some money in one of the Hartford banks although he did not become an officer of the bank.

His time was divided among his business interests in these years.

When Mr. Whale, a teacher of dancing, arrived in Hartford, he was persuaded to open his classes at the coffee house, to teach "the most fashionable steps and cotillions as danced in the city of New York." To stimulate business when times were slack, Joseph brought in oddities and entertainments. In the spring of 1822 he arranged for a grand panorama of the Battle of Plattsburgh on Lake Champlain to be laid out in the assembly room, and invited the public to come and see the show, which was accompanied by music. When Miss Plimpton, a vocalist from Boston, came to town, he encouraged her to use the public rooms for her performance. She gave a concert accompanied by her father and brother on the violin, French horn, and patent six-keyed bugle. The price was twenty-five cents for admission.

Five years is not long for a man to live in a town, but at the end of five years of residence, Joseph Morgan was elected a member of the town committee of the Hartford County Agricultural Society, and four years later he was elected head of the common council of the city. He continued in public office almost all the rest of his life, as a member of the common council and sometimes as selectman.

After 1825 Joseph spent a good share of his time on his farm. That year he served as a member of the inspection committee at the Hartford County Cattle Show, and, incidentally, was awarded a prize of six dollars for raising the best two-year-old heifer shown. He was chairman of the committee on plowing at the cattle show in 1827, and year after year he won some prize for his own cattle, as he showed them.

Joseph Morgan was a good citizen and a God-fearing man, descendant of his ancestors. The Puritan church in New England had given away to the Congregational Church, and it was to that denomination's Center Church in Hartford that Joseph and his family gave allegiance. He bought pew number 21 in Center Church for fifty-one dollars, and every Sunday he went to services with his family, sometimes both in morning and in evening.

He was wealthy enough now to afford the best of educations for his children. Mary, who was twenty in 1828, went to Troy to board at Emma Willard's finishing school for young ladies. Joseph accompanied her part way on the trip. First they went to New Haven, and there took the steamer *Chief Justice Marshall* to New York. In New York, Joseph put his daughter and her luggage aboard another steamer for the trip up the Hudson River and then returned to New Haven by steamer. He took a coach or rode a horse back to Hartford, then, leaving New Haven at one-fifteen in the morning and arriving at home before nine—just in time to go to church, because it was a Sunday.

Daughter Lucy, three years younger, would not go on to Emma Willard for a time, but she, too, would have the advantages of education supervised by the foremost woman educator in the country. Junius was sent in 1826 to his first private academy when he was thirteen years old. He went to Middletown, the home of his maternal grandparents, to board at Captain Alden Partridge's American Literary, Scientific, and Military Academy. It was a large school, housing 295 students, but it was not a very successful one. Junius did not prosper there, either because of the military atmosphere or for some other reason, and the next year he was found to be boarding with a Mr. Bartlett who kept a school in East Windsor. The fault, if there was one with the first school experience, was scarcely the boy's; Captain Partridge's school was so badly run and so unpopular that in four years it was out of existence, and the businessmen of Middletown encouraged the Methodist Episcopal Church to take over the buildings. The church did take the buildings and created a college that was to become Wesleyan College.

With the children away at school, Joseph Morgan devoted even more of his time to business affairs. During vacations he saw to it that they learned the value and humility of hard work. Junius was often sent to the farm at West Springfield on some chore, as in the spring of 1828 when he was dispatched by river boat to take a red cow and a yearling heifer there to pasture, making the trip by himself with this responsibility at the age of fifteen.

By 1829 Joseph Morgan was very much the well-to-do citizen. That year he was elected a director of the Connecticut River Steamboat Company, and he continued as a director of the Aetna Insurance Company.

He had outgrown the Exchange Coffee House and the wearing occupation of innkeeper on a small scale, and in the spring of that year he made another change. He arranged to buy the City Hotel on Main Street, an imposing building of fifty rooms, nearly all with their own fireplaces, which was located a few doors south of the Center Street Church. The hotel had been kept for a number of years by Captain John Bennett, but in recent times it had decayed and had been closed for nearly a year, so Joseph was able to make a good bargain. He made arrangements with local workmen to redecorate the hotel completely, to put new carpets on the floors and new mattresses on the beds and to replace the battered furniture with new. Then he sold his coffee house to Selah Treat for $22,000, part in cash and part in notes, and went off with Sally to New York for what might have seemed a vacation but was really a buying trip. He would oversee the purchase of the new carpets and furniture for the City Hotel.

From the day of it reopening the hotel prospered. The *Courant* commented favorably on the new furnishings and the cleanliness, and was most kind to Joseph Morgan in its general remarks, which set the tone for the success that followed. Joseph continued his farming, adding more and better livestock to his land. He continued his directorates and his interest in public affairs. Indeed, that interest grew to encompass national affairs as well as local. He once bet a beaver hat that John Quincy Adams would defeat Andrew Jackson for the Presidency, and if he lost, why who could blame a man for backing another Massachusetts son?

As he became wealthier, Joseph Morgan did not put on a public display as did some others. Oddly enough, in 1829, when Joseph Morgan gave up his tavern on State Street, another man gave up another tavern in another place, a man whose family fortunes and those of the Morgans would be closely linked in later years. Cornelius Vanderbilt (he called himself Van Derbilt in those days) had been keeping a tavern in New Brunswick, New Jersey, or rather his wife had been keeping the tavern while Corneel ran a steamboat for Thomas Gibbons to compete for the New York-Philadelphia traffic against the old steamboat monopoly established by Robert Fulton and Robert Livingston.

But the moment Vanderbilt decided to go into business for himself in steamboats, he quit the Gibbons company and gave up the tavern. Already for five years while his wife Sophia scrubbed tavern floors, Vanderbilt had lived a private life of his own, disporting himself gaily with the finest carriage in New Brunswick and a double team so celebrated that when the Marquis de Lafayette came on his tour of America the town fathers borrowed Vanderbilt's horses to draw the honored visitor's coach.

There was a basic difference between the Morgans and these others. Joseph bought his first carriage in 1829, a new barouche, for which he paid $450 (the price of a model T Ford a century later when the dollar was worth perhaps a quarter as much in purchasing power). He purchased the carriage, with the harness, from Cooke and Sons in New Haven. It was not a personal toy, but the one outward sign, other than education for his children, that he permitted himself to show that he was a wealthy man. The carriage was purchased for and used by everyone in the family. Whenever Joseph made a trip with the family, they used the barouche. When he traveled alone, he went by wagon, steamboat, or public coach.

In the autumn of 1830 Joseph Morgan took his wife and Lucy on a nine-day trip in that barouche. They drove to Providence, then took the steamer to Newport, then returned to Providence and drove to Boston, where Junius was now living with Alfred Welles, a merchant, and working as his clerk. After three years of boarding school, Junius had elected to go into business, to become a merchant and banker and businessman like his father. Having made that decision, there was no question about his course. In the first half of the nineteenth century young men apprenticed themselves to their elders when they wished to learn any trade or profession. A young man who wished to be a lawyer would apprentice himself to a lawyer. A young man who wished to be a doctor would apprentice himself to a doctor. For the professions the young men often went on to one of the colleges or universities to learn the classics and languages, Latin and German being important in the learning of the professional skills. The clergy of course must know Latin, Greek, and other languages if they were to work with the scriptures of the Christian religion. But the businessman needed no formal education of that type at all. His experience was gained in the countinghouses and in the warehouses and on the wharves or in the factories and stores. For a businessman Junius Morgan had all the formal education he would ever need and more. He was not sent to clerk for Mr. Welles out of any sense of failure as a student, but because in 1829 when he was sixteen years old it was high time for him to begin learning the tricks of trade if he were not to fall behind his peers.

The family was now beginning to sprawl out and separate. In the summer of 1831 Lucy went off to Saratoga Springs for a vacation with relatives, and then she, too, took up residence at Emma Willard's boarding school. Mary, who had completed her education there, scarcely had returned to the family apartment in the City Hotel when James A. Smith, a young clergyman, asked for her hand in marriage. He did it by writing to Joseph, in the fashion of the day. He would have a competency, he said, and would soon have a church of his own (Congregational, of course) at Great Falls, New Hampshire. There was no objection. The young minister was a Hartford boy, two years older than Mary, and she, at twenty-four, was quite ripe for marriage. The wedding was set for the summer of the following year.

Joseph was engaged in many varied affairs in these years. He was an organizer of the Connecticut River Bank. He was a member of the City Board of Health. When the volunteer firemen went out to fight a fire in the cold of winter, Joseph Morgan sent his waiters with them to supply them with food and drink, and when the firemen wanted to hold a meeting or a ball, Joseph Morgan supplied the meeting place and the ballroom.

He was a Whig in politics now, but this did not keep him from rubbing shoulders with the great of other convictions. In the summer of 1833 President Andrew Jackson came through Hartford on his tour of New England. He reviewed the troops. He dined at the City Hotel with Joseph and the other city officials. He paid a visit to the Deaf and Dumb Asylum of which the city was so proud, and witnessed the graduation exercises of the pupils.

Joseph Morgan knew Andrew Jackson. He had met the President in 1832 on a trip he had made to Washington. There Joseph had also met Henry Clay, whom he admired politically, John C. Calhoun, and a number of other notables. He was well and courteously treated by all of them, for he was an important businessman in Connecticut. How important became apparent in the summer of 1833 when Joseph Morgan and a number of his business acquaintances opened a new bank, The Farmers and Mechanics Bank, with a capital of $300,000.

He kept buying real estate and shares in various business enterprises, such as the Enfield Canal Company, which built a cutoff on the Connecticut River between Hartford and Springfield. But he had more time for political affairs now, and he gave his backing to Henry Clay. When Clay came to Hartford he visited Joseph Morgan, and then when Clay went on to Springfield, Joseph went with him to lend such support as his presence would command.

Joseph's life changed greatly during the 1830's. First Mary had announced that she wanted to get married, and did in 1832. The fever seemed catching, for Lucy, who had not completed her education, said that she wanted to get married too, two weeks after Mary. Her young man was James Goodwin, Jr., the son of an eminently respectable Hartford family which had prospered in the tavern and stage line business even before Joseph Morgan brought his family down from Springfield. There could be no real objection, of course, except that Lucy was a little young—but by the standards of the day 21 years old was not too early to marry, and had she not been attending Emma Willard's school she would have found time heavy on her hands as an unmarried spinster of that age.

The weddings were held. Then, in 1834, Junius announced his engagement to Juliet Pierpont, the daughter of the rector of the old Hollis Street church in Boston. This meant, of course, that within a very short time all the children were gone, and Sally and Joseph found that they must make a new life for themselves.

Joseph's answer to this problem was to plunge himself even deeper into business affairs. His particular vehicle was the Aetna Insurance Company. It was the practice of insurance company directors in this period to make personal investigations of claims against the company. This was one reason that Joseph Morgan did so much traveling. Another was that he had interested himself in railroads. He became a charter subscriber to the stock of the New Haven and Hartford Railroad, holding one hundred shares. He traveled to Hartford to a railroad meeting that year, and he went to another in Worcester.

This year Joseph decided to sell the City Hotel and get out of the hotel business altogether. He put it up for sale and sold the lease to John Warburton and Parsons Rose, who had worked for him there. They paid him $8,000 for the lease and the furniture. He took their notes, and gave them guarantee that if the property were sold out from under them before the lease expired he would refund their money at the rate of $1,000 for each year of the lease. He then moved out of the City Hotel with Sally, and they came to the new house they had been building on Asylum Street. It was well furnished, with good new furniture which he had been buying for some time on his trips to New York City. The furniture was not garish or modish, but was as solid and conservative as he himself. For many years he had been picking up pieces that he liked—such as a large Oriental rug he purchased in Boston. He was not a connoisseur of furniture or of valuables, but he liked comfort and good furnishings and now he had them. Yet pleasant as the new house was, it was lonely with just the two of them, and on November 19, 1835, shortly after the move from the hotel, he wrote a few words in his diary wistfully comparing the bustle there with the quiet of the big home on Asylum Street.

For diversion he attended more meetings, made more trips, and generated more business for his many companies.

In the course of bringing new business to the Aetna Insurance Company, Joseph found many businessmen in New York who wanted insurance of their properties. New York City was the largest and fastest growing city in all America. By 1835 its population had risen to 200,000, and there seemed to be much opportunity there. There was also much overcrowding, many slums, and an insufficient water supply. All these drawbacks to life in the city were dramatized on the night of December 16, 1835, in a manner that was most important to Joseph Morgan and the other directors of the Aetna Insurance Company. A fire started in one of the buildings below Wall Street. Because of the cold the mains froze, the water would not run, and the lower part of the city was destroyed. The great Merchants Exchange on Wall Street, just eight years old, was burned down completely, as were most of the other buildings east of Broad Street. Some of them had been put up so quickly and so carelessly that scarcely any mortar was used in laying the bricks and the exterior walls were only a brick and a half thick.

On December 17 Joseph Morgan heard about the New York fire and estimated the losses to the community at fifteen million dollars, which was a considerably larger sum in 1835 than it is today. The Aetna Company was very much concerned because it held policies on many of these New York City buildings.

Many of the insurance companies indicated that they would refuse to pay the claims of the New York policy holders. Where they could not fall back on fine print in the insurance contracts, they claimed the faulty city administration, the poor construction of the buildings, and the inadequacy of the fire safety regulations relieved them of responsibility. To the businessmen whose physical assets had been wiped out by the fire, all that mattered was that either their insurance was good and they were in business, or it was not good and they would suffer the loss.

Joseph Morgan and other directors of the Aetna decided that they would pay the claims against Aetna as quickly as they could, that this was good business in several ways, and that it could not help but profit their company in the long run. They were doing no more than living up to the obligation that was implied, even if it could not be legally enforced.

Not all the stockholders in the Aetna were willing to go along with so radical a proposal, and many of these dissenters were bought out by the braver men. Within a few days officials of the Aetna, including Joseph Morgan, had traveled to New York to investigate claims and make prompt payment where the claims were valid. This news soon was heard by the New York businessmen, and Joseph and his associates discovered that suddenly it was very easy for them to write new business, by the hundreds of thousands of dollars, even though the disaster in New York caused them to triple their insurance rates. The businessmen of New York had found an insurance company they could trust and this was exactly what New York business needed at this hour. The months of December 1835 and January 1836 were a turning point in the story of the House of Morgan. By taking a stroke of fate and making good fortune of it, by doing business on a higher level than any of their competitors, even though they charged heavily for the service, Joseph Morgan and his associates earned fortunes for themselves and other stockholders and established a pattern. It was to be the pattern of the House of Morgan.

CHAPTER

IV

THE YOUNG MERCHANT

J UNIUS SPENCER MORGAN, the sixth generation of his family in the
United States, lived in an atmosphere far different from that
of his grandfather Joseph, who died in 1813, the year that Junius
was born.

All the American Morgans had been primarily farmers until
Junius' father, who was also a businessman. Junius spent some
time on the family farms but after he was four years old he lived
in a city, which by the time he became an adolescent had grown
to a population of nearly 10,000 people, and as an adult he never
returned to the farm. Hartford was small compared to New York,
or even to Boston with 60,000 people, but for the first half of the
nineteenth century it was a comparatively large place. All his life
Junius kept his interest in agriculture but the path he had chosen
precluded active farming. Joseph's was the last Eastern American
generation where a city man could combine working the land
himself with banking and commerce. Twenty years before he died
he had turned the actual running of the farm over to his trusted
employees.

Junius grew up in the warmhearted, busy surroundings of the
Exchange Coffee House and the City Hotel. One family custom,

adopted by Miles from the original Puritans to whom the threat of starvation was reality, was the keeping of Thanksgiving as a family and religious holiday. No matter where they were, if it was humanly possible, the Morgans assembled at the home of the patriarch of the family for Thanksgiving. Christmas was celebrated wherever the family happened to be. New Year's Day was not properly a holiday at all, and three months after his marriage Junius' father had thought nothing of absenting himself from his bride at that time. But no Morgan ever voluntarily stayed away from home on Thanksgiving.

Junius spent his youthful summers either in Springfield or working on the Lord's Hill farm, while living at home in Hartford. During the worst heat of the season he sometimes accompanied his mother to Guilford, on Long Island Sound, where the weather was cooler than in the interior of Connecticut.

On April 4, 1829, ten days before his sixteenth birthday, Junius traveled to Boston to become a clerk in the establishment of Alfred Welles, a merchant, and there to learn the ways of business. For the next five years he served his apprenticeship. Joseph never failed to visit his son while in Boston, where he journeyed often on the business of the Aetna Insurance Company. One day in the fall of 1829, before Mary went away to school, Joseph took her to Boston, and together with Junius they visited Charleston, Cambridge, Bunker Hill, and other points where history had been made. They went to an auction, where Joseph made some purchases of household goods. Junius was home for Thanksgiving that autumn, too.

In the second year of his apprenticeship Junius was given considerable responsibility by merchant Welles. He went on trips to New Haven and New York from time to time, usually managing to route himself through Hartford for a brief visit with the family on one leg of the trip.

Just before his twentieth birthday Junius came home to talk to his father about a serious subject. He had been offered a partnership in the Welles firm and was undecided about accepting it; he also needed cash for investment if he was to become a partner. Joseph was opposed to the idea for reasons of his own and the matter was left unsettled. In November Junius joined his father on a visit to Great Falls, where Mary and her minister husband were living. On the trip Junius must have convinced his father that the partnership was sound because he entered it that year. It did not last long. Perhaps it had been offered in a desperate bid for capital, because in a few months Joseph was forced to assume the obligation of a note of the partnership at the Connecticut River Bank, where he was a stockholder, and also to take deed to a lot belonging to Welles, in discharge of debt. Before the first six months of 1834 were ended, Junius was released from the unfortunate connection and came home for a brief vacation. For his son's next business experience Joseph chose the metropolis of New York, and the banking firm of Morris Ketchum, whom Joseph had known for many years when Ketchum was resident in Connecticut. In July, Junius Morgan went to New York to learn the banking business.

As a confirmed Whig, Joseph Morgan believed in the United States National Bank and in the management of Nicholas Biddle of Philadelphia, who ran the bank. In the 1830's the Jackson administration was committed against rechartering that bank when its charter expired in 1836, partly because Jackson feared the placement of so much economic power in the hands of private individuals, and partly because over a long period of time the President had unpleasant dealings, political and economic, with Biddle and other officials of the bank which caused him to distrust Biddle. In effect, the bank was the fiscal arm of the government. It was more important than the Treasury because it controlled the actual moneys of the government, and placed them where it wished.

In the summer of 1833 Biddle had begun to contract credit in the United States by the device of calling in deposits he had placed with various state banks. This created a "recession" for several months, which gave Joseph Morgan some unpleasant moments because banks where he was an investor were involved. Hartford was hurt but not seriously so in this episode. For the Morgans it was but a passing storm.

There was much money to be made in banking in 1835 and

1836, for credit was heavily expanded when the government took its money out of the National Bank and deposited it in various state institutions around the nation. Even private bankers like the Ketchum company could profit. One way was in speculation in gold: a change in the law by the administration's supporters in Congress brought the ratio of gold to silver from one to 15 down to one to 16, and reduced the weight of gold in the gold dollar. In Europe at this time the ratio of gold to silver was one to 15.75. This meant that it was profitable for speculators to buy an ounce of gold in Europe with 15.75 ounces of silver, and bring it to the American mint for coinage, take the gold dollars, and buy more silver with them and repeat the process.

In February 1836, after nearly two years in New York, Junius, and his father, decided that he had served his apprenticeship. He wanted to come home. When Joseph went to New York to settle the fire claims against the Aetna it was decided that Junius would leave the Ketchum firm and return to Hartford, and in a few weeks it was announced that he had become a partner in the trading firm of Howe, Mather and Company. For Junius' share, Joseph paid into the firm $10,000.

During his business apprenticeship in Boston, Junius had met Juliet Pierpont. She was three years younger than he, the daughter of the Reverend John Pierpont, pastor of the old Hollis Street Church, and member of a family more prominent in both European and American affairs than Morgan's own until this time.

The Pierponts traced their lineage back to Sir Hugh de Pierrepont, Lord of the Castle Pierrepont in Picardy. The name, according to family genealogists, was given when Charlemagne was inconvenienced by the lack of a bridge over a stream near the castle and caused a stone bridge (pierre-pont) to be built. Sir Robert Pierrepont was one of the knights of William the Conqueror who came to England and fought in the Battle of Hastings in 1066. After that Norman victory, Pierreponts were given estates in the captured land, and Sir Robert's share of the loot was in Sussex and Suffolk.

The usual problems of primogeniture affected the Pierreponts, too. After several generations James Pierpont, cousin of the Earl of Kingston, descended into trade. In 1628 he was sending goods to the new colony in Massachusetts, and soon his son, John Pierpont, moved there to carry on that end of the trade. In 1640 John Pierpont married Thankful Stowe and moved to Roxbury, lately deserted by Miles Morgan, where Pierpont purchased three hundred acres of land and settled down to farm.

John Pierpont's son, James, attended Harvard College and became a founder of Yale, where he taught as a professor of moral philosophy. He was also Pastor of the First Church of New Haven in 1688.

John Pierpont was a man of several bents and talents. He had been born in Litchfield, Connecticut, in 1785. He attended Yale in 1804 and graduated in the class of John C. Calhoun. He had been tutor to the children of the Allston family in Charleston, South Carolina—the father was Aaron Burr's son-in-law. In 1811 John Pierpont was admitted to the bar. When in 1810 he married his cousin Mary Sheldon Lord, the famous Reverend Lyman Beecher performed the ceremony.

John Pierpont went into business, and after a brief career as a merchant he was so unfortunate as to fall bankrupt, which destroyed his taste for trade. Soon he felt the call to the church. After attending divinity school in Cambridge, he was chosen pastor of the Hollis Street Church in 1819.

Thereafter the Reverend Pierpont became one of the most controversial and disputatious persons in New England. In 1825 he astonished some members of the Congregational faith by becoming a founder of the American Unitarian Association. In addition to this breach with New England tradition, he became an ardent and constant advocate of temperance and of the abolition of slavery, and he carried his advocacy of these moral matters so far that he aroused a storm within his parish.

Junius Morgan courted Juliet Pierpont with the approval of his own family and the Pierponts, but when the couple decided to marry in the spring of 1836, Father Pierpont could not perform the ceremony. After a particularly heated series of sessions with his vestry and with other churchmen, the Reverend Pierpont left hastily for Europe to recover his aplomb and health, which had been endangered by constant irritation and argument.

Junius took the coach to Boston on April 28, 1836, for the wedding, which was performed by the Reverend Samuel K. Lothrop, who was in charge of the church during Mr. Pierpont's absence. Mrs. Pierpont was on hand.

The newlyweds went to Providence for their honeymoon—just a little over a week—then returned to Hartford and moved into the big house on Asylum Street to live with Joseph and Sally Morgan. Late that summer the Reverend John Pierpont came home from Europe. There was a meeting of both families at Litchfield. Later they went to Hartford to stay a few days with the Morgans.

Junius settled down, then, to become a businessman of promise in Hartford. That autumn, at the age of twenty-three, he was elected to the board of directors of the Hartford Fire Insurance Company. The honor was very much a reflection of his family's position in Hartford and their investment in the insurance company.

On April 17, 1837, the first baby was born to Junius and Juliet Pierpont in the big house at 26 Asylum Street. An astrologer might say it was an omen that John Pierpont Morgan arrived in the middle of the worst financial panic that had ever struck American business. All over the nation banks suddenly refused to honor their paper money, or promissory notes, with payment in gold or silver. In New York City the banking system broke down completely, and a number of banks closed their doors.

The banking situation became so desperate that two weeks after the baby's birth father Junius was forced to leave home and travel to the Deep South on an extensive business trip that he would otherwise have delayed. Howe, Mather and Company dealt in cotton which came from the South and there was no way of making payment and securing shipment save to go to the South with hard money, foreign exchange, or letters of credit on foreign banks.

While Junius was away, Juliet took the baby to Boston to visit her father and mother. She remained all during the month of June. Towards the end of the month, Junius returned to Hartford, wound up his report to his partners about business affairs in a whirlwind four days, and rushed to Boston to join his wife and baby at the home of his father-in-law. John Pierpont Morgan was baptized early in July in what was, strictly speaking, still a Congregational church.

There were frequent exchanges of visits between the Morgans and the Pierponts in Boston. When Joseph traveled to Boston on his innumerable business trips, he made it a point to stop and see the other grandparents. He was loyal enough to attend a lecture at the Odion one November night, where the Reverend Pierpont talked about his experiences and travels around Constantinople.

In 1838 Junius and his family moved to a house of their own on Church Street, and the next year began construction of a large rambling house and barn on the Morgan property, Lord's Hill, on Farmington Avenue.

In 1839 Sarah Spencer Morgan was born to Junius and Juliet and the house building was half finished. It was a hard year. Flood carried away two hundred feet of the great bridge across the Connecticut River, a bridge in which Joseph Morgan had a financial interest. Snows, fires, and other disasters hurt business so much that the Aetna company was swamped with claims and suffered losses of $128,000 in the second half of the year. Cornelius Vanderbilt's steamboat *Cleopatra* came up the Connecticut, carrying, among other things, chimney pieces Junius had selected in New York for the new house, but then the crew was frightened off by ice in the river and went back down to New Haven to discharge the cargo, much to the family's disgust.

The depression was not a serious threat to the fortunes of the Morgan family—their holdings were beyond that. Joseph complained about the plight of the Aetna, but he paid workmen cheerfully enough for building Junius' house and that year Junius Morgan became a director of the New Haven and Hartford Railroad. Baby Pierpont, three years old, had his first train ride on the first train that ran between the two Connecticut cities.

The Morgans were all active in the life of Hartford. They met Charles Dickens when he arrived on the steamboat from Springfield. Joseph and Junius seemed never to stop traveling on the business of their insurance companies, banks, and railroads. Joseph, in particular, took an active part in the sale of securities of the Springfield and Albany Railroad. The family life was warm and family meetings and entertainments were frequent. Both before and after little Mary Lyman Morgan was born to Juliet, Grandfather Joseph Morgan spent much time hauling loads of children to the farm and back, Morgans and Goodwins, to pick apples or bring back a load of garden truck.

For reasons that are not quite clear, Junius Morgan and his family did not join the Congregational Church of their forebears but the Protestant Episcopal Church. The change did not seem to be a matter of family disagreement, for there was no strain between Junius and his father. Perhaps it had something to do with the harsh treatment that John Pierpont was receiving from vestry and congregation of the Hollis Street Church in Boston. Grandfather Pierpont was asked to resign his pulpit because some vestrymen objected to his constant interjection into his sermons of the political or politico-social matters of alcohol and slavery. He refused to resign and demanded a theological trial by his church superiors. The battle continued for half a dozen years.

In 1845 Junius became a vestryman of the Christ Church, the Episcopal Church in Hartford. That same year his father invested another $25,000 in Howe, Mather and Company, buying Junius a larger share of the business, and this year, too, the long struggle of John Pierpont came to an end. He was exonerated of wrongdoing by the church authorities, whereupon he resigned his pastorate immediately and took an appointment to a church in Troy.

Two years later, on July 23, Joseph Morgan died at the age of sixty-seven. Until the very last weeks, when he began to waste away, he had been as active as many young men, taking coach or train or steamboat to Boston and points much farther away. He had visited the Deep South, had made a number of trips to Washington, and had gone as far afield as Kentucky to visit Henry Clay at home.

There was no very coherent public accounting of the fortune of Joseph Morgan. It was appraised by government officials at $102,000, of which $92,000 was in real estate, but this represented only a fraction of the value of the property owned by Joseph Morgan up to within a few months of his death. Perhaps he had transferred some of it, knowing that he was going to die. But he was far closer to being a multimillionaire than these figures indicated. Undoubtedly the probate figure accounted only for local real estate and cash in the bank at the moment of the old man's death. There is no accounting for his stock in various banks, at least two railroads, a steamboat company, a canal company, a bridge company, and his heavy holdings in the Aetna Insurance Company, which was his major business interest during the last quarter of his life.

Two more children were born to Junius and Juliet, a baby boy, Junius; and then a girl who was named Juliet, was born in the winter of 1847, after Joseph Morgan's death. There was now a gradual growing away of the Morgans from the Pierponts. That Christmas there was no exchange of visits between the families, although Troy was not so much more remote or difficult to reach than Boston, and the Pierponts did not come to Hartford either to see the new little granddaughter or to attend her christening in the Episcopal Church. John Pierpont, the minister with strong Unitarian leanings, would not have appreciated his son-in-law's adherence to the Episcopal faith, which was far too close to Roman Catholicism for the more militant Protestants.

The business affairs of Junius prospered. He and his brother-in-law, James Goodwin, administered his father's estate, and one of the first moves they made was to sell the farm that Joseph had accumulated so painstakingly in small parcels thirty years earlier. They offered one hundred acres, the farm house, the barns, the corn house, and three building lots. It was not so much a question of money—they announced that the large part of the purchase could be taken in long-term mortgages—it was that no one of the children was inclined to spend time farming, and they knew that without husbandry the farm itself would go down steadily in value.

Two years later, in the spring of 1850, Junius made his first trip to Europe, the first return of an American Morgan to the country of his forebears. He sailed from Boston on the steamer *America* in

May and returned in August, having completed his business. The breach with the Pierponts was mended somewhat by the Morgans that summer, for they all traveled to Medford, Massachusetts, to spend the day with Grandfather Pierpont, who was preaching in that community, and they all went to church "all day," which meant three services.

In 1850 the name of Junius' trading firm was changed to Mather, Morgan and Company, but elevation to a senior partnership could not long keep the ambitious Junius from looking for more challenging opportunities than he saw in Hartford. The next year he resigned from the firm and joined another partnership of merchants and bankers in Boston. The new partnership was known as J. M. Beebe, Morgan and Company. Now began an awkward and unpleasant period. Junius was forced to spend much of his time in Boston, so he left Hartford early on Monday morning and did not return until the weekend. Juliet found this distasteful and lonely, so she closed up the Farmington Avenue house and moved with the children into Grandmother Morgan's house in Asylum Street until Junius could find suitable accommodations for them in Boston, and, equally important, until he could see how the new business relationship would work out.

In the spring of 1851 Junius decided that the move to Boston would be permanent, so he rented No. 15 Pemberton Square—later to be the site of the courthouse—a few doors from Tremont Street and a few blocks from the heart of the business district. The family came along very shortly, except those children who were old enough to be in boarding school. They remained in their schools for the remainder of the spring term.

Junius began then to sever his connections with Hartford, one by one. He gave up his pew in Christ Church, which he had held since 1839, and bought a pew in St. Paul's Church in Boston. He resigned as director of the Hartford Fire Insurance Company, although he did become a director of Aetna for two years more before he found that too confining. Junius settled down to become a Boston businessman and spent his days in the offices of Kilby Street, his evenings entertaining business acquaintances or engaging in civic affairs. Juliet was an invaluable asset in Boston, far more than in Hartford, because this was her home town. In the days when the Reverend John Pierpont had kept the Hollis Street Church the Pierponts were well known and the minister was admired throughout Boston for his strong stands on abolition and temperance.

The Morgans lived in Boston for several years, Junius Morgan's business becoming ever more oriented to the sea and foreign trade. He traded in cotton and other goods and traveled frequently, often by ship rather than rail or coach, for his voyages were long ones.

In 1853 Junius took Juliet to London on a combined business and pleasure trip. He spent most of his daylight hours on matters of business, while she made the tourist rounds. All the children but Pierpont were taken to stay in Hartford with their Grandmother Morgan. Pierpont had been spending several months in the Azores recuperating from a long and serious illness, and he joined his mother and father on the Continent. They visited France, Germany, and Belgium, and then returned to the United States.

This European trip was decisive in the life of Junius Morgan, for during his extensive calls on businessmen in England and Scotland he and Juliet attended a dinner given by George Peabody, a Massachusetts man who had come to England a number of years before and established himself as a banker and dealer in American securities. During the weeks that followed that first meeting Peabody observed the Morgans and liked what he saw. After Junius and his wife returned to Boston, the banker asked Junius to give up his American business and come to London to be a partner in the firm of George Peabody and Company. The firm was not called a banking firm but a firm of merchants. Morgan would join him in handling the interests of such companies as J. M. Beebe, Morgan and Company in Europe, handle the importation of goods into the United States from England, and take care of all matters of credit and exchange for American clients who traveled in England.

Junius Morgan considered the matter and decided that it fitted his hopes and ambitions exactly. He had not been in Boston long enough to grow roots; he had outgrown Hartford, and he had not been particularly impressed with New York. He decided to move to England and make London his home, as George Peabody had done. A whole new career opened before him and his children.

CHAPTER

V

A BANKER IN LONDON

IN THE SUMMER of 1854 Junius Morgan made preparations to separate his life and those of his immediate family from the long and constant association with New England. The house in Boston was given up. With the exception of young Pierpont, the family was settled in Grandmother Morgan's house on Asylum Street in Hartford for the summer months. J. M. Beebe did his best to persuade Junius not to go abroad to live, but it was useless. Junius was determined, so he sold his share of the business and all else in Boston, even sold his pew in St. Paul's Church to Levi P. Morton, then a Boston merchant.

Junius was eager to be in London for the opening of the fall season. That meant he should arrive before October 1, so the family sailed in mid-September. A house was rented in London, and Junius, Juliet, and the younger children settled down to the life of Londoners while Pierpont went off to school on the Continent. Later the girls were sent to English boarding schools.

The Morgans could not have come to London under a more helpful aegis than George Peabody's. Americans were not regarded very highly by members of London's polite society and the English business world, who looked upon participation in common trade as demeaning. To be sure, certain allowances were made for Americans because they inhabited a Republic. Even so, most of them were regarded as hopelessly outré. Among the Americans acceptable in London, George Peabody led all the rest.

There was reason for his popularity: he had cultivated it in all the ways he could master for a quarter of a century. Peabody was born in Danvers, Massachusetts, in 1795. His titled English friends would shudder to consider it, but he had served an apprenticeship to his brother in a country store at Newburyport until he was fifteen years old. Five years later he made his first trip away from New England, to Baltimore, and settled there in business. In 1827 he visited London, discovered economic opportunity there for a merchant of a very special sort, and decided to stay. He opened an office in Warnford Court to serve Americans almost exclusively. He held deposits for Americans who had come or were coming to Europe, discounted bills of exchange, and negotiated loans for American companies from British capitalists and merchant bankers. As the infant railroads of the United States began to prosper, he began to trade in their securities, in the bonds of states, in the obligations of various canal companies. He made his first mark shortly after his arrival in England when he was appointed by the state of Maryland as one of three commissioners to attempt to restore the credit of that state abroad, after it had defaulted on some obligations. He managed to secure a joint loan from a number of British bankers, enabling Maryland to pay its debts. British investors were grateful, and the Maryland legislature was grateful enough to vote him public thanks.

For a time George Peabody kept rooms in Hampton Court. Then he moved to Richmond. He never owned a house. He was a bachelor when he came to England and he did not marry. It was rumored that he had become engaged to a young woman from Maryland who had been sent to Europe to forget a young man who was quite unsuitable, but even after the engagement she could not forget her original beau and eventually Peabody released her and she returned to the United States to marry the first man and live happily ever after. That story was often told by Peabody when he was asked why he had never married. Whatever the truth, his lack of a hostess made it difficult for him over the years to order and regulate his entertainments.

Peabody was a man of very simple tastes, considering the times in which he lived and the company in which he moved. He ate and drank sparingly, although he entertained frequently, usually in public houses. His annual dinner and reception for Americans in London on the fourth of July became an institution in Europe, and Americans from the Continent sometimes came to London just to attend it.

Peabody's most successful years began around 1850 in the time of the great Crystal Palace exhibition of the fruits of the industrial revolution. Peabody had plumped for American official backing for a United States exhibit at what Londoners called the Great Exhibition, but without success. He dug into his own pockets then, reserved space at the Crystal Palace, and persuaded various representatives of American business and industry to come to London for the affair. The overall American showing was not very impressive, but Samuel Colt came to exhibit his revolver, Alfred Hobbs of Boston showed his new patent clock, John R. St. John of Buffalo exhibited his new compass regulator.

When the exhibition ended in the fall of 1851 Peabody gave a dinner for the Americans connected with the Crystal Palace show at the London Coffee House on Ludgate Hill, where a little less than a century earlier Benjamin Franklin had gathered with friends of the colonies and talked endlessly of reconciliation.

The honored guests at the dinner were Earl Granville, chairman of the Royal Commission which had staged the Crystal Palace Exhibition; Abbott Lawrence, the United States Minister to Great Britain; Sir Henry Lytton Bulwer, British Minister to Washington; Robert J. Walker, the American Secretary of the Treasury; and Thomson Hankey, Jr., governor of the Bank of England.

Many of the other names were scarcely less distinguished and in all there were one hundred and fifty guests, who came to eat turtle soup, meats, fishes, and fowls, and drink wines to suit. They finished with champagne and then a loving cup, which was passed from man to man. It was a huge wooden vessel, made from an oak on the Peabody homestead in Danvers, Massachusetts.

Behind the head table on the wall hung Hayter's full-length portrait of Her Majesty, Queen Victoria, flanked by Stuart's life-sized portrait of George Washington and Patten's life-sized portrait of His Royal Highness, Prince Albert. American and British flags were hung on the walls, wreathed in laurel and surrounded by pennants borrowed from the British Admiralty.

When the guests had feasted and the loving cup was ready, George Peabody arose and proposed a toast.

"The Queen, God bless her," he said, and the band played *God Save the Queen.* Then he toasted the President of the United States, while the band played *Hail! Columbia,* and there were toasts to Prince Albert, the American Minister, the chairman of the Royal Commission, and countless others.

There was very little that could be said for the American exhibition at the Crystal Palace. It had been an almost total failure, because so little was shown, compared to all the European nations. Minister Lawrence apologized, saying that he had seen state fairs where the exhibits were superior to those at London. The next day the London press reported on the banquet and were uniform in praising George Peabody for creating victory from the humiliation of the exhibition. They were generous in praising things American —the new *Atlantic* of the Collins Steamship Line which had just arrived on its maiden voyage, the recent victory of the little yacht *America* over the entire Royal Yacht Squadron summer fleet, which gave it the celebrated 100 Guinea Cup. The newspapers sought reason to praise the Americans, which was a most unusual turn of events in England in the mid-nineteenth century.

Thus, Peabody was accomplishing just what he set out to do, create a climate in which American securities and American trade could flourish in England. He did more for the cause of American business there than any other person, including the entire diplomatic establishment. Later, in 1854, instead of giving his usual private dinner for all the Americans in London, George Peabody allowed the American legation to share the responsibility with him. Previously no one had wanted to do so, but now, with James Buchanan in residence as minister, there seemed to be a new spirit of pride in the American diplomatic group.

The dinner went well enough until the end, when Peabody arose as usual and proposed a toast to Her Majesty. Daniel E. Sickles, secretary of the American legation grew very angry and noisy because Peabody had not first toasted the President of the United States. Minister James Buchanan created the beginnings of an international incident by refusing to rise to the toast. George Peabody was so angry that the joint dinner was not repeated, for he had spent many years cultivating Britons who were suspicious and ill-informed about America, and he could see his work pushed out the window by a nationalism that matched the provincialism of the Londoners.

Not that George Peabody toadied to British royalty. His name did not appear in the "court guide" and he was not interested in acquiring social position except as it assisted him in his business. He was far more concerned that his relationships with Thomson Hankey of the Bank of England remain good than he was in receiving invitations to dine at the home of the Prime Minister.

By the time Junius Morgan and his family arrived to live in London in the autumn of 1854 the repercussions of the Fourth of July Dinner had not ended. The affair had not injured George Peabody's position but had enhanced it, while Minister Buchanan was in serious difficulty with the British government. From the beginning of his stay in London he made a point of abjuring customs of the court to which he was representative. All the other diplomats wore splendid diplomatic uniforms, replete with medals, gold braid, and swords and other ceremonial weapons. Mr. Buchanan insisted that he would appear at court in a black tailcoat that he wore every day. The supervisors of etiquette in the royal household indicated that he would be turned away. This unpleasantness aroused the full fervor of Mr. Buchanan's Republicanism. (In his defense it must be said that having raised the issue he could not back down because of public sentiment at home. He was, after all, just two years short of his successful campaign for the Democratic nomination for the Presidency.)

The argument about court protocol amused some Londoners, but it served to convince many others that the Americans were the barbarians they had been led to believe since the days of the two wars against the recalcitrant colonies. George Peabody did everything he could to offset such calamitous propaganda, and he was successful at least to the extent that he caused British capitalists to have confidence in American investment.

One of the reasons that George Peabody had asked Junius Morgan to come to London as his partner was to relieve himself of some of the onerous details of business affairs. He was nearly sixty years old and he was hopeful of retiring soon from the business world. He felt it important that his position be taken by another man; he hated the thought of leaving a vacuum.

Peabody had selected Junius Morgan to be his partner because Morgan was the best type of American, as seen through English eyes. He was a big man, more than six feet tall, and handsome, with a rectangular face, well-defined chin and broad forehead. His eyes seemed large for a man, but this was an attractive attribute. He wore his hair parted on the right and rather carelessly pulled straight across his head. This gave him an air of youthful casualness that added to his charm. He spoke with the cultivation of a man who has studied the classics—thanks to those few years in boarding schools. He wore an air of confidence in his own abilities and perspicacity. He was wealthy enough to live in proper style in London, and yet he did not force himself upon the rarified society of the young bloods of the court and its environs. He was forty-one years old but he looked younger; he radiated an impression of solidity and decency. All in all it could be said that Morgan had a strong, positive character and this was what was needed for an American banker to succeed in London in 1854.

The importance of character was shown less than three years after Junius Morgan came to work in the offices at 22 Old Broad Street.

When George Peabody had come to London a quarter century before there were more than sixty private bankers in that city. English finance dominated the world, but even the English bankers had their difficulties, as in 1847 when so great an amount of money was sunk into the capitalization of British railroads that a financial crisis developed. Ten years later the pattern was repeated across the Atlantic in the United States. Business conditions in

America had been extremely prosperous for nearly a decade. The Crimean War of Great Britain and her allies created a huge market, particularly for American wheat and cotton. Thousands of acres of land had been opened to cultivation throughout the midwest, and the railroads, seeing this growing prosperity, spun their webs of spur lines out in all directions in order to transport the produce to the seaports where it could be shipped abroad. Promoters laid out new towns even farther west, and businessmen organized companies with heavy loans and small capitalization to begin new industries. Banks—state banks—issued their own paper money.

Suddenly the Crimean War ended and with the peace came a drastic reduction in the needs of Europe for American grains. The price of wheat dropped. The new shoestring industries could not pay their notes. The Western banks that had been financing them could not rediscount the flood of paper in the East, where they had been sending it. Businesses failed by the score, factories shut down, and then the railroads had nothing to ship. A dozen railroads went into the hands of receivers.

Here was the nub of the problem in London. George Peabody and Company, of which Junius Morgan was junior partner, had committed itself heavily in American railway stocks and bonds. With the news that American railroads were failing, one after another, British investors rushed to unload their American securities and eventually the responsibility of upholding the credit of American investment went to George Peabody and Company. The British investors wanted to sell; Peabody had made his fortune by creating and maintaining a market for American securities. Now he must buy those securities back, or the faith of British capital in American investment would be destroyed.

The crisis began in the summer and autumn of 1857 and came to a head that November. George Peabody and Junius Morgan accepted all bills on American firms and all securities that were offered them, trying as best they could to resell these back across the Atlantic in the United States, but funds were so tight in America that their correspondent banks in New York were unable to be of much help or to meet their own obligation to Peabody and

Company promptly. American debt in England amounted to
£32,000,000. Peabody and Junius were paying out their bank's
funds at the rate of £800,000 a day. By November the New York
bankers knew that George Peabody and Company were in difficulties, and this made them even more reluctant to come to the
assistance of the American firm by taking on the glut of securities
that was piling up in the Broad Street offices.

Peabody quietly applied for assistance to several of the private
banking firms in London, who were not nearly so hard-hit by the
panic as his own. The London bankers saw an opportunity to
eliminate a troublesome competitor who had a very heavy hand
on the American market, and they indicated that they would come
to his assistance, lending him money temporarily to purchase securities, but only if he would promise to give up his London banking
business and go home to America.

When George Peabody learned from Junius Morgan that this
was the answer of the London bankers, he flatly refused to have
anything more to do with them, and Junius obviously agreed with
this course. Both men were pledged to the full extent of their personal resources by the end of November, and Junius was so depressed by their prospects that he indicated his belief that everything he had built up in twenty-two years of business was about
to be lost.

Then George Peabody's many years of cultivation of friendship
saved the firm. In 1834 he had made friends with young Thomson
Hankey, Jr., on a ship traveling from America to England. Hankey
had married an American girl, and the friendship had grown
closer. Now, in an unprecedented action, Governor Thomson
Hankey, Jr., of the Bank of England, authorized the lending of a
million pounds to George Peabody and Company.

In New York the correspondent banks, which had been so reluctant to help in Peabody's difficulties, suddenly learned on the
arrival of the steamer *America* of this huge loan, and as quickly
as the next steamer headed for England, their renewed confidence
was made clear in drafts and orders to purchase—now that it was
no longer necessary.

The Morgan move to England was marred by family misfortune.

Juliet Morgan had accompanied her husband and children to London in 1854, but after two winters there she found the damp climate was ruinous to her health. She was not robust at best and had suffered from various ailments, including *roseola*, a painful and disfiguring inflammation of the tissues of the face, which attacked her from time to time, even when the family was living in Hartford. In London all her physical problems seemed to be exacerbated, and so the following year she returned to the United States to recover.

To carry on his responsibilities to the firm and to raise his children properly, Junius Morgan acquired two houses, a narrow five-story town house at 13 Prince's Gate in the fashionable section of London across from Hyde Park, and the other in the country at Roehampton. He lived then very much like the English gentry. It was a very pleasant life, as described by American diplomat Henry White, who grew up in London at this same time:

". . . The landed gentry and the rich commercial families had as yet no apprehension of the levies on property and income that were to revolutionize England a generation later. What with politics, literature, and sport, the pursuits of London and of the country houses provided ample diversion for a set of men and women remarkably homogeneous in their tastes. They electioneered and spoke in Parliament, they looked after their estates, they shot and hunted, they attended horse shows, race meetings, and polo and cricket matches; during the London season they went to regattas, the opera, balls, picture exhibitions, and political receptions. Except to France and Switzerland they traveled little abroad. The 'season' in London was from May until the August grouse shooting began. Then sport called the men to the country and they stayed till the sport had ended, Parliament reopened, and the round in town was under way. It was a society based upon rural life, with country rather than town houses as the centers of its activity. It was also a society where work, paid or unpaid, was not a constant preoccupation, but where every man was expected to do something or to be somebody.

"Into this social sphere, though in no sense a closed one, the ordinary American could penetrate only with difficulty, and even when inside he would find it as strange as Henry James's hero, Christopher Newman, found the French *grand monde*. It was a society of closely knit and personal interests, and peculiarly English —not cosmopolitan. But now and then an American with special advantages of personality or of background would be taken into the society at an early age and in the course of a few years find it completely familiar. . . ."

Immediately Junius Morgan fitted himself into this life, keeping the advantage he brought with him from America, as George Peabody had kept it: he was willing to work far harder at his banking business than his English counterparts. Every business day at ten o'clock in the morning, Junius and George Peabody were at their desks in their counting room on Broad Street. They remained there, supervising the activity until twelve o'clock, and then received visitors in their offices until after one. They went into their banking offices and remained there doing business from one until two. Then they went to the London Exchange where they remained until three o'clock closing, returning to their desks to work until four, the end of the business day.

Business was a great leveler and provided Junius with an advantage over Juliet in integrating himself into London's daily life. Juliet was forced to rely on the American community for entertainment and companionship during the long days. Since George Peabody was unmarried, there was no one in London with any real responsibility to help her or guide her as a wife of his might have done. Life must have been almost unbearably dull for her when she and her family remained in the city, keeping the house for Junius, while all their business peers were out of town.

Pierpont Morgan described their life at home in a letter he wrote his cousin Jim Goodwin in Hartford, during a brief vacation he was taking from his Continental school, on September 5, 1856:

"I have now been at home nearly three weeks without much of interest having occurred. London is now very dull. Nearly everyone is out of town, and Americans are now very scarce. Mother was taken quite sick a week ago last Tuesday and obliged to go to bed and as yet has not been able to make her reappearance below stairs, but I am in hopes that she will be able to dine with us tomorrow. She was to have done so today but as it is 'Steamer Night' we do not dine at home." (Steamer night was the night before the regular biweekly steamship left London for Boston and New York. The day and night before the sailing were times of intensive activity in the George Peabody offices. There were letters to write and accounts to close at the very last moment so as to bring them to date and still catch the steamship.)

Shortly after that letter was written Juliet Morgan returned to America aboard the *Baltic* of the Collins line. George Peabody had gone before her, making his first trip to his homeland in more than twenty years, and when he returned it was as a conquering hero—this was the summer before the panic of 1857. Bankers and other businessmen in New York, Baltimore, Atlanta, Charleston, Hartford, Boston, and other cities urged him to come to visit them, and offered to give him testimonial dinners. Such was the return on the investment he had made for so long—entertaining every American who came to call on him—a practice he had passed on to Junius.

George Peabody refused all social engagements except those planned in his native Danvers. There on October 9 civic leaders held a magnificent testimonial dinner for the American banker from London. Edward Everett gave the address. Professor Louis Agassiz, the celebrated naturalist, came. The president of Harvard College was there, as was Peter Cooper, the New York philanthropist and civic leader. The mayor of Boston and the governor of Massachusetts attended together with the Reverend John Pierpont and his daughter, Mrs. Junius Morgan.

Juliet remained in Hartford over that winter, and through the dreadful business year of 1857. She was in New York City in the spring of 1858 when twelve-year-old Junius, Jr., died suddenly in London. She was prostrated and became ill again but recovered sufficiently by late spring to return to London. From that time on Juliet Pierpont Morgan lived the life of an invalid or a recluse, playing very little part in Junius' business affairs or entertainments.

In the winter she lived at the Prince's Gate house, and in the spring and summer she spent much time at Dover House in Roehampton. This was to become one of the best-known gracious country houses in all England because Junius undertook George Peabody's entertainment functions and gave dinners and parties for thousands of Americans and British business friends at the country house. It was a big Georgian house, with a gatehouse in the road entrance and a large lawn across which could be seen the valley of the Thames and the boy's school at Harrow over the river. Here Junius conducted a model gentleman's farm, with greenhouses and stables and barns, including a dairy which supplied the estate. As had his father in Hartford, Junius purchased land, field by field, until finally he owned ninety-two acres here.

The banking firm continued to be known as George Peabody and Company although among the merchants of London Junius Morgan was becoming very well known as a partner.

When the Civil War broke out in the United States in 1861, there was much sympathy for the Southern states, particularly since the British traded with the South for cotton. From the beginning, Peabody and Company took a firm stand for the Union, and bought quantities of the securities issued by the North to finance the war. There were difficulties. Northern prestige was never lower than in 1861 when the Confederate commissioners, Mason and Slidell, were removed arbitrarily by an American naval officer from the British steamer *Trent;* war between the United States and England really threatened for a time and the sale of American securities in England was very difficult.

The value of United States securities ebbed and flowed quickly and irregularly during these years, depending on the war news, but by taking a stand in favor of the North, and never wavering, George Peabody increased his fortune and, of course, so did partner Junius Morgan. There were difficult periods such as that in 1862 when Prime Minister Gladstone said that the independence of the South was certain to come. But as the war turned in favor of the United States forces the prices of American securities rose, and George Peabody and Company held considerable sums of these on their own account. To show how the trading went here is one example. Shortly after the war began, United States 6 per cent bonds with a par value of 100 dropped to 40 in London. Each time the North won a victory the bonds rose, sometimes as high as 73. Each time the South won a victory the bonds dropped, back as low as 40 again. They never achieved par during the Civil War, and were climbing back at the very end, when President Lincoln was assassinated, and they dropped four points on the receipt of the news.

Those who bought United States bonds at 40 or 50 and held them, or even speculated in them by selling with Union victories and buying on Union defeats, were bound to make money. Throughout all Europe new fortunes were created and old banking houses renewed their fortunes if they sided with the Union. Only those houses which staked their investment on the Confederacy lost.

In 1862 George Peabody made ready to retire and began to put his affairs in order. In March he announced a splendid gift to the people of the country where he had earned his large fortune. He gave more than a million dollars—eventually he was to give more than three million—for homes for the working poor of London, the unfortunates who did their best to earn their livelihoods but found it impossible to find a decent place in which to live.

The plan called for the construction of four blocks of buildings in Islangton. There would be 155 tenements, housing 650 persons. The apartment houses would contain "free baths for those who desire them," gas in every room, and laundry rooms for the tenants, and the buildings would be surrounded by grounds which might be used as parks. They were for printers, painters, laundresses, letter carriers, and dressmakers—the artisans who did not earn enough money to afford decent housing. These first flats were built in 1864 and then four other squares of buildings followed. Elsewhere philanthropists followed. In New York the merchant Alexander Turney Stewart copied the idea and laid plans to build similar tenements for poor New Yorkers. He was forestalled in this, settled on a hotel for single women, and later began an ambitious development at Garden City, Long Island, for commuters.

If George Peabody had previously been accepted by English businessmen, now he was lionized. He was given the Freedom of the City of London by the Lord Mayor. Bankers and businessmen held testimonial dinners in his honor. Sir Curtis Lampson, one of the trustees chosen for the Peabody buildings, said grandly if not quite accurately that if the money was honestly administered for two hundred years it would accumulate enough interest and generated capital to provide for three quarters of the "industrious poor" of London.

The tenements were built under supervision of Sir Curtis and Junius Morgan, who was also a trustee, and they were opened in 1865 for public use. A poor working man could have two rooms for five shillings, or three rooms for six shillings a week.

The next year George Peabody increased his benefactions to the people of London and also gave money to establish various American charities. In all he gave away $8,500,000. Three million dollars went to establish a Southern educational fund, which was to be used largely to educate the newly freed Negroes of the Southern states and prepare them for citizenship. Phillips Academy in Andover, Massachusetts received money from him, and so did Harvard and Yale Colleges. Peabody Institutions were established in Baltimore and elsewhere. A Peabody Institution was established in Boston, to become a museum.

Old George Peabody had retired now, and his banking business was in the hands of Junius Morgan. Peabody spent most of his time with his friend Sir Curtis, American-born, who had sought British citizenship and become a baronet.

When Peabody's benefactions became noticeable, amid the various honors heaped upon him came a summons to court from Her Majesty, Queen Victoria. What could she do to show her gratitude and the gratitude of all England for his benevolence, she asked. She could not put him on the honors list. She could not honor him with membership in one of the knightly organizations. She could not even bestow a medal on him for he was not a British citizen. Clearly, here was an invitation for this man who had spent his life among the English to rectify what they considered now to be a mistake of birth. George Peabody wanted none of it, however. He was an American and he would remain an American. He asked the Queen for a portrait of her and a letter, and she gracefully supplied both. Then he went back to such pursuits as distributing prizes at the Workingman's Exhibition at the Guild Hall and accepting the freedom of the fishmongers company from the fishmongers.

In 1866 he made another trip back to America and distributed his American benevolences. In 1867 he was asked to become a candidate for the Presidency, an honor he declined.

No matter where he went, now he was followed by an entourage, usually composed of people who wanted something from him. While in New York he received four thousand private applications for relief, all of which he burned. On his return to England the letters continued to come from all over the world at the rate of one thousand a month, but he ignored them.

Junius now was becoming noticed in London by the press as well as by his business associates. The *Times* sought his opinions on the workings of the Atlantic telegraph and on the improvements in the mails to Malta. George Peabody, with his thousands of begging letters following him, and his very definite ideas on the management of business, was becoming a trial in those last years. He had grown crotchety and willful. It was with great restraint that Junius managed to avoid a breach, so demanding did the old man grow, but Junius was as much the diplomat now in his middle fifties as George Peabody had been fifteen years before, so the amenities and friendships were preserved. Finally, in December 1869, George Peabody died, and there was public mourning in England. He was given the unusual honor, for an American, of having his remains taken to Westminster Abbey for mourning before the body was shipped back to the United States for burial, and he was accorded the unusual honor for a banker of having a statue erected to his memory within the confines of the city—the only banker to be so honored.

Now, in 1869, J. S. Morgan and Company became the foremost American banking firm in Europe, and Junius became the most important American banker.

PART TWO

A Banker Emerges

CHAPTER

——⋆◈⋆——

I

SCHOOLBOY

Junius morgan had grown up in far more sophisticated surroundings than any previous representative of the Morgan
male line, but his eldest son was to surpass him in sophistication at
a very early age and, indeed, to become a citizen of the world. By
the time J. Pierpont Morgan reached maturity, he could conduct
business in three languages, he had traveled more than most men
who considered themselves civilized world travelers, and he was
more familiar with European art and culture than anyone he knew
save the handful of Americans with whom he had studied abroad.
It is strange that this aspect of Pierpont Morgan's character has
been so neglected by biographies because it explains a great deal
about the man and his adult mores and interests.

Pierpont's independence of spirit began in the autumn of 1846
when he was nine years old and his father took him from Hartford
to Cheshire and entered him in the Cheshire school as a boarding
student. This was the year in which his grandfather Joseph's health
began to fail, and so Pierpont spent much time at home, but still
he had moved that year into the world of loneliness and enforced
independence of the boarding-school student.

From his mother Pierpont had inherited a weak constitution and he was often ill, unlike most of the Morgans before him. As a little boy he was sick much of the time, suffering from vague, unnamed illnesses that kept him for some time from going back to Cheshire school after that first year. Altogether he spent part of five years in that school and the remainder of this period at local day and boarding schools, particularly the Pavilion School. He spent a few months at the Hopkins Grammar School in Hartford. One reason for the changes was his own illness, and another was the illness of his mother, who could not cope with the demands of the five children in spite of the help given her by servants.

The boy was known as Pip among his Hartford and school friends. He was slender and erect, with dark brown hair and the large eyes and mouth of his father. He was a leader among the boys: his name was first on the list of a group of ten who petitioned the principal one day for a vacation from classes so they could go into Hartford to see the "great managerie" which was to be exhibited there.

At eleven, disillusionment with the dreams of childhood began to set in. He was boarding at the Pavilion School just after the birth of his third sister. Christmas and New Year's came and went without a present from his Grandfather Pierpont, and then one night when he was at dinner in a rather sulky mood, not eating properly, the wife of the headmaster said that she had a present for him which she would give him if he would eat his dinner. He did eat a little of it and received the present and a letter from his grandfather.

Grandfather Pierpont had been remiss, but he said in his note that he expected Santa Claus to get the gift, a pen, to Pierpont by New Year's.

In due time Pierpont replied:

". . . I am sorry to say that I shall not like Santa Claus any more because he did not do as you wanted him to do about getting it to me on New Year's Day which he did not do until Monday 3rd. Therefore if I was in your place I would not trust Santa Claus any more to bring presents. . . ."

Three months later he wrote to his grandfather again, very much the eleven-year-old boy. The purpose of the letter was to secure some help for a coming oral examination. Grandfather Pierpont was a writer of some note in New England and a poet. Pip wanted him to write a piece of prose that he could speak as part of his examination. The letter began with an enthusiastic note about Pip's coming visit to his grandfather in Troy, made the request for the piece of prose, noted the passage of the remains of John Quincy Adams through Hartford, and a few other bits of family gossip, and ended with a postscript asking his grandfather to be sure not to forget that piece of prose.

That year he and other boys formed a secret society whose mystical works were never made public. The next year he and his cousin Jim Goodwin organized a business partnership to exhibit a diorama of the landing of Columbus. J. Pierpont Morgan kept the books on this business enterprise, which apparently involved an investment of one dollar and forty-one cents and at least broke even so the investors saw the return of their capital.

During these early years at the primary school level, Pierpont Morgan was not among the best students in his class in arithmetic, spelling, and English grammar. His marks in Latin went from only tolerable to excellent in a few months. He was not a shining student but neither was he a dunce in any department save perhaps penmanship, where he could never please his teachers.

He did not like to be called Pip Morgan, for he was a solemn and dignified youngster. Even to his grandfather and other relatives he signed his letters formally, J. Pierpont Morgan, and in 1850 when he was attending the Hartford Public High School, when he became convinced that he was being treated unfairly by a teacher, he was so disturbed that he wrote her a daring letter, addressed as follows:

Miss Sophia C. Stevens
Teacher, Public High School

Present

(Very Important   from a persecuted pupil
in my mind)

The letter enclosed read:

Miss Stevens:

I should like to enquire of you the reasons why you as a teacher and of course over me only a scholar should treat me in such an unhuman manner as to send me out of the class for laughing a little too loud which I can assure you I am perfectly unable to control and which no punishment will cure me of. You cannot deny that I have tried to behave better in class lately. If I wanted I could sit still (without saying a word) in a corner and suppose all the class were to do it would you not think that all the class were very stupid indeed and you would have to do all the talking the scholars saying nothing. If I cannot be treated well with DII (the section) rather than be treated as I have been I shall next term go into E II which recites to Miss Torrey or else omit History and Grammar altogether. I do not say this hastily in anger but you cannot say but what I have stood it a great while and I think that upon reflection you cannot say but what I have been treated unjustly. I hope before the term ends we shall be on better terms than at present. Going into E II is a long contemplated step.

J. Pierpont Morgan

Please give me your opinions.

Shudder as she might at the lack of punctuation and sentence structure, Miss Stevens was impressed by the sincerity and anguish of this pupil. She put the letter away and finding it some years later she sent it to Junius Morgan as a keepsake.

Pierpont was a serious boy, although he had his moments of gaiety. He was also a leader among the children, both at home and at school. His best friend was cousin Jim Goodwin, and it says much about Pierpont that they were "best friends" during the early years when a few months of age makes all the difference in behavior, and Jim Goodwin was two years older than Pierpont.

He went to dancing school, with the other boys of good family. He went horseback riding. He learned to play chess, and sometimes played in the evenings. His father helped him with his homework and even talked to him about political affairs sometimes. Following the lead of Grandfather Joseph, the family sympathized with the Whigs, although Junius shared none of his father's in-

terest in the art of politics. (Joseph was the most politically inclined Morgan in the history of the clan.)

Like his grandfather, Pierpont kept a diary, which chronicled
the important matters of his life, as he saw them. He noted when
his father began business in Boston and made the long commuta-
tion trips to spend weekends with the family. He noted the
weather, when it was good or bad for skating and sliding. He
noted his own trips and sometimes his expenditures.

In 1851 Pierpont returned to Cheshire Academy as a boarding
student. He had two close friends there, but otherwise was rather
stand-offish, although not rude. His friends were Fred Eldridge
and Joe Wheeler, who later became a Confederate Army officer
and finally a United States Army general who fought in Cuba in
the Spanish-American War. The other boys knew him only slightly.

Young Morgan began to show some signs of the character of the
man he would become. At Cheshire Academy he boarded with
the Reverend Seth B. Paddock, who had been headmaster of the
school until the spring of this year when illness forced him to
become inactive.

Another boy who attended Cheshire boarded with a family
farther down the road from the school, and every day on his way
to classes he passed the Paddock house, where he either fell into
step with Pierpont as he came out of the garden or spoke to him
as Pierpont sat swinging on the gate.

Dr. Paddock's illness was a matter of common concern and
every day the other boy would ask Pierpont how the doctor's
health was.

"Oh, he is just about the same," Pierpont would say.

One day his companion came by and asked the usual question.

"Oh, he is just about the same," Pierpont said, thinking of
something else, and the other boy walked on. "Oh, I forgot," said
Pierpont suddenly, the question sinking in, "Dr. Paddock is dead."

Pierpont's habit of turning his thoughts inward to the exclusion
of all else obviously began at a very early age.

Pierpont was not an athlete in school but he was very active
physically, and was anything but a conformist. Cheshire men and

boys cherished certain traditions about their school, in the manner of boarding-school students everywhere. One of these concerned the school bell, to which was attributed a vague and mysterious past as the ship's bell of a Spanish galleon. The bell hung high in the belfry, and from very early days had been an object of the student hunger for immortality. The brave boys climbed the belfry without the aid of a ladder and carved their initials in the beam from which the bell was suspended. After this had occurred several times the school authorities placed severe penalties on those boys who were caught. If a boy fell, his parents would hold the school liable; and if enough boys carved their initials, the belfry might collapse.

Thus the game was doubly dangerous and all the more attractive. In Pierpont's day only the brave climbed the belfry in the dead of night. He and Joe Wheeler did so one night, carved their initials with gusto, and descended, undetected, to brag about their exploit. It was truly worth all the risk, for they were established as heroes among their peers.

The spring of 1851 was a busy time for Pierpont. He began studying Greek at Cheshire Academy, about which he wrote nothing in his diary, and he spent five days in Boston with his father, touring the points of interest and attending a play at the Howard Athenaeum, about which he wrote much. This spring he took his first interest in the matter of ecclesiastical government, which was to become one of his major interests in later life. He was only fourteen years old but he went to Waterbury to attend the Episcopal Convention and wrote in his diary of the election of Dr. John Williams as an assistant bishop.

This was his last year at Cheshire. When his father found the house at Pemberton Square, Pierpont joined the family in Boston and lived at home, attending the English High School on Bedford Street which had been founded by Grandfather John Pierpont and other public-spirited citizens.

Pierpont managed a very respectable record at the high school, standing eleventh in his class of seventy at the end of the first two months. He collected autographs, and somehow managed to get several signatures of Dr. Oliver Wendell Holmes. He sent several copies to Jim Goodwin in Hartford, suggesting that he might have others in return. He particularly wanted a Prince Albert and a Henry Clay. He collected copies of the *London Illustrated News,* the finest pictorial magazine published in the English language, and he had them bound. He and Jim Goodwin shared an interest in genealogy with a large emphasis on family seals, which fascinated them, and Pierpont knew a man in Boston who would look up genealogies and paint pictures of coats of arms for from two to twelve dollars.

During the winter of 1852 Pierpont suffered from colds, inflammations, and inflammatory rheumatism of the hip and knee, which half crippled him. He attended school only sporadically, and in the late spring, when students registered for the fall term, he gave no indication that he would return that year. By spring his illness was so severe that one leg was drawn up in muscle spasm and it was feared that he would be lame all his life.

All during these formative years Pierpont attended church regularly. At first, when Grandfather Joseph Morgan was alive, he sometimes went to church three times on Sunday, as was the family custom in the last days of the old man's life. After his grandfather's death the family almost always attended church on Sunday morning and again on Sunday evening. Pierpont accepted this as a way of life, and it became habitual with him.

In the summer of 1852 his father and mother decided it would be helpful for Pierpont's recovery to get out of the city and into the fresh country air. He was sent for part of the summer to Medford, Massachusetts, where Grandfather Pierpont had come to take a pastorate after he left Troy. Coolness between the families still seemed to exist, but there was no outright breach. Pierpont visited his grandfather often over the years, but there is no account of lengthy family reunions after the birth of little Juliet.

In the summer of 1852 Charles W. Dabney, member of an old Boston firm of merchants, and American consul at Fayal in the Azores, happened to be visiting in Boston with one of his daughters. At the Morgans' the question of Pierpont's health came up in conversation and Dabney suggested that a few months in the warm dry air of the Azores might be just what the boy needed.

He offered to take Pierpont back to Fayal with him and to look after the boy once they arrived. So in November 1852 the fifteen-year-old Pierpont went off on a foreign adventure, sailing on the bark *Io* with the Dabneys.

Pierpont had never been to sea before nor had he shown any particular interest in sailing. Yachting was then a very new sport in America, so there was no reason why he should be interested. On this trip, however, he learned something of the art of navigation, studied winds and currents and interested himself in the reading of nautical charts. He was very lame when the *Io* sailed, so sick that he was carried aboard the vessel in a litter from the family's carriage, but the complete change of atmosphere soon seemed to make him well and in a few days he was actually on deck, limping about.

The voyage to Horta, the principal port of Fayal Island and the Azores, took eleven days. Then Pierpont went to live at Silva's Hotel, plunged, really alone, into a totally foreign atmosphere where the people spoke Portuguese and kept customs which would have shocked the citizens of Hartford and of Boston.

Pierpont showed from the first an equanimity of spirit in adapting himself to the ways of others. Donkeys were the principal means of transportation in the Azores, and although he had never ridden a donkey before, he started off immediately by hiring one to ride around the island.

The change in atmosphere seemed to be just what Pierpont needed. Less than a month after he was carried aboard the *Io* he was kicking a football with other members of the foreign colony, taking long walks in Horta, and playing billiards.

The center of Pierpont's world in Horta was Bagatelle, the family home of the Dabneys. He went there on Sundays to religious services and remained for dinner. He met a Doctor Cole who was staying at the hotel, and they played chess, whist, and billiards together. He met the ships as they came to port, to secure news and newspapers, and no ship left for Boston without a letter from him to his father and mother.

He was a tall boy, very slender, perhaps the result of his illnesses. His thick brown hair was parted on the left and worn long.

He had the heavy brows that were the regular features of the Morgans, with firm chin and mouth, but a little heavier in the lips than his father, and a nose that was much larger, after the Reverend John Pierpont, perhaps. He dressed formally in coat, waistcoat, large bow tie and wing collar, and wore a watch fob. He wrote long informative letters, telling about the flowers and plants, the food and the cost of his board and room and washing. He made judgments constantly, noting that his collars cost two cents apiece for laundering, that the washing of them was not nearly so well done as at home, but that it was done as well as any washing and ironing in the Azores.

His watch was spoiled during the trip over on the *Io* when water ran into his berth through the bull's eye during a storm and he treated it by putting it in sweet oil to preserve the works from rust. He sent it home aboard a ship for repair because he did not want the local watchmakers meddling with it. Through the weeks that it was gone he told time by the sun.

He bought a blackbird and two canaries, to have something to take care of. He wandered about the island. When he was bored he visited the Dabneys, where he had been given the run of the house, and if there was no one at home he walked into the library and sat down for an hour or so with a book.

His health improved. When he arrived at Horta on November 20 he weighed 126 pounds, but a month later he had gained twelve pounds. Two weeks after that he was complaining that he had outgrown his trousers and could not button two pair of them "within at least an inch and a half." By March 21 he weighed 150 pounds and began writing to his father about coming home, as the object of his visit had been attained. He wanted to return to Boston by way of England, and his father acquiesced, so on April 15 he boarded the steamer S.S. *Great Western* for Southampton. Six days later he was in England, sight-seeing first in Southampton and then in London.

Junius and Juliet came to England that season and met Pierpont at Manchester, where Junius was doing business. They traveled to Stratford-on-Avon and then went back to London, where Junius went about his business affairs for the Beebe-Morgan partnership and his wife and son spent their days in sight-seeing. This was the trip on which Junius met George Peabody for the first time and so impressed him.

The Morgans made a part of the grand tour of Europe on that trip, and sailed home on the steamer *Niagara*. Pierpont entered the English High School again and was put into the same advanced class as his old classmates, although he had missed a year. The principal said he had kept up his studies, and he may have done so, although most of his time abroad was spent in anything but that type of study. It may well have been that the principal believed his year's experience in travel had given him as much as he might have had in his third year of high school. He kept on with the class of 1854, although it was hard work for him in this final year, as he wrote Jim Goodwin:

". . . The lessons which I have to get now are not only very hard indeed but very dull. Some of them are Paley's *Evidences of Christianity*, Paley's *Moral Philosophy*, Paley's *Theology*, Astronomy, etc. I have to study about all the time, thus having no time for recreation or exercise. I scarcely ever touch my pillow before 11 or 12 o'clock at night. Rather different hours from what the scholars used to keep at the High School in Hartford but the only consolation I have is that this is the last year."

Yet his life was not quite so bleak as he indicated. He went to concerts, which he enjoyed because of the presence of young ladies in whom he was interested, to ship launchings, and to visit the captain of the *Io* and other ships that had called at the Azores when they came into Boston port. He became thoroughly familiar with the points of historic and artistic interest in Boston, the Athenaeum, Faneuil Hall, and the State House. He became interested enough in state politics to go to the office of the *Atlas*, a newspaper, to hear returns and he made a prediction in a letter to his cousin that the Whigs would elect the next governor of Massachusetts.

By November, when the first grades for the year came in, he had a very creditable standing, with 494 points as compared to the 540 of the first boy in the division. This was the second division

of the class, but Pierpont was also making up for that lost year.
By graduation in the summer he stood third in his class.

All his life he enjoyed the company of girls and women. He
wrote frequently about various female friends to Jim Goodwin,
and he spent much of his free time in Boston skating and riding
horseback with them. He was positive and aggressive in everything he did and was obviously as attractive to the young ladies
he knew as they were to him.

He was something of a dandy in these days, although a hard-
headed one who wanted to get exactly what he paid for, as he
indicated in a letter in December 1853 to his cousin, who had
written him about the problem of acquiring clothes:

". . . In regard to the coat, considering the remark you made
that 'economy is necessary with the present state of your funds'
my humble opinion is that you would have saved considerable
if you had found out of Mr. Smith the lowest price for which he
would have made your coat with you furnishing the cloth, and
have procured it at J. N. Ball and Co. Or if you had doubted it
you might easily have tried it. I have ordered of Mr. Rice for myself a pair of French boots to cost $9, and you had better believe
that they are to be nice ones. He has sent my measure to Paris, and
they will arrive about the 1st of January. . . ."

During all these years, no matter where Pierpont traveled or
lived, the center of his life was still Hartford. Grandmother Morgan lived there, and the custom of coming "home" for Thanksgiving continued. Pierpont made many more trips than that to Hartford, and whenever Junius and Juliet traveled, or when there were
problems in the family, the girls and younger children went to
Hartford to stay with Grandmother. Pierpont had been dragged
away from there, but his memories and talk in his letters to his
cousin indicated that Hartford was where his heart lay.

Pierpont was also thinking of the future even now. He spent
much time at the Boston waterfront talking to ship captains, for
his interest in the sea and in ships was very real after his trip to the
Azores. He planned, for a time, to make the East Asia trade his
life's work. There were many persons in Boston's port who could

spin brave tales of days on the China seas, but Pierpont's interest was more specific than that. He had no thought of doing anything but going into the mercantile business, and he considered the China trade the most lucrative and fascinating of all.

The Boston English High School offered as good a secondary education as any school in America, with a special emphasis on mathematics. Pierpont's standing when he graduated showed how well he had taken advantage of the opportunity given him. He had studied arithmetic, art, science, geography, and enough higher mathematics to be able to survey or navigate a ship. He spoke French well enough then to deliver an oration in that language on Declamation Day. How much Portuguese he had learned in his months in Fayal was never revealed, but his way of life there, in the English and American colony, indicated that he had little but possibly a pidgin Portuguese at his command. Still, in 1854, when he graduated from high school, he had a far better education than his father had enjoyed and as good a one as any young man of seventeen in the United States. In the coming two years he was to be exposed to European culture to a degree not shared by many young Americans.

CHAPTER

II

CADET

WHEN IT BECAME CERTAIN that the Junius Morgan family would move to Europe to begin a new life, Junius sent Pierpont on a summer's trip with his cousin Jim Goodwin. It was not exactly the father's idea, for Pierpont and Jim had made the plan the previous year, but the boys might not have been allowed to go alone on such a journey had not the departure of the Morgans been set for fall.

The boys started their tour from New York City. They rode the new Erie Railroad to Buffalo, then went to Niagara, and on to Albany, Saratoga, Lake George, and Lake Champlain. By stage coach they rode through the Green Mountains to the White Mountains of Vermont. They were planning to go to Maine, but they began to run out of money in Vermont and had to shorten the trip. For the first and only time in Pierpont's life he had a fear of having no money at all. It never quite came to that, however. By missing a meal here and there, and doing some walking instead of riding, the boys managed to make Portland, Maine, and traveled by steamer to Boston. They did not have enough cash left to take staterooms, and so sat up during the night. They arrived in Boston broke, a matter soon rectified by a trip to the Beebe and Morgan offices. At last they returned to Hartford, where the elder Morgans were visiting Grandmother Morgan at the house on Asylum Street.

When the family sailed for Europe, it was already settled that Pierpont would attend the Institution Sillig, at Vevey on Lake Geneva, owned by Monsieur and Madame Edouard Sillig. This school specialized in teaching foreigners the languages of Europe as well as the other studies. Pierpont had graduated from an American high school, but without French and German he could not expect to do well at a European university. It was decided to send him to a Continental rather than an English public school, perhaps for the cultural advantages this would give him.

Pierpont went from London to Switzerland and settled down in the totally unfamiliar atmosphere of a continental boarding school. His studies were French, German, algebra, and geometry. He did not live at the school but lodged in a chalet just beyond the school grounds because he had been entered so late that the school lodgings were filled.

Pierpont did well at Institution Sillig, although M. Sillig complained in his comments on the student that he was too lazy to speak French as much as he ought to, and spent much of his time in conversation in English with other American boys. Pierpont was very popular among the Americans. He was always leading an expedition to hike in the mountains or walk around the lake. The boys had a regular regimen of school exercise, including calisthenics, gymnastics, rowing, and swimming in the lake in the proper season.

All went well until the Swiss winter set in. Pierpont was ill in January and February with symptoms so disquieting to the school doctor that consultations were held with others. His unnamed illness lasted nearly all winter. He recovered by spring but showed evidences of bad temper. Here, as earlier in his life, the word "sulky" appeared in reference to Pierpont's conduct. When he did not feel well or was somehow disturbed, he might go for many hours with a glum look on his face, not talking at all or answering only in monosyllables. In these periods he was extremely bad company for anyone. He made up for it, however, by his exuberance at other times, and he was not disliked by his companions, although some of them found him hard to understand.

Pierpont became sufficiently fluent in French to appear in the play *Le Médecin Malgré Lui*. He also acquired some German, but his best study was mathematics. He came to know several of the socially prominent young men of Vevey and was invited, with another wealthy young American, to join in organizing a series of private balls. He was particularly attracted to a Miss Hoffmann, and when she agreed that she and her mother would go to the balls, he joined in, although the sponsorship cost $5.75 for each one of them: ". . . that is dirt cheap when you can laugh, talk and dance with such a beautiful girl as Miss H. as much as you choose."

Pierpont was very much pleased with his life and with himself, and he showed perceptions beyond those which his nineteen years would indicate.

"Besides these balls," he wrote Jim Goodwin in Hartford, "I have been invited to several others; one on the 14th ult. given at the large hotel here by a Monsieur Monnaret, which was very pleasant. Another on the 29th ult'o. at the Baron de Roeder's which was a most splendid affair as far as women and costumes were concerned, but rather too stiff to suit my taste. The gentleman who gave it is a Russian Baron who lives here having under his charge a Prince of Prussia who is a little cracked, and the King, wishing to get him out of the way, pays the Baron a very large sum to keep him here and especially to prevent his marrying for fear that his children should lay in a claim to the throne upon the death of the reigning monarch. They live in a grand style about a mile from Bellerive (the school)."

He began that year to suffer periodically from skin eruptions like those of his mother and Grandfather Pierpont, which turned his face red and puffy. He accepted this ailment, and seemed even at nineteen to hold very little hope that he would be cured of it, for he talked of going to Paris to see if anything could be done for his face in a way which indicated that he did not believe so.

He was an apt student of European politics, commenting on various events in his reports home and to his friends. He wrote many long, varried letters at this period of his life, setting down his adventures and discussing all the subjects that interested him. His life consisted of study, balls, champagne parties, teas, and "at homes." In the winter of 1856, his second in Vevey, he wrote of attending four balls in January and being invited to several others, three in February, and more in March. He described a birthday party for Madame Sillig celebrated by 130 people who journeyed by funicular railroad to the hotel on top of Mont Pelerin at Chardonne, where they dined in a splendid room overlooking the upper part of Lake Geneva, the Rhône Valley, and the Savoy Mountains. At this last party a spoiled Pierpont was very much disappointed because he was forced to sit with other boys instead of "next to some charming damsel to whom I might play the agreeable."

In April 1856, after a year and a half at Vevey, Pierpont Morgan was ready to enter a European university. He and Frank Payson, an American youth who had been studying at Sillig's, left Vevey for Paris. They had been up until four o'clock that morning dancing and drinking, and saying goodbye to their friends. They traveled to Lausanne where they spent the night, then took a private carriage to Paris, arising at three o'clock in the morning and traveling all that day and all that next night. They arrived in Paris at five o'clock on the morning of the second day. Pierpont's mother met them there and spent six days with them, going to the theater, seeing the city, dining in cafés. Then Pierpont left for Göttingen, where he was to enter the university. He had chosen Göttingen because in 1856 this university was celebrated for its courses in mathematics and science.

He registered for the course in *Philosophie,* and for the summer term he signed up for lectures in trigonometry and chemistry. For a few days he stayed at the *Gasthof zur Krone* but then took rooms at 85 Weender Strasse.

As at Vevey, Pierpont entered with enthusiasm into the social activities of the student corps at Göttingen. There were two organizations, the *Hannovera* and the *Bremensia.* Pierpont joined the *Hannovera,* but not as a full-fledged member, for that would have meant dueling, and while a dueling scar on the face was regarded as a mark of honor in Germany, this was not true in London or

Hartford, and Pierpont had no desire to become disfigured in the eyes of his friends.

On matriculation at the university, Pierpont received a huge diploma which said that he was a student of philosophy and a small card which he was instructed to carry in his wallet at all times. This card was a police identification card, given so that the students involved in the frequent high-jinks could be identified if their activities became so much out of line that the police were called.

Pierpont's German was not good enough for his studies, so he took private tutoring in the language. He found it very difficult, but he was determined, as he wrote:

"Next week the dancing parties commence and I shall have a chance to practice German conversation with the young ladies, but fear I shall make bad work of it, but as my maxim in the matter is 'sink or swim, live or die,' or rather learn German in six months or else not learn it at all, I am decided to do the best I can."

Shortly after Pierpont's arrival in Göttingen the students celebrated the birthday of the King of Hanover with a party at the *Gasthof zur Krone,* where much beer was drunk and many songs were sung. The party lasted four hours. There were dances, and Pierpont was delighted to learn that the Göttingen girls were fond of Americans because of their strange and wonderful accents in German. In the summer he attended Garden Concerts and dancing parties. He went on the *Kneipe* of the *Hannovera:* the boys would hire carriages and drive out to some country inn where they would drink beer in the garden all afternoon.

About every three months a *Jahrmark* or fair was held in the town, and the students would attend. Sometimes they became raucous and sometimes they were thrown in jail for breaking the crockery or turning over a farmer's load of melons. It was never the town jail into which they were put, but the special one maintained by the university to police its own ranks. Pierpont was circumspect enough to avoid the embarrassment of jailing.

Pierpont's father had sent him to school on the Continent so he could acquire fluency in French and German. Pierpont talked about going home for the long summer vacation at Göttingen that year, but his father urged him to stay on and perfect his German. It would be essential to him in his future position, Junius wrote to his son. Obviously Junius planned that Pierpont would become associated with him in the merchant banking business, and at this time Pierpont was thinking about joining a European house for a while, perhaps in the Netherlands, where there seemed to be both stability and opportunity for an American concern.

As spring wore on, Pierpont considered spending the summer months and perhaps even the winter at Berlin or Dresden. His father suggested that he travel to St. Petersburg for the summer vacation, thus broadening again his knowledge of European affairs. There was some talk of Pierpont's entering the counting room in London that autumn, but Junius was not very much in favor of it, and hoped that his son would take full advantage of this educational opportunity. Pierpont decided to go to London for the vacation instead, and he did so.

During that vacation Pierpont and his father talked about the future. It was planned that he would return to the Continent again to study. His father wanted him then to join a Continental firm, but Pierpont was not very eager to do so. He wanted to go home to America.

Also during the summer vacation Miss Hoffmann arrived in London from Vevey for a visit. Pierpont was at least half in love with her, but she was Swiss and he did not ever seriously consider marriage to anyone but an American. He had considered such matters very seriously and had laid the plans for his life, as he wrote his cousin:

"Your career in life, like mine, depends on our own individual exertions, our courses though widely apart will both be the mercantile sphere and from this cause it becomes our duty to select for our wives those who, when we go home from our occupations, will ever be ready to make us happy and contented with our homes." Speaking of a wife, he had this to say: ". . . It is necessary that she be domestic, her heart must be at home with husband and children, not in the world."

Pierpont escorted Miss Hoffmann to the theater, to the Royal Mint, to the Queen's Mews, and several times to dinner. Then the

Hoffmanns left for a visit to America, and Pierpont confided to his cousin that he knew no young woman like her. "She has gone now. I may never meet her again. But if I should live many years, I am sure I should not see her equal."

At the end of the long vacation he returned to Göttingen and, with his better German, began to take a more active part in the university life. He began studying fencing, embarrassed a little bit at his inability to meet the Germans on their own ground, but when winter came on and he found himself with his usual miserable winter cough, he gave up the lessons, since they were held in a drafty gymnasium.

By December he was well pleased with his progress in the German language and said that he could converse quite fluently. His Corps gave a party for some of the professors, and staged several comic plays which he knew he could watch and enjoy.

This year, besides mathematics and chemistry, Pierpont took a course in European history, and another in French drama and literature.

His interest in European affairs lagged, however, because it was settled that he was to go into business in America. This must have been his own idea and not that of his father, for his father complained at about this time that he did not know quite what to do with Pierpont, and the reason for it must have been what seemed to him an unreasonable insistence on going home.

When summer came and the end of the term, Pierpont prepared to leave Göttingen forever. His mathematics teacher, Professor Ullrich, suggested that he remain and that after another year he could receive an appointment as an assistant and instructor. Eventually, the professor said, Pierpont could possibly hold a chair of mathematics in such an institution as this university.

This was high praise for a professor at Göttingen to lavish on a student, particularly an American student who had attended the university for so little time, but Professor Ullrich was convinced that Pierpont would be throwing his life away if he returned to America and went into trade.

Pierpont, of course, never had any other ambition but to go into business, and there was no possibility that he might give up his heritage for an academic career. He appreciated the honor, however, remembered it, and later sometimes talked of it.

When it came time for the term to end, Pierpont gave a farewell party at the *Gasthof zur Krone,* inviting members of his student corps, his professors, and all the Americans at the university. Much beer and wine were drunk that evening. Pierpont arose and made a farewell speech. His tongue a little thick, the departing one stood up to his full six feet and in emotional tones wished his companions *unglücklichkeit,* smiling sadly, at the thought of the happy hours they would spend while he was toiling in a countinghouse.

His toast brought down the house in cheers, for it was the very first time that one of their number had parted from the university with such a burst of humor. He had, quite in error, wished his friends long, continued sorrow, and they loved it.

CHAPTER

III

HOME TO AMERICA

O N LEAVING the University of Göttingen, Pierpont traveled to
Berlin, where his friend and cousin Jim Goodwin was waiting. For more than a year Pierpont had been persuading Goodwin
to come to Europe at least on a trip, and now he proposed to show
him the sights. They went to Cologne, Antwerp, Brussels, Paris,
and Vienna. While they were in Vienna, Pierpont received a letter
from his father. Alexander Duncan of the firm of Duncan, Sherman
and Company, was in London at that moment, his father wrote,
and they had been discussing Pierpont. If he wanted to go back
to the United States to go into business, this was the opportunity
for the kind of training he would need. He must, however, be
prepared to go to America immediately, and to come to London
without delay to discuss the matter.

Pierpont cut short the holiday. He and Jim returned to Paris
and then to London, and Pierpont met with Alexander Duncan.
It was agreed that he would leave as quickly as possible for New
York and would work in the offices of Duncan, Sherman and Company for two years, learning the mercantile and trading businesses.

Pierpont returned to New York. Since he arrived a few days
before he was expected to go to work in the office of Duncan,

Sherman and Company, he went to Newport, then becoming a center of summer social activity for wealthy families in the New York area, and visited at the home of William S. Wetmore for a week, where he met the Jonathan Sturges family, including two daughters, Virginia and Amelia, and their sons, Henry and Frederick.

After that week of entertainment, Pierpont Morgan settled down in New York to apprentice himself in the business world. He went to live with Joseph Peabody, a relative of George Peabody, in rooms on West Seventeenth Street, off Fifth Avenue. They had met and become friends in London. Every day Pierpont made his way by horsecar, cab, or foot to the Duncan, Sherman offices at 11 Pine Street, in the business and financial district near the tip of Manhattan. He was given a small desk in the counting room, working under Charles H. Dabney, a cousin of the Dabneys he had known so well in the Azores. Immediately, then, Pierpont was among friends. Now it was up to him to do his best and show how well he could master the affairs of business.

Dabney was a partner in the banking firm and a trained accountant. He taught Pierpont the skills of bookkeeping and cost accounting, matters which were relatively easy for a young man who could do problems of higher arithmetic in his head.

New York was a city of more than five hundred thousand people when Pierpont Morgan came there to begin his business career. The population of the nation was nearly thirty million and both the country and the largest city were growing so rapidly that Junius Morgan might well have had second thoughts about the advisability of Pierpont's beginning business in Europe rather than his own country.

The fashionable district of the city, in which Pierpont was entitled to move through his family connections, was located around Washington Square. The Brevoort Hotel, just off the Square, was considered an "uptown" hotel. Delmonico's restaurant, the smartest in Manhattan, was located far downtown on Beaver Street, and it was not unusual for parishioners of Trinity and St. Paul's Churches, who perhaps lived around the corner or up Broadway, to go there for luncheon after church. Northern Manhattan was still largely an area of small farms and country houses, and northern meant above twenty-third Street. Five miles north of this line of demarcation between city and country there was a suburb called Harlem, but it was quite separate from New York.

Pierpont worked hard during the week. He spent the weekends in the company of friends, and Sundays, in particular, with various families to whom he had letters of introduction from his father.

Pierpont's mother was in America during the early months after his return. He traveled to Hartford to visit her and to see Grandmother Morgan. He visited Jim Goodwin in Hartford, and Jim visited him in New York. His social life was active and varied. He would spend a dollar for dinner, and thirty cents for lunch, perhaps $2.65 for a trip to Hartford, and then he would give ten dollars to the Five Points Mission, or spend $13.62 on what he called a "sleighride." He was meticulous in the keeping of his accounts.

Pierpont had been in New York City less than six months when the panic struck in the financial world, and devastated American interests in London even more severely than those at home. It was serious enough in America: the Ohio Life Insurance Company failed; so did the Collins Steamship Line and a number of banking firms. Pierpont was very much concerned at the gloomy tones of his father's letters. Pierpont said that under the circumstances he ought to stop accepting Joseph Peabody's hospitality and get out and shift for himself. He promised to be very economical in his expenditures, and said he felt it was time for Duncan, Sherman and Company to offer him a salary.

In the spring of 1858, after the crisis had been surmounted by the loan from the Bank of England, Pierpont's mother came down from Hartford to visit, and stayed at the Everett House, a fashionable hotel on Union Square. She had been suffering from several illnesses, including jaundice. Another attack overcame her while at the hotel and she was taken to the house of the Babcock family in Chelsea on Twenty-third Street. They were friends of the Morgans, where Pierpont spent a number of his Sundays and evenings, playing whist or singing hymns and popular songs around the piano.

There Mrs. Morgan received the news of the death of little Junius. She collapsed and became quite ill again for a time. Pierpont went into mourning for his brother, and did not go out in the evenings or on weekends, except to look after his mother until she returned to London late in the spring. He was not much of a hand for visiting the billiard parlors and saloons along Fourteenth Street, even though many of them were eminently respectable places where the young men of good family spent their time.

By midsummer, mourning had become a burden, and he began to go out into the country for weekends. He went to Westport, Connecticut, sometimes to visit Morris Ketchum, members of whose family had been partners with his father in Junius' brief career as a New York banker. The oldest daughter of the Sturges family—whom he had met at Newport—was married now to William H. Osborn and was living in a cottage near West Point. Pierpont was invited there to visit one weekend and he again saw Amelia Sturges, who was two years older than he but not nearly so worldly. Soon he was calling her by her family name of Mimi. When the summer ended he had transferred his weekend and evening allegiance from the Babcock household to that of the Sturgeses on Fourteenth Street just off Fifth Avenue.

The Sturges household was a center for a group of talented young amateur musicians and artists. Pierpont was a welcome guest because he was so much more cultured than most young men of New York, and he knew so much more about European art and literature than his fellow "businessmen" from downtown.

Although she was older than he, Mimi Sturges seemed to have all the attributes that Pierpont Morgan had set down as essential for the wife of a young man in the mercantile business. She was refined and quiet, home-loving and sweet. She was not a raving beauty. She wore her hair in a very severe fashion and dressed severely, too. Yet she was attractive, and particularly so to Pierpont, who at twenty-two was very much ready for marriage.

Junius Morgan came to New York on a visit to Grandmother Morgan for what would be the last time, to see his son, and to conduct business for George Peabody and Company. Pierpont's courtship of Mimi Sturges could not have been concealed had he wished, and there was no desire to conceal it. Junius called at the Sturges house, where Pierpont was virtually an evening boarder, and both heads of family liked what they saw. Junius found Mimi Sturges completely acceptable—the girl whom he wanted Pierpont to marry. Parental blessing on the match was sealed by an invitation from Junius to the Sturgeses to visit the Morgans in England.

Mimi Sturges accompanied Mrs. Morgan back to England in February 1859. The other members of the Sturges family followed in April. Pierpont Morgan remained in New York and continued about the business of Duncan, Sherman and Company. He was committed to remain in that company's employment as apprentice until the summer of the year.

Pierpont traveled to Cuba that winter, a welcome relief from the New York cold, and then to New Orleans, where he was to spend several months learning the cotton business. Cotton was an important part of the trade of any mercantile firm that dealt in general merchandise in the foreign market; Pierpont's father had dealt heavily in cotton in Hartford and had spent much time in the Southern states. If he was to be connected with George Peabody and Company, he must learn the cotton business, and, apparently, Duncan, Sherman and Company felt this would be useful to them while he was in their employment, too.

Pierpont worked in the offices of the correspondent company in New Orleans, and through mutual friends he was introduced into the busy social life of the city. But it was not for his accounting ability or his social prowess that the New Orleans stay became significant in the story of his life. In New Orleans Pierpont made his first independent business move, and showed why the worlds of finance and trade had fascinated him.

The cotton bales were shipped from the plantations to the port of embarkation. They came down the Mississippi and its tributaries on steamboats and ended up in the warehouses and on the wharves along the levee in New Orleans. There they were sold and transshipped in steamships and sometimes in sailing craft to all parts of the world where American cotton had made its mark. Pierpont wandered among the ships of the harbor on business, but that was not his only reason. Since the days in Fayal and Boston he had been fascinated by ports and the ships that go to sea, and he liked to go aboard the sea-going vessels and yarn with their captains. He was particularly attracted to sailing vessels. His first adventure had been aboard a sailing ship, and for romance there was no comparison between a bark or schooner and a noisy, floating warehouse powered by steam.

One day Pierpont was at the levee when he saw a schooner just in from South America. He fell to talking with the captain and soon discovered that she was loaded with coffee consigned to New Orleans. Either the receiving firm had become insolvent or there had been some mistake; no matter, the captain of this sailing ship was saddled with a cargo that no one seemed to want. He wanted to unload and take on other cargo and be on his way. When Pierpont spoke to him the captain had received orders from his owners to sell the coffee at the best price he could get. The captain was not at all pleased with the prospect of peddling coffee up and down the streets of New Orleans.

Pierpont took samples of several bags of coffee and went back to the business district of the city. There he began selling the coffee, not as a cargo, but by the order, so many bags in each order.

It was perfectly good coffee, the captain said, bagged by a reputable Brazilian firm. All it wanted was a negotiator who would take the trouble to break down the cargo and sell it as a merchant, which the ship's captain was not equipped or inclined to do.

Pierpont purchased the coffee cargo from the captain of the ship, using the name and credit of Duncan, Sherman and Company. He informed the New York office of what he had done, and received an indignant telegram, ordering him to get out of the mess as quickly as he could, and indicating disapproval of his misuse of the company name.

Within twenty-four hours Pierpont was able to report that he had sold the entire cargo of coffee, reaping a profit of several thousand dollars. When he returned to New York he received a share in the profits for his gamble.

The risk he ran was not so great as it seemed, he later explained to an acquaintance. He had sold the cargo from those samples even before he had made the commitment to the ship's captain. His real risk was that the captain might have been lying to him about the quality of the entire cargo when he represented it as coming up to the standards of the samples. Here Pierpont had relied, as he always would, on his reading of a person's character. He had not been wrong.

CHAPTER

——◄◆►——

IV

MARRIAGE AND BEREAVEMENT

AFTER HE RETURNED from New Orleans triumphant in the success of his first independent venture in business, Pierpont Morgan secured a long leave of absence from Duncan, Sherman and Company and went to London to see his family and Mimi Sturges, who was still there with her mother and father.

Pierpont was very pleased to discover what friends the Morgan and Sturges families were. He embarked on a round of sight-seeing and entertainment, because he was on vacation from his work and he wanted to show Mimi Sturges the sights of London with which he had become familiar on previous visits. It would be wrong to think of Pierpont as very deeply touched by the residence of his family in London; he had never spent more than a few weeks there at a time, and actually was far more familiar with Switzerland and Germany than with England. He was as eager as anyone else, then, to go sight-seeing when he came to London, particularly given the company he now had.

Pierpont spent a long time with his family in the houses at Prince's Gate and Roehampton than he had enjoyed since the summer of 1854, before the family moved to Europe. He did not return to the United States until December 1859, when he came on the Cunard liner *Persia* with the Sturges family.

If Pierpont ever returned to Duncan, Sherman and Company it was for a very brief period. Duncan, Sherman had done what they said they would do: had made a place for him and trained him in business, almost an apprenticeship program. They paid him very little, if anything, but undoubtedly in the beginning he was not worth very much to a merchant banking firm. By the time he had secured the experience necessary to carry out the coffee speculation, he was ready to strike out on his own.

The Pierpont Morgan of 1860 was a handsome young man and he appeared at his very best at this time. He was not yet twenty-four years old. He was still slender. Occasionally he was afflicted with the skin eruptions that had troubled him for four years and occasionally he suffered fainting spells, which bothered him far more, for he never knew when he might collapse. He was a high-spirited young man, physically strong. He was gay, and in London or New York or at the Sturges country home in Fairfield, Connecticut, he was the organizer of the activities of the youthful, planning sessions around the piano, dinner parties, sleighing or skating parties.

He went horseback riding for exercise. Sometimes he brought a horse down from a stable near his lodgings, now on East Twenty-sixth Street, kept the animal all day in another stable near his office room, and then rode back in the evening.

In the winter of 1860–61, as the states of the South began one by one to secede from the Union, Pierpont Morgan went into business for himself. He opened an office at 54 Exchange Place. It was not his office but the room of James Tinker, an Englishman who had become a representative of George Peabody and later of Junius Morgan. They shared the room, and soon began to share certain business affairs of the George Peabody Company of London. In effect, under a watchful and protective eye, Pierpont was becoming his father's representative in New York.

When the war broke out in 1861 a number of young men in the Northern states of the Union sought military appointments as officers and went to war. Pierpont Morgan did not. His failure to enlist in the ranks or become an officer was not at all unusual. The Civil War, in the beginning, was very unpopular in New York, particularly among New York businessmen. Even if Pierpont had not felt any qualms about his fainting spells he still might not have volunteered for military service. President Lincoln's first call in 1861 was for 75,000 three-month volunteers. Well-to-do young men were rarely found in those ranks, and even later, when the course of war demanded larger sacrifice from the North, thousands of men of military age hired substitutes to take their places when they were called. This was deemed quite acceptable within the Northern community. Only in the later phases of the Civil War was patriotism a factor in military service, and by this time Pierpont was very much involved, emotionally and otherwise, in problems that made him quite oblivious to the need for soldiers.

The summer of 1861 was a most difficult time in the life of Pierpont Morgan. He had learned earlier that Mimi Sturges was suffering from weakness of the lungs. She had contracted a cold that spring and had never recovered properly from it. By midsummer it was apparent that her condition was growing worse. She must escape the climate of New York, not to England but to a dry warm area such as the Mediterranean coast.

It had been common knowledge within the families for several months that the pair would marry, and there was no question in Pierpont's mind about delaying the wedding. Meanwhile Mimi remained at the family summer home in Fairfield, and Pierpont visited her nearly every weekend, staying sometimes with his friends, the Ketchums, in adjoining Westport.

The summer of 1861 was a trying time for anyone who lived anywhere in America. Until late spring, even after the firing on Fort Sumter, there were some who hoped that the difficulties between the states could be adjusted without further conflict. When the minor skirmishing began in spring these hopes persisted. They were dashed, finally, at the first battle of Bull Run, where a force of nine thousand Confederates routed thirty thousand Union soldiers. The Union Army and much of the civil populace were demoralized. Where the war was unpopular it became more unpopular than ever. In the South this first major victory redoubled the determination to fight on, and the triumph of the Confederacy seemed to some to be very near.

One problem shared by both sides at the beginning of the conflict was a shortage of weapons. Before the war the standing army of the United States numbered only sixteen thousand men. More than twice that number were engaged at Bull Run alone, and the demands of the Union armies for weapons found the supply dangerously short. In the middle of the summer, even before Bull Run, Major P. V. Hagner was sent to New York City to begin buying arms from private contractors, but he discovered that he was not the only agent purchasing arms for the Union forces. Agents of state militia organizations were buying. So were agents of cities and special defense committees established by private citizens. It was a seller's market, and into this market had crept any number of middle men who saw a way of turning a fast dollar.

A man named Arthur Eastman approached the government with a proposal to modernize some weapons of a type known as Hall's carbines. They were perfectly serviceable but old-fashioned. Eastman proposed to make changes that would improve their effectiveness. The Secretary of War refused to bother with these carbines but authorized their sale to Eastman for $3.50 each, although they cost the government $17.50 apiece. To buy them Eastman had to take all the guns on hand, damaged and undamaged. Even after Bull Run, when the need for every weapon was apparent, these guns were sold. It was testimony not to corruption, but to the thorough confusion of the Union military organization.

Eastman had bought the carbines, but he had no money with which to pay for them, so he made contact with a man named Simon Stevens. Now it was July 29, the disaster at Bull Run had simmered on the front pages of the newspapers for a week, and all the North knew the nation was in for a real war.

Stevens contracted to buy the carbines from Eastman for $12.50 each. Stevens did not have the money to buy them, either, but now he had a contract of purchase with Eastman as did Eastman with the War Department. The guns were still in their grease packages in boxes on Governor's Island.

Stevens then looked around for some way to raise money. The agreement with Eastman said that Stevens had to find $20,000 within five days and the remainder of $37,000 within twenty days. (That first $20,000 was necessary to get the carbines from the government.)

Stevens knew that he would have to borrow the money. He also knew that to borrow it he would have to have a buyer. So he wired Major General John C. Frémont, commander of the newly formed but yet unorganized Western department of the army, who was as much engaged in the frantic search for arms as any official of the American government. Stevens offered five thousand carbines at $22.50 each to the United States Army.

(Now at that moment the United States Army still owned those carbines, but they were not in usable condition. In order to take the modern cartridges that were then being used by the government, the Hall carbines must be rifled and otherwise altered. This could be done; it was what Eastman had originally suggested before Bull Run.)

General Frémont accepted the proposal immediately, offering to pay all extra charges and asking Stevens to devote himself to this business alone.

Stevens and Eastman now had an opportunity to make a huge profit without capital or goods or any asset save shrewdness. Eastman had thought he was doing well to pay $3.50 each to the government for the five thousand carbines and sell them to Stevens for $12.50 each. This meant a profit for him of $40,000, estimating a cost of one dollar per carbine for the rifling. Stevens then proposed to turn around and sell the carbines to Frémont for $22.50 each, having altered them. This gave him a profit of $50,000.

What was needed now was money to buy the carbines from the government for $17,500 so that they could be altered slightly and sold back to the government for $110,000. But where was the money to come from?

Stevens went to see J. Pierpont Morgan in the young man's

new offices on Exchange Place. Why Morgan? Stevens knew H. H. Babcock, who was apparently a relative of the Babcock family where Pierpont had spent so many happy evenings in his early years in New York City. Also, Stevens was the brother of Miss Sophia C. Stevens, who had been Pierpont's *bête noire* when she taught him arithmetic at the Hartford Public High School in 1850.

Pierpont was yet a very young man. Proud as he was of his ability to read character, he was not yet able to discriminate between the balances of inheritance and environment in the molding of this character. Stevens came to Pierpont for a loan of $20,000, explaining that he had a chance to buy carbines unwanted by the government, but had no money. All this was true. He told Pierpont that he was buying the arms from the government; there is no indication that he told the young banker he was also selling them to the government.

Pierpont made the loan of $20,000. He charged interest of 7 per cent and an extra commission of $5,400. By this time, it did not make any difference what he knew. He was involved in this unsavory transaction. At some point he must have learned that a contract had been made by the government to sell arms that were being bought by the government. The only salve to any honest man's conscience could be that the War Department had earlier refused to make the alterations of the carbines for its own use, preferring to sell them. The turnabout in climate in Washington occasioned by the debacle at Bull Run had not changed these facts.

The young banker's position in this affair was not a comfortable one. The money was gone, committed and delivered. All he could do now was protect his investment, which he did by holding a lien on the arms until the loan was repaid. In order to consummate the deal he had made, Stevens needed more money, because Eastman must be paid within twenty days of the date of their contract for all the carbines. Stevens owed $37,500, which he did not have.

Stevens went to Pierpont Morgan again but Pierpont refused to have any more to do with this deal, and, instead, demanded the repayment of the loan he had made.

Now, others entered the scene, all bent on making quick and easy money. A Major Hubbard had entered the arrangement by introducing Stevens to Eastman. He expected a fee for this service, and unless Stevens paid Eastman quickly his interest would be lost with Stevens'. Major Hubbard then introduced Stevens to Morris Ketchum, senior partner in the Ketchum and Son banking firm. Further, he brought them together through George Opdyke, a prominent Republican businessman and politician who would soon be elected mayor of New York.

Ketchum was impressed with the bonafides of Stevens and the company he kept, so he made a large loan to Stevens, which enabled Stevens to complete his transaction. On September 16 Pierpont collected $26,343.54 from Stevens for the $20,000 loan, which represented interest and an additional profit for Pierpont of what was apparently one dollar each on all the guns.

Stevens did not do very well in the end. Eastman, who had profited by $40,000 already, charged Stevens another $3,700 for shipping boxes, bullet molds, and other appurtenances. Eastman had gotten the idea for the extra charge because the government submitted a bill to him. Stevens paid Eastman, but Eastman never paid the government for these "appurtenances."

Banker Ketchum lent Stevens well over $50,000, for which he charged interest at the going rate of 7 per cent, plus a commission. Before the financial arrangements could be completed however, government investigators stepped in, and within a few months the Hall Carbine Affair was a national scandal. By March 1862 so many scandals had been uncovered that Simon Cameron resigned as Secretary of War and a special commission was established to deal with the claims against the government. Of $50,-000,000 in claims, the commission threw out $16,000,000 for fraud and dishonest dealings such as that of the Hall Carbine Affair.

In the end of that affair Stevens and Ketchum had to go to court to collect their claim after the war, and by this time Stevens' profits had been eaten into heavily by Ketchum's interest and commissions, and Ketchum's capital had been tied up for four years. Pierpont was not involved in the case following repayment of his loan and the payment of charges he had made to Stevens.

By the end of the summer it was apparent that Mimi Sturges had developed tuberculosis, or consumption as it was then called, and that she must leave the damp climate of the East Coast. Pierpont decided that they would be married immediately and would go abroad so that Mimi could recover her health. He went to his cousin Jim Goodwin and persuaded Goodwin to give up his own business and take on management of Pierpont's affairs at the office on Exchange Place. That done, and the money collected from Stevens, Pierpont and Mimi were married at the Sturges household on Fourteenth Street, in the back parlor. She was so ill that the doors between the back and front parlors, which were opened in order that the ceremony could be seen, were closed immediately afterwards, to preserve Mimi from the ordeal of greeting the guests. Pierpont then carried his bride downstairs and to a taxi, which took them to the Fourteenth Street pier. There they boarded a tugboat he had hired, which carried them out to join the *Persia,* which had just steamed away for Liverpool.

Pierpont's father and mother did not attend the wedding, as it was held on too short notice for them to make arrangements to come to New York. Nor did the bride and groom linger in London to visit the family. Pierpont took Mimi immediately to Algiers with the finest doctors he could find. The warmth and sunshine should have helped, but Mimi faded quickly. Early in 1862 he took her to Nice, hoping against all indications that she could be saved. Mrs. Sturges was informed of her daughter's grave condition and she sailed just before the end of the year. Mimi died on February 17, but it was two months later before Pierpont could pull himself together enough to come back to the United States, and when he returned, he was a changed man. He was wearing black in mourning—black coat, black trousers, black waistcoat, black necktie, the severity relieved only by the white of his stiff-collared shirt. His hair was long and unkempt. He had grown a mustache which served to make him look older than his twenty-four years, but the real change was in mouth and eyes. His mouth had grown somber, his eyes piercing and tortured. His frame had filled out, and so had his face, even though it seemed now haggard. The difference between the Pierpont of 1860 and the Pierpont of 1862 was remarkable. A boy had married Mimi Sturges. A man was her widower.

CHAPTER

V

ADVENTURES ON WALL STREET

ANOTHER MAN might never have come back to New York City after so debilitating an experience, choosing instead to start life anew in totally different surroundings. It is a measure of Pierpont Morgan's character and simplicity of purpose that he returned to business as usual after his period of grief. He went back to Exchange Place without fanfare.

Pierpont and Jim Goodwin talked over the future, and Pierpont persuaded his cousin to remain in business with him for a time. They opened offices at 53 Exchange Place, and inserted a notice in the newspapers in September saying that the new firm of J. Pierpont Morgan and Company was going into business. They also roomed together, keeping house with a cook and housekeeper named Bridget, and a butler and valet named Henry.

In the fall they took a house on Twenty-first Street. Not long afterward, Pierpont was stricken with a disease diagnosed as varioloid, a mild form of smallpox, and he was very ill for several weeks. He was nursed at first by Mrs. Sturges. Later his mother came from London to stay with the young men in the little English basement house on Twenty-first Street. Pierpont spent most of his evenings at home. He did not go out socially, except

to visit the Sturgeses. He also spent much time at St. George's
Episcopal Church on East Sixteenth Street at Stuyvesant Square.
He had been confirmed and had become a communicant at St.
George's in 1861, shortly before his marriage to Mimi. Now he
attended the services there regularly, to hear the eloquent preach-
ments of the Reverend Stephen H. Tyng. He had purchased his
own pew in the church in 1861, and most of his nonbusiness activity was now devoted to matters of the church. Here, too, he met the
Charles Tracy family with whom he became friendly. Besides the
parents, it consisted of six daughters and one son.

In the spring Pierpont's mother returned to London. That summer he came out of mourning, taking a vacation trip with several
friends to the White Mountains of Vermont. He made all the arrangements and supervised the tour. His party included Edward
Ketchum of the banking firm and his wife; Cornelia Ketchum,
Edward's sister; a Miss Saltonstall; Pierpont's brothers-in-law,
Arthur and Harry Sturges; and Colonel Pride, who was General
Grant's chief engineer at the siege of Vicksburg, which had just
been concluded successfully.

They took the train to West Point and then went to Lake
George and the Fort William Henry Hotel, old Morgan stamping
grounds from the French and Indian wars. Then by stage they
traveled to Lake Champlain and crossed by ferry to stop in
Burlington. Pierpont hired a four-horse stage to carry them into
the mountains to the Profile House, where they spent a week
fishing and climbing. Pierpont was in better spirits than he had
shown in a year.

It was through his friend Edward Ketchum that Pierpont was
engaged in some extensive dealings with Ketchum, Son and Company that year. The firm was one of the largest and most successful New York banking houses of that Civil War period. In 1861
when Secretary of the Treasury Salmon P. Chase sought a $9,000,-
000 loan to finance the war, Ketchum, Son and Company was the
largest single subscriber, taking $1,875,000 in Treasury notes at
85 (as compared to par of 100). The profit seemed high, but the
risk was also great, and the federal government at that time, not
wanting to increase taxation, found the price palatable. Later

there would be much complaint about the profiteering of bankers during the war, but in 1861 there was still too much confusion for any definite policies to be established (nor was the financial market of New York ever brought completely under control during the war).

Jay Cooke of Philadelphia revolutionized war finance a few months later when he undertook to sell war bonds at a very low commission for the federal government. He did not like or trust Morris Ketchum and his son and was reluctant to do business with them. This reluctance caused the Ketchums and their friends to take even less interest in the Northern cause than most businessmen. The Ketchums were not the only bankers left out. Drexel and Company of Philadelphia was also ignored very largely in the war finance plans, and took the policy as an affront.

The competitive attitudes of bankers and businessmen did something to explain the almost total lack of restraint with which various profiteers sought to make capital of the Union's difficulties during the war. Unfortunately J. Pierpont Morgan was so ill-advised as to be drawn into this group. The specific matter was gold speculation.

In the first year of the war the federal government borrowed $8.52 for every dollar it raised by taxation. This was obviously inflationary. In the second year of the war, the government continued to borrow heavily, and also to issue "greenbacks," paper money that was not redeemable in gold or silver. Very soon these "greenbacks" slipped in value, until they finally sank to about thirty-three cents on the gold dollar.

When the currency began to decline in value, a gold exchange was established. Pierpont was familiar with the daily problems involved here, for he dealt primarily in foreign exchange at this time. All merchants who traded abroad and all importers found a gold exchange vital if they were to continue business. Prices had to be computed in terms of something more stable than the fluctuating national currency.

New York was the home of the foxes of speculation, and among these the Ketchums ranked high, particularly young Edward Ketchum, who was just hitting his stride as a banker, as was J.

Pierpont Morgan. Early in 1863 young Ketchum and young Morgan decided that they would make a killing in gold. Given his particular background, it is difficult to believe that Pierpont Morgan did not realize he was helping the enemies of the Union in what he was doing. With his understanding of financial problems and arithmetic, there was no reason why he should not have known that someone was going to bear a loss if he garnered a profit in speculation in money.

Ketchum and Morgan were far from alone. The Gold Room was the center of speculators from every city in the country, rich men and men who were not even particularly well-to-do, because one could buy gold in 1863 with a 10 per cent margin investment.

After the issuance of the "greenbacks," in the spring of 1863, the price was 163, or 163 per cent of a dollar, but a number of Union victories caused this price to drop to 130 and less during the month of September. Those who believed in Union victories sold the gold they held. If they were right, and the price fell still lower, they could buy back gold at a lower price to meet their foreign obligations.

Ketchum and Morgan saw how they could make a neat profit from this situation. If the military situation remained stable the price of gold would remain relatively stable, unless something disturbed it. The way to manage a disturbance would be to buy up secretly a tremendous amount of gold. If this could be done, then gold would become scarce and the price would rise.

Ketchum proposed that the pair buy $4,000,000 or $5,000,000 for the gold, which they could do if they could raise $400,000 or $500,000 and buy on the 10 per cent margin. They could cut the need for cash by splitting the purchase. Half of it could be shipped to Peabody and Company in London, where the price was certainly not less, and some of that could be used to pay outstanding obligations to Peabody and Company. The success of the matter was all in the timing.

By careful purchasing, the two young buccaneers accomplished what they set out to do. The price of gold rose, to 135, then to 140, then to 143. At this point there was rumor in the streets, but the newspapers indicated that there was no particular cause of the rise—meaning that there was no Union disaster to account for it. The price rise, as *The New York Times* put it, was based on "a disposition to speculate on the current demand of customs and export." True, but the disposition to speculate was in the hands of two hungry young men.

On October 10, 1863, Wall Street learned that $1,150,000 in gold was shipped to England by J. Pierpont Morgan and Company. This represented about ten times Pierpont's usual dealings in foreign exchange during any one week.

The gold market panicked when this large speculation was exposed, for although it was not a corner on gold by any means, the amount shipped in that one day represented a large share of the outstanding gold available, and with the end of the year approaching, those who had been delaying payment of outstanding foreign bills would be called upon to make good.

More important than the effect of the amount of gold shipped by Pierpont was the psychological effect of what he and Edward Ketchum had done. They had caught the market napping, and the speculators now began to believe the situation was far more serious than it actually was. Nor did the other speculators and merchants know that Pierpont and young Ketchum were in league. The price of gold began to rise. It went to 145, to 150. Others were selling gold and some were selling short, but Ketchum bought much of the gold that was offered and threatened to lie loose on the market. So the price continued to rise. In mid-October, after gold hit a high of 156, Pierpont and Ketchum sold their gold holdings. Very shortly thereafter gold dropped to 145. The young buccaneers shared a profit of $160,000.

There was an outcry in the press. More than that there was criticism of this maneuver from many within the financial community. Jay Cooke was open in his contempt for the Ketchum firm, and in this attitude at least he and his competitors, the conservative Drexels, agreed.

At about this time the firm of J. Pierpont Morgan and Company was dissolved. Charles H. Dabney, old friend of Junius Morgan in London, formed a new firm to represent the interests of George Peabody and Company. Dabney was senior partner. J. Pierpont

Morgan was junior partner. The firm was known as Dabney, Morgan and Company. It did not speculate in gold.

Young Ketchum continued to speculate in gold, and so did his father. In 1864 Congress retaliated by passing what was known as The Gold Bill to curb speculation. This prohibited the trading in gold futures, but it also placed severe limitations on dealings in foreign exchange which curbed the legitimate business of the Peabody-Dabney, Morgan relationship. The gold room was closed, but speculation continued when the traders found another place to meet, called along Wall Street the Coal Hole. Foreign exchanges were demoralized, the New York Chamber of Commerce protested the bill, and a group of bankers, of which Pierpont Morgan was one, also protested. The gold bill was abandoned by Congress as unworkable, but speculation continued and with more inflation and bad war news (Spotsylvania, Petersburg, Cold Harbor, and Chambersburg) the price rose until finally it hit 285. The Ketchums were involved in gold speculation all during the war, but after this one affair, which was followed by an immediate reorganization of "his" company, Pierpont Morgan speculated no more.

Really, he had a narrow escape, this young man who prided himself so much on his judgment of character. His friend and traveling companion, Edward Ketchum, continued to speculate in gold even beyond Morris Ketchum's knowledge. In 1865, when it became apparent that the Confederate cause was lost, the price of gold began to plummet. Edward Ketchum could not believe it. He continued to buy, on margin, and he had heavy holdings.

So heavy were they that when the price plummeted, even on 10 per cent margin he could not cover the losses. He took nearly $3,000,000 in funds and securities from his father's firm, and then, when this was still not enough, he forged $1,500,000 in gold checks which he then circulated as collateral for loans. Pierpont Morgan accepted some of these as collateral for a loan of $85,000, which was lost in the crash of young Ketchum, and then of his father's banking firm, because of the losses. At that time it was the largest defalcation in the history of Wall Street.

If Pierpont had actually earned $80,000 for his share of the shoddy gold transaction in which he engaged with Edward Ketchum, he came out slightly the loser anyhow.

In 1863 when the Union was feeling most sorely its need for trained soldiers, Congress passed a conscription act, which made all men between the ages of twenty and forty-five liable for military service. Quotas of men were established for each state. Still, a man could avoid entering the army by either securing a substitute or paying $300, which the army then used as a "bounty" to encourage enlistment. Pierpont paid the $300, as did many of the young men he knew. Not all of his friends avoided the war; one of the Sturges boys became a soldier, and one of the Tracy girls married a soldier of New York's Seventh Regiment. The war did not fail to touch the wealthy families of New York City, but as far as the draft was concerned, in the first draft in 1863, 292,000 names were drawn all across the country, 164,000 of these were exempted for physical disability, and more than 100,000 found substitutes. So of the draftees, only a few thousand ever served at all.

If Pierpont needed to make further excuses for himself, he could point to his uncertain health, to his successful business career, to his connection with George Peabody and Company and the share he had in helping government finance by purchasing United States securities for that firm.

In the autumn of 1863 Pierpont Morgan became a frequent visitor to the Tracy house on Seventeenth Street, around the corner from St. George's Church. He had recovered from the tragedy of Mimi's death, it seemed. Nearly every night in their house on West Twenty-first Street, Pierpont and Jim Goodwin were either out for dinner or giving a dinner at home. They moved the next year to a house on Madison Avenue near Thirty-eighth Street, and there the gaiety continued. On March 17, 1865, Pierpont and Frances Louisa Tracy became engaged. They were married at St. George's Church two months later, on May 31, with Joseph Peabody serving as Pierpont's best man.

Two weeks later Pierpont and Frances Louisa—Fanny, for that was what she was called—sailed on the *Persia* for England, for she had never met her parents-in-law. They visited the elder

Morgans at the Prince's Gate house, and then moved on to Paris, to Switzerland, where Pierpont took his bride to meet the Silligs at Vevey, and then to France. They sailed home in August and moved into a house at 227 Madison Avenue. A year later their first child was born. It was a girl and they called her Louisa Pierpont, after mother and father. She was christened in St. George's Church, where the young Morgans went to service every Sunday. On Sunday evenings they gathered around the piano with any guests who might be present and sang hymns, Pierpont always singing with great gusto if very little tonal accuracy. Just before Christmas 1865 J. Pierpont Morgan was elected to membership in the Union Club, one of New York's most conservative and well bred. He had long been a member of the Young Men's Christian Association, and now he sat on the board, giving good advice on how to attract young men to the organization (spruce up the rooms and the furniture). He was junior partner in a very successful merchant banking firm, whose profits brought him an income of $50,000 that year. He was a young man on his way, twenty-eight years old, happily married and in the process of raising a family, successful in business, and holding all the right connections for the future.

Pierpont also became a member of the board of St. Luke's Hospital. Soon he would help form the Metropolitan Museum of Art and the American Museum of Natural History. He would join the board of the Society for the Suppression of Vice. He would be sought for committee after committee, because he was a rising young man in business.

In the summers he and Fanny moved to the country, first renting a house in Irvington-on-Hudson, and then in other communities on the river and he became a summer commuter on the local trains. Levi P. Morton, the old family friend from Boston, and his father's one-time partner, had come to New York to go into the banking business. Morton went to Europe in 1867 and Pierpont rented his house at 243 Madison Avenue, but he maintained his relationship with St. George's Church downtown, and became a vestryman there in 1868. The Morgan's second child,

John Pierpont Morgan, Jr., was born on September 7, 1867, and the family settled in more tightly than ever.

In 1864 George Peabody had retired from his banking firm and it became known as J. S. Morgan and Company. Pierpont might look forward to taking over his father's business in London one day. In the meantime, there was quite enough to be done to handle the firm's business in New York in 1865, and to see what opportunities reconstruction of the damages done by the Civil War would bring in business.

PART THREE

The Making of the Financier

CHAPTER

I

THE FIRST RAILROAD

GREAT BRITAIN was the wealthiest nation in the world; British investors had become vitally interested in railroads in 1825 and that year 206 private bills were enacted by Parliament to form joint stock companies, most of them dealing in some way with railroads. British investors turned to American railroads ten years later when those roads began to issue stock and mortgage bonds, but investment waned in 1837 and American railroad shares went off the Stock Market of London. The stock of the Camden and Amboy Railroad was traded in London, however, after 1838.

After the Civil War, when Congress made railroads a gilt-edge investment by giving many of them huge chunks of the public lands for their rights of way and thus guaranteeing real estate values, British capital returned to America. Railroads and United States government bonds were at this time the only securities the British investors really trusted; railroads were more highly regarded than state government securities because the railroads had not defaulted, and too many states had done so over the years.

This pattern was to become important in the history of American railroads and in the development of the career of J. Pierpont

Morgan. As far as he was concerned, railroads first became important just after the end of the Civil War, when the great Eastern roads began to consolidate.

During the war years Commodore Vanderbilt, the nation's most important steamship and steamboat operator, had quietly divested himself of most of his shipping empire and was concentrating his fortune and his talents as an organizer on the amalgamation of several small railroads. By 1864, in fact, Vanderbilt had created the nucleus of the important New York Central System, putting together the New York and Harlem Railroads and the Hudson River Railroad. Although the New York legislature at first refused to sanction the amalgamation, Vanderbilt ignored the legislature and ran the roads as he pleased. Eventually, through bribery and influence, he managed to secure his way legally as well as in fact.

In 1866 Vanderbilt persuaded a young lawyer named Chauncey Depew to give up an appointment to the foreign service in Japan and become a railroad man. He also took control of the little New York Central Railroad, which linked a number of towns around Albany, and when the dust had settled it was discovered that Vanderbilt had outflanked the older Erie Railroad and had created a system that naturally funneled from the Great Lakes into the city of New York along the Hudson River. Vanderbilt then began to consolidate and strengthen his transportation empire.

One of the Commodore's first moves was to buy many tons of imported iron rails from Britain, for the British made the finest rails in the world. He used the banking firm of J. S. Morgan and Company, through their subsidiary, Dabney, Morgan, and Company, to buy rails at $125 a ton, and he bought by the thousands of tons. Pierpont, in 1866, became aware of the large potential of railroads for banking profit in several ways. Iron rails might yield a banking house $100,000 a year in profit. Now that the war was ended and British investors had overcome their shyness, railroads offered an attractive investment to them too. The railroads were eager for cash to finance their expansion. This cash was largely secured through mortgage bonds sold at home and abroad.

Railroads were becoming the nation's most important investment in the 1860's and every major banking house was considering railroad finance. Jay Cooke, who had come out of the Civil War as the nation's leading banker, refused to help finance the Northern Pacific Railroad in 1866 because the project seemed too risky, but Drexel and Company of Philadelphia was deeply involved in the Pennsylvania Railroad, and other houses were taking up the bond issues of the various Western roads.

Bankers now began to travel across the country to learn something about the area west of the Mississippi River where so much activity was suddenly generated. Jay Cooke traveled to Duluth, was convinced to back the Northern Pacific, and then became a Minnesota land speculator in addition to his other enterprises.

If he was to represent the interests of J. S. Morgan and Company properly, it would be wise for Pierpont to learn more about his own country, so in the summer of 1869 he organized a trip west. The children were left at home with a great-aunt and Pierpont, Fanny, her sister Mary, and his cousin Mary Goodwin set out for the wild West. They went to Chicago and stayed at the Sherman House for nearly two weeks, sight-seeing. Pierpont visited the stockyards and the railroad stations and talked to railroad men. They all went to church on Sunday, of course, at St. James Episcopal Church, and then left for the adventurous part of the trip to the far West on July 19 on a Pullman car called Minnesota.

They crossed the Missouri on a ferryboat, remaining in their railroad car, for this was before the building of the great railroad bridges. They saw what they thought was a Pawnee war party from windows of their train, and there were a number of American soldiers. They rode the train as far as Uintah in Utah, and took a stage to Salt Lake City where they called on Brigham Young. Pierpont declared that Young had taken a fancy to Mary Tracy, his sister-in-law, and indicated that he feared the party might have to leave her behind to become the Mormon leader's twenty-first wife. They scoured Salt Lake City for a church on Sunday and discovered a little Episcopal mission, working at its hopeless task. A stage coach took them to California where they boarded

a Central Pacific Railroad train and rode to Oakland, on San
Francisco Bay.

They were among the first tourists from the East. They traveled
into Yosemite Valley by coach, with Pierpont riding horseback
much of the time. They slept in log hotels where the partitions
between the rooms ran only seven or eight feet above the floor,
not nearly to the ceilings. They did not complain, although for all
of them, including Pierpont, it was the first taste of anything short
of luxury in their lives. They came back again by private Pullman
car. One Sunday they were on the road and Pierpont read the
morning services to the group.

During that spring and summer, while Pierpont was discover-
ing some of the potential of America, his father was busy in London. Junius became involved, as a banker, in attempting to settle
the claims of the United States government against Great Britain
that rose out of the Civil War. At the beginning of the war, several
ships were built for Southerners in British yards. One of these,
known at Laird's shipyard in Birkenhead as No. 290, was obviously being converted to become a man-of-war. In the summer
of 1862 the American legation discovered that this ship was to be
a warship and would be used against the Union, and the legation
protested that this was a violation of British neutrality. The British
government was sympathetic to the cause of the Confederacy and
while action was officially taken to stop the launching of the ship,
it was done so slowly that she escaped. Her armament was brought
to her in British ships, sailing from Liverpool to the Azores, where
she lay at anchor. Then, as the *Alabama,* this warship did serious
damage to American shipping until she was sunk in the summer
of 1864. After the war the American government began to make
claims against Britain for the damages done by the *Alabama,*
Florida, Shenandoah, and other Confederate raiders which were
constructed, launched, and armed by British citizens. The argument began to grow heated, and a coalition of bankers resident in
Great Britain stepped in to help settle the quarrel. Leader among
these was Junius Morgan, whose position in England was more
respected than that of any other American, following the death
of his old associate George Peabody.

That spring Junius met a young millionaire railroad man and bridge builder named Andrew Carnegie, who had emigrated from Scotland to the United States and was building his fortune. Carnegie was thirty-four years old. He was involved in a number of enterprises: an iron company, a locomotive works, railroads, and the Keystone Bridge Company of Pittsburgh. In 1869 he held a contract from a group of businessmen, who had organized a bridge company, to build a bridge across the Mississippi River at St. Louis. He secured an option on $4,000,000 of first mortgage bonds on the bridge company, and took it to London. There he called on Junius Morgan, who agreed to take part of the bonds with an option to take the rest, after some changes in the wording of the issue. Thus began an association between the young promoter and the banker that was to last for a number of years, with Pierpont, on the American side of the water, handling the details but not the negotiations. Carnegie referred to Junius as the greatest banker in Europe. Obviously this was exaggeration but Junius was an important international banker by 1869. At this period the basic position of Dabney, Morgan and Company was to serve the London office. Some trading was done on the responsibility of the American firm, and some loans were made, but by and large Dabney, Morgan existed to do the bidding of the British customers of J. S. Morgan, and to buy and sell on the J. S. Morgan Company's account.

Late in the 1860's, as railroads grew and prospered, a number of speculators and manipulators began to close in on the small lines, hoping to put together several of them and thus create a "system" which could dominate some area of the country. Among the most flamboyant and successful of these manipulators was Jay Gould, who constantly surprised Wall Street and Washington with the spread of his interests and the shallowness of his morality. Gould was shrewd and bold, and he had a knack for finding men of ability, if not of high character, to work with him. At one time he offered Andrew Carnegie, offhand, the presidency of the Pennsylvania Railroad and half the profits if young Carnegie would devote himself to the management. Gould did not even own a substantial amount of Pennsylvania stock at that moment, but had Carnegie assented, Gould would then have begun a campaign to take over this road, as he had taken over the Erie in a fight in which even Commodore Vanderbilt came off licking a few wounds.

Gould controlled the Erie then through Jim Fisk, a more flamboyant, if less thoughtful character than Gould himself. Gould lived on the edge of respectability, personally. Fisk was a denizen of the world of saloons and the *Police Gazette*. He was the leader of Gould's bully boys, who did not hesitate to beat up the opposition and wreck their headquarters when this seemed necessary.

In 1869 Jay Gould coveted the Albany and Susquehanna Railroad, a little line that ran for 142 miles. It was important because it connected with the Delaware and Hudson, the New York and Pennsylvania, the Erie, and the Delaware, Lackawanna, and Western. To Gould it was particularly valuable because it connected the Erie with all these other roads. Control of the Albany and Susquehanna would give him the opportunity to work out traffic agreements with the other roads, and also put him close enough to them that he might be able to enlarge his empire by taking control of some or all of the others.

The Albany and Susquehanna was a cooperative venture, formed by the communities along its right of way, and backed by them financially through bond issues. The capital of the road had actually been subscribed by the cities involved, by issuance of general obligation city bonds. The stock was held by the municipalities and each city was entitled to a member on the board of directors.

Gould immediately saw the weakness of the Albany and Susquehanna system, in a financial way. No one really had a stake in preservation of control of the railroad, because no one had a personal financial interest. The last mile of track was completed in December 1868, and the line was officially dedicated in January 1869. By the time the first train ran along the tracks, Gould was already at work to gobble up the line.

Jay Gould had managed to secure a representative on the board of directors of the Albany and Susquehanna because through the

Erie Railroad he had great influence with the Delaware and Hudson Canal Company. That company had lent a considerable sum of money to the Albany and Susquehanna and was given a seat on the board to protect its financial interest. Gould's influence with the Delaware and Hudson Canal Company was such that the director from that firm became in effect Gould's director.

As Gould and Fisk began buying railroad stock from the twenty-two communities that held control of the little railroad, they secured support for their position. They bought $45,000 worth of stock. During the spring, railroad president Joseph H. Ramsey saw that the Gould plan seemed to be succeeding. Nearly half his fifteen-man board of directors had turned against him and could be counted on to vote for Gould. If nothing was done, Gould would soon control the line. Ramsey's first move was to issue 9,500 more shares of stock, with the approval of the majority of his board of directors. This stock was kept in the control of the friendly members of the board, and Ramsey hoped, thus, to stave off the attack of Gould. He paid only 10 per cent cash—or his stockholders did—and this was financed by money borrowed with company bonds as security.

The annual meeting of stockholders of the railroad was scheduled for September 7, and exactly one month before that date the stock transfer books were to be closed. Ramsey issued three thousand shares shortly before the closing, then planned to close the books, and to protest the transfer of stock from the towns of Oneonta and Worcester, which Gould was buying. This would maintain Ramsey's control handily.

Gould discovered the plan through his connections on the board of directors. He went to see Judge George G. Barnard in New York City, a state judge who had the power to issue court orders that should be obeyed throughout the state. Judge Barnard issued an injunction voiding the three thousand shares that Ramsey had added to the Albany and Susquehanna stock book. Another injunction suspended Ramsey as president of the railroad. Still another appointed Jim Fisk and Charles Couter as receivers, who would take charge of the operation of the railroad until the ownership question could be settled.

These rulings, in effect, placed the Albany and Susquehanna in the hands of Jay Gould. The judge who made the rulings had been known rudely as "Vanderbilt's judge" during the Erie war. He had issued injunctions against Fisk and Gould in that fight. Now he was issuing injunctions that favored them. Yet the use of the railroad's own bonds to borrow money to issue new stock to maintain control was hardly proper. Thomas G. Shearman, who was one of Gould's attorneys, carried these injunctions to Albany, and presented them there. President Ramsey was not in, so a director named North, who was one of the Gould men, took possession of the offices and locked the doors. Superintendent Van Valkenburgh, who was a Ramsey man, broke them down. But while the doors were locked the stock books were stolen.

Ramsey's attorney then went to Judge Rufus W. Peckham, sitting on the State Supreme Court bench at Albany, a judge with the same power as that of Judge Barnard, except that he was also on the scene. The railroad management's attorney secured one injunction which suspended four Gould directors, and the treasurer of the company, so he could not do as Gould ordered. The judge appointed an Albany man named R. H. Pruyn as receiver of the railroad, and Pruyn put Superintendent Van Valkenburgh in charge of the offices in Albany.

Soon Jim Fisk arrived at the offices of the railroad, bearing his court appointment as a receiver, and accompanied by a gang of roughnecks. After a fight, they were thrown out of the offices and Fisk was "arrested" by a man who claimed to be a policeman. He was not held, however, and soon returned to the railroad offices. There, it is said, he encountered President Ramsey and offered to settle the fate of the Albany and Susquehanna by playing a hand of seven-up. If Ramsey did not accuse him of carrying marked cards at least he did not play.

Backed by a court order from Judge Barnard in New York City, the Gould men seized much of the rolling stock of the railroad and one end of the line. The Ramsey men seized the other end of the line and the rest of the rolling stock. The dividing line between territories was a tunnel near Harpursville, with Gould men on one side and Ramsey men on the other, and the tunnel itself as no-man's-land.

Violence broke out as each side hired toughs to harry the other.

A locomotive manned by Gould's men was derailed at a switch, and captured, along with its crew, by the Ramsey men. The Ramsey men captured the tunnel, and the Gould men drove them out. The danger to the public grew so great that Governor Hoffman called out the militia and placed the railroad under martial law. General Robert Lenox Banks was put in charge of the company, and Major General James McQuade was made operating superintendent of the line, until civil control could be re-established through the courts.

The courts were in a disgraceful state. On August 12 Judge Barnard in New York City issued a court order vacating all the orders in the case issued by Judge Peckham in Albany. On August 13 Judge Peckham issued an order vacating all the orders issued by Judge Barnard. It was apparent that the railroad was in sore distress, that the only people who were making any money out of the situation were the lawyers, and that justice must first disentangle itself before it could serve the public. What President Ramsey needed now was a banker, not a lawyer, for only money and power could disentangle this knot.

President Ramsey realized this well before the stockholders' meeting, and sought the advice of Samuel Sloan, president of the Delaware, Lackawanna, and Western Railroad, who had no use for Gould, and was involved in this affair because his subsidiary coal company had a stake in the preservation of the independence of the Albany and Susquehanna. (He competed with the pro-Gould Delaware and Hudson Canal Company, which was now really a coal company.)

Samuel Sloan had come to know J. Pierpont Morgan during the summer when Pierpont commuted to New York City from Irvington-on-Hudson. Sloan knew that Dabney, Morgan and Company was backed by one of the strongest banking houses in the world, that of J. S. Morgan in London. He knew and liked Pierpont as a forthright young man of sturdy disposition and temperament, who was uncommitted in the railroad industry.

So President Ramsey went to see Dabney, Morgan and Company and ask their assistance. Pierpont consulted his attorney, who was Charles Tracy, his father-in-law, and agreed to take a hand.

The first move was for Dabney, Morgan and Company to acquire six hundred shares of Albany and Susquehanna stock, which they did. The next was to hire the best lawyer they could find in Albany, which they did. His name was Samuel Hand.

On September 3 Judge Barnard in New York City issued an injunction restraining Dabney, Morgan from receiving the six hundred shares of stock, and restraining the railroad from selling any stock. On September 6, the stockholder's meeting one day away, Gould's attorneys filed the nuisance suit against President Ramsey and the other officers of the road, so Gould men could serve these officers with warrants of arrest as the stockholders meeting began, and thus keep them out of action.

Pierpont went to Albany. There he conferred with Attorney Hand and they prepared their arsenal. They would rely on absolutely proper procedure. They checked out the ownership of the shares of stock, making sure that the stockholders friendly to their cause would appear to vote or would give up legal proxies. They prepared minutes and other papers.

Hand, quite by accident, discovered that Jim Fisk and a gang of plug-uglies were on their way to Albany for the meeting, and President Ramsey was informed. So warned, the defenders were ready for anything.

The next day Ramsey was arrested and so were other Albany and Susquehanna stockholders. They managed to return in time for the election, however, and vote their stock. Fisk, his mustaches waxed, showed up with forty roughnecks, each carrying a proxy and playing the role of a legitimate stockholder.

These toughs were not allowed to vote in the Albany and Susquehanna stockholders election supervised by Pierpont and Attorney Hand, so they held their own stockholders election. The Ramsey men returned the Ramsey board and Ramsey control. The Fisk men, in their voting, returned the Gould board and Gould control.

Immediately after the meeting, Fisk headed back to New York to report, and the next day Judge Barnard issued injunctions to restrain the Ramsey board of directors from acting.

But this time Gould was outfoxed. Pierpont Morgan had been elected vice-president of the Albany and Susquehanna Railroad. At a board meeting immediately after the stockholders' meeting the board of directors also voted to accept a proposition the new vice-president made: they would lease the Albany and Susquehanna Railroad to the Delaware and Hudson Canal Company for ninety-nine years, thus pulling one of Gould's props from under him. This would be very profitable because the Delaware and Hudson had agreed to accept a valuation of the railroad of $7,000,-000 and would pay 7 per cent per year. Since the little Albany and Susquehanna was only earning $450,000 a year with the expenses of operation, this would mean far more profit and far less corporate expense, let alone freedom from operating problems.

Pierpont went to New York and made the arrangements. Meanwhile, when the new injunctions of Judge Barnard were brought to Albany, they were matched by injunctions of Judge Peckham, and the entire matter was thrown into the state's highest court, with Governor Hoffman's men continuing operation of the railroad in the interim. In a few weeks the high court ruled in favor of the Ramsey board, and the leasing arrangement was approved, and went into effect.

CHAPTER

II

THE NEW ALLIANCE

M UCH OF Pierpont Morgan's time in the last few months of
1869 was taken up by what the newspapers called "the
Albany and Susquehanna war." The high court did not hand down
its decision until December and meanwhile all avenues of action
were considered.

Pierpont's personal fortune and his future seemed secure
enough to him in the autumn of 1869 that he purchased the family's first house, a town house at 6 East Fortieth Street, next to the
southeast corner of Fifth Avenue, where William Henry Vanderbilt lived. It was long and narrow like most of New York's houses.
It was furnished comfortably, fashionably, with overstuffed furniture, oriental rugs, candelabra, and paintings, mostly landscapes,
that Pierpont and Fanny purchased.

Under Charles Dabney's direction, Pierpont had learned to
avoid the recklessness that characterized so many of the other
young men in the financial world. In the summer of 1869 Jay
Gould was perhaps paying less attention to the Albany and Susquehanna struggle than he might otherwise because he was engaged in heavy gold speculation. Gould's method was to persuade
those around President Grant and to try to persuade the President

that it would not be proper to interfere in the "normal" routine of business in Wall Street by tampering with the gold market.

Gould and others then began buying gold. Jay Gould had organized a conspiracy to buy as much gold as possible and run the price up. The price of gold kept rising until on September 24 it hit 162½. At that point there was demand for $250,000,000 in gold, some of it by people who needed gold to fulfill real obligations to foreign customers, but much of it was a demand created by the hoarding of a handful of speculators, who refusal to sell their gold and created an artificial shortage, and by short-sellers, or gamblers, who proposed to buy cheap gold to pay expensive debts.

Although President Grant's brother-in-law had been corrupted and was involved in the scheme, President Grant was finally persuaded that the government must step in and sell gold on the market, buying back its own bonds to drive the gold price down. Jay Gould discovered this decision, but the other conspirators did not. He did not tell them and began selling gold privately.

On Friday, September 24, the crisis came when $250,000,000 in gold was needed, and only $15,000,000 in gold and gold certificates —redeemable at the Treasury—was actually available in the market. Then a group of bankers, led by Brown Brothers and Company began to sell gold they had acquired, and the price began to drop. From Washington came the word that the Treasury would begin to buy gold. When this news reached the market at noon on September 24, the price of gold had been forced back to 160 by Brown Brothers' selling. Now it fell from 160 to 133 in fifteen minutes. Jim Fisk had not been told the secret by Gould, so he was buying gold all this time. He was ruined. So were scores of other brokerage and banking houses. Lockwood and Company, an honest firm with a capital of $5,000,000 and twenty-five years' experience in Wall Street, went down in this crash. Other banking houses fell or tottered, and the bankers and brokers revised their interest rates on securities. New York Central railroad stock was then one of the stout investments in the market; nonetheless the bankers charged 5 per cent *per day* in interest on money loaned against this stock.

Amid this devastation, Dabney, Morgan and Company were serene. Pierpont Morgan had learned his lesson in 1864 very nearly painlessly. This summer and autumn had been the acid test, for the "gold bug" had bitten nearly every man on Wall Street, except Pierpont and his partners. Added to the victory in the Albany and Susquehanna affair, this conservatism added materially to the reputation of Dabney, Morgan and Company in the American financial community, but it had quite an opposite effect on Pierpont personally.

He was sick of the business world. His third child, Juliet Pierpont, was born on July 19, 1870, and he now had a sizable family to support, but Dabney, Morgan and Company had earned several hundred thousand dollars for him and he felt that he could retire from business and live quite satisfactorily. At thirty-three he seemed very young to be talking of retirement, but he was disgusted and he felt that his health was poor. His disgust was easy to understand. He was living in the most lawless community in the nation. On all sides of him he saw corruption: the bribing of legislators by the railroad men, the bribing of city councilmen by merchants and contractors; the corruption of judges and the venality of all the political world. He saw business partner cheating business partner and both cheating their customers. He was distressed by the low level of business morality, and the disorganization of railroads and the financial community.

His health was a matter of grave concern. He did not understand why he had fainting spells. He did not understand the eruptions that disturbed his face, and were beginning to enlarge his nose. He was, however, taking interest in many cultural activities. This year he attended his first diocesan convention as a lay delegate from St. George's Church. He and others were planning the organization of the new American Museum of Natural History which would sprawl along the west side of the new Central Park. But he was not happy with his life.

Pierpont confided this unhappiness to his father in one of his lengthy letters. Junius was at the height of his powers and reputation, for in the autumn of 1870 he engineered a banking coup which brought him a reputation in England to match that of the Rothschilds.

Emperor Louis Napoleon of France had fought the Germans in the Franco-Prussian War until he could fight no more and had surrendered to King Wilhelm of Prussia at Sedan on September 2, 1870. Two days later the news reached Paris, which would soon be surrounded by Prussian forces. That night the Legislative Assembly met and voted to abandon the empire and declared that a Republic would forthwith govern France.

A Committee of Defense of seven men was appointed, and set to work to prepare a defense for the city, expecting an attack. Cattle, grain, salt, hay, and other foods were brought into the city. Every available building was converted to a warehouse.

Walls, bastions, and embrasures were quickly erected around the city, trees outside the city were cut down, including the beautiful ones of the Bois de Boulogne, and the swans and deer in the wood were killed by soldiers. No one expected a siege; they were preparing to resist a frontal attack by the Prussians. For two more weeks the railroads continued to run, radiating out into France like spokes from the capital; then 250,000 Prussians ringed the city, the city's fifty-one gates were closed, and the siege began.

Before the gates were closed, two members of the Committee of Defense, M. Cremieux and M. Garnier-Pages, were sent out of the city to govern the provinces for the Republic during the period ahead. Adolphe Thiers, head of the Committee, was visiting foreign capitals to try to enlist sympathy and funds for the new Republic.

October came. The Prussian troops who surrounded the city prevented word from coming in or going out, except by carrier pigeon or message smuggled through the lines.

Among the members of the Committee left in Paris was Léon Gambetta, a thirty-two-year-old Paris lawyer, born in Cahors in the south of France, of Italian parentage. Gambetta had made a reputation in Paris under the hated monarchy by speaking out against the excesses of Louis Napoleon's rule. Now, in a city made immobile by siege, he longed for action. One day he persuaded the other members of the Committee that the only salvation of Paris lay in bringing help from outside. He wanted to go out and lead the action.

The others were persuaded that Gambetta could bring help, and so a balloon was brought into a courtyard, inflated, and the intrepid politician stepped in, to be wafted aloft and escape over the very noses of the Prussians outside the city gates.

Gambetta made his way to Tours where Cremieux and Garnier-Pages had set up a government in the archbishop's palace. Gambetta now took over. He became Minister of War in this interim Republican government and also Minister of Interior. He called to England for help in France's hour of need, and in response to that call, Junius S. Morgan came to Tours. Gambetta needed 250,000,000 francs, fifty million dollars, in order to raise an army and govern the country while the Republic fought against Prince Bismarck's Prussians. Morgan took the risk. He guaranteed a loan for that amount, in the form of 6 per cent bonds. The cost to the French was high. Morgan bought the bonds at eighty cents on the dollar, but the risk was very great.

How great became apparent very shortly.

At Christmas time Gambetta was raising and training two armies, the Army of the Loire and the Army of the Jura. But in Paris people were feeling the pinch of hunger. Here is the menu of a Paris restaurant saved from Christmas Day 1870:

Soup from horse meat
Mincé of cat
Shoulder of dog with tomato sauce
Jugged cat with mushrooms
Roast donkey and potatoes
Rat, peas, and celery
Mice on toast
Plum pudding

The Rothschilds distributed $20,000 worth of clothing, but fuel grew almost nonexistent. The American Sanitary Commission had sent a hospital to Paris for the 1867 Exposition Universelle. This was set up, but soon the supplies of opium and quinine were exhausted.

Outside Paris, Gambetta and his armies moved, but General Bazaine, a royalist leftover who had another force of 170,000 men, surrendered to the Prussians at Metz for no apparent reason. Gambetta's men moved up the Loire, and at one time seemed near to compelling the Prussians to lift the siege of Paris. But the surrender of Bazaine enabled the Prussians to throw another 150,000 soldiers against the city. On January 27, 1871, after four months, Paris surrendered.

As affairs worsened in France, the sale of the French bonds fell off in London and when the surrender came Junius Morgan was forced to buy back a number of them to protect his investment. With the surrender, came a demand from the Prussians for a $40,000,000 ransom. The Republic government agreed to pay and the Prussians withdrew. The Republic then was overthrown in favor of a bloody Commune, and Morgan's position appeared to be desperate.

Then, the Commune was itself overthrown. The Republic was declared once again. Gambetta came back in glory as one of the most respected figures in all France, and in June 1871, when the French Republic appealed for further loans of 2,000,000,000 francs at 5 per cent, secured by bonds which would be purchased at 82½, the loan was oversubscribed by a pool of bankers in a few days. Junius Morgan's 6 per cent French bonds at 80 were already gobbled up on the news of the fall of the Commune.

In this heady atmosphere of success, Junius Morgan did not show much sympathy with Pierpont's expressed *weltschmerz* or his plaint that his health was gone. He wrote to Pierpont that he had recently visited with A. J. Drexel, of Drexel and Company, Philadelphia. "It is possible he may want to see you about a certain matter," Junius said, "and if he does I hope you will go to see him."

This was in the spring of 1871. Pierpont was just cleaning up the affairs of Dabney, Morgan and Company. The stipulated time limit for the partnership was about to expire, and Charles H. Dabney wanted to retire from business altogether. Jim Goodwin wanted to go back to Hartford to take over his father's business affairs. Partner George H. Morgan wanted to go into business for himself. This Morgan was a member of the "other branch" of the family, a descendant of old Miles Morgan by his first wife. George Morgan had married Pierpont's sister Sarah in 1866, and then had come to America to join Pierpont's firm.

Pierpont was half set on quitting business altogether, no matter what his father said, when the letter referring to Drexel came in the mail.

The Anthony J. Drexel to whom Junius had referred was the son of Joseph Drexel, founder of the most important banking house in Philadelphia before Jay Cooke had come along with his whirlwind bond-selling tactics. Cooke had now established an international banking house with an office in London managed by Hugh McCulloch, who had been Secretary of the Treasury under both President Lincoln and President Andrew Johnson. There the firm was known as Cooke, McCulloch and Company. Drexel had an office, or partnership, in Paris, where it was known as Drexel, Harjes and Company, but none in London.

In London, Junius Morgan had welcomed the idea of an alliance with the Drexel firm rather than competition against it. He and A. J. Drexel had discussed the possibilities of such an alliance. From Drexel's point of view it would be most helpful to have a strong New York connection, and this could be supplied by Junius' son, Pierpont.

Pierpont did not have all this background in his mind, however, and was somewhat mystified as to what Anthony Drexel should want from him, when he received a telegram asking him to come to Philadelphia to see him. Pierpont went to Philadelphia that day and dined at the Drexel house. After dinner Drexel asked Pierpont to join his firm as a partner.

At first Pierpont Morgan said that he could not think of it, that he was about to retire from business altogether because of his ennui and his health. Drexel said he thought this would be a mistake, and he painted so glowing a picture of the prospects for the future that Pierpont was half-convinced, and went so far as to stipulate that he must have a year off if they agreed on any arrangement.

Drexel agreed to this and outlined the terms offered on the back of an envelope. Pierpont took the envelope along as he left that evening for New York. It provided for the establishment of a New York partnership to be called Drexel, Morgan and Company, with the Drexels contributing half the capital and the Morgans contributing half the capital, with the profits and liabilities to be shared equally. Pierpont would also become a partner in Drexel and Company of Philadelphia.

By the next day Pierpont had thought the matter over and was inclined to accept. He wrote his father about it, seeking his views. Since it was Junius' idea in the first place, there was very little question about approval, and so the arrangement was made. This move created a strong alignment. The Drexels were an important force in Philadelphia. J. S. Morgan and Company was strong in London. Drexel, Harjes and Company was influential on the Continent. Now, with the Drexel and Morgan names and Pierpont's demonstrated abilities to make order from confusion, Anthony Drexel and Junius Morgan had hopes that a powerful combination could be achieved. They might even have suspected that the brawny thirty-four-year-old Pierpont, who was so worried about his health, would one day come to dominate the entire combination.

CHAPTER

III

INTERLUDE

Pierpont Morgan contributed $727,649.21 in capital in the summer of 1871 to begin the Drexel-Morgan partnership. Much of this money came from his father. Pierpont's earnings during the past decade had been high, but not nearly high enough to give him such a great surplus. As for Junius Morgan, he could now afford to contribute very well, for on the French bonds alone he had earned a profit of at least $5,000,000. This was the reward for great daring, for he had staked his personal fortune on Gambetta and the Third Republic.

Business was slow enough in America so that there seemed to be no reason why Pierpont should not be absent for a year. He packed up Fanny and the three children. He arranged with his loyal and forbearing cousin Jim Goodwin to close up the affairs of Dabney, Morgan and Company before he returned to Hartford. Drexel, Morgan and Company opened offices in the Morgan rooms at 53 Exchange Place, and Joseph Drexel of the Philadelphia firm came up to supervise the new establishment. By the end of the second week in July, Pierpont and his family had sailed on the Cunard liner *Scotia* and a few days later they were inside the doors of No. 13 Prince's Gate, overlooking London's Hyde Park.

Pierpont rested and went driving in his father's coach. He was nervous and did not sleep well. He did not seem to improve very much in London. Perhaps that was because Junius was busy and the air of bustle communicated itself through the house.

Junius was a leading financial lion of London. Hundreds of promoters now came to him. He was busy with the *Alabama* arbitration, as well as the sale of United States government bonds and railroad securities. He was also earning good profit with very little risk by dealing in acceptances of bills against American firms for railroad rails.

All this activity was not what Pierpont had come to Europe to seek; he might have remained in New York for that. The young Morgans and their children therefore took the boat train to Paris. They stayed at the Hotel Bristol, operated by Junius Morgan's one-time butler, Morlock, but they did not stay for very long. Pierpont was too nervous to stand the noise of Paris, so he packed the family up and took them to the spa of Pau. Nerves again, plus the terrible heat of summer, were too much for him and in a few days they were back in Paris. Pierpont seemed to be most improved when he was either traveling or planning a trip, but the constant movement was most wearing on the rest of the family.

Fortunately Pierpont's next move was to lead to more relaxation for all. He was persuaded to go to Karlsbad, one of Europe's famous watering places, and to take the baths and the cure. This meant that the family stayed at a Karlsbad hotel. Pierpont consulted a doctor there and was given the prescription for the cure. This consisted of long walks, baths in the mineral water, minimums of tobacco and alcohol, plenty of sleep, massages, and regular morning pilgrimages to the drinking rooms to drink several glasses of the laxative mineral water.

After Pierpont had taken the cure he felt much better. (He was impressed enough with this method of counteracting city living that he continued it all the rest of his life.) The family now toured the Austrian Tyrol. At Innsbruck they met Junius and Juliet Morgan, and Pierpont went with them on a trip to St. Moritz to visit the Engadine. Fanny took the children to Salzburg to rest. During the remainder of the summer they visited Vienna,

Munich, and then moved south through Bavaria and into Italy as
fall approached. By December they were in Rome, then went to
Egypt for the coldest part of the winter. Pierpont chartered a
dahabeah—Nile boat—and began a trip up the river. The slow
sailing disturbed him, and he transferred his party to a Cook's
river steamer, which took them up to the first cataract and back.

They were in Rome again in March, where Fanny fell ill briefly
with fever. When she recovered they moved up to the lake country
of the north, and then through Switzerland to Karlsbad again,
where Pierpont repeated his cure of the year before.

It was now the summer of 1872. In August, while they were
at the hotel in Karlsbad, Pierpont learned that a house on the west
bank of the Hudson River, at Highland Falls, was to be sold because the owner had died. For several years he had been renting
a house about half a mile north of this one, and he knew it well.
It belonged to a Mr. Baldwin and was called Cragston. It was a
large Victorian building, overlooking a long, spacious lawn, with
a fine view of the Hudson below. In the past, many times when
they had been out walking from their rented summer quarters,
Pierpont and Fanny had wished that they owned this house. Now
came the chance to acquire it.

Pierpont made some rapid calculations about Hudson Valley
real estate, and came up with a figure that he considered to be
a fair one, even on the high side, since he was eager to have the
house. He telegraphed the offices of J. S. Morgan in London,
telling them to make an offer and then waited anxiously to see if
it was accepted.

A few days later came the word that a contract had been signed
by his agent in New York and that the house was his. Not until
much later did Pierpont learn that his father had sent the message
to New York to buy the house and had said nothing about price.
Pierpont knew much about the banking business in 1872, but
Junius Morgan knew that if a man wanted something he ought
not to let the problems of money get in the way.

CHAPTER

IV

MORGAN THE MILLIONAIRE

The possession of his new house on the Hudson exorcised any remaining demons that were troubling Pierpont Morgan. His old zest for life returned. He and Fanny began to buy furnishings and bric-a-brac for the new home, and they spent hours talking about what they would do to renovate it for their own use.

In the autumn the young Morgans visited Junius and Juliet again at Prince's Gate and Dover House, and then they sailed for home on the *Scotia,* the ship that had brought a tired and dispirited Pierpont across the Atlantic. That Pierpont had disappeared in favor of a robust thirty-five-year-old man who could scarcely wait to get back to business and his civic affairs.

In Pierpont's absence, the Drexels had built a six-story white marble building at the corner of Broad and Wall Streets, in the center of the financial district, and this building was very nearly ready for occupancy when Pierpont returned from Europe. There were a few weeks of work in the old offices at 53 Exchange Place; there were goodbyes to be said to Jim Goodwin, who now, at last, could go home to Hartford; there were rounds of Christmas entertainment and social calls at New Year's. Then, the holidays over

139

and his rest behind him, Pierpont plunged into the world of business again.

His first move in the new surroundings and new company was to travel to Washington with Levi P. Morton and other New York bankers to protest the government's manner of refinancing its Civil War debts. While Pierpont was on vacation in 1871 the Treasury had attempted to refund $200,000,000 in Civil War bonds which would soon come due. The government wanted to call these in to exchange them for long-term bonds. Jay Cooke and Company had become the foremost American financial house in the handling of government bonds. They had taken and sold bonds during the war when no other house could or would do the job so well, and they had financed the war on a very low level of profit to themselves. In 1871 they had expected to be given the chance to handle the refunding.

They would not get it without a fight. Anthony Drexel began to make representations that other firms should have the opportunity to handle these bonds. Levi Morton agreed and went to Washington to try to get the loan for himself and his English house. In the struggle, Congress became aroused and decided that the Treasury would sell the bonds directly, without using a financial house at all. In March 1871 the Treasury appointed a number of financial houses as agents for the bonds. As agents, these houses would be paid only a fee for selling the bonds. What they wanted was a chance to bid on them, to buy them at perhaps ninety or ninety-five cents on the dollar, and then to have for their own profit the difference between the price paid and the market price. (It was conceivable that the bonds could go immediately to 110 or 115 per cent of par.) The sale was to last for about three weeks, for that should have been plenty of time to dispose of the total amount. But at the end of that time only $20,000,000 had been subscribed in the United States and $80,000,000 in England. (England was by far the most important financial market in the world at this time.)

Dabney, Morgan had been an agent. So had J. S. Morgan in London. But no one was much interested in this business when other business was so much more profitable to handle. After the

Junius Spencer Morgan, 1890.

Mrs. Junius Spencer Morgan, 1861.

"Pip" at 10, with his sisters Sarah and Mary.

Pierpont, 16, at Göttingen, 1857.

From J. Pierpont Morgan *by Herbert Satterlee*

Above: Cragston-on-Hudson, near West Point. *Below:* Woodcliff, a family summer house in Irvington-on-Hudson.

Above: An early picture of the Morgan houses on Madison Avenue. *Below:* The library at 219 Madison Avenue.

At the Temple of Karnak, 1877. J. P. Morgan on a picnic. He wears a helmet and knickers and stands between his wife and son Jack.

At an excavation in the Libyan Desert. The Omdeh of Khargeh and J. P.
Morgan talked in sign language for over an hour.

J. P. Morgan on a priest's throne in a Coptic cathedral in Sakkara, Egypt, 1909.

Courtesy Pierpont Morgan Library

J. Pierpont Morgan, 1888.
Portrait by Frank Holl.

Courtesy John P. Morgan, II

J. P. Morgan at the Villa
Albani, 1907.

Courtesy Pierpont Morgan Library

Above: The West Room of the Pierpont Morgan Library about 1910.
Below: The Pierpont Morgan Library.

Mrs. J. P. Morgan, 1902.

Courtesy Pierpont Morgan Library

"The Corner," Drexel Building. 1871-1913.

The House of the House of Morgan, 23 Wall Street. This replaced "The Corner" in 1914.

The House Party at Nuneham Park, 1907. King Edward sits at center, Morgan is the fourth from the top on the stairs.

Courtesy Pierpont Morgan Library

Above: Corsair II, about 1892. *Below:* J. Pierpont Morgan, J. P. Morgan Jr., and Louisa Morgan Satterlee going to the "Pujo Committee" Hearing, Washington, 1912.

J. Pierpont Morgan, Jr.,
"Jack," 1915.

Ann Pierpont Morgan,
President of the American
Friends of France, and her
secretary, 1944.

Wide World

Harvard College, 1939. Junius Morgan, who graduated from Harvard 25 years earlier, J. Pierpont Morgan, Jr., who graduated 50 years earlier, and Henry Sturgis Morgan, who graduated 16 years earlier.

failure of the government attempt, a syndicate was organized by Jay Cooke to sell the remainder of the bonds, which it did at a profit to the syndicate of $3,000,000.

In 1872 the government wanted to refund another group of bonds, and Jay Cooke suggested that he be allowed to sell $600,-000,000 worth of new bonds. This would have brought more huge profits, but there was much objection to giving Cooke the business. Drexel, Morgan and Company objected and so did many other competitors of the Cookes. Consequently no refunding at all was done in 1872 and no bankers made any money from new federal bond issues.

In January 1873, when Pierpont and Levi Morton went to Washington, it was to persuade Secretary of the Treasury Boutwell not to give all the bond business of the government to Jay Cooke and Company, but to spread it around among the various banks. The attack took two forms. First was the trip to see the Secretary and state the case. Second was a campaign against Jay Cooke and Company launched by a group of Philadelphia bankers backed by Drexel. This campaign was conducted on Capitol Hill in hearings before the House of Representatives Committee on Ways and Means.

In the end the Treasury split the bonds. A syndicate was formed. It was led by Jay Cooke and Company, which received the handling of $150,000,000 in government bonds, while another group, led by Levi Morton and Pierpont Morgan, would take the other $150,000,000. The success of this depended very largely on the foreign sales, and this meant English sales. The key firms were Morton, Rose and Company, Baring Brothers, J. S. Morgan and Company, and, on the Cooke side, the Rothschilds, and Cooke's English house. This was why Drexel and Company had been so eager to form an alliance with the Morgans; the immense prestige and sales power of J. S. Morgan and Company in Britain could make the difference between success and failure in any bond or stock flotation.

In this bond issue there was no question of the government's selling the obligations below par. There was no drastic need. Congress had authorized the bond houses to take a commission of one half of one per cent. On $300,000,000 of bonds, this would mean that commissions of $150,000 could be split. There was another inducement to the banks: they would be allowed to keep the money they received from the sale of the securities in their hands for three months without paying interest on that money. This could be the equivalent of another $4,500,000 if the sales were quick. Thus there was a total profit of $6,000,000 at stake for the various banking houses; such an amount was certainly worth fighting over.

For Jay Cooke at this time, success and speed were essential. He needed guaranteed profits and he needed them quickly. His banking house was desperately involved in the financing of the Northern Pacific Railroad, which was badly and wastefully managed, and which had not shown anything like the activity he had expected. Cooke had also gone heavily into other investments in the Northwest, and none of them was working to be the bonanza he had expected. Just before Christmas there were times when his house was overdrawn by $150,000 and more at the New York clearing house, without assets to meet the obligations. On at least one occasion a debt was paid by having the Secretary of the Treasury advance the date on payment of a check due the house.

At this time, in Cooke's desperation, the European houses, Rothschilds and Morgan, and the rest, took it upon themselves to delay in the sale of these bonds. They held an option until December 31, 1873, and they saw no reason to put on a Jay Cooke type of whirlwind campaign. Such a campaign might work in America, but in England it would only cause investors to worry why there was so much fuss.

Everybody, it seemed, was in the money market, and everybody was trying to make too much money too quickly, and everybody was nervous. The queasiness of the money market is illustrated in a tale told by Andrew Carnegie:

One day Colonel William Phillips, president of the Allegheny Valley Railway at Pittsburgh, came to the New York office of Carnegie and said that he needed money badly. He wanted to sell $5,000,000 worth of bonds for his company, at ninety cents on the dollar, with interest at 7 per cent. They were a good investment because they were guaranteed by the mighty Pennsylvania Railroad, but they were a bad bargain for sale abroad because they were payable in United States currency and not in gold. Colonel Phillips told Carnegie that he could not sell any banker on the idea of taking them, and he had been nearly everywhere in Wall Street, which meant to Drexel, Morgan and Company as well as other houses.

Carnegie was quite sure that the American bankers were holding out among themselves for their own conditions in this issue. They wanted the railroad to give them the bonds for eighty cents on the dollar or maybe eighty-five cents. Such profits were not unusual in these postwar boom days. Carnegie saw, however, how he could turn this problem to his own profit. He knew that the Pennsylvania Railroad held a large amount of Philadelphia and Erie Railroad 6 per cent bonds in its treasury. He telegraphed John Edgar Thomson, president of the Pennsylvania, and proposed that the Pennsylvania trade $5,000,000 in those bonds for the 7 per cent Allegheny bonds, and that the Pennsylvania loan the Allegheny Railway $250,000 with interest. So Colonel Phillips' problems were solved temporarily. In gratitude he gave Carnegie a sixty-day option of the $5,000,000 in Philadelphia and Erie gold bonds that he had acquired by the trade, at ninety cents on the dollar. Carnegie then took a ship to Europe and went to the Baring Brothers banking firm. He made an agreement with Baring Brothers to take the bonds, and to lend the Pennsylvania Railroad $4,000,000 at 5 per cent interest until the bonds were sold. The Barings would take a two and a half per cent commission on the sale of the bonds.

Carnegie figured his profits. He had earned more than $500,000 in the deal—by selling the bonds at par when he was taking them at ninety cents on the dollar. The deal was made and all was settled when it was learned that the elder Mr. Baring was coming to London the next day. It would only be proper to allow him to approve the transaction, and so as a courtesy the signing of the papers was laid over until the following day.

Carnegie sensed that something was wrong as he left the Baring offices. He walked the four miles back to the Langham Hotel.

When he arrived, he found a note from the Barings saying that Prince Bismarck had put a £100,000,000 under lock and key at Magdeburg, and that the financial world was in a panic. The Barings were sorry but they must withdraw from the transaction.

Andrew Carnegie then went to see Junius Morgan and sold the bonds to him, although he did not get nearly so much for them because of the depressed money market of London. Thereafter, he said, he always offered J. S. Morgan and Company everything first.

Carnegie then had another idea. He knew that the Pennsylvania was always in need of money for extension and rebuilding. Before he broached the idea, however, he asked Morgan a question:

"Mr. Morgan," he said, "I will give you an idea and help you to carry it forward if you will give me one quarter of all the money you make by acting upon it."

Junius Morgan laughed. "That seems fair," he said, "and as I have the option to act upon it or not, certainly we ought to be willing to pay you a quarter of the profit."

The idea was to take those Allegheny Valley bonds that the Pennsylvania held and offer them on the foreign market. They were 7 per cent bonds, and they were backed by the credit of the great Pennsylvania line. By a carefully worded prospectus, the fear of the English investors about the repayment provisions ought to be allayed. Carnegie offered to write the prospectus himself.

He had made this offer because he saw in London then an apparently unlimited demand for American railroad securities. Morgan took the idea and decided to act upon it. Carnegie went to Paris, where Pennsylvania president Thomson was visiting, and secured his approval of the transaction at a price that was profitable to the Pennsylvania—a high price. Thus about $10,000,-000 in Allegheny bonds was placed on the market.

Business conditions in the United States were very spotty in the spring and summer of 1873. A number of banking houses and brokerage firms in New York were heavily extended in railroad finance, which had been so attractive and so profitable for the past five years. Few seemed to know it, but the railroads were generally undercapitalized and overmortgaged, and they had been bled heavily by their owners and managers, who inflated their capitalization simply by declaring new stock issues on the basis of totally artificial valuations—the practice called stock watering. Jay Cooke, theoretically the strongest of banking houses, was actually on the brink of ruin in the summer of 1873. All, or nearly all, could be laid at the door of the Northern Pacific Railroad, which owed Jay Cooke's various houses $6,957,592.43 on August 15.

The summer of 1873 was almost a copy of the summer of 1857. The building of railroads had absorbed the nation's free capital. It had stimulated the iron industry, which had absorbed more capital. The new areas opened to grain production had caused farmers to grow more grain, and this summer there was a glut of wheat and a drop in the price. America was borrowed to the hilt abroad—the English, for example, had held $200,000,000 in United States securities in 1866, and now the sum had increased by several times. With investment and stock watering, the capitalization of American railroads had increased from $2 billion in 1869 to $4 billion in 1873. In Europe the demand for American agricultural products had decreased, and this suddenly showed in a huge drain on the nation's gold supply. Perhaps all these problems might have been weathered, but since 1869 the public had been reeling under a series of shocks: exposure of corruption in the Grant administration in a dozen major scandals, the Credit Mobilier scandal which destroyed much public confidence in the financing arrangements of *all* railways, the Tweed Ring's fall and exposure, the Erie scandal, the battle of the Allegheny. Pierpont was not the only one who had been disgusted, but he happened to be one of the few who had the option to leave the country if he became disenchanted. Others could not leave, and they reacted by withdrawing into cynicism, pessimism, and negative action.

All these negative factors came into focus in Wall Street in the second week of September 1873. First came the word that the New York Warehouse and Security Company had failed. This house was the financier of the Missouri, Kansas, and Texas Railroad, and when that railroad was unable to meet its obligations the banking house was bankrupt. Next was Kenyon, Cox and Company, in which Daniel Drew was involved. On September 17 the Cooke partner in New York realized that Jay Cooke's situation was desperate. The next morning he called on the heads of several New York banks and laid the problem before them. They refused to help, and just before eleven o'clock that morning came the word that Jay Cooke and Company's New York house was closed.

This was bad enough, but when Cooke's parent Philadelphia house failed, and the First National Bank of Washington succumbed because it had been too generous in loans to Cooke, the American financial community went into panic. Loans were called by banks without notice. Depositors withdrew their money from the banks. Business was paralyzed. The New York Stock Exchange closed its doors on September 20 for the first time in history.

Worse, this was not just a money market panic but a national financial illness. That year 5,183 business firms closed their doors with a loss of more than $200,000,000. A depression began which would last for five years.

The Morgan firms were far less seriously hit by the panic of 1873 than most financial houses. In his detailed biography of J. Pierpont Morgan, son-in-law Herbert L. Satterlee does not even mention the panic. The impression given in those pages is that the years from 1872 until 1881 were simple, quiet, normal business years. That impression probably is a correct one so far as the Morgan-Drexel combination was concerned, because their international interests were an almost sure guarantee against financial trouble, as long as the houses kept their investments spread properly and worked on a conservative basis in their risks.

One incident involving Andrew Carnegie indicates how cool and unconcerned the Morgans were during this crisis that was so terrifying to others.

The sale of those $10,000,000 in Allegheny bonds had not gone far in 1873 when the panic struck. Andrew Carnegie was canny enough to keep his house in order in the panic, but he was short of cash as was every other capitalist in America, a fact which Pierpont obviously made known to his father. One day Pierpont called on Carnegie. "My father has cabled to ask whether you wish to sell out your interest in that idea you gave him."

Carnegie recalled that he was to receive a quarter of the profits on the Allegheny bond deal.

"Yes, I do," he said. "In these days I will sell anything for money."

"Well," Pierpont said, "what will you take?"

Carnegie said he recalled that the last statement showed he had $50,000 to his credit, so he would take that plus $10,000 to get out. The next morning he called at the Drexel, Morgan offices, and Pierpont handed him checks for $70,000.

"Mr. Carnegie," he said, "you were mistaken. You sold out for ten thousand dollars less than the statement shows to your credit. It now shows not fifty but sixty thousand to your credit, and the additional ten makes seventy."

Carnegie offered the extra ten thousand dollars back to Pierpont.

Pierpont waved the money away. "No, thank you," he said, "I cannot do that."

Whereupon the relationship between the Morgans and Carnegie was absolutely cemented.

In his autobiography, published in 1920, Carnegie had this to say about the banking house that Junius Morgan was building with his son's assistance and the world in which they lived:

"A great business is seldom if ever built up, except on lines of the strictest integrity. A reputation for 'cuteness' and sharp dealing is fatal in great affairs. Not the letter of the law, but the spirit, must be the rule. The standard of commercial morality is now very high. A mistake by anyone made in favor of the firm is corrected as promptly as if the error were in favor of the other party. It is essential to permanent successes that a house should obtain a reputation for being governed by what is fair rather than what is merely legal. A rule which we (Carnegie) adopted and adhered to has given greater returns than one would believe possible, namely: always give the other party the benefit of the doubt. This, of course, does not apply to the speculative class. An entirely different atmosphere pervades that world. Men are only gamblers there. Stock gambling and honorable business are incompatible.

In recent years it must be admitted that the old-fashioned 'banker' like Junius S. Morgan of London, has become rare."

The Morgans in 1873 were obviously relaxed and doing business as usual without pressure or strain. President Grant came to New York to confer with financial leaders about the crisis, bringing Secretary of the Treasury Richardson. They picked up General Hillhouse, who was in charge of the Subtreasury in New York, and they went to the Fifth Avenue Hotel, where they conferred for a long time with Commodore Vanderbilt, the most powerful man in New York. Vanderbilt was not much inclined to be helpful; he offered to put up $10,000,000 in securities of the New York Central or the Lakeshore Line if the government would put up $30,000,000. The government solved the crisis in a little different way, by purchasing some $20,000,000 in government bonds, thus putting more greenbacks on the market.

The year 1873 was disaster for many, but for the Morgans it was another good year. Pierpont that year contributed $202,253.03 to the capital reserves of Drexel, Morgan and Company and in no sense did he stint on his personal expenditures. There was Cragston, the house at Highland Falls, to be refurnished and made ready for summer occupancy. The family moved to Cragston early in the spring of 1873. Pierpont purchased a steam launch, the *Louisa*. He took the train up Commodore Vanderbilt's Hudson River division on the eastern shore. He was met at Garrison by the steam launch and ferried across the river.

This was a quiet summer, marked in family matters by the birth of Pierpont's fourth child, daughter Annie Tracy, and in a business way by concentration on the business of J. S. Morgan and Company. The next year was the same; much of Pierpont's investment and lending was in the matter of government bonds. Depression still gripped the country and little expansion was undertaken, so neither capital nor generalship was in demand. The summer of 1875 was little different, except that this year the children were left at Cragston for several weeks while Pierpont and Fanny and a party went to Maine for a child-free vacation. They picnicked and hiked on good days, and Pierpont and some of the other guests played cards on rainy days.

Pierpont fell ill again in 1875 with his mysterious ailment, which not only inflicted pains and fevers but made him nervous and irritable. This year, his thirty-eighth, he was noticeably burly in the body, and the rare skin disease from which he suffered, *acne rosacea,* had begun to deform his nose, broadening and thickening it. The blotchiness and the disfigurement were sources of never-ending embarrassment to Pierpont, but he must either bear it or retire from the world. Now, in 1875, he was committed to a business life. He had always enjoyed the perquisites of wealth, but now he enjoyed the perquisites of economic power, and he found it exciting to exercise that power among men. He exercised it in good cause and with restraint. He became treasurer of the American Museum of Natural History this year. He joined the vestry of the Church of the Holy Innocents at Highland Falls and became a member of the finance committee.

Business life was very quiet, again, and consisted of attending to the routines of the merchant banker. Even Matthew Josephson, scourge of American capitalists who coined the term Robber Barons to describe them, could find nothing to complain about or even to write about Pierpont in these years. The radical socialist Lewis Corey later wrote *The House of Morgan,* which purported to unmask the strangulation of society by a banking combine with the appearance and fearsomeness of an octopus. He, too, could discover nothing in the public life of the Morgans in these years to interest him.

At the end of 1875 Joseph Drexel retired from the business world and from the Drexel, Morgan partnership. Two new partners were brought into the firm in 1876, Egisto P. Fabbri and Charles H. Coster. Coster through the years was to become the master of detail of the Morgan partnership in New York, as much a "chief of staff" as could be said to exist in a business organization of the Morgan kind.

Pierpont traveled in 1876. He took Fanny to Washington in the spring, and the entire family went to Europe in June on the Cunard liner *Scythia.* Together with the elder Morgans, they went to Dover House for the summer. Pierpont joined his father at the J. S. Morgan offices in the city, driving there each morning in a coach and out in the evenings. In August all went north to the lake country to escape the heat, sight-seeing in the daytime and singing around the piano in the evenings. They visited Scotland and stayed for a time. The vacation was interrupted for Junius and Pierpont by business affairs. They rushed back to London to settle some pressing problem and were occupied with it for two weeks, then rejoined their families in the Highlands and continued to travel. It was September before they were back in London and the men were at their desks.

In October, Pierpont took the younger Morgan family to Paris. Intermittently, all during the summer he had suffered from blinding headaches. Now he came down with the grippe. Between illnesses he moved back and forth from England to the Continent doing business and playing the tourist. In December, Pierpont decided to take his entire family, plus his wife's cousin, on a trip to Egypt. He made all the arrangements, and they set out.

They traveled to Milan, then to Venice, and finally sailed from Ancona for Alexandria. They spent Christmas in Cairo, at the Grand New Hotel, where they had all the trappings of a home Christmas except a Christmas tree. Pierpont filled the children's stockings himself, and found an English chapel where they could go for services.

Then Pierpont decided to go up the Nile. The manner of their travel was a mark of the change in his mode of life, when compared to the trip of six years earlier. He chartered a steamer, the *Beni Souef*. He employed a physician, Dr. Bouigors, a tall man in a boiler-plate shirt, to look after everyone's health. He had brought along the small lively Caesar, a trusted courier who worked for J. S. Morgan but always took care of the younger Morgans when they were in Europe. He had also brought the formidable Mrs. Gibbons, the ladies' maid, and Abby, a rather vacant young lady who was the children's nurse. There was the bearded dragoman, Ibrahim, in his checked suit and fez, who dealt with the Egyptians, half a dozen Egyptian servants, a French waiter with wonderful black mustaches that rivaled Pierpont's own, pert Cousin Polly, as Mary Huntington was known; Fanny, who was becoming very matronly; young Jack, who was manly and important in his topee, short-pants suit and long stockings; the three girls ranging from pre-adolescent Louisa to pudgy baby Annie; and splendid Pierpont, who at this time looked very much like a young Teddy Roosevelt. A picture of the entourage, taken at Karnak in January 1877, shows Pierpont and his family and servants, he with a stout stick standing in his topee against the background of the temple. He is wearing a lightweight suit of wool with knickerbocker trousers, heavy gray woollen stockings, high-topped walking shoes, a stiff wing collar, a cravat with a stickpin, a heavy gold chain and watchfob ornament, and a flower in his buttonhole. He is very much the man of substance, proud, even when relaxed with one hand in his trousers pocket.

Pierpont began to collect antiquities this year. One could buy them readily then from the villages and shops in Cairo and other cities. The problem was to discern between the real and the manufactured, and with some help from his doctor and other experts Pierpont began to be able to discern treasures from fakes. The doctor taught him to play the French card game *piquet*, and they played every night.

Pierpont was a magnificent organizer of tourist trips. When the party reached Aswan, which was the end of their southern voyage on the Nile, he organized a camel trip to the ruins at Phylae. At night he brought out fireworks and organized demonstrations to the delight of the party and the natives. When they started downriver, he had the steamer stopped wherever he saw anything of interest and organized a trip inland to see it better. He organized entertainments for everyone they met, including Lord Lindsay, an amateur English archaeologist. When they returned to Cairo he immediately organized a trip to the opera house to hear *Aida* that same night. He organized shopping excursions on which they bought rugs, jewelry, and oddments for their houses. He organized affairs so that Fanny and Cousin Polly could get into several harems, although he could not go in himself.

It was not that Pierpont was a busybody. He was suffering from his old nervousness and restlessness, and he was cranky and uncomfortable unless he was moving around. Fanny came down with fever again in Rome, and then Pierpont slowed the pace.

They took it by easy stages to Paris, and remained there for a number of weeks. Fanny spent much of this time at the couturier establishment of Monsieur Worth, then the unchallenged world leader in the field of expensive clothing for women. Scarcely any Americans had ever heard of Worth or even of a couturier in 1877. Pierpont and Fanny were introduced there by Junius. It was a sign of Pierpont's sophistication that he took a close interest in the styles and even materials offered, and in later years whenever he was in Paris he stopped to buy something from Worth's for every girl and woman in his household.

The Morgans spent the "season" of the spring of 1877 in Paris. The Prince of Wales was there. So were assorted other members of royalty and wealthy families, and the Morgans gave much time to entertaining and being entertained. In May they moved back to London, for Pierpont had work to do in the offices of J. S. Morgan and Company. In the evenings they attended the Covent Garden Opera, or dined out, or entertained at 13 Prince's Gate. They were a part of London society, courtesy of Junius and the status of the firm. Pierpont was forty years old that April, and he was living the life of a millionaire. Except for his headaches and troublesome complexion, he was enjoying every minute of it.

CHAPTER

V

MORGAN THE NEGOTIATOR

T HE YEAR 1877 marked several changes in Pierpont Morgan's
affairs. The first of these, and a very noticeable one, was
personal. Pierpont and Fanny were settling down to the customary
lives lived by the rich married people they knew. Pierpont stayed
in the city on Tuesdays and Fridays so he could write his long
letters to Junius and get them off on Wednesday and Saturday
steamers. He kept a room at the Fifth Avenue Hotel, and on the
nights that he stayed in the city he usually dined at Delmonico's.
He spent Thursdays in the country with the family and went to
the country on Saturday afternoons to spend Sundays with them.
But this was different from the way in which the family had lived
until this time; it represented a growing independence of Pierpont
from the daily routine of domestic life.

One reason for this change was the demand on Pierpont's time.
Business had picked up in 1877; not that it had been bad for the
Morgans at any time; Pierpont had contributed $325,000 to the
Drexel Morgan reserves in 1874 and $200,000 in 1875. Now, how-
ever, there was important American business to be done in the
financial world. That year the Drexel and Morgan firms joined
a large syndicate of banking houses in America and London to

undertake sale of a bond issue for the federal government. Jay
Cooke was now out of business and there was no squabbling. The
syndicate sold $235,000,000 in bonds, earning a profit estimated
by the *New York Tribune* at $5,000,000 for the Morgan firms.

If that profit seems high, it represented years of acquired knowledge, skill, and the high character that the bankers needed to
instill trust at home and abroad. Also, there was always a certain
amount of risk in selling any bond issue, even a government issue.
Current events played a very large part in the bond market, and
the failure of a firm to sell its share of the bonds would mean
losses, for the selling expense continued whether or not it was
successful.

Unlike many of the American financial houses, Drexel, Morgan
and Company showed a sense of responsibility to the public at
large that was higher even than that of the United States Congress in 1877.

Following the disputed election of 1876 the waving of the
"bloody flag of the rebellion" was brought to an end by a compromise under which Republican Rutherford B. Hayes was
awarded the Presidency of the United States and the Democrats
were awarded the return of the South to American society and
of Southern representatives to Congress. The Southerners came
back to Washington with a healthy disrespect for the United
States Army, which, after all, to them was still the Union Army,
which so lately had been occupying their county seats and other
places of government.

The Congressional session began in December 1876 and ended
just after the inauguration of President Hayes in March 1877.
Congress adjourned after heated debates on many subjects, and
one subject of debate and anger was the employment and size of
the United States Army. The Southerners effectively blocked action which would give the American soldiers their pay.

All was well until June 30, the end of the fiscal year.

After that date there was no budget, no appropriation, and
no authorization for the Treasury to pay out any money for soldiers' pay. The soldiers would not be paid between July 1 and

December unless President Hayes chose to call a special session of Congress, which he did not choose to do.

Pierpont Morgan came to the rescue of the American Army. He wrote Secretary of War McCrary that the Drexel, Morgan firm would advance the money to the soldiers.

"It is not our intention to offer to lend the money to the government for the purpose and thus establish what might be considered an objectionable precedent, nor should we wish to do anything to place the officers and men in the light of beneficiaries . . ." the letter began. He proposed to cash the pay vouchers of the soldiers, charging the actual costs of handling the transaction. When Congress met again, he would hope that the Congressmen would appropriate the money to repay the capital outlay, plus the legal rate of interest for the use of Morgan's money. The War Department was not eager to accept private financing of the Army, but there was very little else to be done. The Army had no credit of its own. The offer was accepted.

Drexel, Morgan had to put up more than $2,500,000 to carry the Army for five months when Congress was out of session. They also had to send disbursing officers at their own expense to at least a dozen major cities, and undertake the vast administrative task of paying the troops. They charged about four per cent to the troops for handling the vouchers.

Drexel, Morgan did this job. If, after the appropriation was made, and they counted up the expenses and profits from interest, they earned any money at all, it would have been surprising. Money or profit was not the matter at issue here. As Pierpont put it, the firm had an "obvious and sacred duty" to the nation's defenders. A young soldier named Hugh L. Scott recalled that incident many years later when he was a Major General in the United States Army. He had been in Montana on the expedition against the Nez Perce Indians and had not been paid for six months when he rode into Helena where the paymaster's office was located. The paymaster took him to a bank, where his pay voucher was cashed on the strength of Pierpont Morgan's guarantees; Helena was one of the points where Drexel, Morgan maintained disbursing officers. "When we needed a friend," Scott said later of Pierpont Morgan, "he was that friend."

The prestige and acclaim that this transaction brought to the Drexel, Morgan name cannot be exaggerated. Pierpont Morgan was not now a young man on the way up. With this transaction he had arrived as a figure in American affairs to be counted in his own right.

Any tendency Pierpont might have to self-inflation because of such exploits was rudely exploded in the family circle. Pierpont was active in the church, and he loved to sing hymns, but Fanny's sisters claimed that he could not carry a tune. This matter became the subject of family argument and something of a sore point with Pierpont, who did not like it to be said that he was a failure at anything. One of the young ladies made the outrageous (to him) statement that he could not tell the difference between "Home Sweet Home" and "Yankee Doodle." At family parties when these charges were made he either engaged in heated argument or retired to sulk. One evening he went to the Tracy house to a party, and before many strangers Fanny's sisters began to play on this theme. He became angry, and then, determined to defend his singing honor, he offered a bet that he could hum twenty-five different hymns in such a manner that those present could recognize them. He did it, too, and won the bet. The girls still said he couldn't sing worth sour apples.

Pierpont worked hard in the last years of the 1870's, but he could not work too hard for too long, lest he begin getting headaches and fevers. He made frequent trips around the country and to Europe, some of which combined business and pleasure and some of which were purely for pleasure. Each year Pierpont traveled to England at least once to see his father and go over affairs of the Morgan companies. Twice in these years Junius came to the United States. The first of these trips to America was in the autumn of 1877, when a testimonial dinner similar to that given George Peabody was arranged for Junius in honor of his many years of service and entertaining of American clients of J. S. Morgan at 13 Prince's Gate and especially at Dover House. The second trip involved the most important railroad transaction in

Pierpont's career at that time, and one of the most historic transactions in Junius' career, for it changed the course of American railroad history.

For some reason the mythology of the American business world has built images of J. Pierpont Morgan either as the greatest genius of finance in the history of the nation, or, more popularly until recent times, as king of the buccaneers of Wall Street, and in doing this the mythmakers have placed the beginning of Pierpont's independent career as November 1879, when this railroad transaction was brought about. The facts, however, are not at all as they have been depicted in Wall Street legend.

In the autumn of 1879 the Pierpont Morgans were living their usual quiet lives. On November 1 Fanny and the family moved down to 6 East Fortieth Street from Cragston. The next day Pierpont took twelve-year-old Jack down to Quarantine on a tugboat to meet the steamer on which Junius Morgan was arriving from England. They escorted him to the Brunswick Hotel, where he stayed when he was in New York.

Then, after this November 2 arrival, the Morgans, father and son, began to negotiate with William Henry Vanderbilt, Pierpont's neighbor and now proprietor of the immense Vanderbilt railroad holdings, for a large turnover in Vanderbilt railroad stock.

What had happened to bring about the negotiations was this:

In January 1877 old Commodore Cornelius Vanderbilt died, at the age of eighty-two. Until the day of his death he had maintained personal control of what was then the most important transportation empire in America. On the day of his death he was the wealthiest man in the United States. One of the policies he followed absolutely was to maintain iron control of any enterprise that was important to him. Thus he owned outright the comfortable majorities of the stocks of all his railroads. He owned 90 per cent of the common stock of the New York Central Railroad. He borrowed money on bond issues and preferred stock issues and sold some common stock, but never enough to endanger control. Even in his will he left bonds and other securities to his wife and most of his children; he left the common stock to William Henry, his major heir.

Less than three years later, William Henry Vanderbilt decided he was sick of the never-ending work of operating railroads. Since his earliest youth his father had kept a heavy hand on his shoulder, first consigning him to a Staten Island farm as a dunderhead, and then, slowly, gaining confidence in William Henry's abilities and giving him some responsibility, but not very much authority, in the management of the railroads. William Henry was a decent, heavy-handed man, fifty-eight years old, suffering from high blood pressure, who wanted to enjoy himself. After his father was decently buried he had begun construction of the most pretentious house in America, at 640 Fifth Avenue.

His demands for luxury were very great, and so were those of his nine children, all of whom lived in the way they thought millionaires ought to live. Sometimes even William Henry felt short of cash, living in these surroundings.

It was not a need for cash alone that drove William Henry Vanderbilt to think of divesting himself of absolute control of the New York Central Railroad system—for that is what he was planning in the fall of 1879. In the past two years he had gone through a strike of the Central's men, which he put down in a manner that some would describe as ruthless, with the aid of militiamen called out by Governor Robinson. He wanted to travel. He wanted to collect art. He wanted to be free of the nagging need to watch the stock market and plan every financial move—activities which had delighted his father. He was also tired of the bad publicity he and his family received.

"We get kicked and cuffed by Congressional committees, legislatures and the public, and I feel inclined to have others take some of it, instead of taking it all myself," he said one day.

That was a clear statement of the reasoning that led William Henry Vanderbilt to seek the sale of part of the stock of the New York Central Railroad system, and a truthful indication of what went through his mind before he called in J. Pierpont Morgan, the young banker, and told him what he wanted to do.

Pierpont was not chosen by accident. Such activities as his work for the Metropolitan Museum and the American Museum and his other charities brought Pierpont to the powerful William

Henry's favorable attention. Pierpont's skills as a banker were becoming known through such actions as the Battle of the Susquehanna, the Army payroll arrangement, and his skill in handling the Morgan share of the government bond issue of 1877.

The integrity of the Morgan banking houses was above reproach, and this was a very important factor in so delicate a maneuver as William Henry wished to accomplish. Equally important was the relationship of young Morgan to his illustrious father in London, for it was Junius who would have to carry out the plan.

After William Henry had explained to Pierpont in outline what he wanted to do, Pierpont was in touch with his father in one of those long letters he wrote twice each week to London. When his father came to New York, the Morgans began meeting William Henry Vanderbilt to determine how best to fulfill his wishes.

By mid-month there were rumors in Wall Street about an impending sale of a large quantity of New York Central stock. They were denied stoutly by William Henry in the interest of keeping the price up, but they persisted.

On November 26, at two forty-five in the afternoon, the press was on hand when a large group of bankers and railroad officials emerged from the white marble Drexel, Morgan building at the corner of Broad and Wall. Then the news was revealed. The Morgans, father and son, had organized a banker's syndicate to take over 250,000 shares of New York Central stock. The syndicate included August Belmont, the American representative of the Rothschilds; Morton, Bliss and Company; Winslow, Lanier and Company; L. von Hoffman and Company; D. O. Mills, Cyrus W. Field, Russell Sage, and Jay Gould (this last name represented a truce in the railroad wars).

During November, Junius and Pierpont Morgan had arranged the sale of most of this stock in England, so quietly that the market never did break, as William Henry had feared it would. On the day that the bankers assembled on the steps of Drexel-Morgan, it was all over. The bankers had bought 150,000 shares of New York Central stock at 120, which gave William Henry Vanderbilt $18,000,000. At that moment, the stock stood at 135 on the

New York Stock Exchange, which meant the bankers had a possible profit of $2,250,000. They also held an option on another 100,000 shares of New York Central at the same price.

The names of the other bankers and financiers were important names, but as it worked out they were largely window dressing. Most of this stock had been placed by the J. S. Morgan Company in England, which meant that a very important interest in the New York Central Railroad was now held by English stockholders. Since these stockholders could not attend meetings and send their representatives across the Atlantic to attend board of directors meetings, J. Pierpont Morgan became the representative of the English stockholders on the board of directors of the New York Central. Further, the house of Drexel, Morgan and Company became the fiscal agent for the New York Central Railroad, which meant that Pierpont would have that road's banking business and the handling of its stocks and bonds. On a continuing basis, it was the most important piece of business that had yet come to the Drexel, Morgan firm.

The millions of dollars that changed hands by no means represented the real importance of the arrangement just concluded. It meant an entirely new direction and consideration in the matter of railroad and other corporate finance, where ownership would be spread widely and bankers would become managers as well as financiers of railroads and other businesses. Here was the beginning of a marked change in the system of American capitalism. William Henry Vanderbilt still owned the controlling interest in the New York Central System, but the way was paved for him to relinquish his absolute majority of stock, and for the control to become diluted.

In 1880 then, Pierpont Morgan became vitally interested in American railroads. That year he headed a syndicate which bought and sold $40,000,000 in the 6 per cent gold bonds of the Northern Pacific Railroad, on which Jay Cooke had stubbed his toe seven years earlier. Drexel, Morgan made a very careful survey of the line before investing; that was their way. They investigated the entire system, noted that in spite of the huge expenditure of the past the road extended only to the western side of Minnesota, and saw that by extending it to the Pacific as planned, the railroad could enjoy a prosperous future. So it was done, and with the enormous prestige of the Morgan banking firms the issue was sold out.

Pierpont was traveling alone more these days than in the past. Fanny was not well. Sometimes one of the children would accompany him on trips, sometimes he went alone. He was seen on occasion at St. George's by himself on Sundays, passing the plate. He joined the Whist Club, and Saturday nights became his card nights. He attended the meetings of the Thursday Evening Club, and of the Mendelssohn Glee Club. Even when he went abroad, at least once a year, he might take one of the children, or he might go alone. At this time and for many more years Pierpont Morgan's name would be linked with many lovely women of stage and society. There was no question about it; he engaged in many affairs, all conducted with great generosity. None of the women with whom he was associated ever found cause for public complaint, either about his treatment of her or the manner of his leaving.

This aspect of Pierpont Morgan's life was carried out with Victorian delicacy. There were many Victorian aspects to Pierpont Morgan's character; he separated his life into compartments and he did not let one part seep into another. Women of the family, for example, were never welcome at the Drexel, Morgan offices, except when the firm's doors might be opened on a holiday, which occurred on New Year's Day, when the earnings of the previous year were computed. The children were brought up with strong personal supervision and were sent to the best schools, as Pierpont had been. He was tender and loving to all his family. For all their life together Pierpont sent Fanny flowers on the day that they became engaged, and when he went anywhere on a trip he did not fail to bring her presents.

He was living a very full and busy life after 1880. At Cragston in the summer, he now visited the family on Wednesdays and Saturdays, staying over Thursdays and Sundays. He always crammed a week of living into those few days. He began fancying collies, after their trip to the Scottish Highlands, and brought his first, Shep, from Scotland and then brought others. His dogs took many prizes in dogs shows around America.

Other wealthy Americans were building castles in these days. All the Vanderbilts did so. William Henry Vanderbilt spent $3,000,000 on his palace at 640 Fifth Avenue, and it took six hundred workmen a year and a half to build. William K. Vanderbilt, his son, built one nearly as grand across the street on the northwest corner of Fifty-second Street and Fifth Avenue. Cornelius Vanderbilt, Jr., built another mansion at Fifty-seventh Street and Fifth Avenue. Alexander Turney Stewart, the merchant, built a marble mansion on Fifth Avenue. So did Mrs. Collis P. Huntington.

The building of a millionaire's row on Fifth Avenue was very much in progress in 1880 when Pierpont Morgan decided they had outgrown No. 6 East Fortieth Street and sought larger quarters. He did not even look on Fifth Avenue. Instead he bought the Phelps house at 219 Madison Avenue, at the northeast corner of Thirty-sixth Street. His one move in common with the Vanderbilts and the other moths in pursuit of fashion was to employ architect Christian Herter, who also built the William Henry Vanderbilt house. Pierpont employed Herter, however, because he was competent. Herter's job was to make the interior of the house what Pierpont wanted, change the front door around from the Thirty-sixth Street side, and otherwise leave things as they were.

No. 219 was a big square house of three stories, built of the brownstone that was so famous in New York. Pierpont wanted comfort, not show. The upstairs rooms were for the family and the servants. On the first floor after the remodeling there was a large drawing room, which ran the length of the house, a reception room, dining room, study, and library. A conservatory was added. The library was Pierpont's room, and it was also the center of family life when he was there. When he was at home, he was very much the home body. On Christmas Eve 1880, as he had before, Pierpont dressed up as Santa Claus, climbed into his carriage with Jack, and drove around the city distributing Christmas gifts to friends and relatives.

CHAPTER

VI

MORGAN THE MEDIATOR

I N 1880 Pierpont Morgan took over the financing of the Northern Pacific Railroad and in 1881 he again organized a syndicate to sell $20,000,000 in Northern Pacific bonds. This time, so high was the prestige of the Morgan banking companies, that the loan was oversubscribed three and a half times, mostly in Britain.

During these years the railroad men who wanted to rule or ruin the American transportation system became extremely active and prominent among them were Jay Gould and Henry Villard. Villard acquired control of the Northern Pacific, while Jay Gould set out to wreck the New York Central.

Using as a nucleus a little railroad called the Ontario and Western, which ran from Oswego, 250 miles south to Middletown, New York, Gould joined forces with the Pullman Company to create a new railroad system. George Pullman had no love for the Vanderbilts because they had backed Senator Wagner's attempts to take over the sleeping-car business. The new road was to be called the West Shore Railroad because it was to run up the west shore of the Hudson River, paralleling the New York Central, starting from Weehawken, New Jersey, across the river from Manhattan Island, and running to Buffalo. The company raised $15,000,000 in

Wall Street, leased land in Weehawken, and began building northward. Among other evil consequences of the building of the West Shore, was the ruin of the summer for those who had homes in the Highlands area of New York State along the Hudson, for the construction crews were working below the bluff, creating a dreadful racket day after day, even blasting the windows out of the houses.

Pierpont went to Europe in December 1881. He spent the Christmas holidays with his father, then joined a group aboard the steam yacht *Pandora*, of the Royal Yacht Squadron. The cruise was a leisurely one and they did not return to England for several weeks, having toured the Holy Land and stopped at a number of Mediterranean ports. Pierpont remained in England. On return from this expedition he bought a yacht of his own. He cabled New York to buy a ship he had been offered earlier. She was the *Corsair*, a single-screw steamer, 165 feet long. When Pierpont came back from Europe on this trip he was met by the *Corsair* down the bay, and that day she steamed up to Cragston to take him home. Fanny and the girls came home from Europe, where they had joined Pierpont that spring, and he now met them in the *Corsair* and took them up the river. Only Jack missed all these festivities because he was busy studying at St. Paul's boarding school in New Hampshire.

That autumn Pierpont was busy with many affairs. William Henry Vanderbilt had relinquished control of the Western Union Telegraph Company, and Jay Gould had bought control. This bothered Pierpont, because his confidential messages and those of other bankers were carried across Western Union wires, and he did not trust Jay Gould. The important messages were sent in cipher, but given time perhaps Gould could have the ciphers broken. Knowing his man, Pierpont knew that such a move would not be out of character. Pierpont began buying Western Union stock on the account of his own company, and bought enough to secure himself a place on the board of directors so he could watch Gould.

This was also the period in which Pierpont became interested in Thomas A. Edison's scheme for electric lighting. He was not interested at first as an investor but as a householder. In the renovations of 219 Madison Avenue, he ordered the installation of an electric lighting system, the first private system in the city of New York. It was not connected to the Edison power station downtown, but ran off a generator that was placed in the basement under the stables. The electric lighting system was not a notable success in the beginning. An engineer was hired to run it. He came to work at three o'clock in the afternoon and quit at eleven o'clock at night unless someone told him that he ought to stay on. The Morgans often forgot to tell him to stay on, and so at eleven o'clock, no matter if there was a party in progress, the lights would go out. The neighbors complained of the noise of the dynamo, and one protested that the smoke from the machine tarnished her silverware. Everybody in the neighborhood, it seemed, complained because in the winter the dynamo kept the roof warm and all the stray cats in the alley would gather there.

A year or two after the first Edison station had been built at Pearl Street, Pierpont and his partners financed the second station, Pierpont putting up half a million dollars himself and his partners matching that amount. A number of the partners were interested in the Edison company before Pierpont, and by this time, in 1883, the directors meetings were being held in the Drexel, Morgan building at 23 Wall Street.

In 1883, for the second summer in a row, the builders of the West Shore ruined Pierpont's season at Cragston. This year it was worse than the year before because the rough workmen were wandering about the village of Highland Falls, and the children had to be supervised by an adult whenever they went off the Morgan grounds. Some of Pierpont's associates participated in the financing of the West Shore, but he would have nothing to do with it. For one reason, he disapproved of a railroad that ruined his summers. This was justification enough for objecting to the construction of the line as far as he was concerned.

That he did not hesitate to act upon his complaints is exemplified by his feud with the Cunard Line. On one of his trips to Europe a few years before, Pierpont had become angry with their service. His ship had landed at Liverpool on the afternoon of

Christmas Eve. The crew was so eager to be home for the holidays that no arrangements for porters or any services were made for the passengers. Pierpont had spent a thoroughly miserable and exhausting time that day rounding up taxis and luggage and transportation to London for himself and several ladies he knew, for whom he felt responsible. He had not arrived at 13 Prince's Gate until the afternoon of Christmas Day. He had said nothing to the Cunard Line officials. That was not his way. He transferred his patronage to the White Star Line which he would later assist in its competitive efforts against Cunard.

There was another reason, of course, for Pierpont's refusal to deal with the West Shore line. He was a member of the board of directors of the New York Central System. He was not very pleased with the manner in which the New York Central was being operated, but he would not help an organization that was setting out to wreck the road.

In 1884 Pierpont's interest in railroads was rather shallow, that of a banker alone. He declined re-election to the board of directors of the Northern Pacific Railroad because he did not like Henry Villard. He disapproved very strongly of William Henry Vanderbilt's abnegation of responsibility for the New York Central lines. Vanderbilt was stripping himself of his railroad stock, buying government bonds and other "safe" investments with the money. By 1883 Vanderbilt had cut down to 80,000 shares of Central stock, which made him far from the majority stockholder.

The West Shore line was opened in 1883 with a train that ran from Weehawken to Buffalo. Within twelve months a rate war was in progress between the West Shore line and the New York Central. The West Shore sold an excursion ticket which was good for rides anywhere on the line for a month, at twenty dollars a ticket. The Central retaliated by cutting its rates to a quarter of the old rates. Both roads lost money, and the stock of the West Shore dropped to a fraction of its old value. The stock of the New York Central began to drop too.

When the West Shore's stock and bonds began to decrease in value, George B. Roberts, president of the Pennsylvania Railroad, began buying up the mortgage bonds of the West Shore line.

These mortgage bonds were a primary obligation—that is to say, if at some future time the railroad were to go into a complete decline, it was possible that the bondholder could take possession of the railroad without regard for the stockholders at that time. It might be possible for Roberts to take this line over and connect it with the Pennsylvania in New Jersey. Then he would have a line that could compete with the New York Central.

Seeing this, the operators of the New York Central began construction of a railroad known as the South Pennsylvania, which had no economic reason for existence, but was simply a New York Central move to build a line that could compete with the Pennsylvania in that railroad's own territory. Andrew Carnegie contributed $5,000,000 to start this road.

By 1885 the West Shore line was bankrupt, but the Pennsylvania was in control of it. George Roberts was very angry with William Henry Vanderbilt for trying to move into his territory. The South Pennsylvania was building across the Allegheny Mountains, paralleling the Pennsylvania from Philadelphia to Pittsburgh. In previous years the New York Central was famous for making special arrangements with important shippers. In 1879 a New York State investigating commission discovered that the Central had six thousand such agreements, which meant that its published rates meant very little. This, obviously, was why Andrew Carnegie had been willing to invest $5,000,000 in the new Vanderbilt venture.

Actually, the venture was not strictly a Vanderbilt one. William Henry had taken to spending much of his time in Europe, and Chauncey Depew was running the railroad almost singlehandedly by 1885.

By this time the rate war between the bankrupt West Shore line and the New York Central was depressing the value of Central stock, and the change was of prime importance to Pierpont, because he sat on the board of directors of the Central as the representative of the English stockholders.

In March 1885 Pierpont went to Europe to discuss the problems of the New York Central with his father. They decided that he should come back on the steamer with William Henry Vanderbilt and try to talk sense to him, persuade him to stop this needless competition that was ruining the Central as an investment.

William Henry was not eager to return to the business world. He was weary of strife. A few years before, on his way to Chicago, he had subjected himself to an interview with a young reporter and when that reporter had questioned a Vanderbilt decision, asking what Mr. Vanderbilt thought the public would say about it, William Henry's blood pressure had boiled up and he had uttered his immortal statement, "The public be damned." He would never be allowed to forget those words.

The usual practice in cases where a nuisance railroad was begun by capitalists to harry an existing road was for the owners of the existing road to buy out the owners of the new line. Such forays had been made a number of times before, both against the New York Central and the Pennsylvania, and Vanderbilt and President Roberts were experienced men. Both, however, were also stubborn men. Consequently Pierpont's fear was that the railroad war that seemed imminent would destroy the investments of those who held New York Central stock, and this, in turn, would ruin the confidence of English investors in the house of Morgan.

On the steamer Pierpont persuaded William Henry Vanderbilt of a responsibility to preserve the New York Central Railroad. When William Henry returned to New York he began buying New York Central stock ostentatiously, which gave confidence to the investors.

Still, the problems of the West Shore and the South Pennsylvania existed. Vanderbilt was willing to listen to reason, but George Roberts did not seem to be. He would not discuss what he intended to do with the West Shore line, although Pierpont went to Philadelphia several times to see him, and so did Chauncey Depew, president of the New York Central.

Pierpont called meetings at 23 Wall Street. He cudgeled his brains, trying to find a solution. Then, one day, he invited George Roberts and Frank Thomson, vice-president of the Pennsylvania Railroad, to come up to New York and go for a trip on the

Corsair. They could talk privately, he said, in the cool of the river and ocean breezes.

Roberts and Thomson came to Jersey City and boarded the *Corsair* at the Pennsylvania Railroad's pier around ten o'clock one morning. Pierpont was there. So was Chauncey Depew.

The rakish black yacht with its single funnel slanting backwards headed up the Hudson, towards Garrison. Pierpont talked about the wastefulness of competition and proposed that the New York Central take over the West Shore line, while the Pennsylvania take over the South Pennsylvania. All the details, he said, would be worked out and the financial arrangements would be handled by his firm without cost, or commission to the parties.

All day long Pierpont stated the case, Chauncey Depew chiming in enough to show his acceptance. All day long George Roberts listened, not committing himself.

The *Corsair* turned at Garrison and steamed back down the river, out to Sandy Hook, turned again, and steamed up to Jersey City. By this time it was seven o'clock in the evening and Pierpont had talked himself out. The Philadelphia men had to get back, and their train was waiting for them.

Only as he got off the *Corsair* did Roberts say anything. He stood on the gangplank and shook hands with Pierpont and Depew.

"I will agree to your plan and do my part," he said.

So what could have been a ruinous competition between two major railroads was averted.

After this conference, many in Wall Street and the newspaper circles of New York City started to invest Pierpont Morgan with strange and wonderful powers. From this time onward began the manufacture of legends about his persuasiveness, and many people began to stand in awe of this forty-eight-year-old banker. There were several reasons for this awe and the growth of legend. First, Pierpont had been pushed by circumstances into an entirely new position for an American banker. Merchant bankers and others traditionally dealt in money and securities. Because the English stockholders must be represented and protected in New

York, Pierpont assumed a role in the management of the New York Central Railroad that began as a responsibility to them but soon transcended that. He could not protect the stockholders' interests without taking an active part in the establishment of railroad policy. Thus was developed a new role for bankers on the American scene.

The trend was not occurring in the railroad industry to the exclusion of all others. At this time, many corporations were developing, because the industrial revolution brought the need for new products. Experts, such as Thomas Alva Edison, could produce these products but did not have the money to back their work or to market the results. The broad-based corporation offered much in this regard, and it also encouraged bankers of the Morgan type to take an active part in formulation of corporation policy.

The essential ingredient in the philosophy of business of Junius and Pierpont Morgan was the elimination of waste, which in the railroad industry meant cutthroat competition. Theirs was a conservative position.

The details of the West Shore-South Pennsylvania settlement were complex. Morgan placed the problem in the hands of former Judge Ashbel Green, who first said that he did not think the arrangement could be worked out legally. Pierpont was brusque. "That is not what I asked you. I asked you to tell me how it *could* be done legally," he said.

This brusqueness was a second reason for the growth of the Morgan legend of Wall Street. Partly the brusqueness came from power, the important economic power Pierpont now had through the success and growing wealth of Drexel, Morgan and Company and the much greater importance of J. S. Morgan and Company in London. Backed by such power, Pierpont found it easy to fall into the habit of acting and talking in shorthand, dispensing with the usual courtesies between men. But there was another reason for his brusqueness, which many did not even suspect. This was the coarsening and enlarging of his nose, where the *acne rosacea* had now settled. Pierpont was very sensitive about his deformity and became very shy with strangers. With his family he was as loving as ever. With his friends he was as loyal as ever. He had formed a *Corsair* Club, because he now used the yacht as his home when he remained in the city overnight, and five men were asked to become his companions, to dine with him and spend time playing whist and other card games on the yacht. For many years Charles Lanier had been Pierpont's dear friend. When the West Shore was building, Lanier became involved in the sale of securities and in the backing of this line, and when it fell into trouble, he was in trouble too. Pierpont wrote him one night, telling him that Lanier could count on Morgan no matter what came. "I say this because I feel that you are surrounded by men in those companies without the least particle of honor who will not hesitate to put you in a false position if by so doing they can shield themselves or secure for themselves any benefit whatever."

These were important words, for they told a great deal about Pierpont Morgan's philosophy of business. From his father and from Charles Dabney he had learned that integrity meant more than money or position. He was now practicing this philosophy, and he had very little regard for many of the men he saw around him in Wall Street. This, too, contributed to his brusque manner, and to the legends that were growing so rapidly about him.

In the settlement of the New York Central-Pennsylvania dispute, Pierpont created a new method of corporate organization. The matter became more complicated when a stockholder sued to prevent the Central from buying the West Shore. This was a simple attempt at holdup: the three men involved wanted to sell 339 shares of stock for a million dollars. Pierpont would not deal with them, or, rather, he would have dealt with them only if Vanderbilt had asked him to do so and would have put it down in the accounts as payment of blackmail.

But, in the end, some blackmail was paid by Chauncey Depew to end the stockholders' suit. Pierpont was sick in bed with influenza in December when the West Shore matter was in the courts at Albany, where it must be settled. Chauncey Depew got him up one day and they took a train to Albany, carried out all the legal actions that had to be taken (as it worked out Pierpont bought the West Shore and sold it to the Central), and Pierpont's illness vanished. Three days after the West Shore arrangement was completed, William Henry Vanderbilt died of a stroke. His two sons, Cornelius and William Kissam, took over the railroads, and, in their lack of interest in railroad affairs, Pierpont Morgan assumed an even more important position in the New York Central organization.

Within the next few years Pierpont was called on to help with the reorganization of a number of railroads. Again, his interest was prompted by the growing disgust of foreign investors with American railroads. The reason for the disgust was the cutthroat competition. Backed by various bankers who saw a way to make a quick profit by starting a railroad, selling stock in it, and then forcing the existing line in the territory to buy out the competitor, many such roads came into existence in the 1870's. By this time nearly all the useful railroads had been built, nearly all the markets were tapped, and the building of new lines almost signaled a buccaneering move.

In 1879, sixty-five railroads were foreclosed by mortgage holders. A year later bankrupt railroads represented 20 per cent of the total mileage in America. Foreign investors owned $251,000,000 in bonds that had been defaulted by the railroads involved.

The Bankers' Magazine estimated that European investors in six years lost $600,000,000 in bankruptcies, fraud, and mismanagement of railroads in America. In a sense the reputation of the Morgans rode with the reputation of American business, and Pierpont felt a sense of responsibility here. This accounts for his calling of a meeting in the library of his house at 219 Madison Avenue, to which were invited all the major bankers who participated in railroad finance and all the heads of the Eastern railroads. Various railroad officials spoke frankly about their troubles. George Roberts of the Pennsylvania castigated the bankers who lent money on blackmail propositions. This meeting lasted two days. The result of it was the formation of various regional railroad associations. It did not sound like very much of a development, but it was all based on what Pierpont Morgan called "gentlemen's agreement." The parties agreed verbally to cooperate with one another, and the system was successful enough that press and public picked up Morgan's term and added it to the vocabulary of American business. The associations that were formed out of these meetings were trusts, combinations of corporations agreeing to cooperate and not to compete. In a later period they would be dissolved as violating the Sherman Antitrust Law. But in 1886 there was no Sherman Antitrust Law, nor was there any other useful regulation of American business. Pierpont's method could certainly not be practiced by government, but until government began to take responsibility for the public's stake in American industry, practically no one else did. Pierpont Morgan's basic concern was to protect the rights of the stockholders he represented, and to satisfy his own innate sense of order in business. The concept of a great public weal, over and above the interests of the owners in railroads did not escape him, it simply never occurred to him to believe that what was best for business could possibly be inimical to the interests of the public at large. One could not doubt his public spirit and his sense of responsibility to the people of America. The soldier's pay plan showed that he would act in the public interest when no other private banker would consider that he had any responsibility. Herbert L. Satterlee, Morgan's son-in-law, had this to say about Pierpont Morgan's attitude toward public responsibility:

"In every phase of his plans to improve the transportation facilities of this country, Pierpont gave proof of his absolute belief in the future of the United States and of his conception that public service was a duty to be performed whether it affected an individual's private affairs adversely or not. He never did a thing, except the buying and selling of securities or foreign exchange, simply to make money from the doing of it, and he never hesitated to do a thing that might put him into bankruptcy if it failed, provided always that he believed it was right and ought to be done."

The result of Pierpont's activities in reorganizing transportation facilities was what his adverse critic Lewis Corey referred to as *Morganization* of the industries he touched. Morganization involved three phases, by Corey's definition.

First was the financial reorganization of the company, or railroad, to put it on a paying basis and thus resolve the immediate problem.

Second was what Corey called "consolidation and community of interest." This lessened competition among the railroads either by consolidation or by establishing harmonious relations between railroads based on a community of interest. This was done, Corey noted, by Pierpont's participation or that of his representatives in the directorates of the reorganized companies.

The third phase, according to Corey, was control. The House of Morgan retained control of these businesses (Corey spoke here only of railroads) by securing a voting trust, stock purchases, and interlocking directorates. This was done to insure the reorganization in the beginning, but later as an "expression of deliberate Morganization."

So, it became a question of examining Pierpont's character and Pierpont's motivations. Was he the dictator that Corey would have him be, or was he the angelic spirit that Satterlee would have him be? The railroad reorganizations could not be drawn to prove either point really, for as has been shown, in undertaking to end the ruthless battles between the Central and the Pennsylvania, Pierpont was primarily concerned with the interests of his and his father's banking clients. Junius in London was not usually very outspoken about his son's accomplishments, but he did make one statement about the negotiations in the West Shore matter. Pierpont had handled this, the old master said, even better than he could have done it himself.

CHAPTER

VII

THE BUILDER

PIERPONT MORGAN was not the only man in the United States who was concerned with the rampages of untamed capitalists. His particular interests were largely bound up in railroads for reasons that have been made clear, but there was much other than railroads in the American corporate picture in the 1870's. Fortunes were being made in petroleum, steel and iron, sugar refining and distribution, manufacture of whiskey, lead and other nonprecious minerals. The men of wealth who controlled these industries were no less selfish than the railroad men, no less interested in looking after their own. As early as 1870 the bustling millionaire John D. Rockefeller buttonholed Amasa Stone, vice-president of Vanderbilt's Lake Shore and Michigan Central Railroad and demanded a rebate on all the oil shipped by his company over the Lake Shore line. Rockefeller's was then the largest of some thirty oil refineries in Cleveland. His business was important to the railroad, and he got his rebate, which put him in an enormously advantageous competitive position.

The Rockefeller company had been incorporated in 1870 in Cleveland, as the Standard Oil Company of Ohio. John D. Rockefeller dreamed a dream of monopoly. With his railroad rebate in the first year he forced four competitors out of business. Then there were twenty-six.

Rockefeller planned to buy out all his competitors in Cleveland. Two years later he organized the South Improvement Company, which consisted of the largest refiners in various districts of the country. Each member of this cabal agreed to help the others stamp out competition in each area, and split up the shipping business among three railroads, taking rebates from all three. Within two years Rockefeller had swallowed all the twenty-six refineries in Cleveland.

This kind of trust, or industrial combination dedicated to the stamping out of competition, did eliminate some marginal operations and blackmail businesses. It also stamped out legitimate competition, and in the West, in particular, the states became upset by restraints on trade placed there by the millionaires who were in control of the means of production. In the 1880's Americans were becoming generally as disgusted with the masters of capital as Pierpont Morgan had been a dozen years earlier when he considered giving up the business world altogether. The solutions of the public, however, were not the solutions of the Morgans. States had tried to regulate business but had not been very successful in the task. New York's legislature had made some efforts, but New York's legislators of this period were notable for their inability to act on almost any subject that involved large amounts of money because of the proclivity of some legislators to accept bribes.

The first effective means of controlling the depredations of business on the common weal was the Interstate Commerce Act, which was passed in January 1887. It forbade rebates of the kind that Rockefeller was demanding, or any other discrimination against one of a number of competitors. It established a government commission to check on freight and passenger rates. In effect, one might say that the Interstate Commerce Commission law was a railroad law, although in future years it was to be broadened in its scope very greatly.

The Interstate Commerce Commission law was not much of

a beginning. The commission had very little scope. But it was handwriting on the wall.

Pierpont Morgan did not like the Interstate Commerce Commission, or the act, or the state of mind that brought it into being. He believed that the railroads and other industries were perfectly capable of policing themselves. He had no high regard for politicians. Why should he have? In his experience most politicians had proved to be either venal or "takers" whose palms could be greased with money by men like Vanderbilt and Gould. Pierpont knew that all politicians were not of this make—he deserted the Republican ranks in 1884 to vote for Grover Cleveland whom he respected, against James G. Blaine, whom he did not. Yet in the nineteenth century there was an innate conflict between politicians and businessmen, and Pierpont shared the business point of view that he governed best who governed least.

The meetings at 219 Madison Avenue in December 1888 that established the railroad associations did not resolve the problems in the railroad industry. Pierpont managed to persuade all the important railroads of the country and the important railroad bankers to come to his house in January 1889 in order to secure agreement among the roads that they would not cut rates, not build unnecessary lines, not engage in ruthless and wasteful competition. He had his agreement. The associations of railroads agreed to live up to the Interstate Commerce Act. But they did not do so. Particularly the Western roads were engaged in the same type of competitions that the Eastern roads had suffered ten years earlier.

Pierpont worked by himself and with others to do what he had asked the railroad men to do. He and a syndicate rescued the Reading Railroad.

He rescued the Baltimore and Ohio, putting out a $10,000,000 bond issue and a $10,000,000 preferred stock issue as the head of a syndicate. Because Pierpont Morgan was involved, these securities had a high market value: his name now was synonymous with railroad reform. He became a board member of the New York, Providence and Boston Railroad. He was a board member of the Sioux City Railroad and his banking firm held proxies on two-thirds of the stock when that railroad was taken over by the Illinois Central under Edward H. Harriman through a legal maneuver which made the Morgan stock voteless in the annual meeting. Morgan never forgave Harriman for this, nor Stuyvesant Fish, who was also involved in the transaction. This was an aspect of his character which grew more pronounced in middle age: he never forgot friend or enemy. Anyone who did Pierpont a good turn would be rewarded more than doubly if the time came for reward. Anyone who did him a bad turn would be destroyed if it was within Pierpont Morgan's power to destroy him. He would not put himself to great lengths to carry out a vendetta, but no one who offended him could retrieve the error. For the remainder of his life, Pierpont Morgan distrusted Harriman and would have nothing to do with him, until one final meeting when Harriman was dying and they met to resolve their differences and say farewell.

Pierpont rescued the Chesapeake and Ohio, formulated the plan for reorganization of its financial structure, and handled the financing. Many of the shareholders of the line were unable to put up more money for improvements; an examination of the plight of the railroad showed that it had been so badly drained by profiteers that its physical assets would stand no more credit expansion, and when it was decided by the Morgan partners that stock assessments would have to become part of the cost of reorganization, some stockholders could not meet the demands. Pierpont and his partners put a large majority of the stock, then, into a five-year voting trust. They took over the stock whose owners could not meet the assessments, and paid the assessments.

Morgan and Company financed the New York, Lake Erie and Western Railroad and the Richmond and Allegheny Railroad in 1888. In this, as in all the major railroad reorganizations after the West Shore arrangement, the details were handled by Morgan partner Charles H. Coster. He made himself an expert on railroad finance, inventing many of the new wrinkles. Pierpont ceased to handle the details; he was far too involved in too many enterprises, for now business was coming to J. P. Morgan and Company as rapidly as the partners could handle it.

In 1890 there came a new panic in American financial circles. In England the Baring Brothers banking firm collapsed. Morgan sailed through these problems serenely, untouched by difficulties that were miring and sinking other men. The reason, simply stated, was that he was not involved in stock market speculation or in speculative enterprises except on the highest possible level. Morgan was quite willing to stake his fortune if he believed in the future of the enterprise in which he was involved at the moment. He had done this in the West Shore transaction, for at one point in that complex maneuver he had personally owned the West Shore Railroad, which in any hands but the Vanderbilts was nothing but a major liability. He had done all this without consideration of profit—he had strictly ruled out profit in the arrangement—and all he ever received for it was a letter of thanks and a gold dining service from the New York Central.

How did Morgan make his money, then? He made it in the same way that Junius S. Morgan had been making money for many years. He undertook the marketing of government securities. He undertook the management and marketing of new issues of stock and new issues of bonds for railroads and other corporations. The management of a new issue of stock or a bond issue would yield high profits in terms of numbers of dollars, because huge amounts of money were being handled. In 1891, for example, the Union Pacific Railroad needed money and issued $5,500,000 in gold collateral trust notes through J. P. Morgan and Company. It was a very small transaction. The Morgan company might have profited at only a half a per cent in handling it. Still, this would be $27,500, and if it was multiplied a hundred times during the year, here was a large amount of money.

A very important reorganization carried out by Pierpont and his partners was that of thirty-five separate corporations into what would be called the Southern Railway, the largest railroad in the South.

The key firm in this region was the Richmond and West Point Terminal Railway and Warehouse Company. Since the Civil War it had been in financial difficulties time and again, and had become a primary target for stock speculators. A handful of men owned a large share of the common stock, and so Pierpont decided that he would not attempt to reorganize the railroad unless they would all deliver their shares into his hands while the reorganization was taking place. That was the only way he could be sure that they would not speculate on the shares while he was trying to build up the line's position.

The major owners came into the Drexel, Morgan offices at 23 Wall Street and were escorted into the partners room, a large private room—with a long sofa and a number of chairs and table— in which conferences were held. Pierpont explained what he must have if he was to do the job. W. P. Clyde, one of the owners, said that he had bought Richmond Terminal stock several times in the past few years at seven and sold it at fifteen. He proposed to do so again, and he would not go along.

Neither would Pierpont. He abandoned the plan for reorganization of that line, knowing that it could not be successful until he had control of the men who owned large shares in the company, or they were replaced by others.

The reorganization was undertaken by the Central Trust Company, and it failed, as anyone might suspect it would, since several of the men heavily involved in the company were opposed to its best interests. Only when the situation grew bad enough that the major owners agreed to temper their cupidity and deliver their stock into safekeeping would Pierpont undertake the reorganization. This was, of course, one of the secrets of Pierpont's success in reorganization of companies. He insisted absolutely that voting control be in his hands while the task was being done, and that afterwards it never again fall into the hands of speculators who would ride the stock down, by rumor or by encouraging waste or by actually destroying business for the line they owned. When the stock hit low points, the speculators would buy heavily. This buying would show others a confidence in the line, the stock would rise, whereupon the speculators would dump it at large profits to themselves. No railroad or any other company could prosper under such conditions. There was no regulation of these conditions except that which was brought by strong men. In the 1890's Pierpont Morgan became the strongest of all these men, and he saved the companies in which he was interested from riding the speculation toboggan simply by refusing to allow it, as with Richmond Terminal.

When Pierpont moved back into the Richmond Terminal situation after the Central Trust had failed, he found the following situation: this was the hub of a system of half a dozen railroads, which ran as far afield from Richmond as Cincinnati. Management had been so poor, and speculation so vicious for twenty years, that the railroads were bankrupt, although together they were in an excellent position to drain a large market and do a profitable business.

In 1893 the various railroads were in receivership. The receivers, who represented banks in large part, called upon Drexel, Morgan and Company for reorganization, based on the reputation Pierpont had achieved in his previous efforts. Pierpont then put into effect his formula for the reorganization of sick railroads.

First, he sent in his own experts, Charles Coster and Samuel Spencer. They estimated the minimal earning capacity of the system they wanted to create. This was a very complicated job in itself, because the system included more than thirty different companies, with aggregate securities of $250,000,000.

Coster and Spencer did the legwork, and then they went over the results of this work with Pierpont. J. P. Morgan and Company then reported to the receivers for the railroads that they would undertake the reorganization if the holders of a majority of every class of securities would deposit these with the Morgan company to assure against an attempt to break away in mid-passage.

The next step of the reorganization was to reduce the fixed debt. This was done by devaluing some securities, reducing fixed charges, forcing some bondholders to accept common stock or preferred stock, or bonds which bore lower interest. In the end $135,000,000 in bonded and floating debt was reduced to $94,000,-000. This was done to the point where the earnings of the companies could carry the expenses of operation and still meet the interest on the debt.

Then the stockholders were given the option of accepting an assessment against their stock, to provide new working capital, or getting rid of the stock. (This was possible only where some strong figure such as Pierpont stood in command, and the stockholders could understand that he *would* buy up their stock and make the plan work.)

Third, new stock was issued with an open hand. The object was to cut down the capitalization *problem* of the railroad by increasing the capitalization. In the case of what would become the Southern Railway System, the increase amounted to 27 per cent.

Morgan's price for this was high. J. P. Morgan and Company received $850,000, but the way in which the company took its payment also helped guarantee the success of the reorganization. Morgan took $100,000 in cash, and $750,000 in common stock of the railroad. Thus, the other security holders could reason, Morgan must believe in his plan, or he would not back it with his own investment.

The last part, and a continuing factor in the success of the Morgan reorganization of the railroad, was the establishment of a tightly controlled board of directors. In the case of the Southern Railway it became a voting trust, which meant that for vote-control purposes the railroad was in the hands of J. Pierpont Morgan, Pierpont's friend Charles F. Lanier, and George F. Baker, a friend and president of the First National Bank of New York. Morgan associate Samuel Spencer became president of the railroad.

Among Morgan's enemies much was made of his insistence on such stringent controls with himself or his associates participating. Pierpont knew his financial world, however, and he knew that one did not set the foxes to guarding the henhouse. This, of course, was what made the foxes of finance so angry.

The reorganization of the Southern Railroad was accomplished very quickly, in the early months of 1893, before the Republican Congress and administration went out of power in March, and the Cleveland administration and the Democratic fifty-third Congress came in. Following the passage of the Interstate Commerce Act and the Sherman Anti-Trust Act in recent years, no one now knew what a Democratic administration would do, particularly if it felt impelled to appease the Populists, members of a third party which demanded cheap money and heavy restrictions on business.

During the previous years America's economic condition had grown perilous, and the struggle between Republicans and Democrats over high tariffs versus low tariffs and cheap money versus the gold standard had brought a whipsawing that weakened the currency and the national fiscal position. In May 1893 there came a new Wall Street panic which lasted for a month in the East, then spread west. Pierpont's cash position and investment position undoubtedly shrank during this period, but there was no distress for J. P. Morgan and Company. Colgate Hoyt, then a member of a group of young Wall Street men who were interested in the American Steel Barge Company, the Duluth, Mesabi and Northern Railroad, which was to tap the Mesabi iron-ore range, and the Chicago and Northwestern Railway, was threatened by the panic. Hoyt went to see Pierpont one day in his office at 23 Wall Street. Pierpont sat alone in a back room on the first floor in dark coat, wing collar and ascot. The room had glass sides and he kept the door open, so he could see and hear what went on outside. This also made it seem that anyone could walk in on him—and they could if they were brave enough. They might be ordered out or simply glared out by the piercing eyes and deep frown of the senior partner of the firm.

There was never any problem of getting past a guard or secretary. Anyone who had the courage could go in. Colgate Hoyt did go in.

"Mr. Morgan," he said, "we have got to have some money to carry through."

"How much have you absolutely got to have?"

"A million dollars," replied Hoyt.

"Will it carry you through?" was the next question.

"Yes," was the answer.

"How long will you need it?"

Hoyt named a short term. Pierpont rang the bell on his desk and had a check drawn to Colgate Hoyt and handed it to him, stating that he would charge the legal rate of interest.

After he had thanked the banker, Hoyt said he would bring over his firm's securities so someone could pick out the collateral they wanted for the loan.

Pierpont looked at Hoyt coolly. "You may need your collateral with the banks. I am lending you the money on your business record in Wall Street and upon what I know your character to be."

This was Pierpont's way. No one in Drexel, Morgan and Company would have thought of arguing with such a decision made by the senior partner, even if the articles of partnership had not given him the last word in any transaction no matter how many partners there might be.

During that summer of 1893 matters grew worse. Panic gave way to depression. The Republican, Democratic, and Populist silver men had forced through Congress the Sherman Silver Act in 1890, which caused the federal government to buy huge quantities of silver. The government had to buy all the silver that was mined, in effect. This would have been fine if there had been a market for silver outside the making of money for the United States. For a time there was some market. Countries like India bought silver for coins. But soon their coinage became oversufficient, and they stopped buying.

And, while here sat America with a huge hoard of silver pouring in, her foreign neighbors wanted payment only in gold. They would not accept silver. Also, while putting up the price of silver, the cheap money men had refused to adjust the tariff. The net result was that the depression increased in seriousness.

In August 1893 the Northern Pacific Railroad became insolvent, and the problem of reorganization was turned over to Drexel, Morgan and Company. That job was finished by October.

That year Pierpont also undertook the reorganization of the Erie Railroad, which was suffering from the depredations of Jay Gould and Jim Fisk. This reorganization was opposed by other financial houses, and by E. H. Harriman. Pierpont had his way, however. He was used to having his way now, and would have it. Harriman carried the case to the courts, but Pierpont's attorneys and his partners had taken the reorganization in their usual fashion, one step at a time, making sure that every move was logical and followed legally upon the one before. The courts upheld the Morgan plan. There were difficulties in this program, due to the general worsening financial conditions, and the reorganization did not work out the first time. Morgan had to step in again. This reorganization earned the Morgan firm half a million dollars.

Pierpont reorganized the Union Pacific Railroad, beginning in 1894. He completed the work on Erie, creating from three lines a two-thousand-mile system.

By the middle of the last decade of the nineteenth century Pierpont Morgan was the most important man in American railroading. He did not control every line in America, but he had a hand in lines in every section of the country, along the Atlantic seaboard, through the New York Central, the Southern System, and other lines; the central section of America, through the Erie, the Reading, the Baltimore and Ohio, the Chesapeake and Ohio; into the West through the Northern Pacific and the Great Northern Railway. In 1889, when he had held his celebrated railroad meeting in the library at 219 Madison Avenue and secured the gentleman's agreement to stop cutthroat competition, Pierpont had been able to secure the presence of men from every section of the country, men who represented the power of the railroads. Six years later Pierpont himself represented that power better than any other man. He never stopped competition among the railroads, but he could and did put an end to the financial manipulation of railroads which had cost small investors and the public many billions of dollars. He did this not as the government would do it, by regulation and the waving of the wand of political power, but by waving the wand of economic power. There is no indication either from the direction of Pierpont Morgan's movements in the future, or from the manner in which he maintained his holdings, that he intended to build a railroad empire, though this belief has been stated a number of times by biographers of Morgan and other railroad men, by Lewis Corey in particular, who referred to Morgan's "railroad empire" constantly in *The House of Morgan*. Corey broke down the American railroad mileage of 1900 into six dominant systems, which he said were controlled by E. H. Harriman, Vanderbilts, Morgan, the Pennsylvania Railroad, Jay

Gould, and James J. Hill. But using Corey's specifications Morgan's hold was far stronger than that: he not only actually dominated a number of lines through partners of J. P. Morgan and Company, but his bank was fiscal agent for the Vanderbilts, and for Hill, and he controlled many coal companies, if his financial power can be said to mean control. Of course it meant control in the sense of veto power. Morgan could prevent any corporation in which he held a large interest from flaunting that interest. He could do it by withdrawing his financial support, or by talking to other bankers who would withdraw their financial support. He controlled, as within his own firm, by exercising the veto power. But his concern was not control for its own sake, or power for its own sake, as would be learned only on his death and would not then be absorbed by Americans. Morgan's concern was always the logical concern of the brilliant student of mathematics: he wanted to bring order to an American business scene that suffered from disorder, and he wanted to do it in the only manner he knew how, by exercise of economic power in the hands of responsible gentlemen whose word could be trusted and who sought only what was best, in their minds, for all the nation. Morgan's basic distrust of all politicians prevented him from understanding that there were political forces at work which would make it impossible for his type of order to be maintained.

CHAPTER

VIII

THE ART COLLECTOR

PIERPONT'S SON-IN-LAW said that it was really the banker's nephew Junius S. Morgan who interested Pierpont in beginning his collection of manuscripts and rare editions of books. The Morgan collection of paintings, armor, and other art objects had begun in a small way even when Pierpont was first in Europe, and after he and Fanny were married he unearthed at one time a whole pile of pieces of stained glass that he had collected all over Europe. Some windows were finally made of these for the Morgan library.

Pierpont was a collector, then, from an early age, and one whose tastes and judgments became ever more reliable. In the nineteenth century Europeans snickered when Americans spoke of art collection. There were too many men like Alexander Turney Stewart, the New York merchant, who filled his mansion on Fifth Avenue with what would later be called "nineteenth-century junk." There were too many, like William Henry Vanderbilt, who commissioned paintings to be done for them, stipulating the size and scene. Human tastes being changeable, it was certain that no matter what a man collected in the way of objects of art, he ran the danger of having public world taste devalue his collection at any time. It happened to everyone. There were days when Cézanne and Degas and Matisse and Van Gogh the mad Dutchman could scarcely collect a handful of sous for their paintings. That was a case in point: these men were fighting the battle of the Paris museums and showcases at the time that J. Pierpont Morgan was collecting art, and yet they never appealed to Morgan.

The manuscript collection began, it seems, about 1888, when one day Junius came into his uncle's office. Junius was the son of Sarah, Pierpont's sister, who had married George H. Morgan of "the other branch of the family."

An English friend named Wheeler, who was a book dealer, had approached Junius about buying a rare manuscript. It was a Thackeray. The price was a hundred pounds. Junius sent the young man to see his uncle, who conducted a typical Pierpont Morgan interview with the young man:

"Are you certain that this is in Thackeray's own handwriting?"

"Quite certain."

"You are too young to be quite certain."

"I think not, sir, because I have been dealing in manuscripts since I was seventeen."

"Very well, what's the price?"

"One hundred pounds."

"Is that cash?"

"No, sir. Ninety pounds cash."

"Very well, my secretary will give you a check. Let me know if you get any more really good author's manuscripts."

A chill look from the startling dark eyes, a brief nod, and that was the end of the interview. In a half dozen sentences Pierpont had managed to ascertain the youth's qualifications as an expert and his acuity in doing business. It was a shocking experience for anyone used to gentle ways but a rapid road to profit if one could stand up to Pierpont Morgan's brusque questionings.

Pierpont took this manuscript to his house and showed it around among the family and friends. When he tired of this game the manuscript went into the basement, to a small storage room where

it was soon joined by others. This became the library vault of
the Morgan household for the next eighteen years.

It was a sign of Pierpont's growing affluence, perhaps, but also
a sign of his interest in collecting art that he would react positively
when his cousin the Reverend Francis Goodwin mentioned the
problems of the Wadsworth Athenaeum of Hartford in the winter
of 1889. Pierpont was visiting Hartford to see his various relatives
when the matter came up. He was now fifty-two years old, but
Hartford was very much in his mind as the scene of his happy
boyhood. When Frank Goodwin talked about the problems of the
combination museum-library-art gallery, Pierpont said that he
thought it would be a very good idea for Frank to come to London
that year when Pierpont was there, to see father Junius Morgan.
Now this was a most interesting observation. Pierpont by this
time was a grandfather, and his personal fortune was such that
he could have given money quite handily to help the Athenaeum,
which was undercapitalized. Pierpont was already being painted
in the newspaper cartoons as a symbol of the bloated capitalist.
Yet in a matter of this nature, one close to his heart, he would not
act without first consulting his father, the patriarch of the family.
It was a part of his sense of family piety, but also it was the sense
of orderliness that led him to work for what he thought was right.

The Reverend Francis Goodwin did go to London and did come
to the house at Prince's Gate when Pierpont and his father were
there in the spring of 1889. The Reverend Goodwin laid out for
his uncle and his cousin the exact needs of the Wadsworth
Athenaeum, and Junius Morgan subscribed $100,000 to assist with
the remodeling. Later, as the Reverend Goodwin was leaving the
house, Pierpont whispered that he would also give $50,000 on
his own account.

In 1891 Pierpont began to add seriously to his collection of
manuscripts and first editions. Young Mr. Wheeler, the London
dealer from whom he had bought that first Thackeray, sold him
a first edition of Defoe's *Robinson Crusoe* and of Spenser's
Faerie Queene and La Fontaine's *Fables*. He bought a manuscript
of the elder Dumas, and a collection of autograph letters from

the kings and queens of England going back to Richard III. He acquired manuscripts of Keats *Endymion,* Charlotte Bronte's *The Professor,* and writings by Zola, John Stuart Mill, Leigh Hunt, Anthony Trollope, Benjamin Disraeli, James Fenimore Cooper—and so many others that in the cataloguing they lose their flavor. He began, in other words, to collect with such intensity that what he was making must become a separate library or it would be meaningless. For example, he liked Dickens, so he bought hundreds of Dickens letters, other correspondence that included copyright agreements, drawings that illustrated the Pickwick Papers, and Dickens' first editions and manuscripts.

Hundreds, then thousands of items were purchased, and all went into the little room in the basement of the brownstone house at 219 Madison Avenue, a room to which Pierpont himself kept the only key.

In his collecting as in all else that he did, Pierpont had a strong sense of history and of obligation to all that had ever meant anything to him, as demonstrated by his support of the Wadsworth Athenaeum. But there his cousin was the supplicant for the Athenaeum. Another incident may be more illustrative of this aspect of Pierpont's character. In 1892 he attended the convention of the Episcopal Church at Baltimore. There was nothing unusual about this, for Pierpont was a regular delegate from St. George's Church to the Episcopal conventions. He had been appointed to the committee that would investigate a professed need for changes in the Book of Common Prayer. When the changes were made, he had 250 extra copies of the new prayer book printed, bound in vellum, and sent to public libraries and to each Episcopal diocese. Among others he sent one to St. Paul's Church in Boston with a letter which said "from a former parishioner, J. Pierpont Morgan."

In January 1893 Pierpont went to Hartford to participate in the reopening of the Wadsworth Athenaeum, and there he learned that cousin Frank, then president of the Athenaeum, was worried lest some Philistine buy the property next to the building. A few weeks later Pierpont bought that property next door for $25,000 and presented it to the Athenaeum. He did this without request or urging and without public acknowledgment. He did it because he wanted to do it and because he felt obligation to these places and people of his birth and youth.

The year 1897 was the one during which Pierpont began to make plans for museums of the future. His large cash gifts to the Metropolitan Museum of Art backed much of the museum's archaeological work in Egypt. He began to make large cash gifts to the American Museum of Natural History and with Tiffany's he gave the Morgan gem collection.

This year Pierpont began collecting Bibles and Church of England Rituals. Two years later he was buying whole libraries. His spending was very heavy, but not only on collectors items. He prowled about and kept up his interests in everything. In fact, in his sixties he seemed to have come into a second wind, and to be healthier than he had been since his early business days. He gave money to the hospital at Aix-les-Bains, France (he never gave up taking the cures of the waters in the European fashion). He gave $10,000 for the establishment of a free library in Holyoke, Massachusetts, which was a part of West Springfield, where the family lived for so long. He gave £5,000 to improve the lighting of St. Paul's Cathedral in London. He gave a collection—the Ford collection—of books and manuscripts about early America to the New York Public Library. And by the end of the year he had bought so many books and manuscripts for his own collection that the little room at 219 was overflowing and he must lend out his new acquisitions, if he wanted anyone to see them, or put them in a warehouse he was now using on East Forty-second Street.

In 1900 he commissioned the building of the Morgan Library, next to 219, on Thirty-sixth Street. He gave the contract to the architectural firm of McKim, Mead and White for a simple, low, classic building. The design took many sessions, some of them held at the breakfast table at 219. He was in no hurry. He wanted a comfortable building where he could sit and admire his collections and where they would be available for the use of scholars.

He continued to buy. He began buying older material now, a Gutenberg Bible on paper, and numberless old printings and vellums. This summer, on his trip to Europe, he bought Benjamin

West's *The Raising of Lazarus,* which he gave to the Wadsworth Athenaeum.

At the gallery of William Agnew and Sons on Bond Street, Pierpont purchased the Thomas Gainsborough painting of the Duchess of Devonshire in 1901 for a price estimated to be $150,-000. He never told anyone how much he paid for it, at least outside the family. Someone asked him, and he refused to answer. "If the truth came out," he said, "I might be considered a candidate for the lunatic asylum."

Among all the paintings that Pierpont purchased, that of the Duchess of Devonshire had an emotional significance to him. In 1889 the portrait was purchased by Agnew's at an auction and shown in the gallery. Junius Morgan dropped in to see it one day and bought it for Pierpont, who, he told Sir William Agnew, was beginning to collect paintings in New York. Junius consented to leave the painting on exhibition for some weeks longer. In that time it was stolen by thieves. It was returned finally, in 1901, when Mr. Morland Agnew went to Chicago and ransomed it from one of the thieves.

Junius' purchase, of course, had never been consummated. What he had promised to pay and even the fact that he had bought it were to be kept secret. Now, in 1901, Pierpont saw the painting and admired it. He purchased it, with the understanding that it would hang in the gallery for a time, and then he had it taken to the house at Prince's Gate.

He bought and bought. He acquired the Mannheim collection of antiques, historic silver, coins, and bronzes, and left it in England as a traveling exhibition because he did not want to pay the heavy importation duties to take it to the United States. He bought a collection of fabrics and designs and tapestries that covered most of the history of weaving, and gave it to the Cooper Union of New York City.

One day while Pierpont was in New York, just before he went abroad, President Eliot of Harvard and other officials of the university called on him. He was busy and said he had very little time to give them. Did they have any plans to show him? They unrolled an architect's drawing of a new complex for Harvard

University Medical School and Morgan quickly pointed to three buildings. "I will build that, and that and that," he said, then turned on his heel and said good day to them.

He confirmed the purchase that summer, by cable, so that President Eliot could read the official news to the alumni dinner on June 26. The central building and two side pavilions would be built in honor of Junius Morgan, "a native of Massachusetts and for many years a merchant in Boston."

There was something about the way in which Pierpont did things that was unlike the activities of his peers, the millionaires of Fifth Avenue. Just as he lived in his own way, so he collected art in his own way. He never—none of the Morgans ever—did anything ostentatiously. There is a statue of Miles Morgan, the first of the line, erected at Springfield, Massachusetts. It tells the Morgan story very nicely. It was erected, its plaque says, in honor of Miles Morgan by "one of his descendants." The Morgans did not believe the public need go into the matter any further than that.

All during the collecting years, and they lasted nearly a quarter of a century, Pierpont Morgan was dogged over Europe by art dealers. Among them were those who produced fakes and misrepresentations for Morgan to examine, and, hopefully, to purchase. Sometimes he was gulled—who would not be if he undertook to buy seventy or eighty million dollars' worth of art work in a lifetime? But gulling Morgan was not usually wise, for no matter how much one dealer might cheat him on one purchase, Morgan would find out that he had been duped. He employed the finest art experts he could discover to authenticate his purchases, preferably before they were made. A dealer could perhaps cheat Morgan once, but when discovered, he could never do business with Morgan again, and word of his deception would spread rapidly throughout the art world.

Take the case of Dr. G. C. Williamson, who had some odd dealings with Morgan. Dr. Williamson had persuaded Pierpont to buy a piece of sculpture which he said was done by the Renaissance sculptor Bertolio di Giovanni, somewhere between the years 1460 and 1470. The asking price was $10,000, the doctor said he could get it for $8,500, and Pierpont said he would pay $5,000 and not a penny more.

When the piece arrived, it was discovered that it was some four hundred years later than it had been represented to be—a faked piece of nineteenth-century junk. The dealer was asked to return the money. He returned $625 and then told tales of how the Prince of Thurn and Taxis, who had owned the piece, was out of town and the dealer from whom it was bought was nearly broke, and so on. Eventually, the amount was deducted from the total bill presented by the doctor for a number of *objets d'art*. So, Pierpont Morgan was not so badly cheated after all in this case.

Pierpont had a good eye. He had been training it for antiquities and European *objets d'art* for forty years. He was not an A. T. Stewart, but a man who could claim as much cultural background as any European banker and as much as most children of noble houses.

With pieces of art, or rare books, money was not an object. Pierpont had learned now what Junius had known before him, that if a man wanted something, price was not important. Pierpont wanted lovely objects of art, first to enjoy for himself, but always to be shared with others. There had never been any other intention in his mind from the beginning.

In 1901 Pierpont began ordering up catalogues of his various collections, and these gave him great pleasure, for in thumbing through the pages of these ornate printings he could recall the moments of his purchase and the first fondlings of the object, or first view of the painting. And now, as he turned from the mundane affairs of business, concerning himself only with the matters of highest policy, he amused himself by collecting and contributing to the salvation of the marks of civilization of the ancients. He bought and bought and bought.

CHAPTER

IX

TWO DEATHS

A<small>T THE END</small> of March 1890 Pierpont Morgan made his usual spring trip to Europe to see his father. Junius now spent much of the winter in Monte Carlo, where he kept a villa, alone. Juliet, Pierpont's mother, had died in 1884 at the age of sixty-eight. Her death was scarcely noticed in London, for a dozen years earlier she had retired into the solitude of her own quarters in the house and saw no one but the servants and close family and friends. She had not played a part in Junius' public life for that long.

Pierpont's plan was to travel to London, then to Paris, and finally to join his father at the villa for talks about the affairs of business and the world. Pierpont's daughter Louisa was traveling with her father this year as she sometimes did. All were looking forward to the meeting, particularly Junius, because he now found himself lonely at times. Frank Harris, the *bon vivant* and editor, said that he often dined with Junius Morgan at this period and had the feeling that Junius wanted him to come more often than he did.

Junius had built a position comparable to that of any banker in London. Now he was seventy-seven years old, and while one daughter had married a young man who had gone into his London firm, his other children had returned to the United States and were bringing up their children there.

On April 4, while Pierpont and Louisa were at sea, Junius went out in his coach, which was driven by his coachman and drawn by a pair of spirited horses. Between Beaulieu and Eze the road ran along the rail line, and here the coach passed just as a train came along the tracks. The horses shied and began to run. The coachman had all he could do to bring them under control. Junius stood up in the coach to see what was the matter, and apparently was jolted out by a sudden swerve. He fell into a pile of stones, striking his head. The coachman did not know that his master was missing for several minutes, and then it took several more minutes to find him.

Junius was rushed back to Monte Carlo and a doctor was called, but he went into a coma and never regained consciousness. He died on April 9.

Pierpont rushed to Monte Carlo. He took charge of the body and had it transported to Hartford for burial, taking care of all the arrangements himself. This attention to detail, which he had foresworn in the business world some years before, was his personal hallmark in later years. Now, as head of the family, he would make the decisions relative to business and personal life and carry them out in the latter. He arranged for the special train that took them from New York to Hartford. He arranged for the funeral and the burial in the family plot.

It was a large funeral. The Morgans were Hartford's most distinguished citizens, and although Junius and George Peabody had been attacked by the newspapers at the time of the Civil War for not doing enough for the Union cause, these days were forgotten.

The funeral was held in Christ Church. All along the way from there to the Cedar Hill Cemetery the shops and stores of Hartford were shut down.

At fifty-three Pierpont Morgan was now patriarch. In the case of the Morgans he was also the head of an important and complicated business establishment. J. S. Morgan and Company of

London and Drexel, Morgan and Company of New York were in no way connected officially. Each operated under the laws of its own land. In fact, however, they were together the House of Morgan, and most people on both sides of the Atlantic saw in the separate entities little more than a legal difference. This belief was given strength when Pierpont came to London to straighten out the firm's affairs, and in the new partnership agreement he became senior partner of J. S. Morgan and Company.

The death of Pierpont's father made a great deal of difference in Pierpont's affairs. For one thing it widened his horizons. Now he must think in terms of world finance more and of American finance less. Now he must spend more time abroad attending to the affairs of the London company. This year of his father's death marked the change; it was the year in which he renewed his interest in Europe and began his plans for the collections of European and Oriental art that would later be characterized as the single most important accumulation ever made by a human being.

The family still spent the months of the winter at 219 Madison Avenue, and for the rest of Pierpont's life this would be home to him. His big library, called by the servants the black library because it was paneled in Santo Domingo oak, was the center of his home life. His son Jack was in business with him in Drexel, Morgan and Company's offices at New York, and was also a partner in the Philadelphia and Paris firms.

Daughters Louisa, Juliet, and Anne were at home with the family, too. In April 1894 Juliet married William Pierson Hamilton in St. George's Church. It was a large, fashionable wedding, and Pierpont had charge of all the arrangements. This was a relief to him. Four years earlier Jack had married Jane Norton Grew, the daughter of Henry Sturgis Grew of Boston at the Arlington Street Church. The family had gone up in a special car lent to them by the railroad. (Pierpont never owned a special car as did so many other important men of the nineteenth century. He found it quite adequate to arrange for the use of one when he needed it.) Jack's was a large Boston wedding, with a breakfast at the Grew house, and Pierpont fretted because he could not control the arrangements.

But in April 1894 it was quite different. Pierpont had the church decorated to his own taste by his own florist, and he selected the foods and beverages for his guests from his own caterer.

Two weeks after the wedding Pierpont was in Europe with Louisa, tending to affairs of the European partnership, which he did for six weeks before coming home.

The family routine was much as usual in these years. Spring meant the move to Cragston, but no longer did Pierpont spend so much time in New York at his desk. He stayed for longer periods at the summer house, and paid more attention to his grounds and hobbies there. One pastime continued to be the raising of prize collie dogs; he also had become interested in trotters, then a common sport among wealthy New Yorkers, and he raised some on the estate. There was a question whether Pierpont was very good or very bad with horses. Some years before, near Cragston, he had narrowly escaped injury in a brush with another team. Once in Europe he had tumbled part way down the side of a mountain with a horse. In 1894 he was driving behind one of his trotters with a friend. They had gone to see West Point and were passing the cadet barracks, just as the evening parade gun was fired. The horse began running away and headed for the railroad station. Pierpont turned him into a wall, which stopped the horse and threw Pierpont and his passenger over the wall. Neither was hurt.

Cragston was a showplace by now. Pierpont bred cattle there as well as horses and dogs. He began with Alderneys but they did not take hold in this country as a milk cow and he turned to Guernseys, which he bred for many years.

Driving, he used a road wagon for the most part. His was called a wagonette. It was as large as an omnibus, and this was the vehicle in which the family drove to church on Sundays, Pierpont in the driver's seat, wearing his frock coat and a straw hat to signify that it was summer and he was relaxing in the country. His mode of transportation to and from the country was very grand. He came and went aboard his yacht, *Corsair*, which served the same purpose that the little steam launch had once done except that now Pierpont never rode the trains.

When he was at Cragston he was always busy poking his nose into public affairs. He organized flower shows for the village of Highland Falls, and he and Fanny worked on the affairs of the Village Improvement Association, which planted flowers behind the town's picket fences and encouraged the villagers to paint those fences.

When Pierpont was at No. 219, church on Sundays meant St. George's. For a number of years he walked on good days, but by the time he was in his fifties he had given up the habit, except for an occasional stroll. He had been an energetic young man, riding horses and insisting on many long hikes, but business sapped him of these habits. He gave up riding in his forties and walking early in his fifties.

Pierpont was always interested in business and household technology. Beside the first electric light system, he had a telegraphy ticker and key installed in his house so that he could get the stock market quotations and also be in touch with the office in the days before the telephone. He liked to speculate in the gold market in the mornings before he started his business day, and he sat at the breakfast table doing sums in his head and writing down his findings. He seldom made much money in this speculation or lost much. It was simply an amusement for him as whist was, and as various kinds of solitaire became in these years. Pierpont was addicted to this form of cards and could be seen playing it day after day on trips or at home. It was said that European art dealers paid large sums of money to cardsharpers to be taught the various games that interested Mr. Morgan, so well known was his addiction to this entertainment.

First Pierpont was a vestryman and then he became a warden of St. George's Church, and even before that he was a power. He was instrumental in bringing a fiery young clergyman named William Rainsford to become pastor of St. George's and he remained loyal to Rainsford, although Rainsford once objected to Pierpont's attempt to dictate the size and membership of the vestry. (This attempt to dictate was a growing predilection of Pierpont's after forty, and few men dared stand in his way.) When Pierpont was unable to have his way, he resigned as warden of the church in a sulk. Rainsford would not accept the resignation. Pierpont did not raise the issue again. If his yielding was without much grace, it must be remembered that by the time his father died Pierpont was not used to yielding to anyone save Anthony Drexel, senior partner in Drexel, Morgan and Company. Actually, Pierpront was the important partner in the New York branch of the firm and the New York branch of Drexel, Morgan by 1890 had outstripped Philadelphia and Paris as producer of income and as an important factor in the financial life of America.

Pierpont's day was a busy one when he was in New York. He developed the habit of holding certain business conferences at breakfast and seeing business aquaintances at home before going down to Wall Street in the morning. He remained at his desk most of the period when he was downtown. He would leave at four o'clock in the afternoon, sometimes to go to the Whist Club or the Union Club for a game of cards. He might pay a call on a friend for an hour. Then he would come home and curl up on the library sofa with an afghan or blanket over him, and take a nap for an hour. If he was to have guests at seven he might sleep until five or ten minutes before the hour and then rush upstairs and don his evening clothes. It was one of his points of pride that he could do this with great rapidity.

The lack of real exercise caused him to put on weight. He liked good food and wines, and as the years rolled on he became heavy, weighing 220 pounds, and more.

Business, family, art collection, religion, and civic duty—these were the preoccupations of the adult Pierpont Morgan. By 1890 business had become an even greater challenge to him than in the early years. As his power grew, so did his sense of responsibility to the business community. He did not have a sense of "public responsibility" in the way that the term has come to be used in the second half of the twentieth century. His morality was that of his era: a man had a responsibility to look out for himself and his family. A poor man might be helped because he had shown some attributes of character to make him worthy of help. Charity was a matter of one's individual conscience and for the religious and charitable authorities. Wealth and what a man did with it were as much his own business as was the way in which he spent his time. Work and responsibility were to be encouraged for their own sakes. Government was needed to carry the mails, to levy taxes and raise common defense forces, to establish unity in foreign affairs, and to maintain a useful currency. Otherwise government ought to stay out of the affairs of business, which businessmen would handle so much more effectively than government. He gave much to public affairs. He joined the board of trustees of the Cathedral of St. John the Divine and helped raise money for the building fund—which meant that he also gave a large sum of money.

In business, particularly in the management of railroads, Pierpont had a single theory, and he had not yet been disproven in it. Many years later, Chauncey Depew stated that theory:

"Mr. Morgan believed that the poorest road, in the most bankrupt condition, and furnishing the most wretched facilities, could, if tied to a trunk line and furnished with capital to develop its territory, be made a beneficent operation for the neighborhood which it served and save the investments of those who had possessed the courage to build it."

This was the secret of a business success that transcended the making of money. Pierpont was declared to be a "bull on America," believing that the natural growth of the nation would justify huge increases in capitalization of business. One could not say in any way that this was a hypocritical attitude. Unlike many bankers, he was content in his reorganizations to take much of his fee or charges in stock in the company reorganized, and what businessman could quarrel with such faith as that?

Pierpont's theory was that given orderly conditions of competition, and preferably noncompetition except on the most general basis, given honest and decent management, given a stable financial system, a company producing what Americans, or people elsewhere needed, or providing a service that was needed, could always be operated profitably and to the best interests of all the nation.

In the panic of 1893, Pierpont and his firm had come to the assistance of a number of their friends, but they had not been called on by the general community to "save the day." To put the firm in proper perspective, it was known as an important American banking firm but it was nothing like the power it was to become in the American world of finance in 1893. Perhaps the word panic is unsubstantial in describing the financial debacle of that year, because it was more than a Wall Street reverse; it lasted for nearly five years in its reverberations. the panic of 1893 unleashed two basic problems: cheap silver money, and the overexpansion of American railroads after the Civil War in the absence of any regulative system. In December 1893 the federal government added up the failures: 158 national banks were gone; 172 state banks, 177 private banks, 47 savings banks, 13 trust companies, six mortgage companies were also gone. Stock values had dropped 50 per cent on the New York market. In many areas and many industries production was at a standstill, which meant that money circulation was slowing down everywhere.

Pierpont had gained considerable national renown for the sale of the New York Central securities in England, for this was pioneering in a new field. He had gained renown for the arrangement by which the West Shore was reorganized and sold, and the experience he gained in this transaction had made it possible for him to carry out the extremely complicated reorganization of more than thirty companies into the Southern Railway System. This last reorganization, as noted, came upon the eve of the panic of 1893. When, in the years to follow, the railroads of the nation realized that here was one man who seemed to be able to make order of the chaos they had brought upon themselves, they began to turn to him. The year 1893, then, was a magic point in the career of J. Pierpont Morgan. Until his father's death, Pierpont had been dominated by the large figure of Junius Morgan. Now he was to be *Mr. Morgan*. There was another factor in the change. On June 30, 1893, Anthony J. Drexel died in Karlsbad where he had gone to take the cure. Now there must soon be a reorganization of the American partnership. Now, too, the last control was removed from Pierpont. He could begin to do exactly as he wished. He was undisputed master of the House of Morgan.

PART FOUR

The Maturity
of Pierpont

CHAPTER

I

THE NEW COMPANY

I T WAS Pierpont Morgan's custom to go to the offices at 23 Wall
Street on New Year's Day and supervise the orderly closing
of accounts, a symbolic finishing of the old and beginning of the
new on a day of business rest. On New Year's Day 1895 there was
more than the usual significance in the closure of the books, for
Pierpont was closing the accounts of Drexel, Morgan and Company forever, and with them an era in the family history. Forthwith the company would be known as J. P. Morgan and Company.

This new company had inherited much from the past. On his
death in 1890 Junius Morgan had been the leading private banker
of England, without exception. Even after his death, the firm's
reputation was strong under Pierpont's guidance. In the last half
of the nineteenth century the British invested heavily in Latin
America, especially in Argentina, which was the second largest
and most rapidly developing of the South American republics.
English investors bought railroad stocks and bonds, government
securities, and in the later years they bought industrial offerings
as well. Argentina's economy was based on grain and cattle, and as
long as the harvests were good, there was no problem in the expansion of credit. The Baring Brothers, in particular, were en-

thusiastic about Argentina's prospect. Between 1886 and 1890, prices and apparent values in the Argentine rose to the point where gold was selling for 320 per cent of its value. Obviously, then, nearly every big speculator in the world was buying gold at 120 or 140 and sending it from the other world markets to the Argentine, where he sold it for whatever he thought would bring him the best return, or invested it in Argentine securities. The temptation was great, even to the most conservative of houses. The Barings, who had withstood many such temptations, succumbed to this one.

In October, in London's Lombard Street, there was much uneasiness, but it was hard to pin down. No one wanted to talk about the situation in Latin America. It was known that "one house" which had heavy commitments in the Argentine was throwing off many normal pieces of business which involved the acceptance of bills drawn against other business houses and the furnishing of cash. This was a good indication that the house in question was short of cash, but no one liked to discuss that matter.

That summer, in June, the Bank of England raised its rate of interest to private bankers from three to four per cent, to slow down the speculation in gold in Argentina. A month later, the figure was raised to the very high rate of 5 per cent. On November 7 the rate was raised to the unheard-of rate of 6 per cent. Now this was not the rate at which the individual businessman borrowed money, but the rate at which the banks borrowed money from the central banking system. Paying 6 per cent themselves, they would have to charge 8 or 9 per cent to individual borrowers. Still, those borrowers were willing to pay that and more, for they could send the gold to the Argentine and reap enormous profits from it—on paper.

By November the word was in: the Argentine crop, again this year, would be threatened by bad weather. This was late spring, and the rains had not come as expected.

Then fell the blow. The name of the house that had been passing on its acceptances for the sure, if unsensational, profit of other houses was Baring Brothers, one of the strongest and most honored merchant banking firms in England. William Lidderdale, governor of the Bank of England, learned on November 8 that the Baring Brothers were insolvent. They had liabilities of £21,-000,000 and unless they received a substantial loan from the bank that day, they would have to suspend payments and close their doors.

In London it was believed that this crisis was temporary and probably overstated. Lidderdale raised a quick £1,500,000 by selling Exchequer bonds to Russia, and the Rothschilds arranged a loan of £3,000,000 with the Bank of France. All this shored up the Bank of England's cash reserves, which had been drained so steadily. Meanwhile, the situation at Baring Brothers was under investigation and that firm was being carried along.

When the investigators pried into Baring Brothers' story, they learned that the firm had plenty of paper assets. Against the £21,000,000 in liabilities, there was £24,750,000 in assets, but a quarter of this was in South American government bonds. At that moment the £7,750,000 in Argentine and Uruguayan bonds could scarcely be sold at all, not even at five shillings on the pound. The Argentine government had defaulted and was not redeeming its bonds, which meant that the Barings' assets could not cover their liabilities if they had to liquidate at that moment. More, it meant that their assets were not liquid enough for them to remain in the banking business, unless someone supplied them with cash, not on their assets, but on their name.

This was done. A pool was begun in the city on Friday, November 14, by the Bank of England, which supplied £1,000,000. An hour later it had risen to £3,500,000. By noon the next day it had doubled, and the governor of the Bank of England could make public announcement of the plight of Baring Brothers and still say that all payments would be made. This prevented a run on the bank. It solved the immediate problem. Pierpont was active in this crisis. Indeed, the press gave J. S. Morgan and Company much of the credit for working out the solution, and the American press gave Pierpont more than was deserved.

The Argentine government had suffered severely. Its problem was at the root of the whole situation. Several years before, in an effort to raise money, the Argentine government had imposed heavy taxes on private banks and foreign enterprises. Since the British were so active in Argentina, they had succeeded in forcing the repeal of these taxes, and then the taxes imposed on the people had helped bring about internal collapse. What was needed was to put the Argentine government back on its feet, which would help all concerned. This was the task to which the Morgan banks addressed themselves. J. S. Morgan and Company guaranteed the sale of a loan of $75,000,000 to the Argentine government to pay off the Argentine national debt and refund it. This was easier for Morgan than it would have been for any English banking house, because the Morgan firm had both Paris and New York and Philadelphia on which to count for support, and the French and American markets in which to sell securities. The international flavor of the American affiliates of the House of Morgan was growing.

This became more apparent. In the middle of the nineteenth century, when France was a great explorative power, she began the building of canals. The Suez Canal was built by the French, although it passed into British hands under Disraeli's influence. The French had begun investigating the Panama and Nicaragua Canal routes in the Western Hemisphere early in the nineteenth century. So had American firms and so had the British. The Americans, led by Henry Aspinwall, built a railroad across the isthmus, and later, when the French canal company, under Ferdinand De Lesseps, was planning its routes, it was discovered that the Americans wanted to sell their railroad. They offered stock for seventy dollars a share. De Lesseps thought that was too high a price. The railroad men made life difficult for the canal men and raised their price to two hundred dollars a share. There, because he had no option if he wanted work to continue, De Lesseps had to buy.

De Lesseps was an artist of a promotor who turned his efforts to canals. He had built the Suez Canal after he visited Egypt in 1854 and saw the possibilities; he had promoted the Corinth Canal in Greece. Then came Panama, which was to turn out to be a mismanaged and corrupt enterprise from the beginning. One director general of the canal company lived in a $100,000 mansion and was paid $50,000 a year. Every time he went out into the line, he received travel pay, which came to fifty dollars a day extra. He traveled in a private Pullman car which cost $42,000. Later, when he wanted a summer residence, he put one up near La Boca. It cost the company $150,000.

The French canal company was purely a French undertaking and it was financed in France. Of the first $20,000,000 taken in from shares sold, $9,000,000 was taken out to be divided as follows:

For the concession (to Panama)	$2,000,000
Preliminary expenses (surveys, etc.)	2,160,000
Profit on Preliminary Expenses	
(promoters and directors drawing accounts)	2,360,000
American Financial Group	2,400,000
(see below)	

The figure given under "American Financial Group" of $2,400,-000 was almost as gross a representation of mismanagement as the taking of "profits" from capital before the canal was completed. In the "profit" section De Lesseps and the other promoters took $750,000 for their personal use before a piece of machinery was shipped to Panama.

The American Financial Group was organized through Seligmann Frères of Paris, and it included the House of Morgan. R. W. Thompson was persuaded to resign as United States Secretary of the Navy and become chairman of this American group. A major purpose of the American committee was public relations, to persuade Americans to accept the idea of a French company's building the canal. There was considerable American opinion against such a move, and Seligmann realized that it would be important to have an American of high repute in charge of the committee. First, he tried to get former President Ulysses S. Grant to take the post of chairman, but Grant would not do it.

The American Financial Group undertook all purchases and transactions on the two American continents in behalf of the French company. The sale of the Panama railroad was accomplished through this group. The leaders were Drexel, Morgan and Company, Jesse Seligmann, and Winslow, Lanier and Company. Each firm received at least $400,000 as a fee for its services.

The conditions of purchase, and particularly the price of the Panama railroad stock, reflected Pierpont's point of view about purchasing. He always believed that price was not nearly as important as acquisition of control of a property and its future. Obviously the Panama railroad was a monopoly, and Pierpont, in recommending purchase at so high a price, was simply restating his belief in the ability of the American economy to carry any given load.

The disgraceful conduct of the French company in misusing funds of French investors was not the responsibility of Pierpont or the other members of the American investment group. Eventually this conduct caused the fall of the French company. Corey, in his study of the Morgan banking firm, berates Pierpont for lack of patriotism and for exhibiting imperialist ideas on the one hand and berates him for taking a position against American interests by working for the French on the other. During the course of Cleveland's first administration, Pierpont was aghast, as well he might be, when war threatened for a time between the United States and Britain over Venezuela's boundary dispute, and Cleveland came forth with a restatement of the Monroe Doctrine which the British rejected. There was a time in 1895 when flags were waving furiously and one could almost hear the sound of men marching in the streets. Pierpont was appalled. He said he had spent his life "trying to build up such relations of confidence between the United States and the money markets of Europe, that capital from there could be secured in large sums for our needs, and here is a threatened disaster that will put an end to our borrowing."

This statement represented a very narrow, banker's view of what American foreign policy ought to be, but it was a thoroughly logical view from the position of Pierpont Morgan in 1895. He had spent his life doing just what he said. His father had spent his life creating a Morgan fortune by working to exactly that same end. There could be no argument from Pierpont's point of view. Any trouble between England, France, and the United States would upset the workings of his banking empire. He was wholeheartedly dedicated to the interests of the United States as he saw them. Just as the railroads had a "community of interest" (a term which he coined and of which he was very fond), so did Pierpont see a community of interest between Western Europe and the United States. Had Pierpont given up his banking business to become United States Secretary of State at some point in his career, he would have seen matters from a different vantage point, for he was quick and apt in anything he attempted. By now, however, in his late fifties, Pierpont's mind ran along a single track in terms of public affairs. Everything he considered was related in some way to banking, and he looked at public affairs strictly from the banker's view. This was certainly not his only view of life. As a collector he was throwing money away in a manner that was disgraceful for a conservative banker, but this was Pierpont in another guise. This Pierpont no more considered the banker's interests than did the third Pierpont, the conspicuous consumer who maintained two houses in England, a house in New York City, a house on the Hudson, a thousand-acre outdoor preserve in the north, and a house at Newport. The two latter establishments received relatively little use, but Pierpont acquired them at about this time. He had every right to do so. He was a very wealthy man and might have been much wealthier personally, had he cared about money for its own sake, as did the Rockefellers. Pierpont really never cared about money per se. He cared about the economic power that money would bring, and he tried in his own way to use that power for good. When he exploded against Cleveland for raising the Monroe Doctrine in the Venezuela case, he was as angry as he felt he had a right to be. The implication was very clear that he felt he should have been consulted before so disastrous a policy was announced. In the years to come, Pierpont was often to feel that the man in charge, down in Washington, was trying to subvert his way of running the economy. This was unconscious, of course. Pierpont would never have admitted that he and the President of the United States were competitors.

To such an implication he would have addressed a cold, hard

eye that would have silenced the questioner, and said nothing at all. That was his ultimate in disapproval. Yet, the fact remains that, as of 1895, when the new banking partnership was organized, Pierpont began to assume the role of economic czar of America and to some extent of the Western world. His firm was the most important banking house in that world, not so much for its own resources, but because of the awe in which this silent man with piercing eye was held by the other bankers of that world. As of 1895 Pierpont Morgan radiated a solidity of character which represented all the best in the banking and financial circles of the Western world. His position in America was akin to that of the Bank of England in that country.

Part of this was the legacy of Junius. Who had financed Cecil Rhodes when he decided in the 1880's that he was going to make the diamond country of Africa into an organized business, eliminating cutthroat competition? None but Junius Morgan, and he did so against the Rothschilds, who were backing Barnett Isaacs, sometimes known as Barney Barnato. Barney Barnato had acquired control of the Kimberly mines at about the same time that Rhodes and a partner had taken charge of the DeBeers properties. Backed by J. S. Morgan and Company, Rhodes began a campaign to knock the bottom out of the price of diamonds, and drove that price down to less than four dollars a carat. Barnato sold out for $25,000,000 and a place on the DeBeers board of directors. He continued to do business as a retail diamond merchant in London, but the mines and production of diamonds were in the hands of Cecil Rhodes, banked by the Morgans.

This was a classic example of the Morgan theory of economics. Competition was wasteful. The creation of a trust or a monopoly, such as the DeBeers Consolidated Mines, was a proper movement. The Morgans always relied heavily on what they saw as the good sense and innate honesty of humanity in their plans to eliminate wasteful competition.

Neither Pierpont Morgan nor his father was easily gulled. During the West Shore fight, Pierpont watched in pain while Charles Lanier allied himself with Henry Villard, Jay Gould, and Horace

Porter, and Pierpont wrote his famous note to Lanier describing these men:

". . . without the least particle of honor, who will not hesitate to put you in a false position if by so doing they can shield themselves or secure for themselves any benefit whatever."

At this time, ten years before the organization of the new J. P. Morgan and Company, Pierpont knew his enemies and the perfidy of mankind. Yet he always believed in goodness as triumphant over evil and in his own innate goodness, and this was apparent in all that Pierpont undertook or did. Neither in the French Panama company nor in any undertaking of his adult years could it be said that he acted other than honestly and honorably by his own lights. The Lanier case in relation to the West Shore is revealing. Charles Lanier, Pierpont's old friend, was facing ruin. Lanier had brought it upon himself, by financing enemies of Pierpont and the New York Central. Many men would have turned their backs on Lanier the moment he allied himself with the enemy, but Pierpont refused to allow Lanier to become an enemy. Lanier was his friend, and when Lanier was in trouble he took the pains to say so, at a time when it counted.

"The time may and probably will come when it will be necessary for you to take a stand against them (the West Shore crowd) and, if so, I know you will not hesitate, and I will stand by you through it and so will everyone else that knows you.

"Call on me at any and all times."

This heavy strength was the mark of character of the man Pierpont Morgan, and it was to be the mark of the international banking company he founded on this New Year's Day, 1895.

CHAPTER

II

THE GOLD AFFAIR

I N THE WINTER of 1895, just a month after the firm of J. P. Morgan and Company was organized, the United States government reached a crisis in its fiscal affairs. This situation was a direct result of the "silver folly" of Congress over what was now nearly a decade, during which the financial condition of the government had been turned upside down.

Grover Cleveland had first taken office in 1885 after he defeated James G. Blaine for the presidency, in an election marked by the switch of a number of members of the financial community from their usual Republican support. Pierpont had been one of these, for he could not support anyone as closely connected to the Credit Mobilier scandal as James G. Blaine; Pierpont knew what the financiers of the Union Pacific Railway had been up to while even at the end many in America only suspected the extent of the crime against society.

Cleveland had proved to be just what Pierpont and his friends had hoped: a sound money man who wanted to run the country on a basis of self-reliance and good banking practice.

In 1887, two years after Cleveland had taken office, he seemed almost impregnable as a political leader. His administration was popular everywhere. The Republicans were gloomy about the prospects of defeating him in 1888. Cleveland had ended the spoils system in government jobs, the depression that followed the panic of 1876 had ended, and if Cleveland had been more politician and less statesman, he would have had no trouble in being elected again in 1888. The President, however, was noted for a quality the Tammany Hall Democrats referred to with sarcasm as "ugly honesty." He was brutal in his tendency to come straight to the point when he saw and understood a problem of government. Like Pierpont Morgan, he wasted no words in political niceties.

Early in 1887 the federal government's surplus of money began to raise problems in the American business world. In 1886 the federal government spent some $250,000,000 but collected nearly $350,000,000 in taxes.

From a business point of view, this was a profitable year. Government, however, is not business.

When the businessman accumulated extra money, he invested it, and then the money went into the banks and into other businesses. The businessman's money, then, was always in circulation somewhere, keeping in motion the processes of buying and selling and producing. When the government accumulated extra money, however, that money was not automatically available to the business world, and had not been since the days of the United States National Bank. The government did not have any businesses, it did not lend money to any businesses, and it did not lend money to banks. For all practical purposes, then, in 1886, nearly $100,-000,000 was taken out of the American economy by taxes, over and above the amount of money the government spent to operate the machinery of public affairs. The money spent in government did not bother businessmen; it went back into circulation. The surplus money did bother them, for it was stored away in the Treasury, where many businessmen could not see that it was doing any good.

If Congress had been extravagant and had set out to spend on goods and services all the money that came in to the government, the extravagance would have created political issues but not economic issues. The money would have been kept in circulation. But, except for the third party movements, no one in government or politics considered a massive program of public improvements of the kind that John Quincy Adams had favored. This thinking had gone out of fashion with the Era of Good Feelings.

President Cleveland and Treasury Secretary Daniel Manning saw this surplus problem and met it in their own way in the first half of Cleveland's first administration. They retired all the government bonds possible. In 1886 the Treasury purchased $50,000,-000 worth of its own gold bonds. In 1887 the Treasury bought back more than $100,000,000 before their due dates. This took American securities off the market, cut down the interest received by bondholders as income, and cut down the income of the financial community from the sale and resale of these securities. It narrowed the financial world, in that sense, and made the market smaller.

The financial community did not like the government policy of buying up its own bonds, and President Cleveland, a reasonable man, could understand the reasons. For many months, he and Secretary Manning tried to find solutions to the problem. Manning suggested that they call in all the "greenbacks," paper money not supported by gold in the Treasury. But there was great agitation against the calling in of the cheap money and decreasing the money in circulation in that manner, much of it from the silver interests, who wanted even cheaper money. Others suggested that the Treasury lend out its surplus to the banks at low interest, thus making the money available for investment and circulation, but this plan was resoundingly rejected by Congress, because it smacked of government involvement in business affairs. So, in the first Cleveland administration, everyone watched with dismay as the money kept piling up in the federal Treasury.

One reason the money piled up was the continued importation of billions of dollars' worth of goods by American business firms. The United States was still primarily an agricultural nation, moving in the other direction too, surely, but not yet able to balance industrial exports and imports. The Republicans, traditionally, favored a high tariff to protect the nation's businessmen and the big farmers and ranchers. The high tariff was the major factor in piling up the money in the Treasury. It became the issue of the election of 1888. James G. Blaine, from Paris, said that through the high tariff, foreigners contributed to American revenues. This was a complete misstatement of the facts. Americans, not foreigners, paid the ultimate taxes on the foreign-made goods by paying costs, profits, and tariff in high prices for those goods.

In 1888, after he saw that the surplus of 1887 had more than doubled over that of 1886, President Cleveland advocated a tariff reduction to cut down the amount of surplus in the federal Treasury and increase the ability of the American people to purchase more foreign goods, thus bringing more money into circulation in the country. His plan would have cut the tariff by $53,000,000 and other taxes by $24,000,000.

The high-tariff men of both parties fought the President on this issue. He won, but lost control of his party, and lost the election of 1888. The Republicans brought to power Benjamin Harrison of Indiana, a simple man who had no understanding of the complications of government finance.

Cleveland's position was vindicated within two years, but another issue arose to plague the common weal. This was the silver issue. The Republicans, in 1888 and 1889, had passed the Sherman Silver Purchase law which obligated the Treasury to buy 4,500,000 ounces of silver every month, paying with Treasury notes that were redeemable in gold or silver. This brought money into circulation all right, but it stacked up huge amounts of silver in the United States Treasury, and with the exception of a few countries, the governments of the world and the businessmen and bankers of the world wanted payment of all debts made in gold. The Republicans had taken a serious but soluble fiscal problem and by their methods of dealing with it, in four years had created chaos.

The chaos was not apparent to everyone, but on the day that Grover Cleveland took office for the second time—March 1893— the Gold Reserve of the Treasury had fallen to $101,000,000, just a million dollars above the limitation set by Congress. What had happened was that many shrewd businessmen had bought silver, and sold it to the government at the prevailing price, and then had insisted on payment of their notes in gold. This caused a drain on the gold supply of the government very similar to that of the

1860's when Pierpont Morgan was involved in his youthful attempt at speculation in gold.

In 1893 the first efforts of Secretary of the Treasury John Griffin Carlisle were aimed at persuading bankers to give gold to the Treasury for paper money. The banks turned over $25,000,000 in gold in those first few weeks, but this did not stop the run on gold at the Treasury, and the silver kept on piling up in the coffers. So the government was showing a surplus of money of the wrong kind, money that was not as valuable as gold money no matter what the Congress said about it.

One day in April 1893, a month after Grover Cleveland's second inauguration, the federal gold reserve fell to $97,000,000. The President began to receive letters of concern from various sources, including August Belmont, the New York banker whose strength lay in his firms' alliance with the Rothschilds. It was noted that the value of the silver dollar on the world market was not fifty-three cents, while the gold dollar was worth one hundred cents. As more and more silver was poured out of the mines of the world —not just America—and sold to governments of the world, the glut was frightful. By this time no government wanted silver, and no banking house would accept it at more than fifty-three cents on the dollar. As Belmont and others pointed out to the President (and there was no need to point it out to *him*), the law that forced the United States government to pay out one hundred cents in gold or paper redeemable in gold for fifty-three cents worth of silver was surely driving the United States to bankruptcy. It was apparent to every banker everywhere in the world and to every investor outside the United States if not in it.

That summer Cleveland managed to force Congress to end silver purchases. It was almost too late. In the previous three years so much gold had been drained from the market and silver had caused so much trouble that, now, no one wanted it. It lay there, tarnishing, without affecting the gold problem.

In 1894 the gold problem was worse. In the first seventeen days of January, $11,000,000 in gold was drained from the Treasury and the gold reserve fell to $69,000,000. That month the Treasury issued $50,000,000 more in gold bonds to acquire more gold. The drain continued. By autumn the gold in the Treasury was only $60,000,000.

Now, those who had worried so much about the surplus created by the tariff wished they had that surplus back, but following the panic of 1893 came depression, which meant that Americans were buying less and tariff revenues had fallen off. In 1894 the federal government suffered a deficit of $70,000,000. The situation faced by President Cleveland had exactly reversed itself in his second term.

In November, Secretary Carlisle came to New York to talk to August Belmont about the gold problem. He proposed to issue another $150,000,000 or $200,000,000 in short-term government bonds. Belmont cabled London and the Rothschilds indicated that it would be most difficult to sell American bonds on the market at that time. The issue was reduced to $50,000,000. It was taken by a syndicate including the Morgan firms.

Belmont was the man to see in the opinion of the Treasury. This is an indication of the standing of various houses of finance. Belmont was highly regarded because he represented the Rothschilds, and while in Europe the Morgan firm was far more highly regarded in relation to American affairs, the new J. P. Morgan and Company was yet to achieve its full stature in the United States.

On January 28, 1895, President Cleveland sent a special message to Congress concerning the gold problem. At that date the United States gold reserves had fallen to a little more than $40,-000,000 and there were rumors in Europe that the United States was facing bankruptcy, which would mean default on American bonds. Cleveland noted that in spite of the two bond issues totaling $100,000,000, which had brought in gold, $172,000,000 in gold had been withdrawn, which, in view of the national depression, put the Treasury in a worse position than ever. He called on Congress to guarantee gold payment of all obligations and to stop the reissue of Treasury or silver notes.

On January 30 William Edmond Curtis, the assistant secretary of the Treasury, went to New York to see August Belmont. Belmont was then in touch with the Rothschilds in London, and the

Rothschilds brought the London office of J. P. Morgan and Company into the affair. They told Belmont to be in touch with Morgan in New York. Belmont called on Pierpont and they crossed Wall Street to the Subtreasury to see Assistant Secretary Curtis. After the meeting, Pierpont cabled London that he had talked with Belmont and Curtis, but that without further Congressional action the federal government could not ask for a loan specifying that it would be repaid in gold, as London wanted.

"The situation, however, is critical, and we are disposed to do everything our power avert calamity and assist Government," the cable read. ". . . We all have large interests dependent upon maintenance sound currency United States. Important use every exertion success negotiation. Great factor is European absorption even temporarily of bonds. Public here keenly alive that feature. We appreciate importance gold instead coin bonds, but no authority such at present. . . ."

By the first of February, withdrawals had reached a fever pitch, as all firms that had obligations abroad withdrew gold so that, in case of national collapse, they (hopefully) would be saved while the government was ruined. By that evening, however, when Curtis went back to Washington, the newspapers and Wall Street had the feeling that a syndicate of international bankers, led by the Rothschilds and Morgans, was coming to the rescue of the United States government.

February 1 was Friday. The crisis was such that some said it must be resolved over the weekend, for the drain of gold was very heavy. In Washington, President Cleveland and his cabinet met every night to try to solve the problem. They arrived at two solutions. One was to give a bond issue to a syndicate of private bankers, who would guarantee the sale. The other was to offer the bonds directly to the public.

Curtis had outlined this suggestion to Belmont and Morgan earlier. They had told him that, in their opinion, this would be disastrous, because the public would not take up the bond issue quickly enough to resolve the problem, and the gold drain would continue until there was no more gold in the Treasury. At the moment when the Treasury refused to pay in gold to a person who submitted a Treasury note, the foreign exchange value of the American dollar would drop to the value of silver money.

On Thursday night, January 31, the cabinet considered the proposal brought to Washington from the bankers. It called for an issue of $50,000,000 in gold bonds with a thirty-year maturity. The Belmont-Morgan syndicate would take them, and guarantee their sale, with the provision that half the gold derived from them should come from abroad. There was not immediately a discussion of the rate of interest.

On Friday the newspapers called vigorously for action—action that was being studied at the moment the call appeared. On Friday, also, the situation seemed much eased, because that day only $1,250,000 in gold was withdrawn and the net position of the Treasury at the end of the day was better than ever, because nearly $2,000,000 in gold was returned. This about-face indicated a return in confidence, and gave rise to some false euphoria in high places.

Everyone now expected a bond issue. The speculation was over the manner in which it would come, and the price to the government of securing this financing.

In the banking end of the negotiations, a subtle change was occurring. At first the officials of the Treasury had sought out August Belmont, because of his Rothschild connection and the need to get gold from abroad. Belmont had called on the Morgan firms, and now the leadership in the crisis moved from Belmont's to Pierpont's hands. This was apparent over the weekend, when Curtis again came up from Washington to talk, and the discussions were held in the black library at 219 Madison Avenue. This discussion centered on the terms of the financing. The public, through the newspapers, was talking favorably about an issue of 4 per cent bonds, priced on the market, to yield the purchaser 3½ per cent. Morgan asked for 3¾ per cent, which meant a difference of $500,-000 in profits. Curtis listened, discussed, and went back to Washington on Saturday evening.

On Sunday, February 3, Morgan sat in the black library, smoking cigars and waiting for a telephone call from the Treasury. He expected Curtis to tell him that the terms were satisfactory and the details were being arranged. He had not quite calculated the mood of Washington at this moment, which was gloomy. There was an underlying resentment of Wall Street and bankers. It was indirectly the result of the plunderings of the Wall Street men over a twenty-year period, more directly the result of the constant whipping of Wall Street and bankers by the numerous members and sympathizers of the Populist movement, by the Free Silver bloc, and by the element of the Democratic party which would follow William Jennings Bryan. Altogether this included a large part of Congress.

As far as the administration was concerned, attempts had been made earlier to avoid a bond issue by asking the banks to deposit gold with the Treasury. The banks had felt their obligations to depositors and investors were stronger than their obligations to the nation, and had not done so. In 1894 James Stillman, president of the National Bank of New York, had led the banking group in floating the November bond issue. He said Morgan had declared then it was impossible to sell more United States bonds in Europe with the low state of world opinion about American credit. If that was true, Morgan now had changed his mind and felt that it was imperative that it be done, in the interests of salvation of the national credit, and, of course, every banking house in America.

Congress had not liked the bond issues of 1894. Both were $50,-000,000 issues, at 5 per cent, and the bonds went on sale at 117 per cent of the dollar value. The government did not receive all this money; the banker-guarantors and the selling houses received it.

Morgan now insisted on a private banking contract between the government and a syndicate of bankers. In the past, this had not been unusual—Jay Cooke financed the Civil War in this manner—but public opinion was very strongly against any private dealings of government with bankers, because press and public believed, with some reason, that the bankers had been earning exorbitant profits at the expense of the public for many years.

The telephone message to Pierpont, when it came that Sunday afternoon, was guarded and vague. Curtis said that he was sending a courier with a detailed message. It came on Monday morning, and it called off the negotiations for a private arrangement. Cleveland had come to the conclusion that the bankers were trying to hold up the government, and he was determined not to be victimized.

Pierpont had told Curtis earlier that he was holding out for 3¾ per cent interest because his firm in London had told him that the bonds could not be sold there for less. He had repeated this in the telephone conversation of Sunday afternoon, but the administration apparently had not believed him, or had decided that public opinion was right. Cleveland had told the Treasury to abandon the negotiations.

Morgan and Belmont conferred. They were concerned from two points of view. They truly believed that to tell the public, at this time, that the negotiations with the bankers were off would be "disastrous" to the national credit. They also knew that the failure of negotiations at this time, over an interest rate problem, would be regarded harshly by the enemies of capital, and among the enemies of capital they placed such strong figures as Bryan.

What Cleveland proposed to do was to announce a bond issue, and offer it publicly to the firm or syndicate that would buy the bonds at the highest price, thus allowing the lowest rate and the lowest cost of achieving the financial assistance. This was anathema to the private bankers, who much preferred to deal outside the spotlight of publicity. Nor could one ignore a real concern on the part of bankers everywhere with the financial stability of the United States government. In his biography of Pierpont, Herbert Satterlee has described the negotiations over these bonds in great detail. The book represents Pierpont's views faithfully in many respects. (It was the only work he ever authorized, and although it was not printed for many years, he knew Satterlee was writing it and helped him with it. Other members of the family made available papers and other memorabilia which are not public material.) If one accepts Satterlee's view of the situation as the view of Morgan, which this author does, then much becomes clear about the man and the problem. Morgan believed that in dealing with Cleveland he was dealing with a politician (he despised politicians) who had no basic understanding of international or national finance. He underestimated Cleveland and Cleveland's problems. Cleveland believed that Morgan was one of the selfish, money-lusting crowd that he saw forever wriggling against the Wall Street skyline. Cleveland underestimated Morgan.

Had Morgan been the man Cleveland believed him to be, the negotiations between the Treasury and the international bankers would have collapsed on February 4, when Curtis' private secretary brought the devastating message to Pierpont. But Pierpont would not have it so. He picked up the telephone and called August Belmont to tell him what had occurred. Then he telephoned Curtis at the Treasury in Washington. Curtis said that President Cleveland had ordered the Treasury to make the public announcement that day. Pierpont was aghast, and he asked that the Treasury at least delay until he could come to Washington to talk to the Secretary of the Treasury and the President. Since he and Belmont had spent many hours and had laid their banking prestige on the line for the government in these negotiations, this was the least consideration that could be shown them. He said to wait until they had at least presented their arguments against such a course.

The Secretary of the Treasury was a reasonable man, and when this appeal was made to him in this way, he acceded in the delay of the announcement. That afternoon Pierpont and August Belmont took the train to Washington. The names of their traveling companions indicated how thoroughly Pierpont had now taken over the problem from the banker's point of view. Francis Lynde Stetson was with them. He was Pierpont's attorney and a specialist in financial-legal matters.

Pierpont's junior partner, Robert Bacon, was there. He was youthful and handsome and wore an aura of honesty and impeccability so celebrated in the Richard Harding Davis type of man. He could be useful. He was also decorative.

When the party arrived in Washington, on the platform stood Daniel Lamont, Cleveland's former secretary and now Secretary of War, who told Morgan that the President had not changed his mind and that he would not see the party. Cleveland was quite aware of the criticism to which he was being subjected even for dealing with the bankers; to invite them to the White House might be political suicide. Nor did Cleveland have a very high regard for the honesty or integrity of bankers. Morgan considered this information for a moment. Then he spoke with the dignity and strength that were his.

"I have come down to Washington to see the President," he said slowly, "and I am going to stay here until I see him."

He then walked away to the taxi stand, one potentate announcing to the minion of another that he would not take no for an answer. His attitude had been privately expressed in a cable to the London office a few hours earlier. "Consider situation critical," the cable had said. "Politicians seem to have absolute control. Shall make strongest fight possible for sound currency. If fail and European negotiations abandoned it is impossible overestimate what will be result United States. . . ."

From a banker's point of view, and particularly that of an international banker, whose component firms had done so much to extend American credit abroad, this point of view might be expected. If the United States was forced off the gold standard—which was the real threat here—it would be impossible, at least temporarily, for the government to borrow money abroad, and since the United States was still a debtor nation, needing large amounts of foreign capital to increase production of goods, Pierpont saw the abandonment of the gold standard as destroying the orderly march of industrialization.

Stetson had been Cleveland's law partner in earlier years. That is one reason he was brought along. He went to the White House to try to see Cleveland and arrange an appointment for Morgan. He failed.

Pierpont made it a habit to stay at the Arlington Hotel in Washington. If he went there now, he realized, the presence of reporters would complicate affairs immeasurably. If the President saw him it would be done amid publicity. If the President did not see him, it would be apparent. And each hour of waiting would bring forth new newspaper headlines speculating, which could not help but must worsen the situation.

Pierpont did not go to the Arlington Hotel. He went instead to the house of Mrs. J. Kearny Warren on K Street (Mrs. Warren was an old friend of his father's) and he sent Robert Bacon to tell Attorney General Richard Olney that he must see Morgan and to tell the others of the party that they were to avoid any show of irritation to the press, and were not to discuss the matter of the visit. Pierpont, then, told Mrs. Warren that he was in hiding and that she must not tell anyone he was in Washington or even that she was at home. Then, it being a chilly day, he sat before the logs crackling in the fireplace and smoked, while Mrs. Warren talked about mutual friends. An hour passed. The telephone rang. Bacon had seen Olney and Olney would see Morgan. Pierpont took a cab to Olney's house, where he secured the Attorney General's promise to talk to the President in the morning and attempt to arrange an interview for the bankers. Then, and only then, he went to his hotel.

Pierpont had callers all evening. He would not see the press, but he saw friends. At midnight he dismissed young Bacon and sat down to play a form of solitaire called Miss Milliken.

Sometime during the night, Pierpont recalled that, during the Civil War, Secretary of the Treasury Salmon Chase had come to New York to talk about gold; had then returned to Washington and persuaded President Lincoln to approve a bill which would authorize the Secretary of the Treasury to issue gold bonds on his own initiative, and that during the pressures of war the Congress had passed this bill.

The next morning he arose and breakfasted with Robert Bacon and telephoned the New York office to secure the news of Wall Street. There was word from Richard Olney, who said the President had agreed to see the bankers if they would come to the White House immediately.

The party crossed Lafayette Square and Pennsylvania Avenue and walked up the White House driveway. Inside, in the President's office, Secretary Carlisle and Attorney General Olney were waiting. The President came in a few moments afterwards. He greeted them and went to his desk. He sat down and began to review the situation. Carlisle presented the latest figures from the

Subtreasury at New York (where the vast gold business was transacted for the most part).

Pierpont stated his case. The President said a public offer had been decided upon, and turned to Carlisle, but did not dismiss the others, so they sat down and waited.

For three hours the President and the cabinet officers discussed the problem, hours punctuated by the ringing of the telephone to announce new large drafts against gold being presented in New York, and other Treasury business. Cleveland left the room for some time, nearly an hour. Pierpont, who was not used to waiting long periods these days, fidgeted and crumbled the cigar he had not been invited to smoke.

Finally a clerk at a telephone connected to the Wall Street Subtreasury handed Carlisle a message he had just received. Carlisle read it aloud to the group. Only $9,000,000 in gold remained in the Subtreasury vaults and there were still several hours to go before the banking day was done at three o'clock. Pierpont said he knew of one $10,000,000 draft that might be presented for payment in gold during the day. It had not yet been presented.

"If that ten-million-dollar draft is presented and you can't meet it," Pierpont said, "it will be all over before three o'clock."

Cleveland turned to him. "What suggestion have you to make, Mr. Morgan?" he asked.

Thereupon Pierpont reviewed his case, stating how he and the bankers had been mistreated. Acting on good faith, they had stirred up their associates in Europe and the other international banking firms in New York. Lazard Frères had stopped shipping gold to Europe. Pierpont's firm had not shipped gold abroad for three years. Belmont was not shipping gold to the Rothschilds. The major bankers were acting in good faith, but now the government had repudiated the agreement reached earlier and this put the bankers in a bad light. Further, there was no time now, as the President could see, to put the machinery of a public bond issue into motion. Not enough gold was left in the Treasury to last out more than another day, even if the $10,000,000 draft was held out.

Now the question of the old Civil War law came up. Satterlee and Cleveland biographer Robert McElroy said it was Pierpont's idea. Allan Nevins, in his life of Cleveland, said it was Assistant Secretary Curtis' idea. It could have occurred to both, independently. It was discovered, when Attorney General Olney went for the lawbooks, that a section of law did exist authorizing the Treasury Secretary to issue bonds to buy coin, Section 3700 of the Revised Statutes.

Cleveland had been very cautious in his approach to the bankers, because while they could live oblivious to public opinion, he could not, and his opinions of bankers were colored by those of the people around him. Now he found that his doubts about Pierpont Morgan's character disappeared. "I found I was in negotiation with a man of large business comprehension and of remarkable knowledge and prescience . . ." he said. He also said this: "If a man needs beef, he goes to a butcher; if he needs gold, he goes to a banker; if he needs a great deal of beef he goes to a big butcher; if he requires a great deal of gold, he must go to a big banker and pay his price for it." This is what Cleveland was now prepared to do.

The President asked Morgan what guarantee the international bankers might give him that, if they adopted his plan, gold would not continue to disappear abroad.

Morgan could not really guarantee that this would not happen, but he did make such a guarantee—which meant that he might be called upon to make good, if the other bankers did not act in good faith. He said he would guarantee that gold would not be shipped out during the life of the banking syndicate that would be formed, and until the contract was concluded and the goal was reached— to put a safe level on Treasury deposits of gold.

So the contract was made. Pierpont Morgan and August Belmont signed, binding themselves and the Rothschilds, to deliver $3,500,000 ounces of gold coin which would be paid for in bonds bearing an annual interest at the rate of 4 per cent per year, payable in coin at the pleasure of the government after thirty years from their date of issue, the bonds to be issued as the coin was deposited in the Treasury. Half the gold was to come from Europe. Morgan and Belmont were to "exert all financial influence and to make all legitimate efforts to protect the Treasury of the United States against the withdrawals of gold." The President then sent a message to Congress, noting that the Congress had failed to grant him the power to defend the public credit, so he had used Section 3700.

Then the outcry began. Cleveland expressed it in terms of politics in a letter to Thomas Bayard, his ambassador to London: "Think of it! Not a man in the Senate with whom I can be on terms of absolute confidence." But, he said, "Our friends at the Capitol have blindly wandered into a close trap on the financial question. Today, the House Ways and Means Committee expect a bill for gold bonds, and the Senate is thrashing about in a way that is pitiable. In the meantime, the administration is lightened from a heavy load by our last arrangement for the procurement of gold. I have not a doubt that we shall be free from anxiety on that score for a good long breathing spell."

From the viewpoint of Congress, the President had acted high-handedly and against their will. William Jennings Bryan said, "I only ask that the Treasury shall be administered on behalf of the American people and not on behalf of the Rothschilds and other foreign bankers." The *New York World* trumpeted that the bankers had earned profits of $16,000,000 on the transaction. Corey said the profits were at least $7,000,000 and perhaps $12,-000,000. Attorney Stetson said the profits were not more than 5 per cent, plus interest. Herbert Satterlee said there was no profit at all.

Much later, author Frederick Lewis Allen was shown the original Syndicate Book of the American syndicate, which took half the $62,500,000 bonds. The American Syndicate's actual holdings were $31,157,000, and these were broken down among sixty-one members, banks and investment houses. Morgan had less than 10 per cent: $2,678,825. When the total was figured and the books were closed, the American syndicate's profit was $1,534,516.72, and if interest on the money was figured in, it came to $2,079,-

776.47. Morgan's share, including interest on the American side, was $295,652.93—far less profit than he had secured with far less effort in many an industrial transaction.

Overall, Cleveland was well pleased. He had saved the Treasury against the united opposition of an unfriendly Congress that seemed to want to wreck him politically more than anything else. Overall, Pierpont Morgan was well pleased too, though he had to undergo a political roasting from a Senate investigating committee which came to New York to hold hearings at the Hoffman House on June 19, 1896. The charges made in press, pulpit, and on the floor of Congress had been too severe. (There were even charges made that Cleveland had "sold out" to the bankers and had taken a share of the profits for authorizing the transaction.) Pierpont defended his actions and his position stoutly, with the conviction of a man who has saved his nation from disaster. He was asked why he had undertaken this transaction. Was it in the public interest, or to make money?

"I will answer the question," he told Senator Platt of Connecticut, "though I do not think it is necessary, in view of all that I have done. I will say that I had no object except, as I have stated, to save the disaster that would result in case that foreign gold had not been obtained."

He told another questioner that no one else could have done what he did that February.

Pierpont would never tell publicly how much profit his firm made on the transaction, and this proved to some questioners that the profits had been exceptionally large. The reason, Pierpont later told his son Jack was that August Belmont, for some reason of his own, had asked Pierpont to keep the details of the transaction secret, and he felt it would be a breach of trust to disclose the figure.

To his dying day Pierpont Morgan believed that he and Belmont, through their own efforts and the economic power they wielded, had saved the credit of the United States. Pierpont was not boastful of this feat. He accepted the responsibility for the credit of the United States personally, as a kind of *noblesse oblige* of the most important banker in the world. He would quite expect the government of the United States to turn to him again in time of financial crisis, and after the publicity and promotion of this particular exploit, for good or bad, he was known as the most powerful banker in America.

CHAPTER

III

WHAT THEY CALLED
"THE MONEY TRUST"

TWO MONTHS AFTER the beginning of the Treasury crisis of
1895 it was all over. As Pierpont had promised, there were no
significant exports of gold from the United States. The bonds sold,
and were oversubscribed by ten times in the offices of the English
bankers. The gold reserves of the Treasury moved steadily upward
and promised to be soon back to the $100,000,000 level Congress
demanded but did not provide for maintaining. Pierpont was ex-
hausted and he went abroad, taking daughter Louisa. Nearly three
months later he returned, and then began a new era of his life,
when industrialists and businessmen came to him not just as a
financier, but as a manager of money and monetary affairs.

The next stage of Pierpont's career that was to be important in
the development of the American nation concerned the West, and
particularly two men, James J. Hill and Pierpont's old enemy
Edward H. Harriman.

James J. Hill was Canadian born but was always identified wtih
the American Northwest. When he was a boy, the area around St.
Paul *was* the Northwest. He moved west with the country, and

in 1873, backed by Canadian capital, he secured control of the little St. Paul and Pacific Railroad which straggled 380 miles west from what are now the Twin Cities. At that time the control was vested in capitalists in Holland.

Hill and his allies reorganized this road, and soon created what was the beginning of the Great Northern Railroad. Hill moved slowly and conservatively in building up his small railroad, but by the spring of 1895 he was ready to take over the Northern Pacific, and in meetings with Pierpont in London that spring the arrangements were made, for Pierpont was engaged in refinancing the Northern Pacific after Henry Villard had fallen into evil days in the panic of 1893.

The reorganization of the Northern Pacific involved the usual Morgan railroad plan. Fixed costs were reduced, and capitalization was increased by trading bonds for stocks. As always Pierpont's solution to the problems that beset the mauled railroads was to mortage the future. (The alternative was to throw the road into bankruptcy, wipe out the original stockholders in favor of the mortgage bondholders, and start over.)

In terms of the Northern Pacific and the Great Northern system the Morgan policy made good sense. A look at the map might indicate how suicidal it would be in the sparsely populated areas of the north to have two or three railroads competing for traffic. If it was to survive, the Northern Pacific simply must be allied with a balanced and profitable road, which was just what James J. Hill had developed in the Great Northern system. He and his associates acquired $26,000,000 in Northern Pacific stock, but control of the line rested in the hands of a voting trust that consisted of Pierpont, August Belmont, and a representative of Berlin's Deutsche Bank. Hill, of course, maintained a balance of power by his control of the Great Northern, but Pierpont became his banker. All this was decided at 13 Prince's Gate in May 1895. When a stockholder brought suit to prevent the consolidation of the competing lines, Pierpont and Hill were charged with attempting to create an unlawful combination in restraint of trade —a trust as defined under the Sherman Antitrust law. The suit itself was actually brought under a more narrow and specific state law of Minnesota which forbade the consolidation of competing parallel railroads. The case was tried in the lower courts and the stockholder won. The case began to make its way towards the United States Supreme Court to which Pierpont and Hill insisted on carrying it as a matter of princple. As a matter of fact, however, they used the approach so often favored by Commodore Vanderbilt in his railroading days: they did in one way what they were blocked from doing in another. There was nothing to prevent the stockholders of the two companies from organizing a new company which would control both companies. They did so. Pierpont organized a voting trust with himself at the head of it and ran the financial operations of the railroad; James J. Hill ran the railroads. And Northern Pacific stock lost its taint and began to rise.

In the summer of 1895 Pierpont also reorganized the Erie Railroad. Later that year the most important man in Wall Street—Pierpont—was asked to visit the White House to discuss affairs of state with the President. Cleveland had then just issued the startling Venezuelan message in which he challenged Britain to stop meddling in Latin America. Pierpont disapproved of the Cleveland position because he did not like anything that threatened to rock relations between the United States and Britain. That was natural enough, in view of Pierpont's interests. But Pierpont was not one to stick his head in the sand. The international situation again affected the financial status of the United States, and the gold drain abroad was stepped up by the fear of war. Oversimplifying a little, it could be said that the foreign investors were simply cashing in, relative to their degree of conviction that war was coming.

After Pierpont visited the White House, he began again to sound out international bankers to form a possible syndicate to handle American government bonds for gold coin. He did not go to Belmont this time. It was significant, in view of relations with the English, that the foreign firm directly represented was the Deutsche Bank of Berlin. This was an indication of the growing power of German financiers as well as the international difficulties between the United States and Britain. It also showed the depth and mobility of Pierpont's financial resources and contacts. After studying the matter for some days, Pierpont wrote the President on January 4, 1896. What would be needed, he gathered, was $200,000,000 in bonds to be sold on the same basis as the contract of the previous year. Was this an attempt to hold up the government—as Pierpont's and Cleveland's enemies would say?

One paragraph of his letter to Cleveland answered that question. After he had offered his solution, Pierpont said:

"At the same time I recognize the effect of legislation which has been proposed and the discussions thereupon in both houses of Congress, all of which might lead you to hesitate to make a private contract and, consequently, in view of the gravity of the situation, I feel bound to say, that if after a conference, in which I can more fully lay the matter before you, and without expressing any confidence in such a mode of procedure in face of previous failures of similar attempts, but recognizing as I do that the responsibility of decision lies with you, I pledge to you every influence and effort in my power to assist the Government in its endeavor to make successful a negotiation by public advertisement which shall result in the sale to the Treasury of 11,500,000 ounces United States gold coin ($200,000,000) and further, I will so far as I possibly can, take such steps as will enable the Syndicate which I represent to join in making the negotiations successful to its full amount."

Cleveland wanted no part of the sale of any more American government bonds to a private syndicate. Those days of American finance were ended forever.

So a $100,000,000 bond issue was thrown open to the highest bidders. And who were the highest bidders? The *New York World* telegraphed 10,370 prominent American bankers, asking them if they would buy the bonds if offered to the public. The *World's* purpose was to show that there was great support for the government and that there was no need to deal with the syndicate. When the chips were down, and the bond issue was thrown open to the public, there were actually 4,635 bids from forty-seven states and territories. Eight hundred and twenty-seven of these were higher than Morgan's bid of 110.6877. Morgan and his associates in this enterprise took $38,000,000 of the total $100,000,000 issue before it was finished. They had done their part: they had made a market for the bonds, either as a private transaction or as bidders in a national auction.

In these last years of the nineteenth century, Pierpont became interested in various foreign investments that had been of concern to the London office before for the most part. He financed the Mexican Telegraph Company, and through his friendship with the organizer of that firm, J. A. Scrymer, he became vitally interested in the laying of a Pacific cable. The United States Senate in 1891 had passed a bill which would subsidize such a cable, but the House had rejected it. In 1896 the Pacific Cable Company tried to secure government assistance but failed. Here was one of Pierpont's imaginative schemes which did not work out.

When the American involvement in the war against Spain brought United States forces and influences into the Pacific, investment followed, but this was not the reason for Pierpont's concern with international banking, as Corey has indicated it was. The Morgans were always international bankers. There was no change in direction here, simply a change in the seat of power and influence from London to New York. In 1899 J. P. Morgan and Company refunded the Mexican debt of $110,000,000 for a commission of one per cent, clearing well over a million dollars in profit for the syndicate. Again the Deutsche Bank was prominent in the arrangement. An interesting development in this period of history was the gradual change of financial operations in the United States. Instead of foreigners supporting American enterprise, now American investors were beginning to support foreign enterprise. Bond issues for Sweden, Germany, Russia, Mexico, and many European cities such as Geneva, were sold in the American market. During the Boer war Britain sought money in the American market, and J. P. Morgan and Company sold some $225,000,-000 in bonds for Britain in the United States. The change had come fully now. Young America, always the supplicant nation, had become the world's central marketplace. Pierpont Morgan, representing the oldest continuity of international banking in the United States, had become banker to the world.

CHAPTER

IV

THE INFANT THAT WAS STEEL

I N THE SUMMER OF 1897 Pierpont finally purchased the thousand-acre piece of forest in the Adirondacks which he would use as his retreat from civilization when he and the family wanted to get back to nature. Originally the camp was the property of W. West Durant. Pierpont had first gone there in 1894 as a guest of Beavor Webb, the naval architect, and he had been much taken by the area. Later, Durant fell into financial difficulties and first mortgaged, then sold his property to Pierpont.

That summer the family visited the preserve, which included all of Lake Mohican. With a fine Victorian literary air they called it Camp Uncas.

When Pierpont emerged from the woods, refreshed, he began to talk about a new kind of business combination. This was the era of the trusts, combinations put together by powerful men in various fields. Standard Oil had created a trust in the petroleum industry. There were dozens of others in other industries. After the Sherman Antitrust Act was passed in 1890 the Department of Justice brought several cases to break up big trusts. In the first eight cases, only one conviction was obtained, because the law was drawn so loosely, and amended so heavily that in the end the government was powerless.

In 1895 the Department of Justice attempted to break the sugar trust, which controlled the production of 98 per cent of American sugar through the American Sugar Refining Company and its associated corporations. In examining the issues the United States Supreme Court ruled that a monopoly of manufacture was not a monopoly of commerce. This was good news to the trust men. Soon there would be nearly two hundred trusts which would control much of the economic life of America.

In 1897 Pierpont's interests in industry outside the fields of transportation and communications were limited. He had helped organize the General Electric Company and several other corporations, but his major personal interest lay in railroad finance, a path along which he had been drawn by his fiduciary responsibility to foreign stock and bond holders. The Morgan firm held directorships in the Illinois Steel Company and the Minnesota Iron Company, and through watching what was going on in the steel industry, Pierpont began to see the need for an amalgamation of some concerns in the wire and nail businesses. There were many of these concerns and they were extremely competitive, in the manner that the railroads had been competitive. Among the leading operators in this field was John W. Gates, a one-time barbed wire salesman who played the stock market and ran his steel wire business with the hand of a buccaneer. Gates had earned the nickname "Bet-A-Million" because he was willing to do just that—on anything. In 1880 Gates had established the American Steel and Wire Company of New Jersey, which was a small concern. Its produce was largely barbed wire. Gates had formed his company in New Jersey because that state in 1889 had passed a law aimed at increasing its tax revenues painlessly. The law had made it attractive to companies all over America to incorporate in New Jersey, because it permitted one corporation to hold the securities of another. This made the holding company legal and served as the basis for the formation of trusts. Through his lawyer, Judge Elbert H. Gary of Chicago, Gates proposed that Morgan back the formation of a holding company which would control the steel wire business and end the sometimes ruinous competition. Morgan agreed in principle, and negotiations began. Under Charles Coster of the Morgan firm the negotiations had proceeded. They stopped at a time when the battleship *Maine* was blown up in Havana harbor and Pierpont was in Europe. Yet whether they ceased because of the conflict in Cuba or because Pierpont suddenly became distrustful of John W. Gates is really the question. Pierpont did become distrustful, and broke off the relationship. Gates then went on to form his holding company without Pierpont, and built an enterprise capitalized at more than $80,000,000.

In 1898 Judge Gary and Gates began talking about forming a steel trust which would consist of concerns that produced iron ore, and others that made finished products. At that time there were a number of such concerns in the Midwest, operating independently on a relatively small basis. The idea was to save money in production by putting them into one corporate structure.

Morgan was approached. He liked the idea. He also liked Judge Gary, but he did not like Gates and so he forced Gates out of the management when the new combine was effected. This brought together ore producers, manufacturers of basic steel, and manufacturers of steel products into the Federal Steel Company. Then Pierpont insisted that Gary give up his $75,000-a-year law practice in Chicago and become a full-time steel mogul. Gary protested, but Pierpont would have his way. "You can select the directors, name the executive committee, and fix your salary," he said to Gary. Seldom was a corporation president offered more in those days before stock options, fringe benefits, and the graduated income tax.

Having entered the steel business, Pierpont began to give some consideration to the problems of the industry as a whole. He backed the organization of the National Tube Company, the American Steel Hoop Company, the American Sheet Steel Company, and the American Bridge Company. By the summer of 1900 the trust idea for steel had gained much acceptance. Most of the steel-making resources of the country were mobilized into only eight corporate groups.

There were several untidy sections of the picture, however. One was the control of iron-ore deposits by the Rockefeller interests. Another was the existence of the Carnegie Steel Corporation, which was the largest steel company in America, and which was also self-contained. It owned or controlled its own iron ore, its own coke mills, its own railroads and steamship lines. Andrew Carnegie, furthermore, believed in competition, not in combination.

Pierpont was in an excellent position to consider the advantages of combination. James J. Hill owned larged quantities of ore lands in the Great Lakes area, and of course Pierpont knew the markets for steel through his long association with railroad enterprises. Examining the field, Pierpont saw how a combination of the steel industry into a large, efficient trust could open world markets to America and open those markets to a new variety of strong American securities, which the Morgan banks could safely handle in the interests of depositors and clients everywhere. The prospect began to appeal to him greatly.

Federal Steel provided a basis for bargaining. It was a $100,-000,000 concern, headed by Judge Gary, who had come to New York to live. Morgan partner Robert Bacon represented Pierpont on the board of directors.

In the fall of 1898 Pierpont began to grow restless. He had turned the problems of steel combination around in his mind for several months. He could see how, under proper circumstances, a strong, united American steel industry could take over world markets, producing at prices lower than the English and German mills could produce. He let his mind wander further, to consideration of the alliance of the American merchant marine to carry the new products abroad. One of Pierpont's great qualities was this ability to let his imagination carry him further than most men would have dreamed of going. Here he had a small steel company in hand, and he was talking about building a merchant marine to carry the products of a united steel industry that he did not have to markets that did not yet exist, in ships that were not built. Pierpont, however, had access to the one factor which could make all this possible: unlimited supplies of money. His problem was Andrew Carnegie. The problem was complicated because Pierpont had adopted an intense dislike of Carnegie, based on Carnegie's methods of doing business. In 1898, while Pierpont laid plans and engaged in discussions about the future of steel as the basis for expansion of American industry and the American securities business, he was not ready yet to engage in an unrestricted argument with the wealthiest man in the steel business and one of the wealthiest men in the world.

In 1900 the eight combinations of steel companies began to compete among themselves in earnest. John W. Gates announced to the Carnegie interests that he was canceling his contract for crude steel and that in the future the American Steel and Wire Company would make its own steel. The owners of Steel Hoop and Sheet Steel and National Tube and American Bridge followed this announcement with similar statements.

Andrew Carnegie had been competing in the steel business for thirty years and he was no longer a young man. But that did not mean he was willing to give up and let his empire dwindle before his eyes. Carnegie was spending the summer at Skibo Castle, the magnificent edifice he had built in Scotland to astonish the world and show how a poor Scots boy could live once he had the wherewithal. He had been watching his balance sheets all summer, and he was well aware that orders from these firms were slowly dying out. When he learned what was afoot, he declared war on the other steel men. ". . . Only one policy open;" he cabled Pittsburgh, "start at once hoop, rod, wire, nail mills; no halfway about these last two. Extend coal and coke roads, announce these; also tubes. . . ."

So war was declared. Charles Schwab, Carnegie's principal production assistant, sailed for Scotland, carrying plans for a huge new steel plant to be built on Lake Erie. Carnegie approved it with an offhand gesture. The war began. As far as Pierpont was concerned, this was none of his doing, but his industries were threatened. Even had Pierpont backed away from the steel problem, he must face the news that Carnegie had also declared war against the railroads, largely because the Pennsylvania, with whom he had long had rebate arrangements, had raised his rates. Carnegie's answer was an answer out of the past: build a parallel and competing railroad and either destroy the Pennsylvania or force the railroad men to their knees.

This railroad problem worried Pierpont. Was Carnegie trying to create trouble so that someone would buy him out? Or was he determined to begin a steel war that would wreck half his competitors and might even wreck his own empire?

Pierpont puzzled over these questions. Fortunately before the year was out he had an opportunity to act. It came on the night of December 12, 1900. A dinner was given in honor of Charles Schwab at the University Club in New York. Morgan attended, to be seated in the place of honor next to Schwab. Schwab made a glowing speech that night on the future of the steel industry, a speech that reflected all that Pierpont had been saying privately to his partners and associates.

After the meeting, Pierpont took Schwab aside and spent a half hour asking him questions, which Schwab answered directly. Then Pierpont went home and Schwab went back to the Carnegie plant in Pittsburgh.

For several days Pierpont puzzled about the next move. He called in Bet-A-Million Gates, then, and asked for help. It was odd that Pierpont would call in a man whom he did not like, but he knew that Gates was familiar with everything and everyone in the steel industry, and he needed some advice on the manner in which he should proceed. He suggested that Gates call Schwab and arrange a meeting. Gates telephoned Schwab, who was reluctant to meet with Morgan without first telling Carnegie, but eventually did so, coming to 219 Madison Avenue one evening for a night-long meeting with Pierpont, Robert Bacon, and Gates. They laid out the whole program for a steel combine in that night's discussions, even determining that Bethlehem, Jones and Laughlin, and certain other firms should remain independent of the trust.

The success or failure of this scheme depended on one factor: would Carnegie sell? Schwab did not know. He had tried earlier to get Carnegie to sell, and Carnegie had toyed with the idea, but in the end he had not been enough interested to make the concessions that would have made a sale possible. Morgan asked

Schwab to go to Carnegie and give him a firm offer to buy and ask the price. Schwab said he would. He went first to Mrs. Carnegie and asked her how to go about it. She suggested a golf game, and that is where it was done, on the course of St. Andrew's Golf Club in Westchester County, New York, or rather, in Carnegie's stone cottage overlooking the course after they had completed their round of golf.

Carnegie at first indicated that he was not at all sure he wanted to sell. Schwab said the offer was genuine, and Carnegie knew that he must either accept or reject it. He stated his price, jotting it down on a slip of paper. What he wanted was an exchange of a dollar's worth of bonds in the new company for every dollar's worth of bonds in the Carnegie company, and a dollar and a half in bonds for every dollar's worth of stock in the Carnegie company. He wanted all bonds, and no stock. He would be a creditor, then, and not an investor. (Also, if the company failed, he would have all of it, including his competitors.) Since Carnegie owned 58 per cent of the company's stock this would mean a payment of more than $225,000,000. Overall, to retire all the stock and bonds of the company it would require nearly $500,000,000.

Charles Schwab took the little piece of paper which outlined the largest transaction in the history of the steel business to Pierpont Morgan. Morgan glanced at it and said, "I accept." It was done. Had he quibbled it might not have been done at all, but Pierpont did not quibble over so small a matter as money. He did not even ask for a written contract of sale and purchase, until later he realized that if Carnegie were to drop dead—he was over sixty-five years old—there would be no way of salvaging the sale unless there was some sort of agreement. Thereupon Attorney Stetson prepared a letter, which Carnegie signed, but even this was most informal for so large a business deal.

Then, one day Morgan asked Carnegie to come to his office at 23 Wall Street for a business chat. Carnegie said that it was no farther to Fifty-first Street than it was from Fifty-first Street to Wall Street, and that perhaps Morgan would care to call on him. At this state of his career Pierpont was not used to calling on people, but he went, and he and Carnegie talked for fifteen minutes behind a closed door. What might have been a vigorous and very expensive rivalry was then ended, on terms suitable to both men. Later when they met, Carnegie indicated that he should have held out for $100,000,000 more than he had received for his company. "Well," said Pierpont, "you would have got it if you had." It was quite true. Pierpont would not consider quibbling over such a trifle. Carnegie had money and bonds, but Pierpont had set the stage for creation of what was to be his most important accomplishment in the field of business organization.

Now came the rounding up of other difficult or maverick companies. Bet-A-Million Gates thought he could hold out for an enormous price for his American Steel and Wire Company. Pierpont was kept waiting all one afternoon at 23 Wall Street, wanting to go home, while his negotiators bargained with Gates and his associates. Finally Pierpont gave Gates ten minutes in which to accept the offer or he would build his own plant. Gates accepted.

The Rockefellers, who owned the Lake Superior Consolidated Iron Mines and huge iron-ore deposits in the Mesabi Range, proved to be another problem. Judge Gary wanted to buy these properties. Pierpont did not. Gary was most impressive in his arguments as to the need for control of them in the future.

"How are you going to get them?" Pierpont asked.

"You are to talk to Mr. Rockefeller," said Gary.

"I would not think of it," said Pierpont.

"Why?"

"I don't like him."

But Pierpont did go to see old John D. Rockefeller and did ask him to name his price. Rockefeller would not talk business that day. John D. Rockefeller, Jr., came to see Morgan at 23 Wall Street a few days later, on invitation.

Morgan, having been piqued by the father, was inclined to be brusque with the son. When young Rockefeller and H. H. Rogers came into the office, Pierpont was talking to Charles Steele, one of his partners. He ignored the guests and continued his conversation. Finally Steele left, whereupon Pierpont fixed his two visitors with his piercing glare. Rogers introduced the twenty-seven-year-old Rockefeller. "Well," said Pierpont, "what's your price?"

"Mr. Morgan," said young Mr. Rockefeller, "I think there must be some mistake. I did not come here to sell. I understood you wished to buy."

The two men stared at each other. Rogers later said he thought the interview was ended right there. But Morgan backed off, as he always did when his rudeness was not successful in dominating the others in the room, and began to talk reasonably. It was agreed then that Henry Frick, Carnegie's associate, would handle the negotiations between the two interests.

As the negotiations continued and the Rockefellers asked around $75,000,000 for their ore properties, Gary wanted to back off. He thought the price was at least $5,000,000 too high.

"Judge Gary," said Pierpont, "in a business proposition as great as this would you let a matter of five million dollars stand in the way of success?"

He accepted the Rockefeller price as he had accepted the Carnegie price, and in the spring of 1901 all the loose ends had finally been tied up, all the wanted corporations had been purchased, and in March it was announced that a new steel company called United States Steel Corporation had been organized under the corporation laws of the state of New Jersey. This new company was made up of components that did at that time 60 per cent of the steel business in America. The company was capitalized at $1,402,846,817, and of this only $800,000,000 could be said to represent tangible assets. Nearly $750,000,000 represented Pierpont's faith in his ability to manage a huge combine and his belief in the destiny of America and American industry.

How well that faith paid immediately was shown in a few weeks. Pierpont's profit in this arrangement came from the House of Morgan's sale of the securities of the new corporation. The syndicate that was formed to sell the securities profited by $57,-500,000, and the House of Morgan's part, including management fees, came to $11,500,000. Big Steel's common stock, which had been offered on the market at 38, rose almost immediately to 55 and Pierpont Morgan became the hero of the financial world and the principal demon of those who feared and hated monopoly.

CHAPTER

V

THE DANGER OF THINKING BIG

A FEW WEEKS AFTER the formation of United States Steel Corporation was announced, when it appeared that all was going well, Pierpont began his usual spring trip to Europe, to look in on the offices at London and Paris, to visit the antique and art dealers wherever he went, and to take the waters at Aix-les-Bains. In the past few months he had accomplished far more than many men accomplish in a lifetime, and he felt he deserved a rest.

Pierpont's accomplishment was not uniformly greeted with enthusiasm. The followers of William Jennings Bryan, defeated at the polls in 1900, cried that the trusts were taking over the nation and that soon, if not at that moment, the working man would be chained to his machine. The president of Yale University predicted that unless the trusts came under realistic regulation America would become a monarchy within twenty-five years. Others at home and abroad expressed a love for competition that they had not acknowledged during the days when the railroad kings were running fast trains on inadequate rails with huge costs in blood. Competition, said the opponents of the trusts, brought with it the benefits of good service and low prices to consumers. That this was not always true and had not always been true they promptly forgot in the face of what they considered to be the greater danger of economic control by a small body of men.

On this trip to Europe, Pierpont was accompanied by his son Jack and Jack's wife and children. They went to London, where there was some negotiation regarding steamship lines, but not enough to cause more than the normal number of rumors about Morgan's next maneuver in the world of finance. They went to Paris to stay at the Hotel Bristol where Pierpont and his party always occupied the same apartment on the first floor. It was as good as having a private house in Paris—better, because the Morgans did not spend enough time in Paris each year to keep a full staff of servants properly employed.

While Pierpont was in Paris a serious storm blew up within his railroad empire, and it became necessary for him to give less time to his consideration of the wares of the art dealers and more to the stack of cables that piled up on his desk.

A few years earlier Pierpont had made the judgment that the Union Pacific Railroad was not worth the trouble that it would take to reorganize its finances and put it back on its feet. Having made that decision he withdrew from attempts to create a profitable line there, and the smaller banking house of Kuhn, Loeb and Company had moved in with his blessing. Jacob Schiff, head of the firm, had discovered that someone was throwing monkey wrenches into his efforts. He had come to Morgan to be reassured that it was not Morgan, and he had finally discovered that it was unprepossessing little Edward H. Harriman. "You want to look out for him," Morgan told Schiff. He always looked out against—not for—Harriman himself.

Schiff and Harriman soon made a truce. Schiff went ahead with the reorganization of the Union Pacific, and, for noninterference, Harriman was promised a place on the board of directors, and the executive committee once the job was done. In spite of his personality, Edward Harriman proved to be an apt student of railroads, and he proved that Pierpont had made an error in judgment in passsing up the Union Pacific opportunity. In 1898, after an inspection trip of the line, Harriman recommended an expenditure of $25,000,000 for rehabilitation. The purpose was to speed up freight traffic and make the Union Pacific the fastest, most efficient line running across the country.

In 1900, when he had been bemused with the steel industry, Pierpont had still been involved in railroads. He watched while Harriman tried to buy control of the Chicago, Burlington and Quincy Railroad, which Harriman wanted because it would connect the Union Pacific with the East. The Union Pacific at that time ran only from Ogden, Utah, to Omaha, Nebraska. Harriman failed in his effort at Chicago, and then turned his attention to the West, to try to purchase the Southern Pacific Railroad, which would give him access to the West Coast.

Then James J. Hill set to work to buy up the C. B. and Q., or Burlington line, so that the Northern Pacific-Great Northern combination would have the Chicago access. In April, as Pierpont interviewed art dealers in London, the Burlington went into the hands of the Morgan-Hill combination. Now Harriman was furious and he set about to buy control of the Northern Pacific away from Pierpont and Hill, and thus to regain the control of the Burlington that he had lost.

The Northern Pacific had 800,000 shares or $80,000,000 worth of common stock outstanding, plus $76,000,000 worth of preferred stock—750,000 shares. Both stocks had voting rights, but the preferred could be retired after January 1, 1902. Common and preferred were in 1901 selling at around $100 a share, which meant that Harriman would have to figure on spending $78,000,000 to acquire 51 per cent if the stock remained static, but when someone began buying heavily the stock would rise, so he would have to have available more than $100,000,000 to make his scheme work. He must also chance the wrath of J. Pierpont Morgan. Pierpont's position was weakened by the fact that Harriman knew Pierpont distrusted and disliked him and that anyone Morgan hated, he hated forever. So Harriman need give no consideration to the social or moral problems involved in raiding the eagle's nest.

The Morgan and Hill groups held only $35,000,000 worth of the Northern Pacific stock, or a quarter of the total. These were days in which it was not the practice of the controlling group to hold an absolute majority of stock. That a plurality was adequate for control had always been the Morgan counsel, since the days when the Morgans sold Vanderbilt's majority interest in the New York Central. This position was perfectly sensible just as long as there was no one else who wanted control of a property badly enough to buy an absolute majority on the public market.

Harriman chose his moment of action with ingenious skill. Pierpont was out of the country, his senses lulled by the success of his heady experiment in steel. Young Robert Bacon was as much in charge at 23 Wall Street as anyone could be. The stock market was booming, buoyed by the great steel combination and its immediate success, and very strange and wonderful things were happening to the most unusual stocks every single day in April. Harriman told Kuhn, Loeb and Company to begin buying Northern Pacific stock for the Union Pacific.

Northern Pacific common began the week of April 22 at 101. A week later it had risen to 117. So unaware was the financial world of Harriman's plan that the Northern Pacific board of directors approved the sale of a block of shares by one of its subsidiaries and the House of Morgan sold ten thousand shares that had come into the bank in another transaction.

The bankers and brokers in New York watched the rise of Northern Pacific stock with equanimity. Pierpont's friends sold their stock, unable to resist the quick profit that they saw as coming from the fluctuation of the marketplace, and intending to buy it back again when the price fell.

Yet one man was not gulled. He was James J. Hill. He had gone to Seattle in April to check on the western terminus of his railroad empire. While there he learned that the price of Northern Pacific was rising steadily, and he suspected that he knew exactly why. He had his special car hitched to a special train, had the tracks of his railroad cleared, and began a run completely across the country to New York City. It was perhaps the fastest trip ever made from coast to coast up to that day. On May 3, Hill arrived in New York, went straight to the offices of Kuhn, Loeb and Company and asked Jacob Schiff outright if he was responsible for this buying on behalf of Harriman. Schiff admitted that it was so—there seemed little reason to try to dissimulate, because he was so near to accomplishing Harriman's purpose that there was practically no chance of Hill's stopping him, particularly with Pierpont out of the country. Kuhn, Loeb now held for Union Pacific $42,-000,000 of the $75,000,000 in preferred shares, or a clear majority. They also held $37,000,000 of the common shares of the $80,000,000 total. Altogether, preferred and common, they held $79,000,000 in shares of a total $155,000,000, or a majority of all the stock.

There are two versions of the tenor of the conversation that was held between Hill and Schiff that day. Schiff's version is that he and Harriman had no intention of taking control of the road away from Hill but simply wanted a say in management to bring about "harmony." The Hill version is that Schiff said he and Harriman now had control of the railroad and offered him the chance to retain his position as chief executive if he would join with them.

It seems apparent that the Hill version is far closer to what Harriman had in mind than the Schiff version, and that was exactly the position that Pierpont took when he learned of the raid. Hill went from Kuhn, Loeb and Company to 23 Wall Street, where he informed Robert Bacon of the danger. On the evening of May 3 Bacon took the first step. He put down the figures: Harriman now had 790,000 of the 1,550,000 shares; but Bacon and Pierpont knew that Harriman did not have a pure majority of the common stock and that the board of directors had previously voted to retire the preferred. Bacon asked permission to buy 150,000 shares of Northern Pacific common stock. Morgan cabled his assent at once.

While this was happening, perhaps Harriman sensed that his enemies were moving. He was at home sick, but on Saturday morning he telephoned Jacob Schiff's office and placed an order to buy 40,000 more shares of the common stock of the Northern Pacific Railroad. This would give Harriman an absolute majority of common stock and preferred stock. There would be no question about the control of the railroad.

When the call came into Kuhn, Loeb on the morning of Saturday, May 4, the office and the stock exchange were open, for in these days the exchange worked a six-day week. Jacob Schiff, however, was not in the office because it was Saturday and he was at synagogue. So, the order to buy 40,000 more shares of Northern Pacific common stock was laid over until Monday morning.

For all his alacrity in cabling, Robert Bacon did not get at the buying of the 150,000 shares on Saturday either. Satterlee says that Bacon did not receive Pierpont's cabled answer until Sunday; whether the fault was Pierpont's or the cable company's remains unstated. Fortunately when Bacon did receive the cable he knew how to act, and although both orders were executed on Monday, the Morgan brokers had their orders in first and actually got stock to assure their majority control of the common. It was not done in a moment: the process took all day Monday and Tuesday. At the end of it, Harriman still thought he had control. Pierpont thought he had control. In fact, neither one of them had a majority of stock certificates, because many of the sellers were "selling short"— they did not actually own the stocks. Had Morgan or Harriman demanded actual delivery of the stock certificates they might have destroyed the stock market forever, and soon both sides realized this. Schiff and Bacon, with Pierpont's concurrence, agreed to let the "short" sellers off the hook on which they had stuck themselves —some of them before the week was out had sold stock at $1,000 a share, and now could not buy it at any price. Eventually it was settled that the short sellers could deliver at $150 a share, which kept many speculators from going bankrupt.

The danger to the marketplace of such unrestricted warfare was never better demonstrated. During this week the shares of U. S. Steel which had been offered on the market only a few weeks before at 38, had begun selling at around 40. But as speculators and investors needed money to buy the Northern Pacific stock that was the rage of the marketplace, they had sold everything else they owned, and steel had dropped quickly from 40 to 26. At one point it dropped to eight dollars a share. At this rate even Morgan corporations would be ruined by Morgan's effort to save control of one of them.

In the end Pierpont prevailed over Harriman, but it was not a very satisfactory victory. Harriman was prevented from taking over the Northern Pacific Railroad, but as the second largest stockholder he was entitled to some places on the board of directors, and this did not please Pierpont, for he wanted nothing to do with Harriman. Pierpont had suffered a defeat in another way; for the first time he had been caught asleep and had been forced to fight a defensive battle. Much confidence was lost in his ability to maintain peace through control by benevolence. He had not maintained financial peace by this control in the Northern Pacific fight. Too many innocent persons had been hurt—not just speculators but small investors.

The war was over but the cost to Pierpont's prestige was immense. He was now subjected to the one charge by the press which really hurt him: he was called irresponsible. There was nothing he could do about it; there was nothing that he would have done differently to protect his interests in the past few days. Those who were hurt were victims of the operations of the American capitalistic system, and there was no way that any individual could guarantee against such eventuality.

It was summer before Pierpont came home, refreshed in body and in spirit, to complete the treaty of peace that had been promised by cable. The treaty involved giving Harriman a place on the board of the Northern Pacific, along with his ally William Rockefeller, and giving Harriman a seat on the board of the Burlington as well. It also involved establishment of a new corporation under the laws of the state of New Jersey, to hold the majority of the stock of the Great Northern and the Northern Pacific Railroads, and make sure that nothing like the Northern Pacific fight ever occurred again.

In the autumn of 1901 the plans for the Northern Securities Corporation were being worked out by Pierpont's lawyers when the news came that President William McKinley had been shot by an anarchist at Buffalo. Just over a week later, he was dead. When Pierpont heard the news, as he was setting forth on an outing aboard his yacht he was so stunned that he took off his hat, sat down in his chair, and said nothing for some time. Then he said the blow was too great for him to discuss. Later that day he did talk a little about McKinley's fine character. He had nothing to say about the future.

THE DANGER OF THINKING BIG

The future was what worried every man in Wall Street. Mark Hanna, McKinley's political manager and a millionaire industrialist, called Theodore Roosevelt, who had been Vice-President, "that damned cowboy." His was the least telling of the epithets the wealthy bestowed on the new President. The extremists of Wall Street worried lest the nation now be in the hands of someone very nearly an anarchist himself. The most level-headed Wall Street men lamented the loss of the "safe" McKinley and the coming of the "unpredictable" Roosevelt. Pierpont was worried because he feared that Roosevelt was too temperamental and would disturb matters by experimenting. He had known Theodore's father well when they served together on the board of the American Museum of Natural History.

In the beginning Pierpont's fears were allayed. The prosperity of the country was sound. Even Theodore Roosevelt seemed sound, for he spoke up in defense of the men who had made America great by investing capital in the growth of the country. He managed to settle the steel strike which had troubled the nation that summer and fall. There was, of course, the old nagging fear: Governor Roosevelt had been prompted into the Vice-Presidency by New York Republican Boss Tom Platt because he was considered to be a reforming nuisance in Albany. As Vice-President, Roosevelt had given a dinner for Pierpont and other important men of business. Still, Pierpont did not know. These were strange times; there was no longer the respect for property that had characterized the thinking of the majority all during his life. The ideas of the radicals had seized hold in very strange and sometimes high places. People of property—millionaires—were supporting new journalistic efforts which exposed unpalatable conditions in a number of industries; Roosevelt was to give these people their name: "muckrakers." By the end of 1901 more than two hundred books had been written on the subject of trusts, and when he sent his first message to Congress, Theodore Roosevelt had devoted much of it to that problem.

For nearly forty years the American people had watched the depredations of the lions and jackals of Wall Street. They had seen men earn millions by shrewd manipulation of the stock market, and others, like Pierpont, earn millions by the manipulation of railroad securities and management. The average American wage earner was making less than a thousand dollars a year, and there was only one basic wage earner in most families. Prosperity was growing—or so the well-to-do said—but prices of necessities were rising. Broken as it had been, the steel strike had reminded the public that men worked over hot furnaces for twelve hours a day, six days a week. The United States Steel Corporation was still too new for them to have forgotten that this was a billion-dollar trust. Then, coming on top of all this was the Northern Pacific debacle, which the public blamed on a battle between giants Morgan and Harriman (quite properly) and the formation of the Northern Securities Corporation. The fact that Pierpont was forming the corporation to prevent just what had happened from happening again was not understood by the public and would not have been accepted had it been understood. For forty years capital had been on the rampage, having its own way, and vigorous men had created fortunes, not by producing goods for the public, but by manipulation. This had gone too far for too long, and politicians to whom votes were more than dollars, saw that the majority of those votes were going to be cast in the next few years by people who would not reason on the subject of business and business manipulation. The capitalistic system might be functioning well economically; politically it had given itself over to excesses; men like Pierpont had been unable to control those excesses as was proven by the Northern Pacific fight; and the public was determined that the politicians would control business.

From the viewpoint of Theodore Roosevelt, though the men of Wall Street distrusted him, he distrusted them far more. He knew them better than they knew him. He knew men and types they did not even consider: cowboys on the plains of Wyoming, farmers from Nebraska who had ridden with him in Cuba; policemen who trod the pavements of New York City and firemen who risked their lives to save the property of Pierpont and his friends. Roosevelt knew these as people, as individuals with hopes and fears and yearnings, where Pierpont and his friends knew them only in the aggregate as "the people." Pierpont could be generous.

His charities showed that. He could be thoughtful of people: at least once he saved a bank whose officials had been bad business-men and worse, simply because the bank housed the deposits of working families for the most part. Pierpont took the position that the poor could not be allowed to make such sacrifice, and he shored up this bank, willing to lose $500,000 or more in the public interest. This was public spirit, but it was not the same as Theodore Roosevelt's public spirit, for Roosevelt truly believed in the power of men to govern themselves. Pierpont never considered government by any but his own privileged class. He had never been forced to consider it and the idea would be anathema to him, for he had never moved outside that arena of privilege for more than a few delicious moments as a boy, and then he had been protected by the certain knowledge that he was no further from help than the nearest bank.

"I do not dislike but I certainly have no especial respect or admiration for and trust in the typical big moneyed man of my country," Roosevelt was to write later. Indeed, he once called Edward H. Harriman "an undesirable citizen" with as much dis-taste as he used in characterizing Eugene Debs, the union and Socialist leader, as an undesirable citizen. Roosevelt believed that the enormous increase in Socialist, Anarchist, and other propa-ganda in the United States at the turn of the twentieth century could be blamed entirely on the depredations of men like Pierpont Morgan and the other very rich. Pierpont and his friends quite properly from their point of view had reservations about Roose-velt. What they did not realize was that the Roosevelts did not identify themselves with the Morgans and Harrimans at all, but with the middle class of America, and the new administration would be marked by the first effort in America to control wealth for the social good as the leaders in Washington saw that social good.

In November 1901 the Northern Securities Company was in-corporated in New Jersey by Pierpont, James J. Hill, Robert Ba-con, Daniel S. Lamont, Banker George F. Baker and others—"all names," said Herbert Satterlee, "to inspire confidence and guaran-tee honesty of purpose and legality of operation." Satterlee may have been quite right that these names *should have* done so. A dozen years before they would have done so among the people that counted. Now the people that counted had changed; it was no longer the people of Fifth Avenue and Shaker Heights and the Back Bay and Peach Tree Street; it was not the stockholders of the Great Northern and the Northern Pacific Railroads who objected, they seemed perfectly satisfied; it was the active men in the halls of government who objected.

One evening in February 1902 Pierpont was called from the dinner table at 219 Madison Avenue to receive a message that the Attorney General of the United States was preparing to file an antitrust case against the Northern Securities Company. The next day the case was filed.

Pierpont was not prepared for this kind of action. He was deeply dismayed, not because Roosevelt was going to demand the dissolution of the trust, but because Roosevelt had not come to him and told him that he must straighten this out; that Roosevelt had chosen to challenge him publicly rather than to meet quietly and arrange this affair between government and business as gentlemen might. Even after the action was begun Pierpont hoped it could be resolved thus. He traveled to Washington to interview the President and protested that Roosevelt might have given him advance warning.

"That is just what we did not want to do," the President said.

If he had done anything wrong, Morgan said, it would have been simple enough for the lawyers to work it out. "Send your man to my man and they can fix it up," he said. He was suggesting in this that the President of the United States dispatch the Attorney General of the United States to New York to meet with the attorney of J. P. Morgan and Company, just as the King of England might ask the King of France to let their ambassadors work out a new treaty. Pierpont did this quite unconsciously, without a thought in the world that he was acting arrogantly.

After he left the White House, President Roosevelt turned to Attorney General Philander C. Knox, who had heard this amazing discussion. "That is a most illuminating discussion of the Wall Street point of view," the President said. "Mr. Morgan could not help regarding me as a big rival operator, who either intended to ruin all his interests or else could be induced to come to an agreement to ruin none."

This was exactly how Pierpont felt about it too. He had asked that a compromise be worked out. Roosevelt had said that no compromise was possible—that the government did not compromise with citizens in such matters or negotiate with citizens as with equal powers. Pierpont left the White House a very angry man, wondering why the government was attacking him personally. He sat down in his hotel room and spent the evening composing a long, angry letter. His trusted associates argued with him for many hours, and finally persuaded him not to send the message.

The trouble, of course, was not with Pierpont and it was not with Roosevelt. It was with the changing of the times. Pierpont and Cleveland could meet. It had not been easy for Cleveland to accept a meeting with Pierpont Morgan, but he had done so and they had reasoned together. The result was not serious from Pierpont's point of view but it was disastrous to Cleveland's reputation; when he was in his grave some Americans still believed that Grover Cleveland had sold out the country to the Wall Street men. Roosevelt could meet easily enough with Pierpont only because he knew what his course must be. There could be no temporizing with Wall Street in 1902, not for any political leader who wished to remain in power longer than his elective term. In the next two years Eugene Debs would quadruple his vote for Socialism; the Democratic party platform and the Republican party platform would both condemn trusts and Wall Street interests. Pierpont's problem was that he was totally incapable of recognizing the change that was coming to America, because it was coming politically instead of economically. Two years later the Supreme Court of the United States outlawed the Northern Securities Company by a close 5–4 vote, as inimical to the idea of free competition. This was the first effective curb that had ever been placed on the adult powers of J. Pierpont Morgan. It came to him as a series of shocks.

CHAPTER

——◆——

VI

A MEASURE OF PEACE

I T IS TO THE CREDIT of both Pierpont Morgan and Theodore
Roosevelt that neither held a serious grudge against the other
because of their locking of horns over the Northern Securities
Company case. If Pierpont did not understand the nature of the
change in the world about him, at least he remained true to his
old principles, and his old principles served him very well because
there could be no question but what they were honest and honorable, if not exactly suited to the needs of twentieth-century
American society.

Principle of Pierpont's kind was called into play the next year,
after Pierpont had returned from a round of princely entertainments in England and on the Continent. He lunched with Kaiser
Wilhelm of Germany at Kiel, used the Imperial railway car to
travel to Berlin, and attended King Edward VII's coronation at
Westminster Abbey as a kind of supernational delegate of good
will. President Roosevelt had extended an olive branch by ap-
pointing J. P. Morgan, Jr., as special representative of the American government at the coronation. Pierpont came home to New
York in midsummer, later than usual, to discover that American
business and the American people faced a bleak and dangerous

winter because the hard-coal miners of the East had been out on strike since May and no real progress had been made toward settling the dispute.

A month after Pierpont's return matters had reached so serious a state that President Roosevelt intervened in the strike between the coal operators and the United Mine Workers Union under John Mitchell. He called operators and union officers to a meeting at the temporary White House on Lafayette Place, which he was using while the mansion across the street was being renovated. President Roosevelt had no legal authority to take any action. Many in Congress and in public affairs resented his interference. Businessmen in particular resented his poking his nose into the dispute and the coal operators as much as told him so. George F. Baer, head of the coal operators' group, called the union men outlaws and indicated that they would not negotiate with them. This attitude dated back to the successful ending of the steel strike without any victory of organized labor. The coal operators did not understand the century into which they had moved, either, and they had very little of the milk of human kindness or any feeling of *noblesse oblige* to bridge the gap between the world of the nineteenth century and the new world blossoming in 1902.

Elihu Root, the Secretary of War, was one of the new type of American politicians with many of the old gentlemanly trimmings. He knew the world in which he and Roosevelt now lived; he also knew Pierpont's world, and he could bridge the gap between them. He went to see Roosevelt with a suggestion that Morgan be asked to help because Morgan in a very real sense controlled the destinies of many of these irritable, insensitive, and hardshelled coal operators. George Baer, for example, was president of the Reading Railroad, and Pierpont could crush the Reading anytime he felt like it. Not that he would consider so low a trick; that was not the point; men like George Baer understood power and nothing else. There was no government power over industry except as outlined elsewhere, the fuzzy power over corporation trusts. The world of business was still ruled by economic czars, and Pierpont was the strongest czar of all. Roosevelt said it was a capital idea for Root to go to New York and seek Morgan's support in the settlement of the coal strike. Pierpont had already shown serious concern. He had given Nathan Straus a check for $20,000 for the purchase of coal to be distributed to the poor, and had also arranged a very good price for it from the operators. He had made arrangements for large quantities of coal to be sent to the United States from Britain on the shipping lines he now controlled, even if it meant a loss in normal shipping traffic.

Root telephoned Morgan for an appointment and came to New York on October 12, a Saturday. He went straight to the Hudson River anchorage of *Corsair* on Sunday morning and boarded the yacht, where he set forth his plan. At three o'clock in the afternoon Pierpont and Root came ashore and drove from the Thirty-fifth Street pier to the Union Club. Root then went to the station to take a train back to Washington. That same Sunday, Pierpont talked with coal operators. He stayed in New York at the Fifth Avenue Hotel that night as his family was at Cragston and the house on Madison Avenue was closed. On Monday he boarded the yacht again and the coal men began to come aboard in small groups. They talked all day long. The next day, Tuesday, Pierpont telephoned Washington to report that Root's basic settlement agreement had been accepted. One point at issue had been that the stiff-necked coal operators would not negotiate with the United Mine Workers Union. They had been persuaded to deal with their own employees, not as union men, but to hear their grievances and to submit to an impartial arbitration of those grievances. Pierpont caught a train to Washington, taking along Robert Bacon, who had been Roosevelt's classmate at Harvard College. All was soon settled as far as the negotiators were concerned, and Morgan and Roosevelt looked at one another, face to face, with far different attitudes than they had shown a few months before.

The coal operators were as pig-headed as men can be when they see the handwriting on the wall and have no ideas as to how they might avoid the destiny that threatens them. They agreed to accept arbitration, pressed by Pierpont. One cannot overemphasize the importance of his effort in pushing this decision. Corey claimed that Pierpont "controlled" the coal operators. He did not; at least he did not control all of them by a very long way, and had he been forced to ruin any of them to press a point, it would have represented considerable future trouble for him and a move against his own economic interests. The fact is that his prestige and economic power made it impossible for the coal operators to be totally unreasonable. They had been unreasonable with Roosevelt and they would be unreasonable with anyone who could not ruin them. These were industrial barons of the nineteenth century, bringing their ways with them into the twentieth century.

The arbitration proposal finally accepted by the operators was this: they would accept a commission appointed by the President, to consist of an engineer officer of the defense services, an expert mining engineer, a federal judge of Eastern Pennsylvania, "a man who by active participation in mining and selling coal is familiar with the physical and commercial features of the business," and finally, "a man of prominence, eminent as a sociologist."

Any twentieth-century student will see what was missing here: a representative of the workers. The Union spotted this in a moment, and demanded a union man and a Roman Catholic bishop, since so many of the miners were Catholics.

All was well, then, except that the operators would not accept a union man on the board and the miners union would not accept a board without a labor man on it. The matter was finally solved when the operators accepted the Grand Chief of the Order of Railway Conductors, a union leader, provided that he came into the panel as "a man of prominence, eminent as a sociologist" and that is what he did and how the strike was settled. It was a triumph of cooperation between the biggest businessman in America and the biggest political leader in the land.

Pierpont's economic power, even at this moment when all the economic power of all businesses was being reduced by government, was greater than it had ever been before. Pierpont was now the most important banker in the world and was so recognized even by his English clients, who were not at all eager to render such acclaim to a foreigner, even an American cousin. In 1902 he headed a syndicate in England which took a £32,000,000 British government issue in combination with the Barings and the Rothschilds. But in English eyes his most important act, and a threatening one to English pride, was to organize the International Mercantile Marine. This was the result, in part, of Pierpont's pique on that Christmas Eve so long ago when the Cunard men had left him stranded at the pier in Liverpool. He brought together the White Star Line, the American Line, the Atlantic Transport Line, the Red Star Line, the Dominion Line, and the Layland Line to make this combination. Its fleet numbered more than 120 ships.

This move raised serious questions in England. The penny press began to speculate on Pierpont's every move, as the American press had been doing for years. On the streets of London jokesters sold "licenses to remain on earth" for a penny. They were signed: J. Pierpont Morgan. In the House of Commons the Prime Minister, Lord Balfour, was asked a question about the recidivism of British shipping and the intentions of the House of Morgan. Was Morgan or Britannia to rule the waves? The British government declared that Morgan had no unfriendly intentions towards British seapower, but this was not enough. The Cunard Line played heavily and successfully on British nationalism and pushed the government into a subsidy arrangement which enabled Cunard to begin construction of huge new liners such as the *Mauretania*. It was a disappointment to Pierpont, but his dream for a great international shipping alliance did not work out well, although it limped along during the course of his lifetime.

Pierpont continued with railroad reorganizations. He saved the Louisville & Nashville line from the hands of Bet-A-Million Gates, and other allies, including Bernard Baruch, and combined it with the Atlantic Coast Line to strengthen both. He saved the Reading Railroad from an attempt at seizure by George Gould, son of Jay. Young Gould and his group controlled the Missouri Pacific, the Denver and Rio Grande Western, and the Wabash Line. If they had secured control of the Reading they would have had very nearly a transcontinental rail line. Pierpont had never liked Jay Gould. Now he contented himself by saying that the Gould management was not economic or efficient, and that to have it control the Reading would be "disturbing."

In 1902, during a temporary financial panic caused by the coal strike and worry over Rooseveltian policies, Pierpont combined with James Stillman of the City Bank and George Baker of the First National Bank to build a money pool of $50,000,000. This, they said, would be used to loan money to companies threatened by the panic. The knowledge that the money was there was quite enough in 1902; no rescue loans were needed.

In 1903 Pierpont began another of his visionary promotions. He decided to take the New York, New Haven and Hartford Railroad and, with it as nucleus, make a great New England Railway system, which would combine all the little roads that ran in and out of culverts and coves and up into the hinterland between New York City and Portland, Maine. He brought Charles S. Mellen, an experienced New England railroad man, to become president of the new road, and he began buying railroads to add to the system. Mellen was just the man, it seemed. He had come up to be president of the Northern Pacific and was obviously closely attuned to Pierpont Morgan's railroad philosophy.

The New Haven competition problem was perhaps more serious than that of any road Pierpont had touched. Steamboat lines must be bought or put out of business. Interurban trolley lines must be bought or forced to go broke. There were franchises outstanding for lines that had not even been built, and these must be dealt with in one way or another. The work began in 1903 to combine all the factors for a New England rail system, in spite of these difficulties.

Yet with the New Haven it was never quite the same as it had been with any of the other lines. The old magic was there. The money was there. If the management was not all it should be this did not seem to be apparent at the time. No, something else was wrong, something more than has been stated elsewhere.

To see what it might be, one could compare the problem of the New Haven with the other brave ventures Pierpont was undertaking at this moment. His shipping line was having difficulties because the English were very much conscious of the source of their economic power and very jealous of their shipping empire. Pierpont was also involved in the financial management of an attempt to bring rapid transit to London. Here he was balked by Speyer and Company, an English firm. One reason for the diffi-

culty with financing English companies or companies in competition with English companies was a growing concern lest the new
world take over the old. For many years Americans had accepted
heavy English and other foreign investment in the industries of
the United States. They were grateful for it, and on this rock the
House of Morgan was built. After 1900 the emphasis was changed,
and although J. P. Morgan and Company was a transatlantic firm,
the English did not forget that it was owned by an American,
primarily, and represented America. In many more ways than one
the twentieth century was offering differences to complicate the
world of the House of Morgan.

CHAPTER

VII

THE COMMODORE'S YACHTS

THERE IS MUCH to be learned about Pierpont and the younger
Morgans by an examination of their conduct of what was to
become the great hobby of the family, the cultivation of ships and
the adventures of the sea. Perhaps with Pierpont this interest
dated back to his nautical baptism on the sailing-ship voyage to
the Azores. He grew up in that period of "in-between" when
sometimes one took a sailing ship across the sea, sometimes one
took a steamer, and sometimes one took a steamer that was assisted by sails. Much of the romance of the sea went out with the
disappearance of sails, and Pierpont was one of the few non-
professionals of his age group who had much opportunity to enjoy
the delights of sail. This, plus the sheer luxury of it, translated
themselves into a strong preoccupation with nautical affairs that
lasted all his life and was apparent in the next two generations of
Morgans.

Pierpont's first yacht had been purchased almost on a whim.
She was not a very comfortable draft, according to those who
spent nights aboard her. The cabins tended to be stuffy, and with
the appearance of grandchildren, she seemed too small and too
slow for Pierpont's purposes by 1890. When he left the United

States in the summer of that year to go to London to settle up his father's estate, he ordered a new yacht. One night he dined with J. Frederick Tams, a well-known yachtsman, and asked Tams to supervise the design and construction of a new boat. She was to be larger and faster than the *Corsair,* but she was still to be able to do ferry duty up to Cragston and turn around in the channel of the Hudson there. Tams undertook the chore with some misgivings, because when he ventured to criticize the old *Corsair,* Pierpont simply stared at him with those beetling brows and that unquivering walrus mustache, and Tams thought he would burst a boiler. This was 1890. Pierpont was just coming into his own as a powerful financier, but already he withered men with that steely glance.

Tams was given a book of blank checks and the instructions that no one else was to have anything to do with the boat. She was built in his name. When she was finished in the fall of 1891, she was 241½ feet long overall, her beam was 27 feet, and she drew fifteen feet of water. She was bigger, and faster, and more luxurious than the *Corsair.* And what was to be her name? When Jack Morgan swung the bottle of champagne against her bow at the christening he pronounced her *Corsair II.* Pierpont Morgan had a perfectly good name for a yacht. He would never change it; that was his way.

Corsair II became much more of a traveling yacht than *Corsair* had been. Pierpont could take a large party aboard her, and the size of the Corsair club was increased gradually until it numbered ten men. Like her predecessor, *Corsair II* was black and rakish, with long stem, slender masts fore and aft, and a single tall buff funnel. Her main deck was almost completely covered for weather with canvas awning. She had an adventurous look about her that must have been pleasing to Pierpont, who, after all, was much the romanticist beneath that hard banker's shell.

As with the first yacht, *Corsair II* was the scene of innumerable business conferences. With the coming of the telephone to business, and the general quickening of the pace, Pierpont saw how intelligent he had been in commandeering a yacht for business purposes. The craft usually lay at anchor near the New Jersey shore at about Thirty-fifth Street, on the Hudson River, and it was easy in those days for a horse-drawn cab to move from Wall Street to the landing. There was another value to having one's own yacht, proved absolutely in the summer of 1895, after the gold contract between the Morgan-Belmont syndicate and the Treasury. So noisy were the newspapermen and the administration's critics in attacking the bond arrangement that President Cleveland had been reluctant to be seen in the presence of Pierpont or any other Wall Street banker. The President did want to talk to Morgan that summer about the state of the European market and to secure the banker's opinions on the future prospects of holding gold on the American shores.

So, one day President Cleveland set out on the yacht *Oneida,* which belonged to his old friend Commodore E. C. Benedict of the Seawanhaka Yacht Club. It was not at all unusual for Cleveland to go cruising with Benedict, and sometimes the Commodore took the Clevelands to their summer home on Buzzards Bay, so the newspapers took no notice in the summer of 1895 when the *Oneida* arrived at Gray Gables, the summer White House on the Massachusetts shore. Cleveland was taken aboard and that was the last the newspapermen saw of him for a time. The *Oneida* steamed down the bay, out past Block Island, and into the Atlantic, then moved to an out-of-the-way cove on the old pirate shore of Gardiners Island. There the sleek black *Corsair II* was anchored a few yards away. Pierpont went aboard what, even to him, must be considered the flagship, and he and the President talked far into the night and played cribbage, while Pierpont made his strongest arguments about the need for Congressional action to assure the maintenance of the gold standard by the United States.

A year later, on the eve of William McKinley's election to the Presidency, McKinley manager Mark Hanna was lounging aboard the *Corsair II* explaining the ways of American politics to Pierpont in the words of a businessman who had become a millionaire in his own right. Of all the politicians he met, Pierpont had more respect for Hanna than any other because he could understand Hanna better. On this evening Pierpont learned something about politics, and again hammered his point about the gold standards.

Pierpont lost *Corsair II* to the United States Navy during the Spanish-American War. After the destruction of the *Maine* in Havana Harbor, Congress began scurrying about for a navy, which it had neglected to supply, and a board of naval commissioners was handed a blank check for $50,000,000 and told to put one together. The commissioners snooped around the port cities looking for fast yachts that could be converted into something resembling warships and could be armed to shoot without blowing out their plating. One of the Navy's first choices was *Corsair II*. Pierpont tried to stave off the Navy by promising to build another yacht just like *Corsair II* if they would leave him alone. (This was a particularly annoying time for the Navy to be coming around because it was the beginning of yachting season.) The commissioners were adamant and Pierpont turned over the yacht, which was armed and recommissioned as the U.S.S. *Gloucester*, a gunboat. She was dispatched quickly to Cuban waters. At the battle of Santiago de Cuba she distinguished herself by helping to destroy the Spanish destroyers *Pluton*, which was beached after the action, and *Furor*, which was sunk by *Gloucester*'s fire. The *Gloucester* was hit but not hurt seriously. Pierpont received a piece of her mast from the Navy, showing where a Spanish shell had struck and a report: the *Gloucester*'s action gave a representative picture of the course of the Spanish-American War.

By 1898 Pierpont was much too used to his yachting routine to change, and so that summer after *Corsair II* became *Gloucester* he chartered the *Sagamore*, a large steamer which was rigged for sail, and made do with her. Meanwhile he set out to duplicate *Corsair II*. When Pierpont Morgan said duplicate he meant *duplicate*, not re-create a reasonable facsimile. The same plans were used for *Corsair III* as had been used for *Corsair II*. Naval architect Beavor Webb was given one latitude: he could do anything he wanted about the construction of hull and engines, just as long as the new yacht *looked* exactly the same as the old. This involved the finding of exactly the same fittings and furnishings, and when it was discovered that the carpet factory had stopped making the pattern used in the rugs, the old patterns had to be set up again especially on the factory looms and the rugs matched for Pierpont's yacht. She was launched in December of that year, a little bigger than the old yacht, a little faster. She was 302 feet long overall and 33 feet of beam, but from her profile nearly anyone would have thought they were seeing *Corsair II* all over again. That was just the way Pierpont wanted it.

In the summer of 1899 *Corsair III* was fitted out and ready for Pierpont when he returned from his spring trip to Europe. He used her a good deal for ferrying up the Hudson to Cragston, as he had used the other yachts. On Saturdays he would run to Highland Falls to see the family and spend the weekend. He would take his guests ashore on Saturday and stay at the house, returning to the yacht on Sunday night at about ten o'clock. The yacht would lie at anchor all night long so the owner and his guests could have a good night's sleep, and early in the morning she would head down the river. She would anchor at just about breakfast time, whereupon Pierpont would appear, look about the familiar New York Harbor skyline with great satisfaction and sit down to a breakfast fitting for an ocean-going sailor. It began with fruit, and included porridge, various breads and rolls, butter, eggs, meats, hash made of smoked tongue, fried fish, and sliced tomatoes. Pierpont always ate almost all of it, which for a man who took absolutely no exercise was a daring feat, scarcely ever matched by his guests. Then, at nine o'clock in the morning the launch was alongside and everyone from the city went ashore, Pierpont taking a carriage down to his office at 23 Wall Street.

At the end of the business day during the week he would board the yacht and steam out to Great Neck to an anchorage inside Execution Light, which was adjacent to a shore colony where a number of his friends lived. Every night there was a dinner or an entertainment aboard, with Pierpont presiding. He might seem to snooze in his wicker chair on deck, particularly in the later years, but he was marvelously alive to the conversation that occurred at all times.

Even in these later years Pierpont was a remarkable physical specimen. He weighed about 210 pounds—sometimes more—and he ate and drank lustily. Half a century later such habits as his would serve as a cardiologist's nightmare. He firmly believed that exercise for its own sake was a work of nonsense, and yet he was willing to undertake the most amazing feats if he felt like doing so. He was too portly for swimming off the yacht and he never cared much for swimming anyhow. One day, in the summer of 1899, he took *Corsair III* out to Quarantine to meet his family, who were returning from Europe on the *Oceanic.* He ordered the launch over the side and when the Quarantine doctor came down into his tug, Pierpont got into the launch and had himself brought alongside the liner as his son-in-law, Herbert Satterlee, watched from the deck. Here is the scene as Satterlee described it:

". . . Word ran around the decks of the *Oceanic* that Mr. Morgan was coming on board, and necks were craned over rails and heads came out of portholes to see him. The tide was swirling by the big ship. He grasped the lower end of the rope ladder, swung up on it and his launch disappeared in the direction of the yacht. The ladder swayed with his weight against the ship's side which was rough with overlapping plates and innumerable bolts. In Mr. Morgan's mouth was a cigar. He looked up once, then fixed his straw hat more firmly on his head, and with his teeth clenched on the cigar, he started up. It was a climb of over sixty feet straight up to the rail. To everybody who was watching him it was quite evidently a foolhardy thing for him to attempt . . . although he never stopped and came steadily upward. Some of those on the yacht turned away, too frightened to watch him. The time was long enough for the sporting element on the *Oceanic* to make bets as to whether he would ever reach the rail. If he should fail, there was very little chance of doing anything for him in that tideway. When his face, dripping with perspiration, appeared over the rail, and he got where he could throw his leg over it, he waved aside all the outstretched hands and asked 'Where is Mrs. Morgan?' and without pausing followed the steward down to her cabin."

Later, Pierpont admitted that when he had found himself at the foot of that ladder and looked up he realized he should never have tried it, but his dignity would not let him give up and shout for assistance. That was not the Pierpont Morgan way, but it was the Pierpont Morgan way never to try that particular piece of foolhardiness again.

In the course of his years of yachting, Pierpont indicated to the world more about this particular avocation than most rich men, although he was never one to unburden himself at length to the press. Once, when someone asked him how much it cost to own a yacht, he replied wisely that if one had to consider the cost one ought not to think about it. On another occasion he told an ac-quaintance who was considering the purchase of a yacht that if he did not have at least one or two men of whom he was fond, who would go anywhere with him at the drop of a hat, then he would be very lonely on his yacht. Pierpont had such men: that was the object of the Corsair Club, but more than that J. Beavor Webb was nearly always available and so was Dr. James Markoe, Pierpont's personal physician.

Sometimes Pierpont took *Corsair III* to Europe, although usu-ally he went by steamer. In 1902 the yacht took a party cruising along the French Riviera and to Venice, then down the Adriatic to Brindisi. That was the summer of the intense social activity, when Pierpont lunched with kings. Three years later he took her to Constantinople on a cruise, where Pierpont had an audience with the Sultan of Turkey. He also visited the King of Italy on that trip, and Pope Pius X, in a manner later to be emulated by other wealthy Americans who traveled abroad. He dropped in briefly to Dover, for his old friend the King of the Belgians had come over on his yacht to see Pierpont and receive some financial advice. For a number of years Pierpont had been giving the king advice without fanfare, something like a free CPA service.

Very seldom did Pierpont go anywhere on other people's yachts in his later years. In 1905 he spent a weekend with daughter Louisa and her husband, Herbert Satterlee, on a yacht they had chartered, but this was a demonstration of family piety. He stayed aboard only two days.

In the last few years of his life Pierpont spent much time cruis-ing on *Corsair III*. He visited the Greek Islands and many other parts of the Mediterranean. As a rule he preferred the rough Atlantic crossing to be made on one of the big liners, but *Corsair* was sent ahead or joined him at some prearranged point and the cruises began.

Pierpont also began to take an active interest in sailing, the rich man's sport, as soon as his position in the world of business was established. In 1882 he joined the New York Yacht Club and the next year he went to Marblehead in the *Corsair* to watch a regatta. Ten years later his position was such within the club that it was not presumptuous for him to donate cups for yachting victories and he established the Morgan Cups, which were given for victories in the squadron's run from Vineyard Haven to Marblehead.

His interest in sailing was stimulated by the controversy that arose during the America's Cup races of 1895, when Lord Dunraven protested a decision of the race committee and made several charges that indicated he felt he had been treated unfairly. Pierpont was chosen, along with several other distinguished members of the club, to consider the charges made by Lord Dunraven. The final result was that Dunraven was dissatisfied and was asked to resign from his honorary membership. The special committee conducted itself with such delicacy that Dunraven lost what little support he had secured in England for the unfortunate and stubborn position he had chosen to assume.

In 1897, his sixtieth year, Pierpont was elected commodore of the New York Yacht Club, and as did many other wealthy men who owned yachts, he gloried a little in the title that was often used to address him thereafter: Commodore Morgan. His elevation to this post accounted for his extreme disappointment, too, when the naval commissioners came around next year to take away his yacht for the national defense. It was just not right for the Commodore to have lost his yacht, but it worked out satisfactorily, for so many commodores lost their yachts that the annual cruise was abandoned in 1898.

Pierpont was elected Commodore again for 1899 and that year he organized the syndicate that financed the building of the *Columbia* to defend the America's Cup against Sir Thomas Lipton, the tea merchant who had challenged with *Shamrock*. *Columbia* won; poor Lipton was never to win that cup although he tried almost until his death. Pierpont gave up the active leadership of the New York Yacht Club after the season of 1899. He was asked to stand again for Commodore but he would not. In two seasons, he had discovered, amateur yacht racing and its social trappings had cost him dearly. He had led two fine annual cruises, but they were not inexpensive to him, and it was time that someone else shared the growing cost of maintaining America's place in amateur yacht racing. He continued his generosities to the club. He gave the land on which to build the new building, he gave cups and yacht models and money, and he enjoyed the good fellowship of the rooms and dinners, but for him yachting was a question of being at sea as often as he could be aboard the *Corsair*. This, quite obviously, was one of Pierpont's greatest pleasures in later life.

CHAPTER

VIII

THE MORGAN FAITH

O<small>F ALL THE MEMBERS</small> of the Morgan family, Pierpont stands out for the manner in which his religious faith has been revealed to the public. No other layman in American history, at least none who was not primarily concerned with the church or with reform, has been the subject of such searching review in so private a matter.

Just as no one could ever accuse Pierpont of ostentation in his use of great wealth, no one could accuse him of sanctimony or of conspicuousness in his religion. True, his religion became a matter of deep public interest and public comment, but the reason for this lay more with the sensational press than with Pierpont, and then the prying was coupled with the revelations of a number of people who had something to do with Pierpont in religious matters, including the late Reverend William S. Rainsford, Pierpont's confidant in the affairs of St. George's Episcopal Church in New York City.

As noted, the change of the Junius Morgan family from the Congregational to the Episcopal denomination was the work of Junius. Pierpont grew up an Episcopalian. He was baptized in the Congregational Church but he was confirmed in the Episcopal

Church in the spring of 1861, a few months before his marriage.

He became a regular communicant, an enthusiastic singer of hymns in his bullfrog voice, and a prodigious student of church affairs on a level far above that of the average layman. He might have sung in the choir had he been asked, but that would never happen, no matter how powerful a figure Pierpont might become in the business and ecclesiastical worlds. There was a limit for music lovers. Still, he probably knew more hymns by the time he was an old man than any but a clergyman, and he regularly exercised his lungs in both his churches: St. George's and the Church of the Holy Innocents at Highland Falls. He had habits in church that must have been disconcerting. For several years he conducted a personal struggle, on the very highest plane, with a local character at Highland Falls named Johnny Strang. Pierpont was a vestryman and perhaps he could have used his power to resolve the problem, but he did not approach it that way. Johnny Strang was a rough-and-ready individualist, a man who lived on the mountain in back of West Point, one of the old mountain men of the region. He had gotten religion somewhere and he came to church every Sunday. He took a certain place near the pulpit which was also favored by Pierpont. Every Sunday in those early years at Cragston, Pierpont would rush the family into the omnibus to get to church early so he could beat Johnny Strang to that particular seat. If Johnny got there first, which happened about half the time, he would not think of yielding his seat to the banker.

When Pierpont was in his seat, particularly in his later years when his power was so very nearly absolute, he displayed very definite views about the music that was presented to entertain and uplift him. He liked certain hymns and did not like others. If a hymn was being played and he liked the music but not the words, he would slam his hymnal shut in the middle of the first verse with a sound that was unmistakable.

If he did not like the tune either he would compete with organ and choir during the remaining three or four verses by loudly jingling the small change in his pocket. He was then warden of both institutions and chief financial support and advisor of both. Needless to say, nobody complained.

Pierpont attended his first church convention in 1869—merely a diocesan affair. He progressed rapidly in the church's lay department, however, and was soon the confidant of clergymen and bishops. He was as true a student of church doctrine as he was a faithful reader of the *New York Sun*, the Bible of the financial world. Yet he was not what one would call a scholastic, who buried himself in the trappings or in the theological arguments because he really had no faith in the dogma. Pierpont was a religious Christian with a strength of belief quite unusual in modern times. He was totally unself-conscious about this, as were all the Morgans about their religion. On a visit to the Holy Land in 1882 he wrote Fanny every day, keeping a journal of his trip. On coming to the Church of the Holy Sepulchre in Jerusalem, he was deeply moved. He wrote: ". . . you find yourself in a vaulted Chapel, built on what is supposed to be the summit of Calvary, a death like stillness pervades, the distant sounds of an organ in a distant part of the church are heard, awestruck and impressed you stand almost breathless upon what must always be the most sacred spot on earth."

In 1886 Pierpont attended his first Triennial Episcopal Convention in Chicago, and after induction into this mighty body he was never to be outside the church councils. He became treasurer of the board of trustees of the Cathedral of St. John the Divine, and was responsible for raising much of the money for the building of that cathedral.

In 1889 for all practical purposes he managed the arrangements for the Episcopal Convention which was held at St. George's, and this was a source of great pleasure to him, for everything was just the way he wanted it to be, down to the seating of bishops and other delegates, and the luncheons, which he planned and ordered every day for three weeks. From then on there was no stopping his management of the convention. In 1895, when the convention was held in Minneapolis, he rented a house, sent Louis Sherry and his caterers to staff it, and took a private railroad car to transport his party, which included two bishops and their wives. He always liked bishops. He found that they were good story-tellers and good company and that they were skilled in their profession, well traveled and positive in their ideas. Also, they were neither afraid of him nor beholden to him. When he was dining with his bishops Pierpont felt among equals as he did seldom among men in the business world. He enjoyed mingling with them as much as he did with princes of only temporal power.

By 1900, when Louisa married Herbert Satterlee, Pierpont was glorying in the rites of the church and his management of some of them in the manner of a bishop. Louisa and her fiancé wished to be married quietly in the little church at Highland Falls, with a reception to follow for close friends and relatives at Cragston. Pierpont would not have it; there were far too many people who must come to the wedding, and he began consulting railroads guides, and looking over maps, and talking about special trains. The wedding was finally held at St. George's, which would hold fifteen hundred people. The reception was held in a circus tent on the lots adjoining the Morgan house on Madison Avenue. This was not exhibitionism in the Vanderbilt or Astor manner, however; it was exuberance and Pierpont's love of a party—providing he could manage it all himself.

In church affairs Pierpont was refreshingly audacious. In 1901, when he was sixty-four years old, he attended the Episcopal Convention in San Francisco, taking a special train, of course, and a bevy of bishops to fill it. The convention was held at Trinity Church. When Pierpont arrived he was disgusted to discover that the New York delegation's seats were back in the transept where he could neither see nor hear. So he grasped the New York banner and marched forcefully up to some empty seats in front, which belonged to the Texas delegation, which had not yet arrived. Pierpont stole their places and kept them.

He had a healthy attitude toward religion, taking the position that among earthly sinners earthiness was to be expected. He was firm in his maintenance of a double standard of sexual morality, as earlier noted. During the Episcopal Convention of 1901, while giving every consideration to the matters of the church's government, he also had delivered to him a stream of telegrams that told him exactly what was happening in the America's Cup races being held back off Sandy Hook in New York Harbor. And after every session there was a large banquet, lunch or dinner, at the home of Charles Crocker, the San Francisco banker who had let Pierpont have his house for the three weeks. And at the end, Pierpont took his special train and his bevy of bishops and ladies up the West Coast for a look at the scenery. They stopped in Seattle and he guided them into a fur store where everybody received a piece of fur as a souvenir of the gay time.

In 1904, between a few weeks in Paris during which he made personal financial arrangements for the United States purchase of the Panama Canal companies for $40,000,000 and the acquisition of some new championship line dogs for the show kennels at Cragston, Pierpont made plans to entertain the Archbishop of Canterbury. He ran down to Bar Harbor and conferred with Bishop Lawrence of Massachusetts, and then with Bishop Doane of Albany—but only after an executive committee meeting of U. S. Steel had been gotten out of the way. There he made arrangements with the resting bishops for the entertainment. At the end of August, when the Archbishop and his entourage arrived in the United States, Pierpont entertained them on the *Corsair* and at Cragston and took them all over the East. They rode a special train to Quebec. They took another special train to Niagara Falls, and another to Bar Harbor. There was a minor accident—it could have been a serious one, for their train crashed into a locomotive. They took another special train to Washington to dine with President Roosevelt at the White House. They went to West Point where a special review of the cadet corps was staged for the Archbishop on Pierpont's arranging. Then they all took a special train to Boston, where the Englishmen mingled with the eighty American bishops and the four hundred delegates, all managed by Pierpont. Was it any wonder that toward the end of his career, when his doings reflected such splendid planning and carelessness of expense that a British prelate coined a title for Pierpont?

It was *Pierpontifex Maximus*.

CHAPTER

IX

THE PANIC OF 1907—I

Pierpont was to rise to his full grasp of public power in his seventy-first year, and to prove even to the most skeptical that no matter by what lights he lived he was basically concerned with the national welfare and would do anything possible to further it.

Pierpont spent the summer of 1907 as usual in a leisurely journey through Europe, buying art treasures and visiting people, places, or events which he thought worth while. He entertained five hundred delegates to the International Congress of School Hygiene at Prince's Gate, subscribed to their deficit for expenses, and announced that he believed in good health because it was important for national business prosperity. He went home on the steamer *Oceanic*, sending the *Corsair* separately, which was part of his new routine.

When Pierpont arrived in New York, however, life changed. He discovered that the nation was on the brink of serious economic difficulty. The years 1905 and 1906 had been prosperous for business and particularly for the speculative business of Wall Street brokerage. Prosperity had achieved a new high and appeared secure. Earlier in 1907 there had been some minor economic illnesses at home and abroad but they had been quickly cured, it

seemed. Now, stock and bond issues lay languidly, unsold, on a
flaccid market. Pierpont went to Washington to consult with
Treasury officials about the state of the market and the national
exchequer. He was told that clouds were on the horizon, but no
one seemed to know what to do about removing them.

Pierpont was interested, but not a great deal more than that.
He had been through sloppy times before. It was the strength of
his international organization that in most crises the trouble came
to one nation at a time, or to one continent at a time. In a way
an international banker was like a big gambler who played
percentages: he always had a safe margin of capital laid off on
sure things in safe places; the total collapse that would ruin Pierpont would also wreck every civilized government in the world.

Pierpont, in the autumn of 1907, was far more interested in the
coming Episcopal Convention at Richmond. He had rented a
house, put in an extra bathroom that seemed indicated, recarpeted
the stairs, and brought daughter Louisa down to be hostess to the
bishops.

When the Convention began, Pierpont was found to be up to
his old tricks. He had once tried to reduce the number of vestrymen at St. George's so he could control the church better; now
he was more ambitious—he wanted to reduce the number of delegates to the Episcopal conventions so they would be more mal-
leable. This measure was resoundingly defeated, which Pierpont
took in good stride. His method was going out of fashion but he
was still trying.

Some of the bishops wanted to play hooky during dull days of
the Convention, and Pierpont did accompany a party to Williams-
burg for a visit. One bishop fell ill, or seemed to; a few hours later
a heart specialist came by, "accidentally" it appeared, to call. A
bishop's wife had to rush back home: she discovered that Pierpont
had bought the tickets, arranged the changes, and had even ordered a taximan to wear an identifying badge and pick her up to
move her between New York stations.

All this while, Pierpont was also watching the market and bank
conditions by telegrams that came to him every few hours from
his partners in New York. Telegrams would be delivered, he would

read them, put them down, and stare straight in front of him. If someone spoke to him, he might not answer. He was concentrating on the problems he could see looming ahead.

That fall a number of speculators had misread or ignored the signs of trouble, or had chosen to fish in such troubled waters where fortunes were sometimes made. It was the usual autumn problem: the shortage of cash in the marketplace with the Western harvests in progress and much cash needed.

Among the speculators of this period was a banker named Charles Tracy Barney, who was president of the Knickerbocker Trust Company. The Knickerbocker was a modern banking institution, which maintained two branch offices besides its main office at Thirty-fourth Street and Fifth Avenue. It boasted eighteen thousand depositors with $65,000,000 in the bank. Its operating statements showed a flourishing business, but some of that business—a large amount—was laid off in long-term loans.

A number of other banks were in similar condition, including the Trust Company of America, which had a large and diffused branch operation that was not totally under central control, and the Lincoln Trust Company, another new and relatively unstable institution.

A speculator by the name of F. Augustus Heinze had gained control that year of the Mercantile Trust Company, aided by Charles W. Morse and E. R. Thomas. No one in Wall Street was quite sure what they were doing with the bank, but it was suspected that they were manipulating its deposits to play the markets in stocks, bonds, and commodities on margin. Heinze, in particular, was trying to use the unsettled conditions of the markets for a quick coup: he was out to achieve a corner on copper stocks. In October he began to run up the price of United Copper, causing other speculators great anguish, and some short sellers began to suspect that they were going to have serious trouble, because short sellers can be called upon to deliver stocks "on call" or immediate notice. Generally speaking nobody knows a short seller from a long seller when the stock is bought or sold. The ordinary or long seller has a stock certificate in hand when he sells. The short seller has nothing but the hope that the stock will go down in price and then he can buy it cheaply and deliver it for the price at which he sold it; very complicated; very dangerous; very profitable, if done with advance knowledge or good fortune; disastrous if done recklessly or in the face of someone else's unknown knowledge of events.

On Saturday, October 12, the price of United Copper had fallen. Then, when it suddenly rose so fast on October 14, from 37¼ to 60, Heinze and his cabal believed they had cornered the market. They called for delivery of the stock certificates of all they had been buying: delivery to be on October 15 at two-thirty in the afternoon.

Heinze and company did not have the corner at all. They had made a fearful miscalculation as to the total stock available. On the morning of October 16 the market opened with the price of United Copper at 60, and it stayed there. There was enough stock to meet every bid. The price dropped a little in fact, because there seemed to be plenty of stock—at least there were plenty of people who "sold" which meant they said they had stock or were confident of getting it at a lower price. So, when the call came at two-thirty and the stock sellers showed up at the desks to turn over their certificates and take the cash, the money began going out of the Mercantile National Bank in huge waves. Soon there was no more money, and Heinze and his friends were selling the stock they had just received as fast as it came in to get money to pay the people who kept on bringing more stock to them. The price dropped from 60 to 36, and then down to 10. Within two days the Heinze brokers were broke, and Heinze was appealing to the New York City Clearing House Association to keep his bank from closing its doors.

While all this was happening Pierpont was in Richmond, apparently enjoying the daily sessions of the Episcopal Convention as much as any bishop. No one but Louisa among his companions understood how deep was his preoccupation at that time with the events that were occurring in New York City, nor were the others even aware of any real trend or danger in those events. Bishop Lawrence said later that he noticed that Pierpont seemed restless and silent at the table, but it was sometimes hard to judge the degree of Pierpont's emotions, even among the bishops, because he could remain silent for a long time. The bishops enjoyed his hospitality and his company because he was a valuable man. No one ever accused him of being an easy man.

As events raced along in the financial capital, few people in America seemed much concerned. President Roosevelt had gone off to the Louisiana canebrake country where some Southern friends had arranged a bear hunt. This absence plus the continued presence of Pierpont Morgan in Richmond was indication to many that there was nothing to worry about.

On October 17 when Heinze and his friends found they had nowhere else to go and came to the Clearing House Association, they had *absolutely* nowhere else to go. In 1907 every bank in America was an independent empire, organized by capitalists who used their own capital if they were honest. There was no central bank, as existed in England. There was no Federal Reserve Banking system, as would exist later in the United States. The Treasury Department was not a part of the American banking system, and there was no way, even if this seemed desirable, that the Treasury could directly assist any bank. The New York Clearing House was a loose association of banks which took care of the mechanics of the daily clearing of checks drawn on one bank and presented to another. This was good business, for the combination of facilities saved all the state and national banks a great deal of time, money and trouble.

The state and national banks of America were chartered, either under the state governments or the federal government. State banks were inspected and regulated by the state banking commissions. National banks were regulated by a federal banking agency. One of the requirements for a state or national bank was a certain fluidity of capital and deposit. A legitimate bank would keep a cash reserve of perhaps 25 per cent against all deposits made in its vaults. The other 75 per cent of the deposits, plus the bank's own capital, could be used for various investments. This is how banks made their money, by accepting care of deposits, paying interest on them, guaranteeing the depositor his cash when he wanted it or within a stipulated time limit of his call, and lending out the depositor's money at 1 or 2 per cent more in interest rate than the bank paid for the use of the money. It does not sound like much breakage for profit margin, but 1 per cent of $100,000,000 is $1,000,000.

Besides their cash reserves, well-managed banks—and this means conservative banks—always maintained a large amount of money, perhaps another 25 per cent of deposits or more in such gilt-edged securities as United States government bonds, which could be taken into the market and turned over rapidly, without much danger of heavy fluctuation in price, even when a large number of bonds were put on sale. All this was the banker's hedge against soft spots in financial activity. It did not take much in these days to start a whispering campaign that this bank or that was low in cash, and then the small depositors and sometimes some large ones rushed to take out their money. A show of strength was always necessary here, to prevent a panic. In Wall Street panic was always just around the corner.

There was one basically weak spot in the financial structure of the banking system. This was a result of a carelessly drawn law in the state of New York which provided for the existence of trust companies as opposed to banks. Trust companies were organized originally to settle estates, handle the financial affairs of various heirs to estates, to administer trusts established for people and institutions. The need for such facilities arose in the demand for disinterested third parties who could manage assets without prejudice or thought of prejudice. There was a legitimate need for trust services, and when banks were slow to fill the need, laws were passed in various parts of the nation allowing the establishment of special financial companies which would do so.

In New York it was quickly discovered that the law was framed in such a way as to give almost the same banking powers to trust companies that the national and state banks enjoyed, without any of the same degree of public responsibility. A trust company need not retain a 25 per cent margin of cash against deposits, or any substantial margin. It was envisaged that trust company operations would be long-range investment for high yield, and with relatively little turnover of cash. Many sharp-eyed citizens then set out to organize trust companies and to encourage deposits, by paying higher rates of interest on deposits than the regular banks. This discovery was made in 1898, and in the next eight years the total deposits in trust companies quadrupled.

In October 1907 the members of the New York Clearing House were very much aware of the weaknesses of their system, but they also were aware of their strength as a group. When Heinze, Morse, and others who were associated with Heinze came to the Clearing House for help, the conservative bankers said they would help the companies if these men would resign all their banking and trust company posts. This is what happened. Within three days Heinze, Morse, and the others were out of New York banking. The Clearing House now announced that all these institutions in which the speculators were involved were solvent and that if there was any problem the Clearing House banks would come to the aid of the smaller banks. This was reassuring. Yet in the need for such reassurance there was ground for doubt about the whole financial system. If bankers had been speculating with their depositors funds to the extent of endangering the banks, then was it not possible that other banks had done so and nobody had yet discovered it? This was the way the public suspicions began.

On Friday it appeared that the threat was ended, for all the obvious malefactors seemed to be out of the way. Yet as the public went home to dinner on that evening, reading in the *Sun* and other newspapers of the bright hopes for the morrow, the heads of the great banks were meeting in almost endless consultation, trying to decide what would be done to resolve the financial troubles that had begun. On Wednesday, when Heinze's firm collapsed, the first thought of the bankers was to bring Pierpont Morgan back from Richmond. Other banks telephoned 23 Wall Street and began to put pressure on George Perkins and other Morgan partners. The presence of Morgan, they said, was as much needed as the presence of the head of every other responsible banking institution. Their world was in crisis.

Of course Pierpont was reluctant to come. He was sure that if he moved from the Convention the newspapers would begin speculating that things were worse than they were. On Thursday, October 16, however, he learned from a special messenger that the problem was worse than he had anticipated. The reason for this worsening was the involvement in the affairs of Heinze, Morse, and associates of one of the most successful trust companies in New York.

That company was the Knickerbocker. The degree of President Barney's involvement with Heinze and his friends was not yet fully understood in Wall Street, but ever more evidence was being unraveled to indicate serious general problems existed.

On learning of this turn of affairs, Pierpont agreed to return to New York on Saturday instead of on Sunday as he had originally planned. This change was announced to the bishops and other guests in the house and the Morgan private cars were made ready for the night train to New York. That night, as the other guests slept, Pierpont sat up late, smoking on the rear platform. The next morning when the train came into Jersey City's terminal, the others found Pierpont at breakfast, singing, happy as a lark as far as all the world could see—even if not one of the bishops could recognize the tune.

CHAPTER

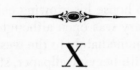

X

THE PANIC OF 1907—II

ONLY WHEN Pierpont had parted from his guests at the ferry
house in New York City did he show any signs of perturba-
tion about the problems of the financial world. The last guest put
into a cab and waved merrily away, Pierpont and his daughter
Louisa stepped into his brougham. He was to drive her up to the
West Shore ferry terminal where she could board a train car
bound for Highland Falls, ferry across the river again, then be
transported by locomotive to Highland Falls and join her husband
and children at their summer home near Cragston. During the
drive uptown Pierpont confided to Louisa that he feared there
would be serious dislocations in Wall Street on Monday morning,
and that he could not come up to Cragston but must stay at a
hotel over the weekend, since the house at 219 Madison Avenue
was closed. Louisa persuaded him to go to her house. There was a
caretaker, and she would send her husband Herbert Satterlee and
the servants down from the country to take care of him. Thus it
was arranged, and Louisa was put on her boat-train. Pierpont then
set out to face crisis. For the first time in many absences from
the city he did not call at St. George's Church, for the habits of

his religion at the moment were subordinated to his concern for the habits of his way of life.

Pierpont's first point of call was the library he had built a few years before next to No. 219 of Thirty-Sixth Street and Madison Avenue. He built it to house his growing collection of books and manuscripts. The library was open although the adjoining house was closed. He went immediately to the west room of the library, a comfortable study with heavy wallpaper, stained glass windows, a high parqueted ceiling, and walls hung with masterpieces from the world of art and lined with leaded glass bookcases to the height of a man's shoulder. There, against the backdrop of madonnas and Flemish burghers, a group of his associates were assembled, worriedly awaiting Pierpont's coming.

In a few minutes the partners had told Pierpont all they knew of the situation, which was very little and which added up to a very confusing story. Pierpont sat before the fire and smoked as he listened. At lunchtime they all went away, and a servant brought a card table and the little silver box in which Pierpont kept two decks of cards which he used to play solitaire. The card table was set up. Pierpont moved to it, the servant went away, and he sat down and began to play.

He did not know what was occurring exactly, or what he must do to save his own empire, first, and the entire order of American business, second. He had come that day from the South without a plan, and still he had no plan. Later that Sunday afternoon men began moving into the library in a slowly growing stream, and when the newspapermen discovered that Pierpont had returned to New York they came in force and remained outside the library, knowing they would never be given access to it. No one gave them any information, so they pieced together what they could from the stream of arrivals and departures.

Pierpont never exhibited much respect for the press, beginning in 1857 when he had first come to the United States as a businessman and representative of his father and had noted what little concern for facts the newspapermen showed when they were building a "story." He wrote his father from time to time, then, in disgust about this financial item or that one, which had been written by someone who did not know anything about the true picture. In later years, when he was deviled by the press, he became bearish, and finally he refused to deal with reporters except to talk to them in his periods of euphoria about such matters as the beauty of his yacht, the America's Cup, and perhaps some particular art acquisition. The press was necessary—that much Pierpont recognized—for the dissemination of information about the financial community—such as the stock market report from the Stock Exchanges. The problem was to keep the press from wild-eyed speculation, and this was one area of his life in which Pierpont failed miserably, because of his refusal to give a little to gain a great deal.

By the end of Sunday, October 20, Pierpont was relatively certain that the House of Morgan was safe from harm. His house was not overextended. The danger that he faced now was the danger of the nation, that the panic would become general and in the swift devaluation of securities his holdings would shrink to a point where much equity would be lost. It was even conceivable that the Morgan companies could be endangered if the American banking structure collapsed. This was Pierpont's concern toward the end of October 20. He studied the banking problem as a whole all evening long.

What happened in the next few days is much disputed by historians and biographers, and the meaning of events has been interpreted by both, according to whose point of view they have chosen. Herbert Satterlee, Morgan's son-in-law and biographer, was on the scene during this time at Morgan's elbow, and his account seems to be the most reliable from Morgan's point of view. For quite a different viewpoint and many different facts, there are other studies of both Morgan and Stillman. Here it is largely a matter of emphasis, plus certain maneuverings to which Pierpont was not a party.

From Pierpont's point of view the next move came in the morning, after a good night's sleep at the Satterlee house. He was down for breakfast at eight o'clock, and partner George Perkins was there to talk to him. The first thing, they decided, was to choose a staff of men who could think and figure quickly and accurately, for they must have access to the most detailed and reliable statistics about the banking firms during the next few days. Pierpont knew then that what he was going to have to do was make or steer a series of decisions about individual banking houses. He did not have the resources to shore up every shaky house. Neither did any other bank or combination of banks. The decisions would have to be made one by one as to which houses could be saved and should be saved, and which would have to be sacrificed.

Morgan and Perkins talked, and Satterlee jotted down some notes. Then Satterlee went to the telephone and began making calls. He was putting together the emergency staff. Thomas W. Joyce would be the man from the House of Morgan; Richard Trimble would come from United States Steel; Henry P. Davison, a man on whom Morgan had his eye, would come from the First National Bank; Benjamin Strong would be lent to Morgan by the Bankers Trust Company. Satterlee called them all and asked them to meet at Morgan's office; Perkins went downtown to Wall Street. Pierpont walked through the alley to the Morgan library where he was to see various bankers who felt that a talk with him would shore up their own situations. He spent an hour talking to various men, then drove down to 23 Wall Street at about ten o'clock.

That morning the president of the Consolidated National Bank and of the Hamilton National Bank both resigned. There were runs on the North America Bank and the Bank of New Amsterdam. Over the weekend President Barney of the Knickerbocker Trust Company had been forced to resign, and A. Foster Higgins had been appointed in his place. Barney, in a last desperate gesture, had come to Morgan's library on Sunday, but Morgan would not see him.

In the afternoon, the officials of the Knickerbocker came to the House of Morgan, pleading for support. Already the National Bank of Commerce, which had cleared checks for the Knickerbocker, had informed the Clearing House that it would no longer take such checks. On receipt of that news, lines began to form outside the Knickerbocker Trust Company offices and to grow ominously longer.

Pierpont doubted very seriously if anything could be done for

the Knickerbocker, but he advised the new president to hold a
meeting of his full board of directors and see if the bank could be
supported through the following day. The meeting was called for
nine o'clock in a dining room at Sherry's restaurant. It might have
been possible to find a more dangerous place for the bankers to
meet, but it was unlikely, for this was a social center of just the
people who would be concerned and likely to act in a banking
crisis. George Perkins attended for the House of Morgan. The
waiters, maitre d's and busboys, cooks and dishwashers attended
for the public. Pierpont went to Satterlee's to await word of the
results of the meeting. The waiters, maitre d's, and busboys had
the results before Pierpont did, and those who had deposits at the
Knickerbocker took out their checkbooks and that night visited
the Night and Day Bank, where checks could be cashed at any
time.

Around eleven o'clock Perkins returned to the Satterlee house
and reported on the debacle. It was, he said, a kind of town meeting, with directors running hither and yon in Wall Street, trying
to find James Stillman or the president of the Hanover National,
or somebody else who might help. The room was in confusion and
everyone in Sherry's knew exactly what was occurring.

Pierpont had left the library that evening because E. H. Harriman and several other men he did not wish to see were waiting
there for him. Now he determined to do nothing more that night.
The Knickerbocker, Perkins said, would open its doors in the
morning.

The bank did open the following morning, to find its doors
jammed immediately with people making withdrawals of their
total accounts. After a quick report from Strong, Pierpont had
written off the Knickerbocker the night before and had moved on
to consideration of the next problem.

On Tuesday afternoon at two o'clock, John Quinn, attorney
for the Bank of Commerce, presented a draft for $2,000,000 on the
Knickerbocker's downtown office and when that could not be paid
the doors of the bank were closed and business was suspended.
That day, too, the reading public learned that the New York State
Commissioner of Banks, who had been in office for two weeks, had

just resigned. This was an announcement by the state government that nothing could be done to help. Secretary of the Treasury Cortelyou, not willing to let it be said that the federal government was taking so desperate a view, came to New York that day to open his temporary offices at the Subtreasury and give such assistance as the federal government might offer.

On Tuesday, Pierpont Morgan evolved part of a plan, or breakwater, to deal with the panic. He organized a group of bankers, who submitted statements, as accurately as they could run them up on short notice, and he began allocating money from the strong institutions in order to shore up the weak, for the general good. He did not get away from 23 Wall Street until six o'clock, and then he went into meetings during the evening until three. By this time a cold which had been coming on since he left Richmond began to get worse.

That night Morgan partner George Perkins made a mistake. He mentioned a specific bank and thus brought public concern to focus on it. Perkins meant no harm, and his words were meant to instill confidence, not destroy it. He had been meeting that night with Secretary Cortelyou. When he came out of the meeting the reporters surrounded him and began firing questions at him. In his answers he named the Trust Company of America as a bank in trouble but said that it had applied for help to the bankers pool and would have it.

And so that night, as the bankers worked late to check the figures of others, the people of New York with deposits in the Trust Company of America began to get the word that their bank was threatened. Long before morning many had made up their minds to go to the bank before opening hours and be sure that they got their deposits out.

CHAPTER

XI

THE PANIC OF 1907—III

ON WEDNESDAY, OCTOBER 23, the morning newspapers printed the story of the difficulties of the Trust Company of America and the lines around the bank grew longer. This morning, Pierpont Morgan's cold was so serious that Satterlee had difficulty in waking him and before he could get up Dr. Markoe had to be called in to administer gargles and sprays. At the breakfast table he drank a cup of coffee and was then ready to face the day. He learned that the governor had just appointed a trained banker named Clark Williams as superintendent of banks, showing interest in the problem of New York. He was pleased.

He saw a few bankers at the library, then drove downtown. He was in his office at eleven o'clock when Oakleigh Thorne, president of the Trust Company of America, came in to say that he must have help or the company would not be able to meet the calls on it. Pierpont then called President Baker of the First National, President Stillman of the National City Bank, and told Thorne to go get securities from his bank for a loan which he would arrange with the other two big bankers. Thorne did. The others came. Pierpont had earlier sent staff members to examine the status of the Trust Company of America. He then met with the presidents of all New York's trust companies, whom he had asked to his office, and advised them to form an association to deal with their common problem, which they did.

Shortly after noon Pierpont asked Ben Strong for a statement on the condition of the Trust Company of America. Strong said it was solvent.

Strong had been at work in the vaults of the trust company since four o'clock that morning, and he had the answers. The surplus might be wiped out by the shrinkage in investments, the assets might be realized slowly because of their nature, but the company was solvent, and its investments were sound. Pierpont then turned to Banker Baker and Banker Stillman and said:

"Then this is the place to stop the trouble."

A few moments later Oakleigh Thorne was speaking on a telephone wire that had been held open between his office and Morgan's. His cash was down to $1,200,000 and going fast. He could not keep the doors open until three o'clock at this rate. Morgan said to come over with his securities, then dismissed the trust company meeting that was going on in another room.

At one-thirty the Trust Company of America's cash was down to $800,000, and at that time Thorne walked into Pierpont's office followed by a line of men carrying black bags and boxes of securities. Baker returned to the First National Bank and Stillman went into another room where he kept on the telephone to his bank. Pierpont took out a pencil and pad and kept track of the values of the securities while Thorne read them off. Then monies were brought out of the Morgan safes and the safes of the other two banks and were delivered to the trust company. This process continued until three o'clock closing time, and at that moment although the cash had dropped to $180,000 behind the wickets at one point, by three o'clock the cash was up to $3,000,000.

Pierpont did not trust Edward Harriman and James Keene, two of the Wall Street men of wealth who kept trying to see him during this crisis.

Harriman was the power behind the Night and Day Bank, which had assisted in fomenting the troubles of the Knickerbocker Trust Company, and whose runners had stood at the sides of

Knickerbocker depositors and led them back to the Night and Day Bank with the deposits they had just removed from the failing company. Keene was well known as a heavy speculator on Wall Street whose practice it was to try to make capital of the troubles of others. When these men waited on Pierpont he avoided them if he could, because he did not want to affront them directly, and yet he felt that they were seeking personal advantage and nothing else from the troublesome situation.

On Wednesday night Pierpont attended a meeting of the trust company presidents at the Union Trust Company and laid down the law. This was a trust company panic and the trust companies must come forward and save the day. He asked for subscriptions, wanted $10,000,000 to be loaned to the Trust Company of America. Before he was through prodding that night he had commitments of $8,250,000, and he said he and the First National, National City, and Hanover National banks would make up the rest.

The next morning, Thursday, Pierpont was feeling better. He was up early and was driving down to Wall Street in a brougham that now became famous all over the world. It was drawn by a white horse. Today, as Pierpont passed, people shouted at him and called out his name and ran behind the brougham. "There goes the Old Man," many of them said.

Thursday was a day of disaster of a different kind. The trust companies were fighting off the ruin that faced them, with the help of Pierpont and other bankers. John D. Rockefeller deposited $10,000,000 at the Union Trust Company. But on Thursday the panic had spread beyond the banks to the securities market. Early in the afternoon the president of the New York Stock Exchange came to Morgan to warn him that he was planning to close down the New York Stock Exchange before the usual hour because there was no market for a majority of stocks and every moment that went by without trading indicated the panic was on and increased its dangers. Pierpont said he must not close the marketplace one moment before the usual hour of three o'clock. The president said the prices were dropping ten points on stocks on each quotation and there were no purchasers at any price. There was no money in the market.

Pierpont then called the presidents of all nearby banks and when they came to his office he told them that unless he had $25,000,000 within a quarter of an hour at least fifty brokerage and financial houses threatened to go under.

In five minutes he had $27,000,000, including $5,000,000 from Stillman's National City Bank. This was turned over to Pierpont to loan on the stock exchange at 10 per cent interest.

When the availability of the money was announced on the exchange floor, the coat of one of the men who made the announcement was torn off his back. He did not care. The exchange was saved. Trading began again and grew stronger as the three o'clock buzzer sounded.

By the end of the day the newspapers and many bankers were saying that the panic was over due to Pierpont Morgan's strong actions. Three more banks had suspended that day; he was not so sure. It depended on national confidence. "If people will keep their money in the banks everything will be all right," he said.

Thursday night Pierpont spent the evening in the west room of the library conferring with little knots of people, largely bankers. The bankers were across the hall in the east room, trying to come up with a plan that would enable them to create an orderly situation in the Clearing House. As of this moment Pierpont had wrested money here and there in emergency measures, but the supply of cash was running low in New York. Western banks were calling for shipment of the reserves they had on deposit in New York. What was happening now was that every safe-deposit box in New York City was rented, and in those boxes, but unavailable to the banks, were millions and millions of dollars in cash. Other depositors had taken their money home to bury and to hoard. The people were not putting their money in the banks and the crisis was far from over.

On Friday it was the same story, with Morgan being called on for money to support this institution and that one. His crew of experts rushed from one place to another studying balance sheets and operating statements. Two more New York banks failed that day, and so did a bank in Providence, Rhode Island. In the afternoon Pierpont had to create another $15,000,000 pool from the big banks to shore up the stock exchange and keep trading going.

He could only get $13,000,000 but that turned out to be just enough.

Here is Herbert Satterlee's description of his father-in-law on that day:

"With his coat unbuttoned and flying open, a piece of white paper clutched tightly in his right hand, he walked fast down Nassau Street. His flat-topped black derby hat was set firmly down on his head. Between his teeth he held a paper cigar holder in which was one of his long cigars, half smoked. His eyes were fixed straight ahead. He swung his arms as he walked and took no notice of anyone. He did not seem to see the throngs in the street, so intent was his mind on the thing that he was doing. Everyone knew him and people made way for him, except some who were equally intent on their own affairs, and these he brushed aside. The thing that made his progress different from that of all the other people on the street was that he did not dodge, or walk in and out or halt or slacken his pace. He simply barged along as if he had been the only man going down Nassau Street hill past the subtreasury. He was the embodiment of power and purpose."

That day the savings bank presidents met and decided they would invoke the sixty-day clause—which meant that savings account depositors must actually give the sixty-day notice their accounts always called for, before they could withdraw. This notice had never before been invoked, but now it was the salvation of the savings banks, even if it worked hardship on their depositors.

The banks this day were issuing clearing house certificates among themselves—which meant in essence that they were issuing a private script or currency for their mutual use, backed by gentlemen's agreements.

On Friday night there was time to examine the panic from a point of view larger than that of the financial needs of banks and stock market. Morgan and his associates had now accepted the responsibility of financing the Trust Company of America and the Lincoln Trust Company through this panic. Both were sound companies; both were overextended in long-term securities. Both could survive if they could be given the cash to meet the demands of depositors.

The problem now was to restore some confidence to the American people. For this Secretary Cortelyou got in touch with Theodore Roosevelt, who issued a statement of confidence. At the suggestion of Satterlee, an old newspaperman, the responsible leaders of the press were taken into the confidence of the group to a degree, and a committee of information was formed to give out selected news about the crisis. Another committee was formed to speak to the clergy and ask them to issue reassuring statements from the pulpits of the land.

Saturday, October 26, was the short workday of the Wall Street week. It began early in the morning at the Satterlee house. Pierpont was up at eight o'clock and reading the newspapers. He received an answer to a cable to England, with the encouraging reply that $3,000,000 in gold would be shipped at once, and this news was given to the press. Then, after a few appointments, the offices closed for the weekend and Pierpont and Satterlee retreated to Highland Falls to their homes for some rest.

On Sunday night it was back to the city. On Monday it was discovered that the city of New York was in serious financial condition, and needed $30,000,000 to meet its payrolls and payments. Pierpont arranged for the clearing house banks to take the city's warrants and give cash and credit for them. The problem still was to make extensive use of credit among the banks, and keep that flow of actual cash from taking all their fluid assets away into hiding.

There were problems, but with the combined help of Secretary Cortelyou, the President, and the bankers led by Pierpont, the problems seemed well on the way to solution by the end of the next week.

The syndicate of bankers organized on a moment's notice by Pierpont had lent $40,000,000. Trading on the Stock Exchange was beginning to revive on Friday, November 1, and it seemed that the two trust companies that were under attack could be saved and the confidence of the public in the money market restored. The outlook, one might have said on that Friday, was restrained but underscored with confidence.

CHAPTER

XII

THE PANIC OF 1907—IV

O N SATURDAY MORNING it was apparent that the panic had not
run its course. The shortage of money on the stock exchange
was broadening the problem. As a series of small pebbles thrown
into a pond will soon put the whole pond into motion, so the bad
news spread—the fall of stocks ten points in a day, the rising cost
of loan money on the marketplace until it hit a rate of 100 per cent
interest, the continued reports of the closings of small banks and
small brokerage houses.

On Saturday came a serious crisis in the important brokerage
house of Moore and Schley. The president of this firm, Grant B.
Schley, was the brother-in-law of George F. Baker, president of
the First National Bank. Cass Ledyard, who was attorney for the
firm, was an old friend of Pierpont's.

Moore and Schley were the principal promoters of the stock of
Tennessee Coal and Iron, a steel company, and Schley, on his own
account, was a major owner of Tennessee Coal and Iron. He and
others had bought their shares through the brokerage firm, buying
heavily on margin, using the shares of Tennessee Coal and Iron
as collateral for the loans and then using the loans to buy more
shares of Tennessee Coal and Iron. On November 2 it became ap-

299

parent that Moore and Schley had very little left in its portfolio except Tennessee Coal and Iron on which it might borrow money, and it did not own these stocks, but was holding them against monies owed the firm by Schley and others. Altogether this represented a most unwise series of transactions by Schley and others who were supposed to be responsible men in the marketplace. They had been speculating wildly, trying to build a fortune in Tennessee Coal and Iron stock, and now their backs were to the wall. The thought of building the fortune was forgotten, and they wanted to attempt to save themselves and their reputations.

This story was brought to Pierpont on Saturday. On Monday some $25,000,000 worth of loans to Moore and Schley would be called. Schley and others had borrowed this money from the firm to buy the steel stocks. If they could not pay, all the Tennessee Coal and Iron stocks would be dumped on the market to satisfy the debt. At the last offer the stock had sold for more than one hundred dollars a share, but if it were dumped suddenly, in this market that was dropping, it could be expected to fall to seventy or sixty dollars or less. Moore and Schley would not be able to pay off all their obligations and the firm would be bankrupt. Schley and his partners in speculation would be bankrupt, and it could be then expected that there would be a run on the stock market to sell and get out. It had been troublesome enough at the end of the week to maintain a market in stocks. If matters became worse, it might be necessary to close the stock exchange, and then the national financial system would be in chaos.

Pierpont had several interests in this matter. First, he felt some responsibility to rescue his friend George Baker's brother-in-law. Second, he knew with absolute certainty how disastrous would be the default of a respectable brokerage firm for so large an amount of money. Third, Schley indicated that they had interested a large number of other firms in investing heavily in Tennessee Coal and Iron and if the price of the stock fell, these firms would be forced into insolvency. Fourth, Tennessee Coal and Iron was a steel manufacturing company which could very easily be integrated into the United States Steel Corporation, and here was an opportunity to do so. This latter consideration was to be given the most serious place in the scheme and reasoning of Pierpont Morgan by critics in later years, but the fact is that if Pierpont had been engaged in trying to create controls for himself in this crisis, there were a dozen ways in which he could have bettered himself—not the least of which might have been to do nothing except sell to protect his own interests. The narrow view was that Morgan acted in the Tennessee Coal and Iron crisis for selfish gain, but this argument does not stand up under scrutiny. No one could say that his scheme was planned in advance, because if there was any truth in what had been happening in these past three weeks it was that nothing was planned, and Pierpont had been rushing around like the boy at the Dutch dike, plugging one hole after another.

If Moore and Schley could be saved they must be saved, in the interests of the bankers and the stock market. If in saving Moore and Schley, Pierpont could do a good deed for United States Steel, he was not going to be unhappy about that. But could Moore and Schley be saved? Pierpont would not rush into a commitment to save an insolvent company even if the advantage to him could be great. He was dealing here not with his own money. As it turned out the money was not his at all, but the money of others, and had he acted as selfishly as later detractors indicated, right then and there his reputation on the marketplace would have been sacrificed, and the firm of J. P. Morgan and Company would never have occupied the same place in Wall Street. Outsiders always have shown much contempt for the Wall Street morality, but the fact has always been that the Wall Streeters knew the jackals among them—the Daniel Drews, Fisks, Goulds, Keenes—and these men never achieved the respect of their contemporaries, no matter how wealthy they became. E. W. Harriman never had that respect, because he was considered to be a sharp operator. Andrew Carnegie did not have it nor did Commodore Vanderbilt. Among the great bankers the Drexels had earned respect because they stood for honesty. To a lesser extent Jay Cooke had enjoyed respect as well as power. Nicholas Biddle enjoyed that respect during the days of the United States National Bank. What Pierpont

Morgan would attempt in this crisis of 1907 would determine his place in the history of his times, and he knew this well enough as he considered the problems of Moore and Schley.

The first thing to be done was to examine the books and see just how badly things were. On Saturday two of Pierpont's staff men went into the offices of Moore and Schley and set to work. By Saturday evening they were ready to report. That evening they came to the Morgan Library to join representatives of the Clearing House Association and of the trust companies, who had been called into session once again.

The representatives of the Clearing House banks were clustered in the east room of the library, and those of the trust companies had taken over Morgan's west room. He had retired to the librarian's private office, where he was meeting with Judge Gary of U. S. Steel and other associates. They were going over the plan for purchase of Tennessee Coal and Iron, and Pierpont was hearing how other affairs had gone that day, from various assistants.

One of these assistants was taking a nap, sitting up on a couch in the east room, when he was called to report to Pierpont in the librarian's office. He was Benjamin Strong, a member of the Morgan task force, specifically assigned to the affairs of the Trust Company of America. The feeling among the bankers was that perhaps another $2,000,000 might be needed to shore up the trust companies that were threatened. Strong had been working all Friday night on the books of the worst-threatened trust company of all, and he went in to explain his findings to Pierpont. It became apparent to those in the librarian's office that far more than $2,-000,000 would be needed.

In the east and west rooms the bankers were becoming nervous. In the past two weeks all of them had been asked to subscribe huge sums, to guarantee millions as if they were making loans of hundreds, and most of them were uncomfortably aware that they had serious responsibilities for their actions to their boards of directors and to the federal and state authorities under whom they were licensed. Some of them wondered if they had broken the banking laws.

Pierpont knew of this nervousness. Perhaps that was why he

now had the key to the front door of the Morgan Library in his pocket. He wanted to make certain that no man could leave that building until the affairs of the night were completed. So he locked the door. All the men he wanted or needed were in, and now none could get out until he willed it. Benjamin Strong made his report to Pierpont. He left the librarian's office and tried to open the front door, feeling that he was finished for the day. Then he learned.

Pierpont sent word into the east room, where the trust company heads were waiting and talking in little groups, that $2,000,000 would not do the job that must be done. He wanted a pledge of another $25,000,000 that night. When this was announced the room broke into noisy sessions. These presidents began to enunciate their fears, their questions of responsibility, the concern of each banker over the assets of his own institution. The trust company men and the other bankers were told something of the problem of the stock market and of Moore and Schley. In the other room, the west room, Pierpont went into the Moore and Schley problem more thoroughly. He asked Baker and Stillman to join with him in each putting up $6,000,000 to purchase the Tennessee Coal and Iron securities from Moore and Schley. As soon as it could be arranged, the U. S. Steel Company would buy these securities from the banks, releasing their capital investment. Baker did not hesitate. Stillman did. He questioned Pierpont's ability to know the facts of the Moore and Schley situation with such scanty information and so little time to study the figures. Pierpont indicated that he had sent Thomas Joyce to examine the figures and condition of the firm. Stillman said he wondered if Joyce knew the whole story. "Well, I know my man," Pierpont said, and that was the end of it. Stillman agreed to take a third interest in the securities too.

Pierpont then went to explain to the trust company men why the trust companies must support their own men and what he and the others were doing in relation to the stock market. Still the trust company presidents hesitated. Pierpont handed them a document which provided that each trust company would put up its share of the needed $25,000,000, depending on its resources.

"There you are, gentlemen," he said.

When no one stepped forward to sign the paper, Pierpont placed his hand on the shoulder of Edward King, the most influential of the trust company presidents.

"There's the place, King," he said, "and here's the pen." He handed King his gold pen and watched while they all signed.

When the door to the Morgan Library was unlocked it was a quarter to five on Sunday morning. Pierpont said goodnight to his associates then. He looked Attorney Ledyard of Moore and Schley in the eye, solicitously. "You look tired," he said. "Go home and get a good night's rest—but be back here at nine o'clock sharp."

CHAPTER

XIII

THE PANIC OF 1907—V

O N SUNDAY the basic concern of Pierpont and his associates of
United States Steel and the House of Morgan was what attitude President Theodore Roosevelt would take toward the purchase of Tennessee Coal and Iron Corporation by U. S. Steel.
Roosevelt had been talking a great deal about monopoly, and antitrust investigations were beginning in Washington. The matter of
finding the money for the purchase was finally settled with Baker
and Stillman. All then that remained was to be certain that the
federal government would not descend on the parties for violation
of the antitrust laws. It was decided to try to find out as much as
possible about this before taking action, and Judge Gary and
Henry Frick of U. S. Steel were dispatched to Washington on the
midnight train, to make every effort to see the President.

Early on Monday morning the two industrialists did see President Roosevelt just after breakfast and when they explained to
him what had happened and was happening and how they proposed to solve the problem, Roosevelt said he could see no objection at all. He suggested that the sooner it was done the better
it would be for the nation, Gary reported. This information was
telephoned to Pierpont at the library on Madison Avenue, and

when the market opened on Monday morning the wheels were put in motion to give Moore and Schley the money they needed to meet their commitments.

Now, to show the extent and limitations of this crisis and the persons involved, it must be seen that not all the leading men of finance in the United States were concerned directly in the events that had centered in the Morgan Library in the past weeks. On Monday, August Belmont came to see Pierpont for the first time since the crisis began. Belmont had not been involved. His firm was a private banking house, as Pierpont's was private, and there was no need for Belmont to involve himself (nor for Pierpont). It was a matter of each man's concept of his public responsibility. Levi Morton called on Pierpont too. He too was an important and wealthy private banker, and he too put in his first appearance on the scene of action during this crisis.

The panic was not over, but the crisis now was ended. Pierpont took time off to go to Albany to the funeral of the wife of one of his bishops. He traveled to Washington to thank Secretary Cortelyou and President Roosevelt for their help in shoring up the position of the banks during the crisis. The bank runs continued, but by this time the banks and trust companies were using a system to fight the runs. They concentrated their stock in voting trusts, borrowed money against the stock from the Clearing House banks, kept after their borrowers to bring in loans, and liquidated assets just as quickly as possible. Toward the end of this third week the bank runs slowed appreciably, and then stopped.

In the aftermath, Charles T. Barney shot himself, on his return from a sanitarium, and several heavy depositors in the Knickerbocker Trust Company also committed suicide. Charles W. Morse was convicted of crimes involved in the downfall of his bank. More change was coming. Pierpont knew that basic change in the American banking pattern must come. He was to spend much time in the next few months with Senator Nelson Aldrich, talking about the needs of the American banking system. As to the American banking system of 1907, Satterlee summed up Pierpont's attitude:

"It was not a good pattern—no one knew that as well as he—but it was the pattern in which he had found it. From that moment he worked to make it better and less vulnerable in bad times or periods of overspeculation. He realized that it must be buttressed against disclosures of dishonesty or irregularity and consequent loss of prestige and the confidence of the public. Security should not rest on any one man."

Six years later President Wilson would create a federal reserve system, controlled by the government, to assure decentralization of banking and an elastic currency. The banks would not like it, they would fight it all the way, but in the end it would be the salvation of many of them, and no matter what else they might say about it, the new system would prevent recurrence of the problem that had faced the banking community in the autumn of 1907. Pierpont Morgan had said that security should not rest on any one man, but it was quite apparent that in the fall of 1907 it had rested on himself. For three weeks without question he had been the most important man in America.

CHAPTER

XIV

THE RESTLESS YEARS

THE NEXT FEW YEARS were restless years in the American financial world. Everyone—bankers, investors, politicians—recognized the serious nature of the crisis that the nation had weathered in 1907. It was the most threatening panic in American history, for in it the signs of approaching national paralysis were unmistakable, before Pierpont stepped in to lead the banking world out of trouble.

Pierpont's remarkable performance was recognized at home and abroad, yet was not appreciated by the American public in the manner that he rather expected it would be. That is not to say that Pierpont sought public acclaim, but he certainly did not expect that by rising to the occasion and saving the economy from at least a serious storm—which all admitted he did—he would bring upon himself and his peers in the world of finance the deep suspicion of the American people. This did happen and it became a source of pain to Pierpont in the last years of his life. The era from 1903 to 1912 has been called the Muckraking Era. It began with S. S. McClure in the January 1903 issue of his own magazine, *McClure's*. Ida Tarbell wrote in that issue of capitalists "conspiring among themselves, deliberately, shrewdly, upon legal advice, to break the law. . . ." In the same issue Ray Stannard Baker wrote of the crimes of labor. There was yet a third exposé in this January magazine. "The Shame of Minneapolis" depicted venal politicians raping a fair city while the people stood by complacent and unalarmed.

"There is no one left," said *McClure's* in an editorial, "none but all of us. . . ." And he indicated that he was going to protect the interests of America. The art of protecting the public turned out to be the turning point in the popular magazine business in the United States, and soon the muckraking magazines surpassed their genteel counterparts and put many of them out of business. *McClure's, Collier's, The Saturday Evening Post,* the *American* and *Cosmopolitan* were leading muckraking magazines of the period and their circulations soared into the millions. One popular misconception of the muckrakers is that Theodore Roosevelt and his administration approved of this manner of resolving the ills that beset the nation. Theodore Roosevelt could not have disapproved more. He coined the very term, but in this context:

"In Bunyan's *Pilgrim's Progress* you may recall the description of the Man with the Muck-rake, the man who could look no way but downward, with the muck-rake in his hand; who was offered a celestial crown for his muck-rake, but who would neither look up nor regard the crown he was offered, but continued to rake to himself the filth on the floor."

Between 1903 and 1912 some two thousand articles of the muckraking variety appeared in the popular magazines, and many of these dealt with Wall Street and competition in the steel industry, both areas in which Pierpont was involved. Pierpont invested heavily in the New York Life Insurance Company stock and in the Equitable Assurance Company. Thomas W. Lawson and other muckrakers "exposed" him, noting that these two insurance companies were controlled by Morgan and that the policy holders had no say in the company. Insiders raked in millions in stock speculation while premium rates rose and dividends declined. (Lawson was familiar with the Wall Street scene. He had been what in other times was called a Bucket Shop Operator, and a Bear, who sought to create a fortune by betting against prosperity on the stock market.)

Some of the muckrakers were sensationalists pure and simple. Many of them were troubled citizens seeking a better life for Americans and a political and economic democracy in which the lower middle class and lower reaches of society could share. This was a concept so startling that Pierpont never grasped it or tried to grasp it. The idea was not of his time. He was past seventy years old when he strode down Wall Street as a lion, settling the worst financial debacle of the era, pushing men along with simple force of character. His lifetime had been dedicated to the service of the capitalistic system, to the preservation of order in the market-place, and this performance in the autumn of 1907 was the crowning business achievement of Pierpont's career. Thereafter he began to take less interest, year by year, in the affairs of the business world. In 1907 and 1908 Pierpont gave a good deal of time to study the ills of the banking world. Senator Nelson Aldrich of Rhode Island headed a committee to inquire into the causes of the panic of 1907. Pierpont counseled with him frequently and bears some responsibility for the nature of the Aldrich-Vreeland Act of 1908 which authorized national banks to issue banknotes for six years, based on the commercial investment they held, plus their government bonds. This provided a certain elasticity to the national credit. Senator Aldrich later headed a commission which investigated a more lasting solution to economic problems and recommended measures that would become a foundation for the Federal Reserve System of banking.

Pierpont continued as senior partner of J. P. Morgan and Company, but he turned more and more responsibility over to others. It was understood that Jack, his son, would become senior partner when Pierpont left the firm. Now Charles Steele was as important to the firm as George Perkins. Henry P. Davison became a partner in 1909, and soon showed himself to be a very important one—the leader of the firm. William H. Porter became the expert on banking and bank management, and Thomas W. Lamont, a former newspaperman, was to come into the firm in 1911. All were able and conscientious men, brought to Pierpont's attention because of stability of character, and brought into his business because he saw in them the strengths he wanted perpetuated to maintain the orderliness of the banking firm.

Pierpont achieved a certain modus vivendi with Theodore Roosevelt, although he never asked Roosevelt for a favor. (He supported Roosevelt financially in the campaign of 1904, a fact which Roosevelt was surprised to learn when the victory had been won.) After their original bristly confrontations the two men began to understand one another a little. Roosevelt invited Pierpont to the White House for conferences, and sometimes to social affairs. He gave an appointment as Assistant Secretary of the Navy to Herbert Satterlee. This was a particularly sensitive post for Roosevelt, because he had once held it himself. Pierpont approved heartily, telling his son-in-law that in government he might very well find the opportunity for useful service. The treaty of peace between Pierpont and Roosevelt was to last.

In 1910 the J. S. Morgan and Company of London became Morgan, Grenfell and Company, which represented the addition of the name of an English partner to the firm. More and more the conduct of the business was being placed in younger hands.

The year 1911 was to begin the period of greatest shocks and disappointments in Pierpont Morgan's long life. President Roosevelt had gone out of office in 1909, after picking William Howard Taft and managing the election of his man as successor. Taft thought he and Roosevelt saw eye to eye, but almost immediately Taft began to do things in his own way. Among other actions, he strengthened the Department of Justice's work against the great industrial combines, and that department began preparations to file a number of antitrust suits against big business firms. In 1911 the Department of Justice brought suit to dissolve the United States Steel Corporation as a trust of trusts, operating to create monopoly and in restraint of trade. Specifically the matter was brought to a head by the purchase of the Tennessee Coal and Iron Company stock during the panic of 1907. Actually, every act and consideration in the domestic and economic sphere of government in all these years since the panic had been taken with that nearly disastrous period in mind. This suit was the logical outcome of the urge to social and economic justice and the distrust of bigness for its own sake, which was just then sweeping the nation. To Pierpont the word came suddenly, without warning from any point. Satterlee described it:

"It was while he was kept at home with a bad cold that the United States Government brought suit to dissolve the Steel Corporation. The compaint was served on him on October 27. He had been told that some man had called at his office, at the library, and at No. 219, apparently to serve a paper on him. At my suggestion he instructed his butler to tell the man to come back to the house that evening. We sat together smoking by the fire when the man was announced. Mr. Morgan stepped quickly out to the front hall, accepted the summons and compaint without a word, and then walked rather slowly back to his chair. For some time, perhaps ten minutes, he sat gazing into the fire holding the printed pamphlet, sometimes looking at the title of the suit on the cover, at other times apparently lost in deep thought. His cigar went out."

In this time Pierpont may well have been reviewing his life, his hopes, his efforts, and those of his father before him and of his grandfather before that to be a part of a growing, building America. In terms of industry he considered the steel corporation to be his finest achievement in a life devoted to the strengthening of business.

Finally Pierpont spoke again to the fire before him and to his son-in-law, putting into one simple sentence his weariness and disappointment that a life so spent should see such an end approaching.

"Well," he said, "it has come to this!" That night he was very tired and walked heavily up the stairs.

It was, in a business way, almost Pierpont's farewell.

Almost, but not quite. There was something else to be done, something that would not be given much credence or much attention by the people of his lifetime, but which would stand forth as the simple statement of belief by one called before the bar of the public after having spent his lifetime in position of great power. As the Roman governors were so often tried on return to

Rome after serving in the far reaches of the empire, so Pierpont was brought to a kind of trial during the following year.

The occasion was a set of hearings held in Washington by the subcommittee of the Committee on Banking and Currency of the House of Representatives. It was part of the inquiry known as the Investigation of Financial and Monetary Conditions in the United States. Popularly the committee was called the Pujo Committee, after Representative Arsene P. Pujo of Louisiana, who was chairman. The investigation was also called "The Money Trust Investigation" because this was the contention of many in Congress and elsewhere—that a handful of men held control of the vast resources of the United States, and were capable of doing what they wished to do with these resources, acting as a group of voracious spiders whose industrial and banking empires were connected through interlocking directorates as would be a giant spider web. Head of this combine of power, said press and public, was none other than J. Pierpont Morgan.

Earlier in the fall of 1912 Pierpont had been called as star witness before a Senate Committee investigating campaign contributions. There had been rumor that Pierpont bought Presidents and Senators the way other men buy ham sandwiches. But in his testimony he explained exactly what he had done. To the charge that he had given $100,000 on demand of Roosevelt for his Presidential campaign against Alton B. Parker in 1904, Pierpont said no. He had given $150,000 on behalf of his firm, but Roosevelt did not know about it; neither did campaign chairman Cortelyou. New York businessman Cornelius Bliss had received the money. (In 1912, Pierpont said, he did not give any money to anyone.)

In December 1912 Pierpont was recalled to Washington by the Pujo Committee. The committee had not had trouble in securing information but many of the witnesses it wanted to receive were most eager to avoid the attention of investigators. William Rockefeller, in particular, played sick, played possum, and played fast and loose with the committee. He never did testify. Pierpont would not stoop to chicanery. This was his government and if the government wished to call upon him for an account of his activities he was willing to submit. That is the attitude he took to the com-

mittee while other capitalists were dodging left and right or sending their minions to do the work.

Pierpont went to a Washington which was decked out for a
Roman holiday. He was to be the sacrifice. The worst of it, from
his point of view, was that he knew it and told his family that
"those people" were out to make a show of him. The show began
on the morning of December 18, with Jack, Louisa, two other
Morgan partners, and a battery of lawyers in attendance. The first
morning of testimony was taken up with forma: identifications
and establishment of activity.

Then came the question of the octopus of financial control. The
Pujo Committee had gathered statistics to show that the Morgan
partnership, the First National Bank of New York City, the National City Bank, the Bankers Trust Company, and the Guaranty
Trust Company held 341 directorships in major banks, trust companies, insurance companies, transportation companies, product-
ing and trading corporations, and public utilities. Of these the
Morgan company held 72 directorships plus control of Bankers
Trust and Guaranty Trust. The Pujo report was filled with charts
and graphs, and eventually the committee members would blame
this group of bankers as the most destructive force in America—
saying their actions were "more destructive of competition than
anything accomplished by the trusts, for they strike at the very
vitals of potential competition in every industry that is under their
protection, a condition which if permitted to continue will render
impossible all attempts to restore normal competitive conditions
in the industrial world." The Pujo Committee, like nearly everyone
else in America, was still thinking of the America of the nineteenth century and had come no further than the panic of 1907.

Pierpont was questioned for a long time, on many subjects. His
relationship with the New York Central Railroad and other railroads was explored. The questioning of Samuel Untermyer, counsel for the committee, indicated the lawyer's search to prove that
Pierpont used his position as fiscal agent of the railroads to control them, and sought membership on the directorates of railroads
primarily to secure the fiscal agencies. Untermyer suggested that
Pierpont's device of the voting trust, through which many large

corporations were controlled, was a means of perpetuating the economic dependence of the railroads and others on the little clique of powerful men. The Southern Railway, where Pierpont and George Baker of the First National Bank were—alone—a majority of the trustees of the stock, was brought up as a case in point. Untermyer asked if it would not be better for the railroad if it was free to sell its securities in any manner that it wished. Here is some of the testimony:

Mr. Untermyer: Take the case of the Southern Railway. During all the years it has been and is still under this voting trust. The fact is, is it not, that Mr. Baker and you, as a majority of the voting trustees, designate the directors of that company?

Mr. Morgan: Yes, sir.

Mr. Untermyer: Don't you feel that in a sense when it comes to issuing the securities of that company and fixing the prices on which they are to be issued, that you are in a sense dealing with yourselves?

Mr. Morgan: I do not think so. We do not deal with ourselves.

Mr. Untermyer: Let us see if you do not.

Mr. Morgan: The voting trusts—

Mr. Untermyer: The voting trustees name the board, do they not?

Mr. Morgan: But when you have elected the board, then the board is independent of the voting trustees.

Mr. Untermyer: That is only until the next election?

Mr. Morgan: It is during that time they act independently.

Mr. Untermyer: You think, therefore, that where you name a board of directors that is to remain in existence only for a year and you have the power to name another board the next year, that this board so named is in an independent position to deal with your banking house as would be a board named by the stockholders themselves?

Mr. Morgan: I think it would be better.

Mr. Untermyer: You think it is a great deal better?

Mr. Morgan: Yes, sir.

Mr. Untermyer: More independent?

Mr. Morgan: Better.

Mr. Untermyer: Will you tell us why?

Mr. Morgan: Simply because we select the best people that we can find for the positions.

At this Attorney Untermyer began to splutter a little. It was not the kind of answer he was seeking. He was looking for evidence of malfeasance or some misdoing, not for simple, direct averment from Pierpont Morgan that because he and his associates were honorable men they would act honorably.

This was the struggle all through Pierpont's testimony. Untermyer was seeking to show selfishness. Pierpont's replies showed an Olympian detachment from pettiness. The men were talking, but they were not meeting on a plane. Here are other selections from the testimony:

Mr. Untermyer: Do you not think it would be entirely feasible that securities of such corporations should be openly marketed and should be sold by competition, just as securities of the United States Government and State Governments and city administrations and municipal bonds of different kinds are sold?

Mr. Morgan: I do not.

Mr. Untermyer: Do you not think there ought to be some kind of competition for them?

Mr. Morgan: There always is competition in the end.

Mr. Untermyer: No, but . . .

Mr. Untermyer: Who decided that J. P. Morgan and Company should be the depository of the United States Steel Corporation?

Mr. Morgan: That was rather *ex officio,* I think, sir.

Mr. Untermyer: You mean you decided it both ways?

Mr. Morgan: When the company was formed, J. P. Morgan and Company had the whole company at that time, and I think that is the way it came.

Mr. Untermyer: You thought it was good business so you thought you would take it?

Mr. Morgan: No, I did not know whether it was going to be good business or not at that time.

Mr. Untermyer: It proved pretty good?

Mr. Morgan: It did. Very good indeed, sir.

Mr. Untermyer: You did not think you were taking many chances when you took it up then?

Mr. Morgan: No, but I began to have doubts when the stock went to $8 a share afterwards.

Mr. Untermyer: Your doubts did not interfere with your buying heavily?

Mr. Morgan: No, I bought all I could.

Mr. Untermyer: You did not have any doubt, did you?

Mr. Morgan: Never; not for one moment.

Mr. Untermyer: You were getting the advantage of other people's doubts at that time?

Mr. Morgan: Nobody ever sold it at my suggestion, sir.

Mr. Untermyer: No, I did not mean to assume . . .

The cutoff of these excerpts with dots as I have made it may seem unfair to Untermyer, who was actually conducting as fair an examination as he knew how, and he was making important points of his own, as he did in a long exchange in which he pointed out how bondholders in railroad reorganizations were at the mercy of the bankers, and that in hands less competent than Pierpont's the bondholders might lose part or most of their investment —more than if they allowed the railroads to go into receivership and be sold at auction. But the point remained that Untermyer showed his feeling that bankers were strangling the nation for their selfish interests, and Pierpont insisted that for himself he had never acted selfishly in any matter that involved public responsibility. Untermyer established the fact that Pierpont had bought a great deal of Equitable Life Insurance stock at a high price that could not have yielded him much as an investment. The implication was that Pierpont bought it for control. Pierpont's answer was that he bought it because he thought he ought to buy it, to keep control of this stock in hands where it would be well held in the interest of the policy holders—his own hands. Untermyer showed how the Guaranty Trust Company of New York was controlled by Pierpont's firm because two of the three trustees were his partners. Pierpont did not even know of this, it was so unimportant to him. Untermyer spoke of one bank voting trust after another, showing how Pierpont had organized these, and, by inference, how he controlled them.

There were other significant exchanges:

Mr. Untermyer: You are opposed to competition, are you not?

Mr. Morgan: No, I do not mind competition.

Mr. Untermyer: You would rather have combination, would you not?

Mr. Morgan: I would rather have combination.

This discussion went on for some time, Untermyer indicating that Pierpont paid only lip service to respect for competition—a little competition that would not hurt the Morgan interests. Then:

Mr. Morgan: This may be a sensitive subject. I do not want to talk of it. This is probably the only chance I will have to speak of it.

Mr. Untermyer: You mean the subject of combination and concentration.

Mr. Morgan: Yes, the question of control. Without you have control, you can do nothing.

Pierpont then went on to talk about the impossibility of controlling the money market. Untermyer was disbelieving. They discussed credit and banking, and that discussion showed that they were talking about different ideas with different philosophies in control:

Mr. Untermyer: I want to ask you a few questions bearing on the subject that you have touched upon this morning, as to the control of money.

Mr. Morgan: Yes.

Mr. Untermyer: The control of credit involves a control of money, does it not?

Mr. Morgan: A control of credit? No.

Mr. Untermyer: You do not think so?

Mr. Morgan: What I call money is the basis of banking.

Mr. Untermyer: But the basis of banking is credit, is it not?

Mr. Morgan: Not always. That is an evidence of banking, but it is not the money itself. Money is gold and nothing else.

Mr. Untermyer: Do you not know that the basis of banking all over the world is credit rather than gold?

Mr. Morgan: It is the basis of credit, but it is not the basis of money.

Mr. Untermyer: I say, the basis of all banking is credit, is it not, and not money?

Mr. Morgan: No, I do not think so.

So they went. Question after question was thrown up. Samuel Untermyer tried to link credit and money and Pierpont would not have it. Untermyer tried to indicate through questioning that a number of men could control the money market; Pierpont said no, money could not be controlled by any one man or group of men. Then:

Mr. Untermyer: Is not the credit based upon money?

Mr. Morgan: No, sir.

Mr. Untermyer: It has no relation?

Mr. Morgan: No, sir.

Mr. Untermyer: None whatever?

Mr. Morgan: No, sir, none whatever.

Mr. Untermyer (trying hard) *: So that the banks of New York

City would have the same credit, and if you owned them you would have the same control of credit as if you had the money, would you not?

Mr. Morgan: I know lots of men, business men too, who can borrow any amount, whose credit is unquestioned.

Mr. Untermyer: Is that not because it is believed that they have the money back of them?

Mr. Morgan: No, sir; it is because people believe in the man.

Mr. Untermyer (disbelieving): And it is regardless of whether he has any financial backing at all, is it?

Mr. Morgan: It is very often.

Mr. Untermyer (disbelieving): And he might not be worth anything?

Mr. Morgan: He might not have anything. I have known a man to come into my office, and I have given him a check for a million dollars when I knew he had not a cent in the world.

Mr. Untermyer: That is not business?

Mr. Morgan: Yes; unfortunately it is. I do not think it is good business, though.

* Parenthetical notes are author's observations. They did not appear in the record.

Mr. Untermyer: Commercial credits are based upon the possession of money or property?

Mr. Morgan: What?

Mr. Untermyer: Commercial credits?

Mr. Morgan: Money or property or character.

Mr. Untermyer: Is not commercial credit based primarily on
money or property?

Mr. Morgan: No, sir; the first thing is character.

Mr. Untermyer: Before money or property?

Mr. Morgan: Before money or anything else. Money cannot buy
it.

Pierpont went on in the questioning to say that no matter how
many bonds a man might have it would make no difference to
him "because a man I do not trust could not get money from me
on all the bonds in Christendom." He also said that it was his
practice at the House of Morgan in the past, when he was more
active, to look over the loans. If he saw a loan to a Mr. Smith
whom he did not trust he would go right to the partner in charge
of that department and tell him to call that loan right away. He
did not trust the man and he would not have that loan in the box.
Mr. Untermyer asked if that was the way that money was loaned
generally in Wall Street.

"That is the way I loan it," said Pierpont Morgan.

And there was really the climax of Morgan's testimony in the
Pujo investigation of the Money Trust. Mr. Untermyer asked a
few more questions, to elicit Pierpont's responses on short selling
and speculation in the stock market. Pierpont said he disapproved
of short selling, but there was no way to stop it, and that he did
not speculate on the marketplace, but that if a marketplace was
to be maintained there was no way to put an end to the human
practice of gambling.

As far as furthering the aims of the Pujo Committee was concerned, Pierpont's testimony had only added confusion to the
picture. The next day the press carried the story of Pierpont's
testimony about reliance on character, going straight to the point
and not missing it or distorting it. The question of how much
of that character existed in Wall Street was quite another one that

the Pujo Committee did not choose to investigate, because it had set its sights on proving that there was a Money Trust and that Pierpont Morgan controlled the trust, and through the trust controlled the business of America and of all the world. Congressman Pujo and his investigators might better have begun their investigation on a broader base. Senator Aldrich had put it this way in 1908 when he was investigating the crash of 1907: "Something has got to be done. We may not always have Pierpont Morgan with us to meet a banking crisis."

The responsible legislators of Congress were really seeking the same ends that Pierpont sought, although they went about it in an entirely different way. The aim was the preservation of order and decency in the marketplace. Speaking philosophically, Congress approached this problem from ideas based on a century and a quarter of combined experience in American government, taking the position that business must be controlled from above because of the innate evil of mankind and because power corrupts; such power as Pierpont wielded must be expected to corrupt a man absolutely. Pierpont always believed in the Christian principle of the goodness of mankind and in the responsibility of the powerful to serve humanity as they saw fit.

By 1912 the gulf between the theories was unbridgeable.

CHAPTER

XV

A FINAL VOYAGE

I N A BOOKLET about Pierpont's art collection and art patronage written half a century after his death, Francis Henry Taylor compared Pierpont to Lorenzo de' Medici, and noted he was repeating one of the accepted cliches of his generation. One basis of Taylor's comparison was Pierpont's regard for wealth as a source of power and moral infallibility, never better stated than in the testimony before the Pujo Committee. Taylor also gave Pierpont credit for changing the attitude of the men of wealth of his time toward the world of art, and although this booklet was published by the Morgan Library to celebrate its fiftieth anniversary, and thus might be suspect of exaggeration, there seems to be no hyperbole in the latter claim. In 1867 a list of important art collections showed only a dozen or so for all New York City with its hundreds of millionaires, and of these Taylor said "virtually nothing in these cabinets except the rare books and manuscripts belonging to (Robert) Hoe and (James) Lenox would be looked at twice today by the curators or purchasing committees of any of the New York museums." The cultural centers of America were Boston and Philadelphia, not New York.

Pierpont began slowly with his collections, but by 1902 he had

322

made his purchase of the important Richard Bennett collection of books and manuscripts, which included some seven hundred carefully selected volumes of the best of Western civilization, and thirty-two Caxton incunabula, which made the collection the fourth largest of this type in the world. This purchase at around $700,000 was the largest Pierpont ever made for the library. He was always depicted by disappointed salesmen as a gourmand of a collector, gobbling up anything and everything in carload lots, but actually after this collection he purchased only two large groups of works, the Wakeman collection of American literary manuscripts, which he bought in 1909, and the Fairfax Murray collection of drawings, which he bought the following year; otherwise, Pierpont's purchases of valuables for the library were made in small lots.

In the house at Prince's Gate, Pierpont kept a treasury of fine arts and added to it each year. A Gainsborough and a Sir Joshua Reynolds, a Romney, a Hoppner, and a Hobbema graced the dining room walls. The hall was the place for statuary and there were numerous statues there. Gainsborough's *Duchess of Devonshire* hung in the drawing room along with Rembrandts, a Van Dyke, a Franz Hals, a Velázquez, and an assortment of valuable miniatures, housed in three tables with shallow drawers.

There were Turners, Fragonard panels, cabinets from Sèvres. Queen Alexandra of England and her sister, the Empress of Russia, were touring the house one day with Pierpont when one of them exclaimed over some chairs in the guest parlor. They had belonged in their family and had been sold without their knowledge.

In the library at Prince's Gate hung a portrait of his father, which Pierpont personally valued above all the priceless works of art. There was Romney's portrait of Lady Hamilton reading, Sir Thomas Lawrence's portrait of Lady Derby, and a thousand other treasures, large and small, to fill the various rooms of the house.

In 1904 Pierpont became president of the Metropolitan Museum of Art. This responsibility coincided with his decreasing activity in the affairs of the banking world. Francis Taylor says that in this year Pierpont decided that he would create in New

York the greatest museum in the world and a library unparalleled. So after this year his visits abroad became longer and his purchasing of art treasures became less deliberate. He was racing against time to do what he wished, and he dealt with any and all dealers who had not offended him. The dealers looked upon Pierpont as the most important person in the art world. Taylor said this:

"The energy with which the dealers sought to find Morgan's Achilles' heel was little short of titanic. For several winters Canfield, 'the perfect gambler' held a special class for the European art dealers who upon their arrival in New York thought it expedient to learn the card games to which Morgan was addicted. Any ruse to get by the secretary or the butler was considered fair game. A. S. Drey of Munich used to tell a story of how he finally established contact with him. The *New York Times* announced one morning that Mr. Morgan, who was about to leave for a Mediterranean cruise on the *Corsair*, had just completed negotiations for the purchase of the *Tornabuoni Princess* by Domenico Ghirlandaio. Drey thought very quickly and that same day caught the *Mauretania* for Cherbourg. He took the sleeper to Florence and went directly to the Grand Hotel where Morgan always stopped. Every day for three weeks he took his post from early morning to sundown in the refectory of the Ognissanti in front of Ghirlandaio's fresco of the *Last Supper*. Surely, he reasoned, a man who had paid such a princely sum for an example of this artist's work would make the pilgrimage to see his greatest masterpiece. Then one day Morgan, who was alone in Florence, walked into the room. In the relaxed manner of tourists before a great work of art the two men fell into casual conversation. The afternoon wore on and they returned together to the hotel for dinner. That evening they played cards and before he went to bed that night Drey claimed he had sold Morgan works of art running into six figures."

Pierpont collected from all periods and all civilizations. He bought half a dozen alabaster reliefs from the Assyrian Palace of Ashurnasirpal at Nimrod. He bought scarabs and jewels from Egypt, sculpture of the Egyptian Eighteenth Dynasty, silver dishes from Cyprus, Germanic art and other treasures of the bar-

barian tribes. He bought Byzantine works, and Roman works, Renaissance jewelry, faïence, a collection of watches, antique plate, and bronze. He bought eleven paintings and several art objects from the Duveen gallery, for which he paid $1,275,000, at one crack.

At first all these objects of art were kept in Europe because the American customs laws did not make any provision for relaxation of duties on art objects, no matter why they were brought into the country. In the first decade of the twentieth century the British government enacted death duties, and this gave Pierpont pause, because he had so much invested in England, in property and art. There was talk about passage of such a law in the United States too. Instead, however, Congress passed a law permitting works of art over one hundred years old to come into the country duty free, and this caused Pierpont to make plans to move his collection to America as quickly as possible.

In 1906 the Metropolitan Museum had decided to send an archaeological expedition to Egypt, with the unenthusiastic backing of Pierpont Morgan who questioned the expense involved. Two parties traveled to Egypt and set to work digging, one in the Nile Valley about thirty miles south of Cairo, and the other at the oasis of Khargeh, in the Libyan Desert, about four hundred miles south of Cairo. Pierpont visited the diggings in their third year, 1909, at Lisht, the site near Cairo on the Nile. He rode over with a party on donkeys one day. They saw the museum archaeologists at work, excavating two pyramids. At the edge of the south pyramid a ruined temple was being cleared by 350 native workmen. Rubble and sand was carried from the ruins in baskets, emptied into little railroad cars, and taken out to a dump. While Pierpont was there the archaeologists were uncovering slabs of painted temple reliefs and many other evidences of the old Egyptian cultures. Pierpont began by asking questions and remained by staying two full days, during which he acquired an understanding and appreciation of the problems of archaeology. Thereafter he began to support the Museum's program for the collection of Egyptian relics.

Pierpont visited the other Metropolitan party that winter and had his picture taken on a divan with Sheikh Mustafa Manad, the Omdeh of the village of Khargeh. As Satterlee put it, although they could not speak to each other they were friendly at once. "Each recognized in the other a man of force and importance, and so they sat down very contentedly and enjoyed the view in silence."

There were few men with whom Pierpont could be at ease now. He had gone, at the solemn request of a dying Edward H. Harriman, to sit with his old enemy and make the final peace. He had returned from that session content and thoughtful. Then Harriman died, and a little bit of Pierpont's life died too.

Albert Lythgoe, director of the Metropolitan Museum's Egyptian operations, took Pierpont around to visit other sights. They went to Luxor and Karnak and to the Valley of the Kings where other expeditions had opened various royal tombs in the cliffs. As the party moved north on their Nile steamer it stopped many times. Lythgoe took Pierpont to visit Mohammed Mohassib, the controller of the antiquity market of upper Egypt. Pierpont waited for several days while the results of a new native discovery were brought in, and Lythgoe bought several pieces of Eighteenth Dynasty art—including an alabaster figure of a dwarf and a Theban statue in dark schist—on Pierpont's behalf. Lythgoe then described Pierpont's reaction as a collector:

"When we reached the river bank I could see Mr. Morgan alone playing solitaire on the brightly lighted upper deck (it was very warm and he was sitting in his shirtsleeves), and I judged that the others had already gone to their cabins to dress for dinner. Then I was soon engaged in showing the contents of the basket to him, placing the objects one by one on the table before him— and I shall never forget his pleasure as he looked long at them and examined them. Some time afterwards, he told me that he could feel the perspiration running down his back from excitement as he saw those things gradually appear out of that basket."

Pierpont added greatly to the collection of Hartford's Wadsworth Athenaeum in these last years and in 1910 attended the opening of the new building there that he had paid for as a memorial to Junius, at a total cost of about $800,000. He also gave

$250,000 in securities to establish an endowment. He established the Laffan professorship of Assyriology and Babylonian literature at Yale University; he gave large sums to the New York Lying-In Hospital and a hospital at Aix-les-Bains. He visited Egypt again and in 1912 had Thomas Cook and Son build a special Nile river steamer, the *Khargeh*, for a trip he took up the Nile, buying antiquities and visiting the digs of the archaeologists of the museum, and seeing his acquaintance the Omdeh of Khargeh, with whom he sat and smoked again in comfortable silence. Pierpont spent more than six months of 1912 in Europe and Africa. Much of the remainder of that year was involved in preparation for or appearances at various government committees.

It is sometimes said that the summoning before the Pujo Committee was the indirect cause of Pierpont's death. A picture of him taken in 1910 would indicate that this statement is hyperbolic, for in that year Pierpont had begun to show his age most markedly. His face and features seemed smaller and he appeared to have lost his bulk. He was grizzled, and where the Pierpont of a few years earlier had been massive, the Pierpont of 1910 seemed slighter and more preoccupied.

He rewrote his will in December 1912, and the following month, on January 7, he said goodbye to Fanny at the house at 219 Madison Avenue and boarded the *Adriatic* for another trip to Africa and Europe. He landed at Naples and then went to Alexandria. Another trip on the *Khargeh* began on February 2, but nothing was right for Pierpont this time. The *Khargeh* was too slow, and Thomas Cook and Son sent a special engineer to see what was wrong with her. They had provided the servants, but neither chef nor waiter suited Pierpont this year, and two new men were rushed upriver from Cairo to replace them. Pierpont fussed and fumed all the way to Luxor, but there, while the others went sight-seeing, he said he felt weak and stayed aboard. He did make a trip to the expedition house that he had caused to be built at Deir-el-bahri, but when he got there and made a welcoming speech at luncheon he was so weak that he had to lie down for a time in one of the rooms. The party went to Aswan aboard the steamer and then returned to Cairo, although a special excursion to Khartoum had been planned and a special train was awaiting them at Wady Halfa. Back at Luxor on February 14, Pierpont had the feeling that he was going to die. He ordered long cables sent to Jack and to Herbert Satterlee in New York. He said he would like to have Jack join him now, but that if Jack came the financial world would take it amiss. Even in this hour of despondency, Pierpont was showing the old sense of responsibility which so many in America could not understand. Jack was to remain in New York. Satterlee was to come to join Pierpont, bringing Pierpont's current physician, Dr. George Dixon.

Satterlee and Dr. Dixon met the party at Shepheard's Hotel at Cairo. Then there were numerous consultations of doctors. It was said that an Italian specialist was paid a fabulous fee to join the group; it is doubtful. Pierpont seemed to improve. He had suffered from indigestion and weakness, but he gained strength. It was decided to take him to Italy and the party embarked on the *Adriatic*. Much was made by the world press of the total cost of the staterooms. That is the way in which the newspapermen were approaching Pierpont. From Naples they went to Rome by special train. In Rome at the Grand Hotel (cost $500 per day) he seemed to improve and soon was out driving and visiting the various tourist spots he most enjoyed. Pierpont would not go out to restaurants, however, and it was difficult for Satterlee and Louisa to persuade him to eat more than a few bites of any meal in his room.

By mid-March he wanted to go home and it was planned that the *Corsair* (cost unknown) would be sent over to Italy to pick up the party. He was very weak but interested in what was going on around him. He wanted to see the American Academy in Rome, to which he had donated heavily, but when taken to the building had to be carried upstairs on a chair. A New York psychiatrist of some note happened to be in Rome and he was called in to see Pierpont. He said he thought the banker was suffering from nervous tension and an accumulation of the strains of very active living over a very long time. The psychiatrist predicted that in a few days Pierpont would be able to travel safely, and then this doctor went off on a motor trip to southern Italy. The next day was Easter Sunday. Pierpont suffered seriously from nervous depression. He left church during the service because he could not bear to sit still any longer. He took a nap in the afternoon and then talked about family and investments and problems that would arise if he died. The next day he was so ill that Satterlee brought in nurses. On Tuesday Pierpont was worse and on Thursday he began to refuse to eat. On Friday he could not collect his thoughts enough to carry on a steady conversation. The psychiatrist was then located in Sorrento and brought up to Rome for consultation. Pierpont kept suggesting that the whole party leave Rome and go to the house at Prince's Gate where he could be at home. The psychiatrist thought that was a good idea, and a special channel steamer and special trains were laid on for departure on Monday, March 31. Just after midnight on Sunday, Pierpont awakened with a very fast pulse and a very high temperature—104½ degrees. He lay quietly, mumbling once in a while, about Hartford school days and the days at Vevey. He pointed upward, looked at Satterlee and spoke. "I've got to go up the hill," he said. Then he lapsed into a coma from which he never came out. He died just after noon on Monday.

PART FIVE

The New
J. P. Morgan Company

CHAPTER

I

THE BANKER'S FORTUNE

B Y 1905 IT WAS APPARENT that the strength of the House of Morgan would lie in the American firm with its English and French connections in that order of importance. This change was a reflection of the strength of character of Pierpont Morgan, but it was not altogether because of that factor. Had Pierpont chosen back in 1857 not to come to America but to remain in Europe, and had an American branch of the firm been established by another, still the importance of banking would have tended to move westward, because the balance of economic power in the world was moving in that direction after the turn of the twentieth century.

This year, 1905, was the year in which Pierpont decided that Jack should come home and take an active part in the American firm. For fifteen years Jack had served his apprenticeship and served his grandfather's and then his father's interests in the London firm of J. S. Morgan and Company. Jack Morgan was thirty-eight years old that September, when he arrived with his wife, Jessie, and the children to settle down in the old Anson Phelps Stokes house at 231 Madison Avenue, which Pierpont gave to him. This was pleasant and convenient to 219 so that Jack could come to the library or the breakfast table for meetings with his father and so Pierpont could see his grandchildren as often as possible. He delighted in the company of all of them; he never forgot a birthday or any family occasion, it seemed, and the children who had not learned that their grandfather was the most important man in American business, adored him because they recognized a kindred soul.

Pierpont's relationship with Jack Morgan—J. P. Morgan, Jr.— was everything that a father could desire. Jack was his good right hand, he never quarreled or complained, and he adored and respected his father as Pierpont had adored and respected Junius. Even at the last, when Pierpont had known he was going to die and had ordered Jack to stay at home and attend to the affairs of the banking firm, Jack had been wretched, but he had accepted Pierpont's wish and had done as he was expected to do.

Suddenly, on April 1, 1913, the House of Morgan had a new head, and one about whom the world knew relatively little, because in the Morgan fashion Jack had never sought publicity and the press of the world had been so bedazzled by the power of his father that he had not received very much attention. What was known was that he was a shrewd businessman with many of his father's strengths. He was an individual, however. He had come to the New York firm after a number of years in England, where he had acquired English real estate of his own (a country house) called Wall Hall in Hertfordshire and a West End town house and many English habits. He liked exercise, which Pierpont abhorred, and when he moved into his New York town house one of his earliest moves was to build a squash court there. He used it, too, playing daily for some time with a professional from the Racquet Club.

Jack was big like his father, and he shared his father's interest in yachting, both steam and sail. He introduced the custom of afternoon tea into the offices of J. P. Morgan and Company. Yet he remained a quieter, more mysterious figure to the American public than his father, and he preferred that it be so.

Pierpont's body was brought back to New York City in April and then to the family plot in Cedar Hill Cemetery in Hartford, where it was buried after a great funeral at St. George's. "He was a great and good man," said Pope Pius X, who had admitted Pierpont to audience a number of times and had discussed art and the state of the world with him.

The state of that world changed remarkably in a few short months, for the most devasting war in history was to come to Europe just over a year after Pierpont's affairs were being decently settled. It was a world that Pierpont would have been singularly unable to handle in his old, familiar way, because from every side the way of life accepted by the Morgans and their friends was under attack. The attack had begun during Pierpont's lifetime, but he had not recognized it as a basic social change. There was no reason for him to so recognize it because the positive was most often hidden under a layer of hysterical charges against the "interests." The real change was that everywhere in the world where men could change their governments without violence they were seeking to bring economic power out of the hands of men of business and place it in the hands of men of politics. The reasoning, in America and elsewhere, was the same reasoning shown in the Pujo Committee: the basic acceptance of the evil of man. The reformers said that control of the economy must be placed in the hands of committees and elected officials so the people could rule.

While Pierpont was in Africa on that final trip, the Pujo Committee made its report, stating the need for control of the "economic interests." The final committee report indicated that the concentration of money and credit was increasing. The committee looked uncomfortably on the consolidations of banks and trust companies, particularly after the panic of 1907. They did not approve of one large company such as United States Steel purchasing the stock control of a competitor such as Tennessee Coal and Iron. They worried, in spite of Pierpont's testimony, about the evils of interlocking directorates. They were concerned, they said, about extension of Wall Street control into insurance companies, railroads, public utilities, and industrial corporations. They did not like the old syndicates or joint arrangements for the purchase of security issues from the source.

Taking the committee's complaints one by one, it was quite

possible to set against every Pujo Committee complaint an action of the House of Morgan in the past fifteen years. What the Pujo Committee said, then, was: abolish the House of Morgan and make it impossible for any other banking firm ever to acquire so much influence and power as this one has had since 1900.

Testifying before the Pujo Committee did not kill Pierpont. The Pujo report would not have killed him. All the same, it was fitting that Pierpont died when he did at the age of seventy-six, because had he lived on another five years he would not have liked what he saw happening to the world to which he had tried to bring his own peace and prosperity.

When the funeral was over and the will was read, Americans were astonished to learn how few were the assets of this man who had been the economic czar of America for so long. First, there was the art collection for which he had spent perhaps $100,-000,000. Art values are like security values, they fluctuate and fashions change. In one decade his acquisitions might be worth only $50,000,000, a half century later they might be worth ten time as much. As any banker knew, Pierpont's assets, no matter what kind they were, could not be measured in terms of money. He had proved the point by having to hold so few assets to maintain so much control of the American economy.

The public portion of Pierpont's estate was valued at slightly less than $68,500,000. That was the estate for tax purposes. He had transferred some properties to members of his family earlier, as many wealthy men did, but not with any particular purpose because the death taxes in 1913 were not an important factor.

Trust funds of $3,000,000 each were left to his three daughters, Louisa, Mrs. Satterlee; Juliet, Mrs. William Pierson Hamilton; and Anne Tracy Morgan. Fanny received $1,000,000 outright, an annuity of $100,000 a year, and the use of the house at 219 Madison Avenue and Cragston for the remainder of her life. Each of the sons-in-law received $1,000,000. A half million dollars was left as capital for the support of St. George's Church and $100,000 was given to the Episcopal diocesan convention for a mission in New York. Dr. James Markoe, director of the Lying-In Hospital was given $25,000, and it was directed that if necessary for support of the hospital the estate pay over $100,000 a year. Nearly every servant and employee of Pierpont Morgan received a bequest in the will. Three million dollars outright and the residuary estate were left to John Pierpont Morgan, Jr., which meant he would have the yacht and the English properties and all the other belongings of his father as well as the securities and money. Besides this, Pierpont left to Jack's disposal the huge art collection that he had attempted to amass. Here is how Pierpont disposed of the collection in that last will drawn a few months before his death:

> This article of the will said: I have been greatly interested for many years in gathering my collections of paintings, miniatures, porcelains, and other works of art, and it has been my desire and intention to make some suitable disposition of them or of such portions of them as I might determine, which would render them permanently available for the instruction and pleasure of the American people. Lack of the necessary time to devote to it has as yet prevented my carrying this purpose into effect.
>
> Unless I shall accomplish it, or make some disposition of these collections, in my lifetime, they will pass to my son, John Pierpont Morgan, Jr., or to his son, Junius Spencer Morgan, Jr., under the foregoing clauses of this will whereby I dispose of my residuary estate. Should either my said son or my said grandson thus succeed to the ownership of these collections, I hope he will be able, in such manner as he shall think best, to make a permanent disposition of them or of such portions of them as he may determine, which will be a substantial carrying out of the intentions which I have thus cherished. It would be agreeable to me to have 'The Morgan Memorial' which forms a portion of the property of the Wadsworth Athenaeum at Hartford, Connecticut, utilized to effectuate a part of this purpose.

For some years it had been understood by the professional museum staff at the Metropolitan Museum of Art in New York City that Pierpont was going to leave his art collection to the museum. This seems to have been Pierpont's intention—at least to donate a very large part of the collection to the museum, still not forgetting the Wadsworth Athenaeum in Hartford. But time and events had interposed a number of difficulties in the way of the disposition of the collection. First had been the disturbing tariff on works of art, but when that was removed other problems arose. From 1906 to 1910 the curator of paintings and then advisor in Europe on paintings for the Metropolitan had been Roger Fry, an intellectual who had devoted himself to fine art and had become an expert on the tiniest details of Renaissance art. At some point before 1910 Pierpont and Fry had disagreed violently over something to do with art. It was indicated that it had something to do with a painting that Pierpont wanted for his collection and that Fry wanted for the museum. But that was only the final breaking point. For years Fry had detested Pierpont Morgan. "I don't think he wants anything but flattery," he wrote. He also wrote of this banker, "so swollen with pride and a sense of his own power that it never occurs to him that other people have any rights," and he referred to Pierpont's "great strawberry nose." Such definition could not help but make itself apparent in their relations. At one time they took a trip together and Fry's contempt for the amateur collector Morgan showed itself very plainly. Fry made the mistake of considering Pierpont insensitive, which was his downfall. It also had some effect on Pierpont's attitude toward the professionals of the museum.

More important, however, was the misreading by the authorities of the city of New York of Pierpont's sensitivities. It was known that the banker intended to give a large collection to the Metropolitan Museum. He had asked, since he was willing to furnish millions of dollars' worth of objects of art, that the city cooperate with him by erecting a suitable house for these objects. The city fathers delayed, however, in making appropriations for a new wing for the museum. Pierpont refused to gather together all the collection and have it shipped to go into storage somewhere, and he was somewhat piqued by the reluctance of the city fathers to show appreciation in a tangible manner. At the time of Pierpont's death no wing had been added, and the art collection was waiting.

The museum had in its hands much of the famous collection in the fall of 1913 and the spring of 1914. The Board of Estimate of New York City indicated its willingness to appropriate money for a new wing for the museum, but it was really too late. As Jack Morgan began unraveling the affairs of the estate, it seemed to him that there was far too little in tangible assets outside the art collection to protect the position of the Morgans in the banking business, and so much of the art collection was sold, over the grumblings and protests of the professionals at the Metropolitan Museum. It would not be until 1918 that the final share of the Metropolitan would be determined, because important matters were to intervene. But when the Duveen gallery bought several million dollars' worth of these treasures, including the classic room of Fragonard panels that had been especially made for Madame DuBarry, there was much complaint about the needs of Mammon.

It was true; the House of Morgan was primarily a banking house and this position must be preserved, whatever the cost to the family in esoteric ways.

CHAPTER

II

JACK MORGAN COMES OF AGE

O N THE DAY that his father died, Jack Morgan was forty-six
years old, quite old enough to become the leader of an important banking and industrial combination, although seven years
younger than Pierpont had been when he became the senior partner in the House of Morgan. Jack Morgan had not been thrust
into leadership in financial and public affairs in the manner of
Pierpont because Pierpont was so commanding a figure that until
the day of his death he ruled the firm; also because the firm's headquarters was now very definitely on the western shore of the
Atlantic and with the growth of industrial power in America New
York was becoming more banker to the world even than it had
been when Jack came home from England.

In the spring of 1913 Jack began assuming the mantle of power.
He was elected a director of the New York Central Railroad, of
the New Haven, and many other corporations in which the Morgan interest had been represented by the senior partner. He began
to assume his father's public trusteeship duties too, with election
to the board of trustees of the New York Public Library. He would
be active in church work, but never so active as Pierpont in the
conventions.

That year the bank refinanced the Boston and Maine Railroad, participated in sale of bonds for the Mexican government, and went deep into the affairs of the Interborough Rapid Transit Company, one of New York's subway systems.

In the summer of 1913 trouble developed along the New Haven Railroad line, trouble that presaged collapse of one of Pierpont Morgan's cherished dreams: the establishment of a strong, unified New England railroad system. Jack Morgan had scarcely been elected to the board and taken his seat when the trouble came.

The Morgan connection with the New Haven went back twenty years and for a decade the Morgans had been most influential in the management of the railroad. Having been brought from the Northern Pacific to the New Haven line, President Charles S. Mellen had been encouraged by Pierpont to buy and buy feeder lines and competitor lines. Pierpont's part in the expansion of the New Haven system from five hundred to two thousand miles had been to produce the money that was necessary to make the purchases. Steamboat lines were driven away or out of business by the New Haven. The New Haven bought control of the Boston and Maine Railroad, and dozens of other properties. In 1903 the capitalization of the railroad was $93,000,000; ten years later the capitalization was $417,000,000. It is questionable whether Pierpont was aware of how far Mellen had gone in running up the capitalization; Morgan had begun the project but he had stepped even more out of the operating sphere of business during those last few years. In his lifetime Pierpont's theory that the American economic system would support the unlimited growth of any given facility was never proved wrong, although he must have had some second thoughts about the maritime empire he was trying to build. Even that was not a fair test of Pierpont's theory or the change in the times that made the theory invalid for there were international problems involved in the shipping business.

The New Haven Railroad represented the dangerous extension of Pierpont's economic theory. By 1912 the New Haven line was in serious financial trouble, and Boston lawyer Louis D. Brandeis was leading a campaign to force a reorganization of the railroad and its operations. It was not generally known, but President

Mellen was trying desperately to shore up his line by paying dividends out of surplus and short-term borrowings. In other words, the New Haven after 1910 was paying dividends without earning profits, and this simply exacerbated the desperate financial condition of the railroad.

Later, in testimony before a federal inquiry, President Mellen would try to shift the responsibility for the operations of the New Haven to the shoulders of the dead Pierpont Morgan. He would say that he was Morgan's man, scarcely more than an office boy, and that he did as he was told, and that he did not stand up to Morgan. Probably that latter point is very truthful, but Mellen carried out improprieties as president of the line that Pierpont would not have countenanced had he been in his prime and paying attention to the New Haven. When Jack Morgan took over in the spring of 1913, he began to investigate the troubles. Mellen was ousted but the ailments continued.

In the summer of 1913 Jack Morgan formed a syndicate to underwrite a new issue of convertible debentures for the New Haven line. This attempt to solve the problem by refinancing created a tempest among the stockholders, who made violent and insulting statements about the conduct of J. P. Morgan and Company. Among other charges was one that the bank had taken excessive profits from its sale of bonds for the New Haven in recent years. It was later revealed that in three years the bank had sold more than $168,000,000 in bonds for the line, with total commissions of only $889,000, or about ½ per cent, which was certainly not high. Profits had been $441,000, or less than a third of 1 per cent of the sales.

When the stockholders made their violent criticisms of the J. P. Morgan and Company methods, Jack Morgan acted quickly. The firm withdrew as fiscal agents of the New Haven line, and resigned all directorships in the New Haven. This was the first action in a new battle that was developing. Pierpont had seen the preliminary skirmishes in the Northern Securities case and the filing of the suit to break up United States Steel Corporation. In the next few years Jack Morgan was to be buffeted and cuffed by an unkind public opinion and by political leaders for reasons that he was never able fully to understand. He was to become the central ogre figure of a target group that would be called the masters of capital. It was true, the bankers were the masters of capital. In many ways they had served the nation well, for its rapid growth could not have been accomplished without inspired banking leadership. Now, in the continued growth, in the settling of the industrial system, and in the turgid political waters of a revolutionary world these same bankers who had been lauded as heroes half a century before became villains. That great sleeping giant—the people—was awakening to the calls of Marx and Freud all over the world. In America the foreign born brought their socialist and anarchist ideas through the immigration ports and added these to the native restlessness of the Populists and syndicalists, and to the agrarian individualism of the West. An enemy figure was needed to serve as the apotheosis of evil by the radicals. And now far more than his father had ever been, Jack Morgan was lampooned by the press and the radical left.

In a way Jack Morgan was in the wrong place in the wrong time in the wrong guise. After St. Paul's and Harvard College, he had spent his later formative years in England. There he had moved among the members of the upper class. He regarded himself, quite naturally, as a member of the upper class, and while he was most circumspect about this attitude when he came back across the Atlantic to the land where classes did not exist—in theory, at least—the leaders of the radical movements spotted him unerringly as the symbol of all they hated in capitalism. His love for grouse shooting, his love for sailing and steam yachting, his clothing, his appearance were all to be lampooned. With his close-clipped mustache, his accent, and his quiet, careful clothing, Jack Morgan was a very English American. Fifty years before, this would have been an asset. Now it was to become a liability and he was to suffer untold tortures for characteristics over which he had no control.

The change in leadership of the House of Morgan coincided, within weeks, with the change in leadership of the United States government. In 1913, for the first time since 1897, the Democrats were in control of the federal administration. There had never been such Democrats as these, either. Cleveland was a Democrat, but he was a man whom a banker could understand; he was a reformer, but to him reform did not mean control of the machinery of capital but the cleaning up of the government. The era of Woodrow Wilson was a new era, and Wilson and the men around him were concerned with social reform of the nation and economic reform of the nation as much as with political reform. At the end of the Pujo Committee testimony the year before, George Baker of the First National Bank of New York, ally of Morgan and a power in his own right, had admitted that the real matter at issue was the character of the men who controlled the financial resources of America. He could see, where Pierpont could not, that if all depended on the character of the men in control, then the nation was walking the edge of the knife:

> Mr. Untermeyer: . . . the safety, if you think there is safety in the situation, really lies in the personnel of the men?
> Mr. Baker: Very much so.
> Mr. Untermyer: Do you think that is a comfortable situation for a great country to be in?
> Mr. Baker (very slowly): Not entirely.

Mr. Untermyer finally had made his point, and he was believed. The nation must protect itself from evil; to protect itself the masters of capital must be curbed, and this was a primary purpose established by the Wilson administration.

Examine the legislation asked by the administration and enacted by Congress in the next few months and consider with each new law how it would have been regarded by Pierpont, based on his long years of experience with government and business finance:

• The Sixteenth Amendment to the United States Constitution was adopted—giving the Congress the power to tax income.

• The Physical Valuation Act gave the Interstate Commerce Commission power to investigate property used or held by railroads, to establish costs and valuations as a basis for rate control.

• The Federal Reserve Act established eight to twelve districts, each containing a federal reserve bank. All was controlled by a federal reserve board which included the Secretary of the Treasury and the Comptroller of the Currency. This board could raise or lower the rediscount rate at the banks, giving it control over the credit supply—much as the Bank of England controlled British credit. The district banks would serve as depositories for the cash reserves of the national banks—which had to join the system, and for state banks if they wished. A member must subscribe to the capital stock of the Federal Reserve Bank an amount equal to 6 per cent of its own capital and surplus. The federal reserve banks rediscounted the commercial and agricultural loans of the member banks and against these the reserve banks could issue Federal Reserve Notes as part of the money supply. This supply could expand or contract, according to the amount of cash wanted or desired in the community. Each reserve bank must keep a gold reserve of 40 per cent against federal reserve notes outstanding unless an emergency came about, in which case this could be suspended. Thus, for the first time, there was created a place for banks to turn for financial aid in time of crisis, and a control, because the banks had to subscribe to the system.

How Pierpont would have hated that!

• The Federal Trade Commission Act established the commission with power to demand annual and special reports from corporations, to investigate the activities of corporations other than banks, to issue cease and desist orders subject to court rules, and to publish its findings.

• The Clayton Antitrust Act prohibited price discriminations which might tend to create monopoly (always a tricky question), interlocking directorates, and the acquisition of stock holdings tending to lessen competition.

By the middle of the summer of 1914 all this had been done. Each of these laws affected directly and immediately the manner in which the private banking firm of J. P. Morgan and Company could do business. The bankers liked these new controls of their activities no better than any social group liked such control, yet did the bankers try to subvert it?

"Its purpose is not, as surface appearances seemed to indicate, to tear business down or to thwart and ruin industry. It has been rather to force all business corporations that are of such great magnitude or importance as to affect directly the great body of the people to be conducted more openly and with more scrupulous fidelity to the interests of both the public and the thousands of small investors who are really the owners of these corporations." That speech, which read like those of New York Stock Exchange officials in the 1960's, was made by Henry P. Davison, second only to Jack Morgan in the Morgan firm in the year 1913, before a group of businessmen. The movement to business reform, however, was suspended in the autumn of 1914 when World War I broke out. Jack Morgan then was suddenly catapulted into a position of the utmost importance in world banking.

At the end of July 1914, when it became apparent that only a miracle could prevent the beginning of a general war, Jack presided at a conference in the offices on Wall Street. Members of the important firms on the stock exchange were there and so were the most important bankers in the city. The problem was whether or not to close down the stock exchange (it was closed for four months) and whether to suspend gold payments to Europe during the conflict. Jack was true to the principles his father had always espoused: that it was the banker's responsibility to maintain the money market. He counseled for maintainance of gold shipments to Europe and won his way. Immediately this became a local problem, because the city of New York owed about $100,000,000 in gold abroad and was not in a position to pay it. Jack Morgan arranged for the financing of this loan.

Not long after war broke out the British Ambassador to the United States, Sir Cecil Spring-Rice, telephoned Jack from Washington. From the outset of hostilities it was apparent that Britain must be able to call on every resource if she was to prosecute the war, and among the resources she needed were two: supply and banking.

Sir Cecil came to New York and met with Jack Morgan in the privacy of the west room of the library on Thirty-sixth Street. Britain needed a banker and a friend in America. For a thousand reasons that have been made apparent in the pages of this book,

Jack Morgan was the logical choice to be that friend. He agreed to assist the British government, and that was that.

Thus, as Pierpont had come to the turn of his career at a time of crisis of the United States Army, when he saw a public responsibility, so Jack Morgan came to the crisis in his career when the land where he had spent those formative business years was threatened.

In the beginning, when the British and French started their purchasing programs in a neutral America, they were paying very high prices and getting very bad service. Government competed with government, and within the governments various purchasing divisions competed, as it was with the Union Army purchasers in New York during the civil war. Late in 1914 Jack asked Henry Davison to go to Washington to see if the British would accept a new purchasing arrangement under which the Morgan firm would handle all these affairs. In the past the British had been paying as high as 7.5 per cent in commissions on purchases. The Morgan company proposed a commission of 2 per cent of sales, out of which it would pay all expenses of handling the work. Lloyd George, who was a member of the British cabinet, indicated his approval of this idea and the government was persuaded to accept it. Then the Morgan company persuaded Edward R. Stettinius, president of the Diamond Match Company, to join their firm to handle this work.

When war came to Europe the general American feeling was that this was a European affair and that the United States must remain neutral. But what was neutrality? Did it mean that both sides should be equally favored in the manufacture of supplies and munitions? Did it mean that nothing should be done for any belligerents?

In the summer of 1914 when Morgan Harjes and Company of Paris received a $6,000,000 credit in gold from the bank of France to open an account in New York, these questions were germane. Jack Morgan asked Secretary of State William Jennings Bryan whether it was legal to accept this credit and set up this account, given President Wilson's declaration of neutrality. Bryan said no, or, rather, that such purchases were not exhibiting neutrality. But Jack Morgan never was neutral in this affair, personally, and neither were many other Americans. In later years some were to charge that the House of Morgan was responsible for dragging the United States into the war, a charge that would have infuriated Theodore Roosevelt had he heard it, because he had been trying almost from the day the shots were fired at Sarajevo to get the United States to take sides with the Triple Entente, against Germany and her allies.

Very quickly the question of selling to both sides in this war became academic, because the Triple Alliance could not control the seas, and except for a few special trips, such as highly touted but not very effective submarine voyages, the Germans were forced to rely on materials that could be brought to them over land, not over sea.

In 1914 the mobilization for war progressed haltingly. No one was sure how long the war would last or what its outcome might be. In the early months the Germans marched on Paris, but their drive bogged down. By the end of the year it became clear that the war was going to be more prolonged than anyone had considered. The allies needed money, and they turned to the marketplace of America for money and for supplies. The sentiment of America began to turn, quite without reference to the Morgans or anyone else. Following the announcement in August that loans to belligerents would not be looked upon kindly by the federal authorities, in October the policy was modified to except short-term loans. The National City Bank made such a loan to France for $10,000,000.

American opinion quite changed after the beginning of May 1915, when the Germans sank the unarmed passenger ship *Lusitania* by submarine torpedo without warning. From the beginning of the war there had been a trend toward involvement of civil passenger ships, because trade was the lifeline of Britain, but this sinking was so unnecessary and so brutal and so costly in civilian lives—1,198 men, women, and children—that American public opinion swung quickly and decisively against the Germans. Soon Jack Morgan and his partners had arranged a $500,000,000 loan through an American banking syndicate to France and Britain, a loan to be used exclusively for the purchase of supplies in the United States. The House of Morgan did not take any compensation or profit from this transaction; Jack termed it "imperative to preserve trade," which was a rather murky way of saying that it was for the good of the nation in his estimation.

Soon the allies were borrowing billions of dollars from the American people, and the Morgans were arranging much of the sale of the bonds supporting these borrowings. Altogether the figure finally reached nearly $2,500,000,000. (The borrowings of the Germans in America, by comparison, came only to about $20,-000,000.) Trade increased month by month in the hands of the Morgan purchasing commission, for that is what it was, under Edward Stettinius. It was charged later that the Morgans had been dealing almost exclusively with companies they controlled, thus making huge profits from the war. Thomas Lamont, a Morgan partner, said:

"The final records as to the British contracts showed that, of the hundreds of different concerns dealt with, there were only eleven in which the Morgan partners held any interest; and the largest interest they held in any one of those eleven did not exceed three per cent of the shares."

After the establishment of this purchasing commission, the British began to worry about putting it in the hands of private bankers in America. Lloyd George, in 1915 the Minister of Munitions, came to America and went to see Henry Davison.

"Look here, my good man," he said, "you must be sure, you know, to try to even up orders between Democrats and Republican producers."

"My dear Mr. Minister," said Davison, "there is no politics in our office on this business of purchasing for the allies. We don't know Republicans from Democrats. We would place orders with a Socialist if he happened to have the best supplies at the lowest prices to our clients."

There was to be profit from the war, for American industry and for the House of Morgan. There was no question about that. All Morgan bankers had always believed in making profits, and they made them now. In 1916 the allies bought $3,000,000,000 worth of goods from American industry. Since the Morgans handled most of that business perhaps they earned a gross income of $50,-000,000 that year in handling the purchasing. No questions were asked by Britain and France. They wanted the supplies.

Or, take the matter of the United States Steel Corporation's profits. In 1913 the steel company earned $11.02 per share of common stock. Business fell off in the United States in 1914 and the company earned nothing per common share. In 1915, U. S. Steel Common earned $9.96 a share and in 1916 it rose to $48.46 per share. All during the war the earnings remained above $22 per share.

So there were plenty of profits and there was plenty of banking business for the House of Morgan and the other big bankers of Wall Street in the war years. More important, from the point of view of the Morgans, was the increased prestige the banking firm achieved by its efficient handling of the huge war business. In the spring of 1913, when Pierpont died and Jack Morgan became the head of the firm, there were many in Wall Street who suggested that the young man was not anywhere near what the old man had been, that the House of Morgan was heading for evil days.

By the middle of 1915 such talk had disappeared in Wall Street. The Morgan banking prestige was higher than it had ever been.

THE MURDEROUS MR. HOLT

B Y THE BEGINNING of World War I, Jack Morgan had suffered from more publicity than he cared to accept, but it was always to be his lot to be in the public eye because of his father's exploits and his own position in American commerce and society. In terms of Society with a large S, the world of social seeking, Jack Morgan played no part. In all of Cleveland Amory's spicy book *Who Killed Society?* Jack Morgan is not mentioned except in connection with his father. In lesser books on the social seekers very often there is confusion about the J. P. Morgans, father and son, which sometimes gives the indication that Pierpont lived to be more than a hundred years old.

For business reasons, Jack lived in a town house in New York City most of the time, or at least kept his headquarters there. From preference, he lived in a large private estate on East Island, near Glen Cove, in what was then the very fashionable district of the North Shore of Long Island. A dozen super-millionaires had built or were building their super-mansions nearby. William K. Vanderbilt, Jr., had built his estate at Lake Success, a little farther in toward the city. He was to tire of it for personal reasons during World War I and move much farther out on Long Island. But W. K. Vanderbilt, Jr., did not go to the office every day, like many

351

of the scions of wealthy families. Among rich men who were rich men's sons Jack Morgan was a leader of the working group; he was not a professional rich man.

After the House of Morgan became purchasing agent for the Western allies in World War I, Jack Morgan was made by the press into a symbol of the "interferer" as opposed to the "neutral." He was lionized by those who believed the United States should come to the assistance of France and Britain, and detested and libeled by those who favored the German cause. His life was now not only busy, but also dangerous.

Just how dangerous became apparent on July 3, 1915, a day that had been planned for a very large party at the Morgan estate and on the Morgan yacht.

On the morning of July 3 the Morgan household awakened at a reasonable hour. The servants were up at six-thirty and seven and breakfast was under preparation in the kitchen; the maids were at work and the big three-story brick house was beginning to come to life. This weekend—for it was a Saturday morning—the Morgans were entertaining Sir Cecil Spring-Rice, Ambassador of His Majesty, King George V, King of the British Isles, Emperor of India, and holder of other titles too numerous to mention. Sir Cecil, Lady Spring-Rice, and the Morgans were in the breakfast room at the eastern end of the mansion, taking their ease and preparing for what promised to be a very busy day.

On the night before, some vandal had set off a dynamite bomb in the Capitol of the United States. It did no particular damage but it aroused Americans to visible anger. This bombing was in all the morning newspapers and it had been the talk of the household, as it was in nearly every household in the land. Everyone suspected that it was the work of German agents. The rash of anti-German feeling was rising, following the sinking of the *Lusitania* and the loss of more than one hundred American lives, including members of the highest circles of business.

This morning, as the Morgans and their guests breakfasted, a man who went by the name Frank Holt was hiring an automobile at Glen Cove about three miles away, and was asking to be taken to the Morgan estate. His name was not Holt but Dr.

Muenter; he said he was a former teacher of German at Cornell; he was also a German nationalist.

When Holt and his hired auto came to the estate the entry was open and they were able to drive up to the front door of the mansion. Holt got out, walked to the front door and rang the bell. In a few moments butler Henry Physick answered the door, whereupon Holt said he must see Mr. Morgan, and extended a card.

"What is your business with him?" asked Henry.

"I can't discuss that with you," Holt replied haughtily.

Henry was used to people who could not discuss their business with the butler and there was not much to be done. The card seemed legitimate enough if not very impressive. It said: Summer Society Directory, Thomas C. Lester, Representing. The next words, however, made Henry suspicious.

"I am an old friend of Mr. Morgan's. He will see me."

If the man had been an old friend of Mr. Morgan's, he probably would have been known to Henry. He did not have the air of an old friend of the Morgans, to say the least. To say the most, had butler Henry Physick possessed X-ray eyes he would have run shouting into the driveway for the cabby and for police. Mr. Thomas C. Lester-Holt-Muenter at that moment was carrying a stick of dynamite in a pocket, and in each of his coat pockets rested a loaded revolver.

Not having X-ray eyes, the butler merely looked querulous at what he saw on the visitor's exterior. Holt became insistent.

"You must tell me the business you have with him," Henry said firmly.

Holt put both hands in his coat pockets. He then took his hands out of his coat pockets, and in each hand was a revolver. He pressed both of them against the butler's body, pushing him back into the doorway and forcing himself past.

"Don't dare and try to stop me," he said.

With two guns in his back, Henry led Holt into the hall.

"You will find Mr. Morgan in the library," he said, with great aplomb, particularly considering those two objects pressing into his back.

Henry walked ahead of Holt toward the library, which was located at the west end of the house, as far away from the breakfast room as any room could be. As Holt went through the library door, Henry stood back respectfully, and when the intruder was inside and the guns were out of his back, the butler ran down the hall in the direction of the breakfast room, hoping that he would not be followed by a hail of bullets.

"Upstairs, Mr. Morgan. Upstairs," he shouted.

He did not approach the breakfast room directly because he did not wish to betray Morgan to the man with the guns. With great presence of mind, Henry Physick ran down the basement stairs to throw the intruder off, and also to find the other servants and secure their help.

Jack Morgan, his wife, Jessie, Sir Cecil and Lady Spring-Rice heard the strange shouts from the hallway and Jack leaped out of his chair, out the door of the breakfast room and up to the second floor of the house by a rear staircase. He was concealed from the intruder by a turn in the hallway of the first floor of the house. He was followed closely by Jessie and the others.

The party went from room to room, searching, trying to discover what the butler's shouting was about. They found nothing. They encountered other servants but they did not know what was happening.

Suddenly one of the servants saw someone ascending a staircase which ran from the downstairs hall near the library, and shouted that a man was coming up the stairs.

Jack and Jessie Morgan hurried to the head of the stairs to intercept this stranger. As soon as he saw Jack Morgan, Holt began to shout too.

"Now, Mr. Morgan," he said, "I have got you." At least that is how the servants heard the shout.

Jessie sprang forward and threw herself against the intruder to push him away from her husband. Jack pushed her aside and when Holt reached the second-floor landing Jack jumped at him.

Holt fired twice, and then the gun misfired. In the hallway, with the smell of burning cordite, could be heard the useless snapping of the firing pin on the defective cartridge.

As the shots were fired Jack Morgan lunged his 220 pounds into the tall, slender Holt and knocked him down. Holt fell with his feet pointing toward Jack and with the revolver he had fired in his right hand. Jack threw himself forward on top of Holt, covering his body, catching the wrist which held the revolver, and forcing the hand loose so that Holt finally had to drop the gun.

Holt had not fired the gun in his left hand, but now he tried to bring it up. He could not. Jack Morgan had Holt's left hand firmly pinned to the floor with his body and he kept it there. Jessie and the servant came forward now and wrenched the second revolver from the assassin's hand.

Now others came forward too. The butler arrived, carrying a heavy lump of coal, the only weapon he could find in the basement. He raised his coal and smashed Holt over the head, stunning him. Jack Morgan lifted himself off the intruder, and other servants came with rope and bound Holt hand and foot.

Jack watched this until he was satisfied that Holt would give no more trouble. Then he walked to the telephone and called Dr. W. H. Zabriskie, who lived about three miles away from the estate. Only when he asked the doctor to come to the house and attend to his injuries did anyone realize that Jack had been shot.

In fact he had been shot not once but twice by the murderous Dr. Muenter-Holt, once in the groin by a bullet that lodged near the base of his spine and once in the groin near the right thigh by a bullet that emerged at the rear of his thigh.

While waiting for the doctor to arrive, Jack went to bed, but not to collapse. He asked for a telephone and when it was brought to him he called Utica, where his mother was staying at that time. He spoke to Fanny reassuringly. He knew the newspapers would soon tell the world that he had been shot and he wanted her to know that his injuries were very slight so that she would not become upset.

Soon the doctor came; and later Dr. James W. Markoe, the family physician, arrived from New York, with Dr. H. H. M. Lyle. The bullet near the spine was extracted without complication.

The Glen Cove police came soon, too, and picked up the assailant. His stick of dynamite was gingerly removed, and the revolvers were picked up and taken with the prisoner to Glen Cove jail, then to Mineola. In his bag they found two more sticks of dynamite and another on the lawn, where apparently it had dropped from a pocket.

Captured, the assailant denied that his conduct had meant anything. It was all a ghastly mistake, he said. He had come to reason with Mr. Morgan about the Morgan backing of the British and French governments in the war against Germany. All he wanted to do, he said, was talk to the banker.

The Morgan household became the scene of much more activity. Police came from everywhere, it seemed, to discover the cause of the excitement and what protection Jack and the British ambassador needed. Junius Spencer Morgan, Jr., Jack's eldest son, had been married a few days before. He arrived with his bride. They were to be guests of honor at a party to be held that afternoon. The young Morgans had not stopped to read headlines or to hear the talk in the streets, and they knew nothing of the shooting until their automobile pulled up at the lodgehouse on the bridge which led from the mainland to the sixty-acre island. The party was canceled—or almost canceled. The guests were sent out on a yacht for merry-making, while their host lay in bed, recovering from his painful but not serious wounds.

It was not very many days before Jack Morgan was back at work, almost, but not quite, as though nothing had happened. Now a barrier was erected at the entrance to the estate and guards were posted to protect the life of the banker. This was a critical period, for the Anglo-French financial committee was in New York, meeting with Morgan and other bankers to decide how best to finance the loans for the war that stretched endlessly ahead, it seemed. The attack was not easily forgotten. A year later one of Morgan's employees ran his car into the barrier stretched at night across the entrance to the estate and sued Jack for damages. (He collected $20,000.)

By 1916 Jack spent his time commuting to Europe in the manner that many wealthy men commuted from New York City to the end of Long Island, but his trips were not for pleasure. He went to wartime England to correlate the financing and supply of the allies as far as these were carried on in the United States. In February 1916 he was in London and then in Paris, discussing supply matters with British and French leaders and Stettinius, and talking with the French about a $200,000,000 loan to bolster the economic condition of the Paris government, as old Junius had done once before in time of crisis.

Jack was not totally concerned with the war, for it was not America's war. As a defender of England he was concerned with the allied victory and war effort, but it was not the same as if his own country was involved. He had plenty of time for business as usual, when he was in New York. He undertook that year to finance the Interborough Rapid Transit Company subway system in New York City. The Morgan firm received a payment of $500,-000 from the Interborough for its financial advice. In the spring Jack sold a part of the art collection of his father, to the outrage of the professional staff of the Metropolitan Museum, who had hoped to have it. Bronzes, Limoges enamels, and majolica pieces went to Duveen Brothers, the art dealers. No one believed it, but as Morgan librarian Belle da Costa Greene said when she was asked why the art treasures were sold, "It seems that we need the money." Money was needed in the banking business if Jack Morgan was to occupy his father's position as head of the firm.

In 1916 Jack expanded the firm's war financing, and began discussions with the Canadian government that would lead to issuance of bonds to be sold in the United States. More than $500,000,000 in gold was shipped to the United States from Britain that year to purchase supplies. The Morgans bought guns, ammunition, trucks, locomotives, railroad rails, cotton uniforms, and woolen goods. It was a drastic change, with Britain importing for her war effort those exact manufactured items that the Morgans had handled for the Americans in years past. The House of Morgan also purchased three thousand railroad cars and fifty locomotives for the Russian government that year.

All this activity on behalf of the allies brought Jack into constant danger. A plot against his life by a man named H. L. Newton was revealed in April 1916, and the number of police guards around his home and office was increased. It was unpleasant living in such a goldfish bowl and yachting helped decrease that feeling of tension. Jack Morgan became a more enthusiastic yachtsman than his father, if that was possible, as well as an ardent sailor of smaller craft.

Jack was asked in the autumn of 1916 to become a trustee of the Cathedral of St. John the Divine, a post his father had filled for many years, and in which Pierpont had raised large sums of money for the church. Jack had neither the time nor the inclination to become so deeply involved in church affairs as had Pierpont, and he declined the honor. He was busier and busier. The trips to Europe continued, but the sailing dates showed how far they were from pleasure trips: he sailed on one such voyage on October 1, and returned on October 24. Estimating almost two weeks at sea, he had spent less than a fortnight in England on the trip, and nearly all that in consultation with British officials about the next in a continuing series of loans.

Jack also suffered in these years from the suspicious attentions of courts and legislative committees on state and federal levels. The suit of the United States government to dissolve the United States Steel Corporation had not been ended. The government lost in the lower courts but appealed. The case was delayed by the war and by legal maneuvers. Jack was called to testify before the New York legislative committee investigating corruption in the building and operation of the subway lines; he was called as a defendant in a suit brought to prevent merger of the New York Central and Lake Shore railroad lines of the Vanderbilt empire. Early in 1917 he was subpoenaed by a committee of the United States House of Representatives regarding leaks of information relative to the United States defense effort.

Notwithstanding all this harassment, he found time to consider the less material needs of the communities in which he lived and with his family was associated. Jack gave $150,000 to Trinity College in Hartford, to which his father had donated. He gave porcelains and paintings and other art works to the Wadsworth Athenaeum in Hartford, plus $50,000 to endow the collection for its upkeep. He gave some three thousand art objects, which represented the bulk of the art collection that was left over, to the Metropolitan Museum.

Jack Morgan had ordered a new yacht from the Herreshoff boat-building firm, and in July 1917 it was delivered. She was called the *Navette* and he was to spend many happy hours aboard her. In the winter of 1918 he was elected Commodore of the New York Yacht Club.

A few months before, when the United States entered the war, Jack had been freed, personally, of the responsibility of carrying the British and French purchasing loads in the United States. A special war purchasing group was organized and Stettinius went to Washington to operate it. This left Jack free to concern himself with the financing of the United States war effort, through the Liberty Loans, and the continued financing of Canada, France, and Britain. He also financed Russia, until her armies were defeated by the Germans on the eastern front and by corruption at home. She signed a separate peace with Germany, became a revolutionary state, and withdrew from the civilized society of the gold standard countries.

During the United States participation in World War I the government did not call on Jack Morgan personally for services, although the firm was used and several Morgan partners found their way into war work. There was a good reason for this passing over of the head of the firm, and that lay in his name. The Wilson administration was extremely careful not to ally itself with any taint of "bloated capitalism," and among the revolutionaries of the world there was no more bloated capitalist than J. P. Morgan. Half a century earlier the favorite whipping boy of the world press had been John Bull. Now it was a figure that dominated the world, and they called it J. P. Morgan. In a way the hatemongers were prophetic, for Jack would come forth in the ashes of World War I to do more for the people of Europe than any other American save Herbert Hoover. Hoover, as head of the American relief program, would bring food and fight starvation. Jack Morgan would lead an attempt to put Europe on its feet again, financially, even as his government moved as far away from world affairs as it was possible for a government to go.

CHAPTER

IV

THE CRASH

THE HOUSE OF MORGAN's war effort was successfully concealed from the unsympathetic world by the Wilson administration, but it was more difficult and eventually impossible to conceal the works of the Morgan partners when the war ended. During the war Henry Davison served as head of the Red Cross, which operated canteens and did everything in World War I that it did in World War II, plus serving as the United Service Organization of the day. Davison raised $114,000,000 for the Red Cross in his first drive after the war began. Thomas Lamont went to London and Paris during the war, even though Wilson insisted that the "unofficial" nature be maintained to the point where the connection of a member of the House of Morgan was kept secret. Lamont might not have gone had not Jack Morgan suggested that he ought to serve the allied cause in any way, no matter what the politicians did.

Lamont served in Europe during the sensitive period when the war was ending and the pattern for the new peace was being drawn. He was in constant communication with the London, Paris, and New York offices of the Morgan partnership, so Jack Morgan, although snubbed from the councils by Wilson because of his name, knew what was occurring in the chanceries of Europe. Edward Grenfell, the Morgan partner in London, was far more privy to the councils of Britain than Morgan in New York; so was Harjes in the Paris office. In spite of the political differences between Morgan and Wilson, in spite of cultural and personality differences between them, Morgan might have helped Wilson in areas in which he faced troubles, and he would have helped in the tradition of his family, had he been so allowed. But it was not allowed. In the spring of 1919 when Wilson returned to America after participating in the Versailles peace conference, which drew the treaty and the plan for the League of Nations, Morgan noted that there was trouble, in a cable to Lamont in Europe:

"Politics is the most awful mess I have ever known it. Congress passed the bond bill fortunately (a delayed loan that was needed desperately to finance the end of the war effort) but declined to pass the railroad financing bill, Army and Navy appropriations bills and various other essential measures. By this act they imperil the financial future of the Government for no purpose as far as anyone can see except to snap at the President. Latter has on the whole done badly since his return, because he has not been intelligent in his answers to criticisms on League of Nations plan, and he has not put it forward in anything like as favorable light as it deserves. Financial conditions are overshadowed by political ones."

So Morgan indicated where he stood. He was not unsympathetic to Wilson. He was most sympathetic to the plan for a League of Nations—he was, naturally, an internationalist at a time when America was preparing to become isolationist.

Jack confined his efforts, as always, to financial affairs and financial management, and remained well away from the political scene in the tradition of the Morgans. In his own way he tried to help the President: he made statements publicly to the effect that the peace treaty must be ratified in the interests of world business and world security. This was widely interpreted in the United States as a J. P. Morgan and Company bid for more business, and for control of the world's banking. These were days in which no

Morgan could do right in the public eye. When there was a leak to the press about the contents of the peace treaty before it was released, Jack Morgan was subpoenaed to testify before a United States Senate committee as to his part in it. He had never seen a copy of the treaty before publication.

Jack was insulted in these years, abused by politicians, and threatened by bomb throwers and bomb mailers. One day just before the war's end a man tried to force his way into the Wall Street office to get to J. P. Morgan. He was captured, arrested, and taken to Bellevue Hospital. After the armistice, on May Day, someone, probably an anarchist or communist, sent J. P. Morgan a bomb. (He also sent bombs to scores of other leaders.) Fortunately they were intercepted and disarmed. A month later a man who had tried to blackmail J. P. Morgan was convicted and sentenced to prison.

Faced with this attention, it is a wonder that Jack Morgan did not retire entirely from the eyes of the American public. Had he wished to do so, there was no reason for him not to. He might have moved to England, carrying on his business from the other side of the Atlantic as his grandfather had done. He did not do so; he preferred to remain in America and fight the battle.

It was a battle and it was to be almost a never-ending one for J. P. Morgan, Jr., because the United States was moving rapidly away from the kind of world that his father had brought him into and the kind of world in which he had grown up.

Only in the international and world financial senses could later generations adjudge Jack Morgan a progressive; or perhaps the more sensible way to have put it was that what he stood for was conservative rational finance at a time when very few others did so, and the United States government least of all. In other matters, J. P. Morgan was a capitalist of the old school, determined that capital should have its way and bound to protect the rights of property. In the eyes of the capitalists of America the first great postwar threat against property was the movement of the labor unions to organize the large industries of the land. Jack Morgan and United States Steel led other employees in refusing to recognize labor unions as bargaining agents of their employees. They were protecting the American principles of liberty—or so they said.

The year 1919 was a boom year for Wall Street, and insofar as Jack and his partners were dealers in securities they prospered from this boom. United States Steel Corporation stock rose from 90 to 104½ as Jack and the others resisted the demands of labor and the International Mercantile Marine, that sick company of the past, rose from 23 to 47.

When the war in Europe ended, the changeover of the financial headquarters of the world was complete. Britain and France—the only two European nations to come out of the war not totally wrecked financially—now had to yield the honors to the United States, the great creditor nation of World War I. And among all the important banks and private banking houses in America the leading house was the House of Morgan. Jack Morgan was half estranged from his own people, not quite understanding the motivations that brought about the demands for change that rang in his ears. He regarded himself as every bit as interested in the future of America as had been his father and the forebears who went back to the days of the *Mayflower*.

During the war years Jack Morgan and his associates had sold nearly $2,000,000,000 worth of bonds in the United States for the allied nations. The United States government during the war had lent another $7,500,000,000 abroad, and Morgan and other bankers had subscribed to and sold another $1,500,000,000 in foreign securities during the last two years.

The end of the war saw the organization of a number of new banking alliances in America to extend American influence abroad. Most important of these was the Foreign Finance Corporation, which was established by the Morgan company and three banks which it controlled: the Guaranty Trust, Bankers Trust, and National Bank of Commerce, plus the First National Bank, the National City Bank, the Chase National Bank. Arthur M. Anderson, a Morgan partner, was president of the Foreign Finance Corporation, and Jack was a member of the board. The purpose of this organization was to multiply the strength of the various banks and groups in order to hold together a syndicate for foreign banking. National City and Chase became the two huge overseas banks, dealing mostly in market expansion for American goods. The Morgans continued to concern themselves with government finance and investment in American securities, a direction they had followed since the days when Junius went to London as George Peabody's partner.

The Morgan bank took a vital interest in affairs in Mexico, where Thomas Lamont was chairman of a twenty-man banking commission established to oversee the interests of foreign investors. The Morgan firm was active in the banking of China. J. P. Morgan and Company became the fiscal agents of the Belgian government in 1919. The House of Morgan headed a syndicate in that same year that floated a Canadian loan of $75,000,000 in bonds which were sold to Americans and others.

There was a considerable difference between the manner in which Jack Morgan ran the firm and the way Pierpont had governed it. As with Pierpont, Jack owned more of the firm—as a partner—than anyone else. It was said that he held a quarter of it himself. That did not represent power, but in a large partnership—sometimes twenty partners—it would be most difficult for anyone to maintain a majority interest, liability, and share in the profits. The control of the partnership, with Jack as with Pierpont, rested in the partnership agreement, which gave him the veto power over investments and activities. But where Pierpont Morgan was an energetic and important figure as an individual, Jack Morgan was an organizer and an executive. He deputed, not just the detail as had his father, but the decisions of the lower orders of business to his partners. He retained policy control, but not nearly so much operating control as his father had held in his strongest days. Partly this was a result of his father's manner of relinquishing control; as it had worked out, George Perkins had been closest to his father for a time, and then Henry Davison had been the most powerful figure in the partnership. The difference was largely a matter of historic change. Pierpont's way of doing business would probably have changed too, had he faced the new situation of being the most important banker in the most important banking nation in the world.

Another difference between the J. P. Morgans, and not so happy a one, was that Pierpont swam with his times, leading the crowd during most of his life and seldom in real conflict with the social wave of the period. Only at the last, when the forces of the common man and egalitarianism began to rise against the forces of property, did Pierpont encounter the kind of difficulty that Jack was to face all his life. Jack swam against the stream. Ironically the House of Morgan achieved its greatest economic power in these coming years when as a force it was out of step with the society in which it existed.

In 1919 and 1920 the House of Morgan exerted the greatest influence of its existence on American foreign policy, by request of the State Department. Specifically the influence was in the affairs of Asia, and particularly of China and Japan.

The problem into which the House of Morgan was drawn grew out of the extraterritorialism of European nations in China. During the last years of the nineteenth century the Western powers and Japan had split China into zones of influence. The British had taken control of most of the rich Yangtze Valley and the south, near Hongkong. The Germans had established the colony of Kiaochow in Shantung province. France had moved into Yunnan province and the southern area that abutted her Indo-China possessions. Russia controlled the Liaotung peninsula. Japan controlled southern Manchuria. Just before the end of the first decade of the twentieth century the various powers began to run afoul of one another in their extensions of transportation and commercial enterprise, and realizing that if they did not work out their difficulties they would soon butt heads, they established what was called the Chinese Consortium, which was to be a council in which important economic moves were to be decided jointly before they were made—in the interest of everyone but the Chinese.

The United States had deliberated the possibility of joining in the rape of China through extraterritorialism and had decided against this move when Secretary of State John Hay developed the Open Door policy of free trade in China. When this Consortium was established, in the interest of American trade it was essential that the United States be represented, and President Taft so told the Consortium powers, so the United States joined the group. In 1909 the American representative was Henry P. Davison of the Morgan bank, representing an American banking syndicate composed of the Morgan firm, Kuhn Loeb and Company, the National City Bank and the First National Bank of New York City. The first move of the Consortium was to float a bond issue to finance the building of the Hukuang railroad, which would connect Chungking in Szechuan province in the far west of China with Hankow in central China and with Canton in the far south. The bonds were sold, a quarter of them in the United States. In 1913 under President Wilson and Secretary of State Bryan, United States foreign policy was essentially isolationist, and the American bankers were informed that they could no longer look upon themselves as semi-official representatives of the American government. Bryan and Wilson wanted no part of the Consortium.

In 1916 that policy was changed, partly because it became apparent with the Japanese conquest of Shantung province that Japan was moving to take over control of China. For the long run, prevention of Japanese control of China was more important to the United States than any event in Europe, and it transcended even the isolationism of the American government. This was seen by Robert Lansing, Wilson's second Secretary of State, where it had not been seen by Bryan, and the American participation in the banking Consortium was again encouraged with promises of full diplomatic support. Jack Morgan then selected Thomas Lamont to represent his company, and some forty other banking institutions in the United States which agreed to participate in the financing of Chinese improvements. Lamont met with other members of the Consortium in Paris during the peace talks, and the next year he traveled to Japan to try to reach some accord with the Tokyo government on the serious questions of Japanese expansion in Asia. Japan had been a member of the old Consortium. Now she seemed reluctant to rejoin, holding out for special concessions. She won them, and the Consortium was re-established, to continue until the Franklin Roosevelt administration changed the banking laws early in the 1930's, to effectively remove American banks from the field of international finance by prohibiting them from underwriting bond issues.

The year 1920 was a most active one for Jack Morgan and his banking house. That year he joined with Pierre S. Du Pont of the powder and chemical firm, to take control of the General Motors Corporation. A dozen years earlier W. C. Durant had sought participation by the Morgans in a banking combine to raise $1,500,-000 which would be used to consolidate a number of small motor car companies and parts companies into Durant's dream: General Motors. The Morgans had not participated, largely because Durant was an unprepossessing and wild figure. They did not care for his character. Now, Durant was forced to sell out and Morgan bought. His interest in motor car companies was thoroughly aroused with the tremendous success of Ford, and he traveled to England to study the Slough motor works there, which Henry Ford was interested in purchasing if it could be financed through the Morgan bank. But all the way, Jack was forced to defend his financial operations in a manner that Pierpont would have considered to be ridiculous. When the International Trading Corporation was established, by the Morgan bank and the Guaranty Trust Company, Henry P. Davison felt impelled to make a public statement, denying that Jack Morgan was trying to create a world trading corporation to dominate the business world.

Jack took certain public actions in 1920, moved by a spirit of public service and perhaps by some hope of making peace with the American political community. He offered the house at Prince's Gate to the United States government to become the United States embassy since a new embassy was needed, and Jack now found it sensible to divest himself of this expensive property. There was, strangely enough, considerable opposition in Congress to acceptance of the gift, and when it was accepted by Congressional vote, the action was taken in so slovenly a manner that it appeared to be in bad taste, for it took nearly a year to persuade the United States government that it should take this well-located property.

The radicals were still up to their violent tricks. They exploded a bomb outside the Morgan bank on September 17, 1920, just at the busy luncheon hour, killing some twenty people and raising the fear of all the workers in Wall Street. None of the Morgan partners was killed or injured, except Junius S. Morgan, Jr., Jack's eldest son, who was slightly cut by glass sent flying through the building when the bomb burst outside. Still he kept a luncheon appointment. The Morgan offices were closed for the remainder of the day of the tragedy, as were many other Wall Street firms. Jack Morgan flatly refused to discuss the explosion with the press, which was his right, but his reticence intensified the animosity with which they treated him.

As Commodore of the New York Yacht Club in 1920, Jack Morgan enjoyed himself as his father had in years before, and in his flagship, *Corsair,* he led the annual outing of the club up Long Island Sound.

In a sense, although the years of Jack Morgan's power in J. P. Morgan and Company were years of economic growth for the banking firm, they were years of retrenchment. After passage of the Clayton Antitrust Act in 1914, Jack Morgan's connection with various other banks was strictly limited. Private bankers were forbidden to serve on the boards of directors of national banks. Therefore, in 1914 Jack withdrew as a director of the National City Bank and of the National Bank of Commerce. In order to avoid charges of "interlocking directorates" he resigned from eighteen directorates, and his partners also resigned from another dozen. This still left the partnership with some thirty-three directorates in various companies whose operations were of vital interest to the banking firm.

As times changed, so did the Morgan interests. The New Haven debacle was a reflection of the overcapitalization of railroads but it was not unique. Railroads were troubled by government regulation ever after World War I, when they were seized in the national interest by the government. The railway labor act, which established grievance proceedings and saddled the railroads with the burden of government influence—and with none of the benefits of government operation—created serious problems for railroad management and made of railroads a growingly thankless investment. In 1921 Jack resigned as a director of the Northern Pacific Railroad, ending a long association begun by his father. This year as always, he was buttonholed by the press, harried by unwanted visitors, threatened by radicals, and he was picketed at home by a lady named Rebecca Dobson who wanted to convince him that lawyers were evil. He was a target of every crackpot in America. Small wonder that he fled when he could during the proper seasons to Europe and to the *Corsair* for outings. One characteristic of Jack Morgan's yachting expeditions is that they were more venturesome than most of his father's. Pierpont had been content to be aboard his yacht, in the open air, away from the office. Jack liked to go places: to the Caribbean, up the Maine Coast, south along the Atlantic coast, to Europe, and threading through the Mediterranean. He spent many happy weeks in such excursions.

The early 1920's were good years for the Morgan firm, although 1921 in particular was a disastrous year in Wall Street for others and for the farming community, especially in the West. The price of wheat fell disastrously, the crop was overplanted, and thousands of ranchers and farmers went broke that year. What happened to the wheat farmers also happened to the beef ranchers and the sheep ranchers; farm mortgages became a glut on the market and the grass grew tall in the ruts of the market roads.

In 1921 Jack and his company issued bonds successfully for the Burlington line, and for General Motors, and they floated a large French government bond issue in the United States. As members of the Consortium, they also backed and sold a Chinese bond issue: this was the purpose of the Consortium, with affairs so confused in China the backing of the representatives of European, Japanese, and American governments was essential to provide the financial stability that would attract investors. This was profitable business for the bankers, and in the next few years for several reasons the House of Morgan turned to international finance. Through Morgan, Harjes of Paris the house financed the Polish and Rumanian governments. Through New York they financed the Cuban government and the Austrian government in 1922 and 1923. In 1924 they loaned $100,000,000 to the Bank of France, and provided money for Japan. They loaned so much money, selling bonds, to so many countries and important business firms that those who borrowed through them were sometimes attacked, as was Premier Herriot of France, for using the House of Morgan. The attack was based on the charge that by selling bonds through that house the French government was actually placing itself under Morganization (the term was still used), or Morgan control.

There were pitfalls and dangers in international finance, and as the years rolled along the Morgans fell afoul of several of them. No banking house could be intimately engaged in the financing of governments without taking a strong interest in the affairs of these governments—simply as a matter of self-protection. The Morgans loaned money to Cuba, and when Cuba's legislature threatened to pass tax measures that would discriminate against Americans the Morgan bank sent a representative to Havana to complain. The Cuban government changed it policy, whereupon the anti-imperialists in the world shouted that Morgan capitalism was running the world, or at least trying to run it.

Another type of problem, inescapable for the international banker, was the decision to finance a government that was not totally popular in the world. Such was the Italian Fascist government of Benito Mussolini. In 1925 Thomas Lamont spent some time with Benito Mussolini and his finance minister, Count Volpi, and then recommended to Jack Morgan that the firm undertake the sale of $100,000,000 in bonds plus another $50,000,000 in loans. The bank formed a syndicate, taking $250,000 for managing it and lending the bank's prestige to negotiating the sale of the bonds. Also, the profit margin for the syndicate was $4,500,000, which made this a very expensive loan for Benito Mussolini to obtain from any source. It was not unusual, however, for the Morgan bank to charge high rates for its services, no more so than for other banks. All the countries of Europe needed money in this period, and the bankers profited from that need. The British government borrowed money from the United States, from the federal reserve and from the Morgan bank, through a bond sale. The charge was 2½ per cent for the private monies, which was regarded as high, but money was hard to come by.

The most highly publicized banking operation undertaken by

the House of Morgan in the years between the two great wars was the loan made to Germany for reconstruction under the Dawes Plan. This was an outcome of the paralysis of the German economy in the early 1920's. In 1923 when the German inflation had become ruinous President Coolidge announced the appointment of a commision to investigate German finances and the means of curing the financial illness of the defeated enemy. A three-man committee was appointed and it made its investigation in the next few months.

In the spring of 1924 the commission proposed the Dawes Plan, named for Charles G. Dawes, a member of the commission. The object was to stabilize the German currency by reorganizing the Reichsbank under allied supervision, to establish a new schedule of payments for the reparations due the allies—the exacting of which had caused the financial disaster—and the support of this program by a huge loan to Germany from her old enemies. Of this 800,000,000 gold mark loan, the United States was to take $110,-000,000, and this was handled by a group of bankers headed by Jack Morgan. One aspect of the Dawes Plan commitment was the operation of the German railroads, which was placed under control of an American commission. Through Morgan, Harjes of Paris, the expert railroad management firm was placed close to this problem.

So they were busy years. Jack enjoyed himself in a fashion made famous earlier by his father—but only during his father's last years of life. Pierpont was born an American of middle class, he attended public schools as well as private schools, and although his father was a wealthy man, the young Morgan did not live in extreme luxury, and wrote in early life about having to make his own way.

There was never any question in Jack Morgan's mind about having to make his own way. His father believed in work, and he was brought up to respect work for its own sake; his children learned to work, and were expected to do so. Yet from an early age Jack Morgan's friends and consorts were the royalty of England and the very wealthy, quiet families of New York. His pleasures were in shooting grouse in Scotland, and in yachting and in all the activities attendant to sailboats and their racing. He owned a racing yacht called *Phryne* and a Q class sloop called *Grayling*. He sailed in yacht club races and in other regattas. He participated in the America's Cup defenses, as a member of a syndicate or on the committee. When the Prince of Wales, who would become Edward VIII, visited the United States, it was said that he became a guest of the Morgans at their home.

When Jack was in England in the autumn, quite naturally he went shooting with the royal family. This was the way he lived; he was born to it and it suited him admirably. It also made many enemies for him of men and women he had never met nor even considered, because he never learned that in the United States one price the public figure must always pay is collected in emotional currency: he must appear to be humble, and the wealthier and more important he is in the American scene, the more necessary it is that he pay lip service to the democratic ideals of equality. If he fails to enunciate his adherence to the ideal or to enunciate it loudly enough, he becomes hated as a poseur.

Jack Morgan was the largest taxpayer in Glen Cove, for example, and he continually believed that he was being taxed unfairly, and yet for nearly twenty years he was unable to secure any satisfaction from the taxing authorities, and when he complained his complaints aroused hoots from the readers of the newspapers. In spite of this he was a good citizen of Glen Cove, he supported the Episcopal church there, and sometimes attended the diocesan convention. He gave Glen Cove a public park; and he built a new summer home there in 1927.

The 1920's were sad years for Jack Morgan in a way. In 1924 his mother died, and after a funeral at Highland Falls, which she really regarded as her home, she was buried next to Pierpont at Hartford's Cedar Hill Cemetery. In 1925 Jessie contracted sleeping sickness and died two months later.

The years were happy in another way. Junius, his eldest son, was becoming quickly adapted to the business after entering it as a partner in 1920. Before he had become a partner, Junius was elected a director of the Liberty National Bank. In 1925 he became a member of the board of General Motors Corporation, and three years later of the board of directors of United States Steel Corporation. Jack's second son, Henry Sturgis Morgan, became a partner in 1929. Junius also took over some of the public chores of the family and the firm. He presented a pension to Dr. S. French one night in 1926, honoring the doctor's twenty-five years of service with the White Star Line, a part of the International Mercantile Marine combine. Unfortunately that combination was due for failure at last—another of Pierpont's dreams which did not come true. In the spring of 1926 Jack Morgan resigned as a director, which was the end of the line for the House of Morgan in that business.

So the 1920's passed with the House of Morgan at a financial zenith now, although not nearly so important in American public affairs and not nearly so much respected as Pierpont had made the firm in the last days of the nineteenth century. Respect and admiration were the keys to the public attitude toward the Morgan house of Pierpont's day; awe was a more descriptive word for the public attitude toward the Morgans in this new postwar world—awe and distrust of great wealth.

In these years the last physical properties of Pierpont Morgan changed hands. Much of the estate on the Hudson River was sold in 1928, and two years later Cragston became a yacht club and country club. The venture failed and it went into the hands of real estate developers. Finally the old house burned.

In 1929 Jack offered the *Corsair* to the government but there was some reluctance about acceptance of a gift that cost $100,000 a year in maintenance. Eventually she was accepted, and became a government ship, renamed *Oceanographer*.

Jack began to buy a few art treasures of his own. He bought a Tintoretto painting and he bought additional manuscripts for the library. He traveled more abroad, sometimes on business, sometimes on pleasure, and in 1929 he attended the Reparations Conference, working out with Dr. Owen Young the Young Plan, forcing through a rescheduling of German reparations payments to make them run another sixty years. Jack was doing for nations now what Pierpont had done for railroads. With a firm and lavish hand he was recapitalizing national debts—a remarkable undertaking, although one not totally appreciated for its finesse by the public at that time. Herbert Hoover appreciated it and when Jack returned from Paris he gave public praise to the banker for his work. It was a brave motion for a politician to make in the twentieth century.

As 1907 was a high point in the career of Pierpont Morgan, so 1929 might have been a high point in that of his son and namesake. Praised by the President for his work at the Reparations Conference, Jack returned home, urging support for the International Bank that had been suggested by European nations to stop the depression that was distressing Europe. He received an honorary degree from Princeton University. He was building a new yacht, said to be the largest and most expensive in the history of steam yachting. He gave $2,000,000 worth of real estate to New York Hospital. He gave $2,000,000 to the Lying-In Hospital, his father's old charity. All this before the autumn of this profitable, bustling year.

Jack returned that spring to a United States that seemed to be running on a continuous belt of prosperity, but as John Kenneth Galbraith has pointed out it was not that at all—the economy was headed straight for disaster:

First, income was being distributed improperly. Jack Morgan and his partners were earning millions of dollars each year. Workers were producing more but not getting more money, largely because of policies followed by the bankers and industrialists. Income taxes for those in the upper brackets were very light, and in 1929 the upper 5 per cent of the people in terms of income received a third of all the personal income earned during the year.

Second, because of the efforts of Jack Morgan and his acquaintances in the banking business, the United States had become the world's leading creditor nation. In 1927 Jack Morgan's bank floated more bond issues than any other house in the country; he was the undisputed leader in the field of foreign finance. As creditor the United States must buy heavily abroad. Failure to import goods would cause the other nations to fall into depression;

they would not be able to pay their debts to America and American business would suffer.

Third, the economy was being manipulated by the owners of corporations through pyramids of holding companies. The Morgans were deeply involved in this; one might say that Pierpont was of the original holding company operators. His reason for having interest in this form of financial operation was maintenance of control; it was possible through holding company operations to control a $100,000,000 company with an investment of about a quarter of that amount, and this holding company if it had a total investment of $25,000,000 could be controlled by another holding company with an investment of a quarter of that amount, and this could in turn be controlled by a company with a quarter of that amount. There were a number of these complicated pyramids, including the railroad holding company empire of the Van Sweringen brothers, in which the Morgans were involved. These holding companies were perfectly sound, just as long as the company at the base was earning profits—for it was the only producing company and all the rest were financial paper houses, representing what Galbraith termed "thimble-rigging," after the old game of shells or thimbles showing the little ball—now you see it, now you don't.

Another weakness lay in the stock market boom, which had been cresting until the spring of 1929. Then there had been some bad days and some people had become cautious and retired from the market. Some but not many. The speculators were in control and they were booming the prices of stocks ever upward. Radio Corporation of America, which had not yet paid a dividend, went to 573 that summer.

This was how matters stood in the fall of 1929. The Morgans were really above the market, as usual. In September the market faltered and some more people were forced out. But again not many. Then, in the week of October 21, the storm began.

On Monday, October 21, trading was fairly heavy and there were some losses, but no one seemed to be worried. On Tuesday, October 22, the losses seemed to be regained, until the last hour of trading, when the losses began again. On Wednesday the fright set in and the tape ran an hour and forty-four minutes behind the trading when the exchange closed at three o'clock. On Thursday, October 24, a block of twenty thousand shares of General Motors was offered first thing in the morning—a very large amount of stock, and similar amounts of other stocks were put up for sale. As the huge sell orders came in, the prices dropped. United States Steel opened at 205½ and soon dropped to 193½.

Many factors combined to bring about panic, not the least of which was the communications failure of the ticker tape machines, which gave only the last digit and fraction of a stock's performance: it might have dropped from 156½ to 83¼ and all the ticker would show was 6½ to 3¼.

But the reasons for the panic were something that could be gone into at leisure, and would be over many years. The problem was to try to stop it.

Shortly after noon on Thursday a group of bankers slipped into the offices of J. P. Morgan and Company to talk about the panic in the market, for they realized that they were facing panic. One of them was Charles E. Mitchell, president of the National City Bank. Another was George F. Baker, Jr. Also, there came Albert H. Wiggin, president of the Chase National Bank, William Potter, president of the Guaranty Trust Company, and Seward Prosser of the Bankers Trust Company. They came, not to see J. P. Morgan, Jr., alas, but to see Thomas Lamont, the most senior of the partners other than Morgan.

It was a situation reminiscent of 1907, but the actions were not the same, just as the actors were not.

After a few moments of conversation the bankers agreed to put up $40,000,000 each to create a pool and save the stock market. They sent word of the commitment to Richard Whitney, vice-president of the Exchange and head of a brokerage house with which the Morgan bank did much business. Whitney went to the place where U. S. Steel was sold especially, which was symbolic enough for a Morgan broker, and bought ten thousand shares of stock offering the last quoted price in each case. In a few minutes he bought some $20,000,000 worth of United States Steel stock and some twenty or thirty other strong stocks. It was about half-past one. In the next hour and a half the market steadied, and steel and some other stocks actually closed at prices higher than they had closed the day before.

So, the banker's pool had resolved the problem for the moment. Next, of course, was the problem of facing the second step, and one might have expected that there would have been meetings held far into the night, with locked door sessions in the west room of the Morgan Library. Not so. The bankers shored up the pool but did not plan any heroic measures. The next day, October 25, they continued the shoring up, and many in the market thought the bankers were in to see it through and hold the Stock Exchange together. They could not have been more wrong. The purpose of the bankers in this case was not the purpose of Pierpont Morgan in 1907. The bankers were together holding the market steady so they could get out themselves and get their clients out without disaster. By the weekend they were out of the market. They met on Monday, October 28, when stocks plummeted further and faster, but they did nothing to halt the debacle.

It is not the purpose here to blame the stock market crash of 1929 on Jack Morgan or any other banker or coalition and bankers. The blame for the crash has been fixed on many persons, depending on point of view. It is certain, however, that J. P. Morgan, Junior, did not behave in 1929 as J. P. Morgan, Senior, behaved in 1907, and really, with all that had happened in his world, why would anyone have expected him to do so? The stock market crash was just the beginning of it, as it turned out, but by the time it ended in the first week of November, the banks were beginning to feel the pinch—and then it was too late to shore up the economy. The House of Morgan really did not try. Its concern was its own investments and its clients. Although 1929 is considered the year of prime disaster in America, as far as the Morgan bank was concerned it was not a disaster at all. When the United States Senate Committee on Banking and Currency began investigating the profits and commissions and operations of the House of Morgan some months later, it was discovered that the partners paid an income tax of around $11,000,000 that year, and the net worth of J. P. Morgan and Company and of Drexel and Company had been increased during the year by more than $27,000,000. Senator Aldrich had been correct. There would not always be a Pierpont Morgan to shore up the American marketplace.

CHAPTER

V

CHANGING TIMES

AFTER THE CRASH of 1929 Jack Morgan was the subject of very unpleasant publicity in the United States. Much of the reason for this was in the times. While men were selling apples in the streets of New York City, he was launching the largest private yacht in the world, the new *Corsair*, which cost $2,500,000 to build and equip. While men were losing everything they owned, he was arguing with the officials of Glen Cove because his house and estate were valued at $1,121,000 for the purposes of taxation. Yet the Morgans had lost too. On November 31, 1929, the net worth of the partnership was $118,000,000. Three years later the net worth was $53,000,000.

Few people knew exactly how deeply involved in the American economy the House of Morgan had become, but the involvement was so deep that a little thought would make anyone realize that no matter how well the House of Morgan came out of the Wall Street crash, its future lay in the recovery of the American investment market. Unless there were investors, unless there was production, there would be no need for bankers, and the economic power that the Morgans exercised because they were *American* bankers would soon be lost. The Morgans had organized United States

379

Steel. They were involved from the beginning in General Electric. They had acquired, with the DuPonts, control of General Motors. They had created Standard Brands from a number of food companies. They had created United Corporation, a public utility holding company. For the short term, the Morgans might prosper even in the disaster of others as they had in the year 1929. For the long term, continued disaster would mean either a revolutionary change in the American system of government and economy, in which they might lose all, including their lives, as Russian and French aristocrats had lost theirs during similar troubles elsewhere, or chaos and the resultant loss of the Morgan position in world banking.

Neither the Morgans nor any other bankers were prepared, however, for the changes that were to be brought into the American economy under the Roosevelt administration. The voice of Samuel Untermyer was yet being heard in the land, and in 1933 he continued to believe that the bankers were responsible for the problems of America. He referred to the "disastrous hegemony" of industry and finance, and if that were not enough he added that J. P. Morgan and Company were responsible for all America's problems, especially the American entrance into World War I. Now that Teddy Roosevelt was dead, there were few who would argue with him.

The Morgans and the other big bankers and brokers of America were now beset by government. When the Democratic administration of Franklin Delano Roosevelt came into power in 1933, the action to control the bankers began. First there was another hearing, of the same general nature of the Pujo Committee hearings of so long before. This time, however, the United States Senate committee was certain that there were serious wrongs to be righted, and there was no stopping the investigators, or turning them away with strong moral position, as Pierpont had been at least partly able to do in the year 1912. The investigation began with a series of questions from the subcommittee about the financial activities of the Morgan firm. The partners protested that eight of the twenty-three questions concerned private matters into which the Senate committee had no right to pry. The Senate committee did not listen very seriously to this complaint. Jack Morgan and ten of his partners were subpoenaed to appear before the committee in the spring of 1933. When they appeared they were subjected to harsh and not always polite questioning. When it came out in the press that Jack Morgan had paid *no* American income taxes in the years 1931 and 1932, the public was not prepared to consider the fact that the Morgan losses in stocks had been huge. Here was a man who represented to the American people all that was meaningful in power and wealth, a man who led the American banking system, and in the time of the people's crisis this man paid no income taxes. Rightly or wrongly this publicity was disastrous to any hopes the Morgans and their allies might have had at this late date that business reason prevail over the demand for political control of the American financial marketplace. The fact was that the lower echelon of American money earners had been overexploited in terms of the production of the individual and the earning power of money. There would be a swing of the pendulum.

When the swing came, first in the Glass-Steagall Act of 1933 and later in subsequent legislation, it brought an end to the House of Morgan as it had been constituted. The Morgan partners had remained in Washington for a long time, trying to protect their interests, spending $2,000 a day in hotel rooms—a figure the press liked to flaunt about. The hearings of 1933 were not dissimilar in scope and content to those of 1907; there had been few major changes in the American financial system except that it had grown larger and more difficult for government to control the financiers with the old laws. There was one difference: a smart press agent somehow persuaded J. P. Morgan, Jr., that he needed some good publicity and the proud banker posed for a picture with a circus midget on his knee. Could anyone consider old Pierpont doing that? It was symbolic of the basic misunderstanding of Jack Morgan and his associates of the changes that were being introduced into American life that he might be persuaded that allowing himself to be made to look the fool would solve any problem or create any climate of good will toward him and his way of life and business.

The change in attitude of those in control of the government at that time was expressed later in a speech before the Bond Club of New York by William O. Douglas, who along with the Senate Committee and Ferdinand Pecora, its counsel, was to revolutionize the system of American finance.

As one probes into the background of particular business failures, he finds reflected in them practices and policies which have preceded the collapse of many enterprises. He finds practices designed to siphon the money both from investors and from business. He sees that high finance has piled holding companies on top of holding companies until investors whose money has been taken have no more than a piece of blue sky for their security. He sees market manipulations. Companies have been merged and consolidated for no sound business reason but only to create profits for high finance. The overhead and costs of finance have been placed on business merely to keep high finance prosperous. High finance has levied its toll by taking watered stock and by unloading that watered stock on the public. The promoters pocket the proceeds. The company gets nothing for the stock it has issued. The public holds the bag.

"It would be an error to denounce all of finance in these terms. Finance occupies an important place in our society, whether its functions are performed by government or by private bankers. But finance moves into the zone of exploitation whenever it becomes the *master* rather than the faithful and loyal *servant* of investors and business. To make finance such a *servant* rather than a *master* becomes a central plank in any platform for reform."

In this brief statement, William O. Douglas outlined the history of American corporate finance from the days of Commodore Vanderbilt, the champion stock waterer, through the days of J. P. Morgan, Jr. There was the picture of Pierpont, the man who had done more than any other in American society to make finance the master of industry rather than the servant. Pierpont had done so because industry had created havoc by its own milking of the public and had left what must be destroyed or rebuilt through finance. Much of what had happened to America in 1929 and the 1930's could be traced back to beginnings in Pierpont's days, and a large share of this to policies and extensions of policies that he had invented. Because others were unwilling or unable to carry out the reforms, Pierpont began to carry them out himself, and the rest was history.

The reforms that came about through the Franklin Roosevelt administration's new policies were drastic. Many businessmen took the position that the Roosevelt administration had somehow turned against business. This was not Jack Morgan's view. He had felt that the politicians on both sides were opposed to business, fundamentally, and had been at least since the days of the Pujo investigation of 1912. He had said as much during the days of the Wilson administration. If he had not been right before, he was right in the 1930's, for the administration, backed by the vast majority of the American people, believed that business had gone too far and had become too powerful and had worked too hard for the profits of the few at the expense of the many.

In 1933 when the Senate Banking and Currency Committee began its fateful hearings on the financial situation, in a way these hearings were a continuation of the Pujo investigation. The law-makers wanted to see where the legislation covering operation of the financial community had broken down to allow the infla-tion and then the crash of 1929. In testifying before the com-mittee, the Morgans offered several statements which showed the extent of their operations.

Between the end of World War I and the spring of 1933 the Morgans had joined with syndicates of bankers to sell more than $6,000,000,000 worth of bonds and other securities. More than a third of this amount represented the bonds of foreign govern-ments. Not quite a third represented the bonds of various rail-roads. A million dollars, or about a sixth of the total, represented public utilities and public utility holding companies. The other sums were made up of industrial bonds and stocks, municipal bonds, and railroad holding company bonds.

The Morgan statements were not simply defensive (although they noted that the Morgan partners had paid some $51,000,000 in United States income taxes since 1917, and that the reason they did not pay income taxes in 1931 and 1932 is that they lost money; and they noted that although there was much talk about their stock operations, stock transactions made up only 3 per cent of the Morgan business). The Morgan partners offered their opinions on the trend of the United States, a note which would sound predictive and more palatable thirty years later than it did in 1933:

> The growth of corporate enterprise has been drying up individual independence and initiative, drying up the life of the big town and the small town and the hamlet. We are becoming a nation of hired men, hired by great aggregations of capital, theoretically controlled by absentee stockholders, who are, however, so numerous and whose individual interest is generally so small that their control is inarticulate and difficult to express. This corporate growth in large measure was inevitable and no doubt desirable. To attempt to reverse it would be like turning back the hands of the clock.
>
> But do we wish to go further and accelerate it? Not merely to grant charters and franchises and immunities and subsidies to corporations, but by law and regulation to stamp out private enterprise and private initiative, the activities of private business men and private bankers, who are ready and willing still, in spite of the subsidized competition of corporate enterprise, to stake their own time and attention to the management of their own businesses?

It was a hopeless fight. The Senate committee addressed itself to the image of the House of Morgan which had grown up over twenty years, the image of a huge spider sitting in the center of its web and manipulating the strings that pulled along the puppets of all American banking and business. It was shown in the hearings that the House of Morgan was represented by 167 directories, 89 corporations. It was indicated that the Morgans controlled in one way or another all the important banking in America, and almost all of big business. The charge was hysterical and ridiculous ($50,000,000 to control America?) but it stuck. This image in mind, the committee recommended and the Senate concurred in legislation that would make it impossible for any individual ever again to have the power or the functions that Junius, Pierpont, and Jack Morgan had exercised as private bankers to the world.

The new laws of the 1930's destroyed the old House of Morgan. The Glass-Steagall Act of 1933 divested all national banks and banks with Federal Reserve affiliation from the ownership or affiliation with brokerage houses. Investment bankers were forbidden to act as commercial bankers. This was the particular part of the law that changed the lives of the Morgans. It meant that the Morgan bank must either become a bank, accepting deposits and lending money directly, or it must become a house to underwrite and sell securities. It could not do both, nor could investment bankers serve on the board of directors of any commercial bank. There were other changes, regarding the issuance of securities, to protect the buyers from misrepresentation, dishonesty, or sharp dealing. As bankers, the Morgans were honest and honorable and their word could be trusted at any time. The change for them was to be the change of function.

After 1933 Jack Morgan took life easier. The days of the huge bank and the huge influence in world affairs had come suddenly to an end. Jack, the father, chose to remain in the banking business with J. P. Morgan and Company and to divest himself of further interest in the financial management of American business, for this is what the change really meant. He called on Franklin Roosevelt at the White House in 1933, but that was probably the last time. Then, symbolically, he went on vacation to the South. When he returned his world was changed and it would never be the same. The Morgan firm would hold its British and French affiliates, it would continue to be banker and protector of its clients, but it could not underwrite securities issues, and this cost the House of Morgan much prestige abroad and much control of investment.

J. P. Morgan, Jr., then, elected to remain with the firm that bore his and his father's name. So did his eldest son, Junius Spencer Morgan, Jr. Henry Sturgis Morgan, however, chose to strike out in the more venturesome part of the business, the part that Pierpont himself probably would have chosen had he been given such a choice. Old Junius certainly would have accepted this role, for it was much like the part of his own role which gave him most pleasure—the constructive use of the banking facility to build businesses. Taken back to Junius' times the illustration was simpler than in Jack's. Junius, for example, inherited from George Peabody the business of the infant McCormick Reaper Company insofar as that business was simply a service banking business for Junius in London. The McCormicks made frequent trips to Europe, and seemed constantly to be changing their dates of sailing and the hotel accommodations that they desired. Junius accepted their deposits and paid their bills, and submitted bills to them. He collected their accounts in England for such few reapers as were sold there. He was travel agent, bill collector, safe-deposit vault, and errand boy for the McCormick family and their employees. Then the business began to change. First came interest by others in McCormick patents, and McCormick's interest in securing those patents abroad. In the beginning of this development, Junius resisted the efforts of McCormick to push him into handling the patents. He referred McCormick to various patent attorneys and told him that these would know much more about the business than the J. S. Morgan firm. McCormick blithely disregarded all Junius' plaintive letters and continued to rely on Junius for all but the technical problems of patents. Eventually this led to the financing of the McCormick Reaper Company by the House of Morgan at home and abroad, still later to the combination of the McCormick Company and the Deering Company and others, and to a huge business for the House of Morgan in deposits, yes, but primarily in the sale of securities to finance the expansion of the companies that joined to become International Harvester.

Now, in 1934 the business of the Morgan bank was split up and J. P. Morgan and Company became a bank in the sense of the word that people who grew up after the depression would understand, without knowing any other sense.

CHAPTER

VI

THE CHANGING SCENE

Following the disappointing actions of Congress and the Roosevelt administration in 1934, Jack Morgan began to withdraw from active participation in the business in the manner that Pierpont had done after the panic of 1907. He was sixty-seven years old, two years past the age that would be considered time for retirement in a society given ever more to consideration of the welfare of every segment of the population. That year, in the winter, Jack went on a long yachting trip aboard the *Corsair*, a cruise very fashionable in that day, to the British West Indies and especially to the Galápagos Islands. The *Corsair* touched at St. Kitts and at Puerto Rico, where she was greeted with suitable awe —the largest and most munificent private yacht in the entire world.

The following season the pinch of depression struck home to Jack Morgan. He laid up the *Corsair* as too expensive to use— along with a dozen other millionaires who either sold or drydocked their yachts indefinitely. The laying up of the *Corsair* represented the end of an era; yachting on the scale of Pierpont and Jack was coming to be beyond the means of all but rajahs and Greek shipping millionaires of the future.

That year Jack sold the Fra Angelico painting *Madonna with*

Child and put five paintings up for sale plus a number of valuable miniatures. He sold paintings by Rubens, Filippo Lippi, Frans Hals, Holbein, and others. He was feeling the pinch. It made little difference to his manner of life, if it curtailed the lavishness of it. Late that summer he was host in Scotland at grouse shooting to the Duke of York.

Although his activity in the business world was diminished, Jack did not retire from the world of affairs. He continued as had Pierpont to be a member of the board of trustees of the Metropolitan Museum of Art, and in 1935 Jack was re-elected senior warden of St. John's Church, Lattingtown, the church for which he had done almost as much as Pierpont did for St. George's.

In 1936, having suffered a heart attack, ill from neuritis and other ailments, Jack was troubled with the feeling of his morality. He began putting his house in order, a much more complicated procedure in the 1930's than it had been twenty years before in Pierpont's time. Most of the art collection and many valuables were sold in order to make the estate liquid. The danger was that if the estate was tied up in properties it would be so solid and unmanageable that much of the value would be lost in the forced selling for tax purposes. There were huge new taxes to be considered now: income taxes, of course, and gift taxes, and death taxes. These latter were established to wipe out inherited wealth more than as a measure for the raising of revenue, although they raised large sums of revenue in wiping out the wealth. In 1920 the death taxes on an estate of $50,000,000 had been about $2,000,000 altogether. In 1938 they would take $28,000,000, or more than half. And in 1944 the death taxes would rise to the point where one millionaire, who died carelessly, leaving an estate of $36,000,000, had planned so badly that his heirs received only $6,000,000 or one-sixth of his holdings.

Nineteen hundred and thirty-six—that was the year that partner Thomas W. Lamont said wryly that money was the root of all evil. No, said Jack cheerfully, it was not the money that was so evil, it was the love of money. This quality was one that no Morgan ever exhibited, quite unlike the Morgan peers in the world of the very rich.

It did not do Jack Morgan much good to look down on money as servant and not master, however. His government continued to suspect that somehow he was sitting by, waiting for a chance to take over everything. In the munitions scandals and investigations of 1936, the Morgans were accused of fomenting World War I and of profiting exorbitantly from it. In 1939 a Senate committee investigating business charged that Jack Morgan maintained a monopoly in railroad finance. The charge was not true, but that did not stop it from appearing prominently in the press, nor did it stop millions of Americans from believing it. Jack listened, heard, and went about his own activities. That summer King George VI was his guest at grouse shooting in Scotland. That summer, too, John Pierpont Morgan, II, old Pierpont's great-grandson through Jack and Junius, spent the summer working as a farmhand in the family tradition of work, now a tradition hardened and expanded.

Jack Morgan's health became precarious in these years and his retirements from various activities came regularly. In 1939 he retired from the board of trustees of the American Museum of Natural History. He resigned as a director of the Aetna Insurance Company, a post that was dear to his heart because of his great-grandfather's part in founding that company and making it into a great institution. This was the year that Jack Morgan took an extensive cruise to Athens and the Greek Islands.

In 1940 the further effects of the new economics of the Roosevelt administration made themselves felt in the banking world and particularly in the Morgan partnership. It had become increasingly difficult for the bank to attempt to compete with the huge corporate banks. The banking laws of the 1930's cut the House of Morgan down to size, but they contributed to the swelling of the First National City Bank, the Chase National Bank, and other corporate banking organizations. To compete, by 1940, the Morgan partners decided it was far better to incorporate. One reason for this, of course, was the ever-growing rate of taxation on personal incomes and partnerships. A corporation was far better equipped to fight for its life in the tax struggle between business and government which had come to dominate all other activity.

The American system now favored the corporation above any other form of business activity and to hold out was senseless. J. P. Morgan and Company severed its old relationship with Drexel and Company of Philadelphia and incorporated to become a trust company as well as a bank. This brought in a new type of business which, in part, offset the loss, four years before, of the very important securities management. The Morgans sold their stock exchange seats, since no banker could also be a stockbroker. The partners all became directors of the corporation.

The *Corsair*, which had become so expensive to maintain, was disposed of at the beginning of World War II by giving her to the British to become an emergency patrol vessel. When the United States entered the war after Pearl Harbor, Jack's two sons entered the service, both as officers in the United States Navy. Junius had been in the Navy before, during World War I when he was but a stripling; on the declaration of war, although he was just out of college and just joining the firm, he had enlisted in the Naval Coast Defense Reserve.

His younger brother, Henry, had been too young at sixteen for that war. In the second war, Junius became an officer in destroyers and served in England, ending the war with the rank of captain. Henry entered service as a lieutenant. He was assigned for a time to the munitions board, working on procurement, since that was a traditional Morgan function, but shortly after the war began he secured an appointment to the newly formed Office of Strategic Services under General William B. Donovan, and spent the war in secret work that was publicly known for its romanticism and heroics.

In the winter of 1943 Jack Morgan had gone to Florida to escape the northern cold, at the Gasparilla Hotel in Boca Grande, an island forty miles northwest of Fort Myers for a fishing vacation. On February 25 he suffered a stroke. On March 2 he suffered another. He was seventy-five years old and this was not unexpected, particularly since he had been ill for half a dozen years. Henry Morgan and his sister, Mrs. Paul G. Pennoyer, came to the island to be with their father. On March 12 he died, a much misunderstood man even to the end, because of his foreign ways, and the history of the business he had carried on in the family name. Jack had held to the family maxim of keeping business on a high level. "Do your work," he had said, "be honest; keep your word; help when you can; be fair." These were his maxims, much as they were his father's, although Pierpont had not stated them in quite this way. But Jack was far better known for another statement. In 1936, at about the time of the Nye investigation into the part played by bankers and munitions makers in fomenting World War I (if any, as it turned out) Jack had counseled against the destruction of the "leisure class." To a world versed now in Thorsten Veblen's writing, it seemed an ugly statement. Jack's hasty addition that anyone who could afford to hire a maid belonged to the leisure class rang hollowly in the land, for in that time anyone who earned one hundred dollars a week could afford to hire a maid for perhaps twenty dollars a month and board and room. Men without property, without money to belong to the leisure class? That was not what Jack Morgan meant, and the world knew it. He had meant, of course, that from the leisure class still stemmed a certain appreciation of arts and literature, but these words fell, in the way that he stated them, on deaf ears. The world's impression of the Morgans did not change up until the day of his death.

CHAPTER

VII

THE END OF THE HOUSE
OF MORGAN

At one time the fortune of John Pierpont Morgan, Jr., had been estimated to be in the neighborhood of $500,000,000. It is doubtful if it ever reached so high a figure, no matter on what basis of the blue sky or watered assets one might consider it, art collection, yachts, and all. With his death the conspicuous consumption of the Morgans ceased almost altogether. The yacht was gone. The Hertfordshire County Council in England took over the Aldenham estate. The Matinecock Point estate eventually became a Catholic nunnery. Jack Morgan's fortune was much diminished by the time of his death. It was said then to be $16,000,000 (largely split between the sons). In 1947, when it was still in process of settlement, the firm gave the figure as less than $5,000,000.

When the war ended, and the two sons of the House of Morgan returned to civilian life, they were going separate ways. Junius was an officer of J. P. Morgan and Company. The bank now fell on less profitable days than in the past, partly because foreign investments in American enterprise were greatly diminished by the Second World War. Another reason was a change in direction in American industry. The old industries had been railroads, steel, and automobiles. The new industries were plastics, aluminum, air-planes, and defense-space. The diffusion of investment among many banking houses cut down the Morgan influence in these industries, and the direct loaning of money by the government to various industries cut it still further. The House of Morgan, the J. P. Morgan and Company bank, when all was said and done, was not the most important banking institution in the United States. It was twelfth most important in size and assets, and had been well down the list even in Pierpont's day. The "control" that the Morgans were always supposed to have enjoyed, much discussed by the radical press, existed very largely in people's minds, and where there was reason for it, much of that control was maintained because of the character of the Morgans and the seeking out of this firm by businessmen for management of financial affairs. In the 1950's, H. P. Davison was president of the J. P. Morgan and Company bank. Junius Morgan was a vice-president.

Junius Morgan's son, John Pierpont Morgan II, came into the firm to become a banker, so in a sense a certain continuity was assured of Morgans in the House of Morgan. That continuity was wiped out, really, in 1958 when the company became a corpora-tion, and then the direction and structure further changed in that year when J. P. Morgan and Company merged, in the fashion of the times, with the Guaranty Trust Company of New York City, an old Morgan bank, but now virtually an independent one. This made the Morgan Guaranty Trust Company the third largest bank in the city of New York and the fourth largest bank in the United States. (The larger ones are the Chase Manhattan, the First Na-tional City Bank, which represented a merger of the old Morgan allies First National and National City, and the Bank of America, an entirely independent and different variety of institution which controlled much West Coast banking.)

All the while, even to the day of the merger, there were voices in America that shouted out charges against the Morgans, and continued to insist that the Morgan firm controlled much of Amer-ican industry and was continuing to try to control it all. Repre-sentative Emmanuel Celler of New York in 1958 was critical of the motivations of the Morgans in seeking merger, and suggested that it was against the national interest. It was the old deep suspicion, restated. In the merger H. C. Alexander of Guaranty became chairman of the board and chief executive. J. L. Cleveland became executive committee chairman, and H. P. Davison and T. S. Lamont were only vice-chairmen. D. E. Sharp was president. No Morgan was even in the top listing of the officials of the new corporation.

When the merger was made, the United States Department of Justice began an investigation of the merger. It would have to do that, because historically the Department of Justice had looked upon the Morgan bank with suspicion since passage of the earliest antitrust legislation at the end of the nineteenth century. But even after exhaustive efforts to discover something that might be wrong the Department of Justice could not find any reason to void the merger, and it was carried out in 1959. It swallowed up the London branch of the bank, and merged with Morgan et Companie of Paris in that year, Morgan et Companie having succeeded Morgan, Harjes on the death of M. Harjes.

There was no shortage of Morgans, of male descendants to carry on the name of the family, or even of the work. Henry Morgan had married Catherine Adams (of the Adams family of Massachusetts) in 1923, and five sons had been born to them: Henry Sturgis, Jr., Charles Francis, Miles, John Adams, and Peter Angus —names (except the last) easily recognizable to students of American history and the Morgan genealogy. As second son, Henry had abandoned the name Pierpont to the other line, but Henry Morgan was to come closer to being a banker in the sense of his lineage than ever could the Morgans of his brother's branch. In the Morgan Guaranty Trust Company, the Morgans would be part of that "nation of hired men, hired by great aggregations of capital" of which the Morgans had spoken at the time of the 1933 Senate banking committee hearings. The heir to the important and lasting part of the Morgan tradition was Henry Sturgis Morgan, who had chosen to become investment banker instead of remaining in the commercial banking field. Investment banking, not commercial banking, was what had made the Morgan name.

In 1934, faced with the immediate loss of the underwriting business of dozens of Morgan companies because of the change in the banking laws, Henry Morgan saw the opportunity and responsibility to carry on this aspect of the firm's affairs. With other partners of the Morgan and Drexel houses (he had been a Morgan partner since 1929) Henry formed the investment banking firm of Morgan, Stanley and Company. At first the firm was a corporation, but this did not suit the firm's activities very well, and so in 1941 it was reduced to a partnership.

The firm had no direct connection with the House of Morgan (in spite of the paranoia of certain legislators) unless one would say that Henry Sturgis' being the son of J. P. Morgan, Jr., and brother of Junius Morgan would make the formation of the firm automatically a conspiracy.

The firm had one aspect of conspiracy, perhaps: it was founded on the old Morgan tradition "of doing only first class business, and that in a first class way." It set out to manage offerings of stocks and bonds to finance new industry, expansion of old industry, and governments of the world. In twenty-five years the firm managed $20,000,000,000 worth of securities, by far the major part of this amount sold to the public at large through various brokerage houses around the United States and abroad. It also participated as member of a syndicate in some $750,000,000 worth of issues. By far the most part of its business was as manager or co-manager, in other words, as organizer of the syndicate if there was a syndicate.

The banking laws of 1933 and thereafter did not prevent the private, investment bankers from dealing in stocks and bonds on the marketplace, as they did the commercial banks. Soon, Morgan, Stanley was buying and selling stocks, too, for its clients—not on its own account particularly—and in later years it was providing "services in connection with the acquisition or sale of companies," a matter of growing importance in a world of continuing mergers.

Morgan Stanley provided another important service: financial advisory services where financing was not directly involved. This meant advice and plans for long-range finance, recapitalization, purchases and sales and mergers and assistance in dealing with the federal and state governments. This was much of a piece with the work of Pierpont in the days of the nineteenth century, although in those days there were not so many names for various services and not nearly so much red tape or complication in the management of business finance.

Here is an indication of the work done by Morgan, Stanley in a quarter of a century:

For the World Bank or International Bank for Reconstruction and Development of the nations of the world, Morgan, Stanley floated $1,135,000,000 in loans. It issued bonds for the Argentine Republic, Australia, the city of Brisbane, Belgium, Canada, British Columbia, the British Columbia Toll Highways and Bridges Authority, the Pacific Great Eastern Railway of the province; France, and Italy. It issued securities for many scores of business firms, including such old Morgan-connected names as DuPont, General Electric, General Motors, United States Steel; and such new ones as Grand Union, Texas Instrument, Bendix, Chemstrand, and Merck. It marketed $3,750,000,000 in telephone company securities of the various companies, and $3,500,000,000 worth of public utility offerings. It was still involved in railroads, including the New York Central, until the Vanderbilts and their allies lost control in 1954. But some old railroad names tied up with Morgan were still there: Chicago, Burlington and Quincy, the Erie, the Great Northern, Louisville and Nashville, and the Richmond Terminal and the other lines that made up the Southern system. Now there was a difference. They also financed the great banks: The First National City, J. P. Morgan, and the Morgan Guaranty Trust. International Harvester, the successor, several times removed, of Cyrus McCormick, was still with the Morgan firm.

The constancy of these associations must have in part accounted for the suspicion with which the Morgan, Stanley Company among all investment banking houses was regarded by the various agencies of federal government. Then, too, by dividing banking as it had done, the federal government had created serious problems of its own.

The commercial banks, except for the issuance of their own securities, and perhaps certain trust company operations, were outside the realm of the Securities and Exchange Commission, which supervised the dealings of businessmen in the stock and bond markets. Their activities would be controlled by the antitrust division of the Department of Justice. But the investment bankers seemed to fall within the purview of both government agencies. And thereby, late in the 1940's, came a great difficulty, arising from the conflicts of interest of the government agencies.

In 1948 the federal government filed a case against the seventeen major investment banking houses in America, charging them basically with conspiracy to control business in the United States. (The charge, of course, was far more complicated.) Two years passed before the case could be brought to trial, and then three years passed in trial, during which the taxpayers' pockets were relieved of the cost of 32,000 pages of transcript and of preparing and displaying 2,500 exhibits. How many hundreds of thousands, perhaps millions of dollars, were spent by the various defendants in lawyers' fees?

The case was tried by Federal Judge Harold R. Medina, who had achieved a reputation for fair dealings on the bench in his trial of various Communist cases in the 1940's. After listening for several months, Judge Medina decided to learn all he could about the securities business. He heard one witness who impressed him greatly: Harold Stuart of the firm of Halsey Stuart and Company. During some testimony by Stuart, Medina asked many test questions to secure fundamental answers and ascertain fundamental attitudes. Finally he decided that he could trust Stuart, and then went to the Halsey Stuart offices to observe the entire process of a securities issue. Then, after more study and consideration, the judge was ready to act.

The federal government charged that the conspiracy among the investment banking houses had existed since 1915. Medina considered all the evidence, all 32,000 pages of it that had assaulted his eyes and ears.

Finally he said this: the charges of the government that a monopoly existed were completely fictional, and they were not even brought in very good faith. The government's attorneys kept trying to shift the ground of the trial as one contention after another was blown up as unsound. It was difficult for Judge Medina

to understand why the case had been brought at all, except for
what he called the "head-on collision of the SEC on the one hand
and the antitrust division of the Department of Justice on the
other."

It was difficult, the judge said, for him to put out of his mind
the thought that the government was trying to cover up the lack
of evidence to support its charges—that was why the government
at the end of the trial kept trying to amend its complaints.

Altogether the case came to a head in October 1953, when
Judge Medina threw it out of court. The government had been
trying to prove that the bankers operated on the traditional banker
concept, which meant the first underwriter had, by unwritten law,
the first chance at the securities of that particular company from
that point on; the historical position concept, which meant that in
a syndicate all the parties would in future have the same lineup for
other syndicates; the reciprocity concept, which meant that if one
banker gave another a part of an underwriting he would expect
the other to reciprocate, and over twenty years the books should
be balanced with equal favors.

Medina threw them all out. He said he saw in the investment
banking business the signs of keen competition. He put it this way,
in terms of O. Otto Kahn, one of the wiliest of bankers and also
one who claimed to be most gentle, and unassuming, and who
looked as though he was incapable of taking candy away from a
baby, or of any argument with anyone.

"Under this façade, however," the judge said, "we shall find
shrewd and ingenious method used to get business of the highest
quality whilst all the time protesting that the firm would never,
never take business away from another banker."

The fact was, as Henry Morgan put it, that the investment banking business was among the most competitive in the world. Many
seemed to be fooled by the Wall Street camaraderie—forgetting
that traditionally in Wall Street everyone is friendly to everyone
else, but is also inclined to watch only curiously if the throat of
a competitor is cut and the blood flows. Many of the men of Wall
Street belong to the same clubs, they drink in the same bars and
eat in the same restaurants and go to the same house parties. They

may participate in syndicates to float the latest candidate for defense of the America's Cup. Yet they are deadly competitors in business, and in matters of business in Wall Street any weapon is considered to be fair, as long as it is gentlemanly on the exterior and does not outrage the community. It does not do to denounce one's competitors in the public rooms of the Bankers' Club; one can do it all so much more genteelly with a handful of statistics spread out on the damask tablecloth in one's own private dining room.

"It matters not whether the members of the team be called 'partners,' 'quasi-partners,' 'joint adventurers' or what not; the significant fact vis-à-vis the Sherman Act is that they are acting together on a single, integrated, unitary, cooperative enterprise, the purpose of which is not 'raising, fixing, pegging, or stabilizing the price' of anything nor the exercise of any manner of control over general market prices, but solely the distribution of a new security in an orderly manner."

That was a part of Judge Medina's 424-page opinion, dismissing the case against the bankers. He said he thought it futile to continue, forever, to "be threshing over the old straw of 1934–36" in considering the activities of banking houses. He might have gone further and said the old straw began souring in 1912 with the Pujo Committee hearings and the never-ending talk about the "spider web" of national and international finance.

Judge Medina's decision was so obviously a learned one, made by the first jurist (or anyone outside the financial community) to take the time to study the banking business and learn it thoroughly. The *New York Times* said editorially that "here is a treatise on investment banking that must be reckoned as at least supplementary reading to any existing textbook on the subject of investment banking."

Were Judge Medina's decision to be accepted and followed by future generations of government officials, perhaps the new House of Morgan could rid itself and the rest of the banking world of the stigma under which they had lived for half a century, and the bankers could be considered as citizens on the basis of their individual contributions to American society.

In the 1960's, the old House of Morgan dead and gone, the Morgans continued to contribute to the society in which they lived. One of Henry Morgan's sons was a captain in the United States Navy, a career officer. Another was a partner in the Morgan, Stanley firm. A third was a musician. A fourth was a partner in the banking firm of Dominick and Dominick, and the fifth, newly out of college, was spending a few years as were many hundreds of thousands of other American youths, as an enlisted man in the service of his country—learning to run an atomic reactor aboard an atomic submarine.

For many years the Morgans had enjoyed wealth and privilege. Pierpont's education was exceptional for his day. Jack's education, at St. Paul's School in New Hampshire, most closely approximated that of an English public school boy of his day. Jack's sons, Junius and Henry, both attended Groton, for the simple reason that Samuel Endicott Peabody, a partner in the Junius S. Morgan firm, asked that they be sent to the Reverend Endicott Peabody's school for boys. It was a matter of family association, and if the Morgan family's associations have long been linked with the course of American history, well that is the way it was.

The Morgans have long been castigated as baronial types who have moved out of the mainstream of American society (to use a phrase the American Communist Party is fond of using). But have they so moved? Have they ever been out of the stream? The record is here for all to see. America is a business community and the Morgans are businessmen above all, and always have been since the days of Miles, first descendant of the line we have studied, as opposed to the other line of the family, which produced diplomats, scholars, sailing-ship captains, and soldiers as well as businessmen.

Following this pattern, John Pierpont Morgan II was in 1962 named a trustee of the Atlantic Mutual Insurance Company and a director of the Centennial Insurance Company. Other Morgans were deeply involved in other affairs, corporate and civic: the Morgan Library, which was a public institution, the Metropolitan Museum of Art, the Carnegie Institution, The American Fund for the Blind. Certainly they belonged to the best clubs of New York

City, the New York Yacht Club, Links, Lunch, Brook, Century Association, Recess, Pinnacle, and San Francisco's Bohemian—in the case of Henry Sturgis Morgan. But so did many others, and that was not the point. The point in the middle of the twentieth century, the only sound fundamental basis for considering this family as a family and worthy of biography as group, was to discover what relationship the Morgans had to American society. The answer lies in these pages, a simple enough answer: they have represented wealth and social position for at least six generations and the continuity of American history since the days of the *Mayflower*. They have been Americans as long as nearly anyone. How they have comported themselves, how their fortune grew, and whether they have deserved what fortune has bestowed upon them, in riches and in slings and arrows, these are matters for the reader to judge.

NOTES

Introduction

The discussion of the place of the Morgans in America, which is carried throughout the book, is the basic raison d'être for the work. The author became interested in the accomplishments of the Morgans and their place in the social history of America, through noting in writings of Cleveland Amory, the historian of what is or is not Society, the observations that Morgans were somehow apart from the majority of wealthy families, both in power and their social proclivities and their use of wealth. The book really is a part of the author's continuing study of wealth and power in American society, of which *The Vanderbilts and Their Fortunes* and *Marilyn* are also parts. With the Morgans, as with these others, there are divergent views as to their places and the tenor of their actions. There always will be divergent views. With the Morgans, in particular, there has been much misreading and misjudgment of the men and their actions, and the author attributes this to the changing morality of American business, or at least the changing moral climate in which American business works, plus the ease with which people of one generation can look back on another and see venality and purpose where neither may have existed.

The Morgans have been placed among the despoilers by the important chroniclers of American business: Gustavus Myers in his *History of the Great American Fortunes,* Ferdinand Lundberg in *America's Sixty Families,* John T. Flynn in *Men of Wealth,* Lewis Corey in *The House of Morgan.* Stewart Holbrook dealt more gently with the Morgans in *The Age of the Moguls,* but even he was bemused by the trappings more than the substance; small

402

wonder, because the age of the American Moguls was an age of enormous conspicuous consumption, foolishness, and waste, which could not but impress itself on Americans of succeeding generations when such waste was considered gaudy and gauche.

PART ONE: The Morgan Clan

Chapter I. Migration

For the general background of the Morgans the author relied on *The Historian's History of the World,* published by Henry Smith Williams, Outlook Company, New York, 1904, and the Morgan genealogies cited in the bibliography. Much of the general information about Massachusetts comes from the authoritative Hutchinson's *History of Massachusetts.* Certain papers in the possession of the Connecticut Historical Society tell of original and later holdings by the Morgans. The story of the Indian uprising and attack on Springfield is compiled from several sources.

Chapter II. The Morgans of Massachusetts

Herbert Satterlee's privately printed life of J. Pierpont Morgan was very valuable in the re-creation of the life and times of these early Morgans as was Hutchinson's *History of Massachusetts.* Various materials relative to the Morgans were found in the Connecticut Historical Society offices in Hartford. The story of Shays' Rebellion comes from Hutchinson. The details, or most of them, of the Morgan family, are from Satterlee's original work, which was compiled with the full use of family papers and a diary kept during most of his life by the third Joseph Morgan of the line.

Chapter III. The Base of Fortune

This chapter was prepared from notes made on the various Morgan genealogies, Satterlee, and papers in the Connecticut Historical Society. At some time in the past someone took considerable interest in Joseph Morgan, to the point of tracing through the pages of *The Connecticut Courant* and *The Hartford Courant* (successor to the former) his purchase of the Exchange Coffee House, the events that occurred there, Joseph's honors and activities as reported in the press, and his purchase of the City Hotel.

Chapter IV. The Young Merchant

The basic sources for this chapter were Satterlee and Corey's *House of Morgan.* Although Lewis Corey was inimical to the Morgans in almost every way he was a good scholar and spent much time in Springfield and in Hartford going through records in his tracing of the history of the Morgans. His conclusions are those of his political and economic beliefs, but as to this early period of the family, his facts, where checked against other accounts, were impeccable. The story of the Pierpont family in America comes from the Pierpont genealogy, listed in the bibliography.

Chapter V. A Banker in London

The reconstruction of the life of George Peabody was made after consulting the various works on Peabody as listed in the bibliography, and with particular interest in Emden's *Money Powers in Europe*, as a guideline for the progress of private and American banking in London. The anecdote about James Buchanan comes from the author's *James Buchanan*, Reilly and Lee, Chicago, 1966. Satterlee was also used in this chapter. The long quotation describing life among the moneyed classes of England at the time that the Morgan family arrived there is from Allan Nevins' *Henry White*. The quotations of Pierpont's letters are from Satterlee.

The files of the London *Times* were also used in this chapter. In the years after 1860 until his death George Peabody's name was often mentioned in the British press, particularly after he retired from business and began his many benefices, among them his remarkable gift of housing for the working poor of London, which represented a gesture unprecedented in English society. Also, in this period, the ebb and flow of history is traced through Morris' *Encyclopedia of American History* and through the work of the Beards.

PART TWO: A Banker Emerges

Chapter I. Schoolboy

This chapter relies very heavily on the work of Satterlee, to whom Pierpont gave access to all his papers in a conversation shortly before his death in Rome. Equal access has not been given to other Morgan biographers, the family apparently feeling that Satterlee has done quite enough with the papers. As far as the young Pierpont is concerned this would seem to be an adequate answer, although any biographer would prefer to go back to the original source books. As far as Pierpont's later works are concerned, and those of J. P., Jr., and the rest of the family it is also understandable why the family might not wish to make papers available: many of Pierpont's actions still were germane to American business and industrial developments of the 1960's; Jack Morgan's actions were certainly too fresh; and publication of intimate details of transactions might be embarrassing or cause loss of money or confidence within the business world. Obviously no banker and no banking family can afford to impinge on the confidential relationship between banker and client. If ever an outside biographer is given access to the intimate Morgan papers, most certainly this will come only after all the Morgans are out of the banking business, and perhaps only when the Morgan connection with the Pierpont Morgan Library becomes remote.

Chapter II. Cadet

Satterlee here is again the primary source, although *Baedeker's Switzerland* was consulted for details about the towns and areas involved and *Baedeker's Northern Germany* (1893) was consulted for certain details about Göttingen.

Chapter III. Home to America

Various histories of the United States were consulted to establish the detail of the United States and New York City in the period of Pierpont's earliest activity in the business world. Previous studies made by the author for other books that dealt with New York City were valuable, and need not be listed here, except to say that the complete bibliography is contained in the author's *The Vanderbilts and Their Fortunes.* Satterlee provided much of the intimate detail of the Morgan family during this period, and Satterlee's version of the coffee coup was used here in preference to all the others, in other books about the Morgans, since it seemed the most logical.

Chapter IV. Marriage and Bereavement

Some of the physical description of Pierpont in this chapter comes from Satterlee; much of it comes from examination of photos of him taken during the years under consideration in this chapter, and some notes come from Frederick Lewis Allen's *The Great Pierpont Morgan.* In this chapter the author has examined the Hall Carbine affair with some detail, after reading all the negative accounts, which began with Myers in 1910, and were transmitted by others who wrote about the Morgans, and examining these against the Wasson account, knowing, of course, that the latter was prepared by a member of the House of Morgan. It is most difficult for anyone outside the business world to understand the motivations of men in business, and a century after the Hall Carbine affair it is probably very difficult for anyone to understand how a man might be involved even on the fringes of an attempt to bamboozle the government for private profit and yet consider himself as acting in a thoroughly honorable manner. Still, the age of shoddy is not ended, nor is the age of cheating on defense contracts, as the newspapers attested during World War II and in the years since that date.

Chapter V. Adventures on Wall Street

The story of Pierpont and Edward Ketchum and their gold speculations was written after checking Satterlee and Corey very carefully. Here again it is hard to understand how a young man could conscientiously speculate in the gold market, knowing as he must that this was causing expense and harm to the Union cause in time of war. It seems apparent from all accounts that this was the darkest financial transaction in all Pierpont's life, and that his father approved of it no more than the reader might be expected to approve, for the rapidity with which Pierpont was put under the parental wing once again attests to more than a need for additional help in New York by Junius Morgan's powerful London firm. The author also consulted various accounts of New York and banking in the Civil War period, particularly the Henrietta Larson work on Jay Cooke and Studenski's *Financial History of the United States*.

PART THREE: The Making of the Financier

Chapter I. The First Railroad

Much of the material for this chapter comes from research done by the author in connection with *The Vanderbilts and Their Fortunes*, Doubleday, 1962. The story of Pierpont's trip to the West is told in some detail in Satterlee. The details of Junius' activities in London come from several sources, including the autobiography of Andrew Carnegie. The story of the Albany and Susquehanna struggles comes from Satterlee and from various other accounts, including the negative Corey account, which is inaccurate in several important respects—but then so is Satterlee.

Chapter II. The New Alliance

The story of the gold panic of 1869 has been told many times, in biographies of U. S. Grant, in the author's book on the Vanderbilts, in books on the Goulds and on Jim Fisk. Several of these were consulted. The story of the defense of Paris comes from Elizabeth Latimer's *France in the Nineteenth Century*, the Encyclopaedia Britannica, and other sources. The source of the tale of Pierpont's alliance with Drexel is Satterlee.

Chapter III. Interlude

This chapter comes almost entirely from Satterlee and *The New York Times* files.

Chapter IV. Morgan the Millionaire

This chapter relied heavily on the Jay Cooke story and the Beards, various accounts of the life of Carnegie, the author's bibliography in the Vanderbilt book, Satterlee, and various newspaper files.

Chapter V. Morgan the Negotiator

Satterlee was the source of the tale of Pierpont's informal loan to the United States government to pay the troops. The author's study of the Vanderbilts is the basic source of the discussion of the sale of the New York Central stock. The author has adopted Frederick Lewis Allen's view of Pierpont's private life—which is that it was his personal business and not germane to the study of Morgan as a public figure in America. Corey and Winkler took a different view.

Chapter VI. Morgan the Mediator

The detail of the various financial adventures of Pierpont in this period comes from the files of various newspapers, the Corey book, Satterlee, and Frederick Lewis Allen's *The Great Pierpont Morgan,* and the author's story of the Vanderbilts.

Chapter VII. The Builder

Material for the beginning part of this chapter came from the various works on the Rockefellers and from the Encyclopedia of American History. That material which relates to Pierpont came largely from Satterlee, except as noted in the text.

Chapter VIII. The Art Collector

The anecdote about the Thackeray manuscript came from Satterlee, as did the recounting of the collection, piece by piece. The story of the trip to Hartford came from the files of *The Hartford Courant,* the Connecticut State Historical Society files, and Satterlee.

Chapter IX. Two Deaths

The story of Junius' death came from Satterlee and from various accounts of the life of Frank Harris, who knew Junius well in the days on the Riviera. Various details about the lives of the Morgans came largely from Satterlee, some from newspaper sources.

PART FOUR: The Maturity of Pierpont

Chapter I. The New Company

The story of the financial crash in London comes from Emden's work on European banking, and the story of the development of the Panama Canal comes from the Marshall book cited in the bibliography, and from various histories of the United States. The tale of Junius Morgan and Cecil Rhodes comes from research acquired by the author in preparation of *The Jewel Hunters*, Atlantic-Little, Brown, 1966. Pierpont's letter to Charles Lanier is from Satterlee.

Chapter II. The Gold Affair

Much of the material in this chapter comes from research amassed by the author in preparation of *Grover Cleveland*, Reilly and Lee, Chicago, 1962, and from various biographies of Cleveland consulted in that work. Some are mentioned, some are not, in the bibliography of this book. The best account of Pierpont's part in this affair is that of Frederick Lewis Allen, who went into the records of J. P. Morgan and Company and was allowed to consult the cable books and other private papers. The author has used this account as a guideline. Satterlee was extremely useful for detail. The Satterlee referred to after 1863 is the Macmillan book that was published for general circulation. The privately printed volume, which covers much of the same material, ends with 1863. It was Satterlee's intention to complete a second thorough volume covering Pierpont's life from the birth of his first child until his death. Unfortunately for historians and biographers, somehow Satterlee was diverted from this task and persuaded to the one-volume work, which telescopes the most important part of Pierpont's career and gives it largely without background.

Chapter III. What They Called "The Money Trust"

The story of Pierpont's relations with James J. Hill comes from Satterlee and several biographies of Hill. Pierpont's relations with Cleveland were traced through study of the various biographies of both men.

Chapter IV. The Infant That Was Steel

Satterlee was a basic source for the study of the formation of United States Steel. So were the various books about Carnegie, Ida Tarbell's *Life of Judge Gary,* and various books on the Rockefellers.

Chapter V. The Danger of Thinking Big

The story of the threat to the Northern Pacific system is told in the biography of Hill, in various biographies of Harriman, by Satterlee, and, in quite a different vein, by Corey. Pierpont's relations with Theodore Roosevelt are described in various books about both men, although, oddly enough, Pierpont is scarcely mentioned in Roosevelt's own voluminous writings.

Chapter VI. A Measure of Peace

In this chapter the author leaned heavily on Satterlee and the biographies of James Stillman and George Baker.

Chapter VII. The Commodore's Yachts

The meeting between Pierpont and Cleveland is described in Satterlee and in Nevins' account of Cleveland's life. The stories of the various *Corsairs* come largely from Satterlee, with some reliance on the newspaper files; the tale of Pierpont climbing the rope ladder up the side of the *Oceanic* was as impressive to this author as it had been to Frederick Lewis Allen, and was used for that reason. In a sense, this exploit of 1899 seemed to have the first indication that he was not as young as he used to be.

Chapter VIII. The Morgan Faith

Pierpont's religious activities have been detailed thoroughly in Satterlee, and Frederick Lewis Allen used the relationship with St. George's Church to do what he called "triangulate" Pierpont's character in *The Great Pierpont Morgan*. The author has relied mainly on these two accounts of Pierpont's activities within the church, although at one time the author had some minute connection with St. George's, which was the neighborhood church of the Stuyvesant Square section of New York City even in the 1950's, and some members of the congregation still talked about Pierpont Morgan.

Chapter IX. The Panic of 1907–I

The Satterlee account of the Morgan activities on the eve of the panic of 1907 and during that upheaval is quite thorough, and in this particular instance Satterlee played a role himself, as a secretary to Pierpont during the days and nights of intensive activity. The author has consulted other sources, but where it was a question of what Pierpont was doing at any given time, Satterlee certainly can be relied on, for he was there most of the time. As to motivations, one can find those that he wishes, from Satterlee's hero worship to Corey's iconoclasm, to James Stillman's grudging admiration. The study of the general financial structure of the United States and the banking system comes from a number of sources; from Grayson, and from many sources consulted by the author in his study of Wall Street for *The Tempering Years*, Scribner's, 1963.

Chapter X. The Panic of 1907—II

For the personal story of Pierpont Morgan here Satterlee is again the mainstay. The newspaper files of the New York City Public Library were also helpful.

Chapters XI, XII, and XIII. The Panic of 1907—III, IV, and V

Satterlee was the basic source here, along with Ida Tarbell's life of Gary, Allen, biographies of Roosevelt, and the newspaper reports.

Chapter XIV. The Restless Years

Various studies of the muckrakers and the period, as cited in the bibliography, were used to prepare this chapter. Tarbell was essential, as well as Satterlee, which here functions almost as a diary. The Pujo Committee reports of Congress were studied carefully, and extracted rather extensively, to show the differences in point of view that were emerging in America.

Chapter XV. A Final Voyage

The Taylor work on Pierpont and his library was vital to this chapter. Satterlee, as usual with anything that concerned Pierpont, was important to the story. Some perspective was given by the author's study of the secretive career of Alexander Turney Stewart, the merchant king, who collected expensively to very little avail. He was inclined to buy paintings by the yard, and although he became a patron of Rosa Bonheur, not too much more can be said about Stewart's collection, which was typical.

PART FIVE: The New J. P. Morgan Company

Chapter I. The Banker's Fortune

With Pierpont's death Satterlee's account ends, and since Satterlee was a member of the family, and privileged to use personal information, he was

able to give much to the world about Pierpont Morgan. No such availability of information has yet been offered by the Morgan family about J. P.
Morgan, Jr., and the following members of the family. If they kept diaries
or their private papers for the world to see, it will be some time before the
world sees them. If there seems to be a change in the tone of the book, from
the time of the death of Pierpont, this is a reflection of the paucity of personal detail available about the younger members of the family. Pierpont
learned to shun reporters and he taught his children and grandchildren the
same rule. They followed it ever after. The delicate nature of the banking
business, and its lasting effects on society, and the ever-present dangers of
government interference in what bankers consider to be private affairs,
through antitrust legislation, or government prosecution—all these would
naturally militate in favor of a banking family keeping its affairs to itself.
Almost entirely the subsequent chapters of this book depend on public
sources of information.

Chapter II. Jack Morgan Comes of Age

Sources here were the newspaper and magazine accounts of J. P. Morgan,
Jr.'s career, various books that deal with the Wilson administrations, the
Pujo report, Thomas W. Lamont's book on his foreign experiences.

Chapter III. The Murderous Mr. Holt

The New York Times account of the attack on Jack Morgan was basic here,
although it was checked against other stories, too. Corey and other sources
were useful for different views of the Morgan participation in the war effort,
and Lamont was used extensively.

Chapter IV. The Crash

The author leaned very heavily on his earlier research for *The Tempering
Years* in preparation of this chapter. Quotation of the discussion of the postwar political situation came from the Lamont book. The general atmosphere
was represented in William O. Douglas' speeches, as listed in the bibliography.

Chapter V. Changing Times

Newspapers and the Douglas book were important here, as were other
works cited in the bibliography of *The Tempering Years*, which deals entirely with this period of American social history.

Chapter VI. The Changing Scene

Again the newspapers and the author's study of the 1930's in America were vital to this short chapter.

Chapter VII. The End of the House of Morgan

The material for this chapter came from various contemporary sources, from discussions with people who know a considerable amount about the Morgans but who wish to remain anonymous, from such sources as *Who's Who in America, Current Biography,* and the files of various news magazines, and from the Morgan Stanley Company's progress reports, published for private distribution by that company. The study of the conspiracy case against the investment bankers comes largely from *The New York Times* files of that period.

SPECIAL BIBLIOGRAPHY

(The more general bibliography of times and affairs is included in the Notes. The special bibliography represents works which deal specifically with the Morgans or some time or place of Morgan activity.)

Allen, Frederick Lewis, *Lords of Creation*, Harper and Bros., New York, 1935.

Allen, Frederick Lewis, *The Great Pierpont Morgan*, Harper and Bros., New York, 1949.

Allen, Frederick Lewis, *Only Yesterday*, Harper and Bros., New York, 1931.

Amory, Cleveland, *The Last Resorts*, Harper and Bros., New York, 1952.

Amory, Cleveland, *Who Killed Society?* Harper and Bros., New York, 1960.

Anonymous, *The Mirrors of Wall Street*, G. P. Putnam's Sons, New York, 1933.

Baedeker's Switzerland, Leipzig, 1905.

Barnum, Mary Pierpont, *Genealogy of the Pierpont Family and Connections*, edited by Arthur Edwin Boardman, James Allen Crosby, Boston, 1928.

Baruch, Bernard, *My Own Story*, Henry Holt and Co., New York, 1957.

Beard, Charles A. and Mary R., *The Rise of American Civilization*, 2 volumes, The Macmillan Co., New York, 1927.

Behrman, S. N., *Duveen*, Random House, Inc., New York, 1952.

Bishop, Joseph Bucklin, *Theodore Roosevelt and His Time* (2 volumes), Charles Scribner's Sons, New York, 1920.

Bridge, James Howard, *The Inside History of the Carnegie Steel Company,* Aldine Book Company, New York, 1903.

Brome, Vincent, *Frank Harris,* Cassell and Co., London, 1959.

Brooks, John, *The Seven Fat Years,* Harper and Bros., New York, 1954.

Burr, Anna Robeson, *The Portrait of a Banker: James Stillman,* Duffield and Co., New York, 1927.

Chalmers, David Mack, *The Social and Political Ideas of the Muckrakers,* Citadel Press, New York, 1964.

Commission on Money and Credit, *Private Financial Institutions,* Prentice-Hall, Inc., Englewood Cliffs, New Jersey, 1963.

Corey, Lewis, *The House of Morgan,* G. Howard Watt, New York, 1930.

Curney, J. L. M., *A Brief Sketch of George Peabody Through 30 Years,* Cambridge University Press, 1898.

Current Biography, 1943.

Douglas, William O., *Democracy and Finance,* Yale University Press, New Haven, 1940.

Emden, Paul H., *Money Powers of Europe in the Nineteeth and Twentieth Centuries,* Sampson Low, Marston and Co., London, no date.

Encyclopaedia Britannica.

Encyclopedia of Connecticut Biography, American History Society, New York.

Farley, James A., *Jim Farley's Story,* Whittlesey House, New York, 1948.

Flynn, John T., *God's Gold, The Story of Rockefeller and his Times,* Harcourt, Brace and Co., New York, 1932.

Flynn, John T., *Men of Wealth,* Simon and Schuster, Inc., New York, 1941.

Forman, S. E., *A History of the American People,* George Allen and Unwin, Ltd., London, 1922.

Grayson, Theodore J., *Leaders and Periods of American Finance,* John Wiley and Sons, Inc., New York, 1932.

Griscom, Lloyd C., *Diplomatically Speaking,* Little, Brown and Co., Boston, 1940.

Hanaford, Phebe A., *The Life of George Peabody,* B. B. Russell, Boston, 1870.

Harris, Frank, *Latest Contemporary Portraits,* Macauley, New York, 1927.

Hendrick, Burton J., *The Life and Letters of Walter H. Page,* Doubleday, Page and Co., Garden City, New York, 1922.

Holbrook, Stewart H., *The Age of the Moguls,* Doubleday and Co., Garden City, N. Y., 1953.

Hoyt, Edwin P., *The Tempering Years,* Charles Scribner's Sons, New York, 1963.

Hoyt, Edwin P., *The Vanderbilts and Their Fortunes,* Doubleday and Co., Garden City, N. Y., 1962.

Hutchinson, *History of Massachusetts.*

Jones, Jesse and with Edward Angly, *Fifty Billion Dollars*, The Macmillan Co., New York, 1951.

Josephson, Matthew, *The Robber Barons*, Harcourt, Brace and Co., New York, 1934.

Kelen, Emery, *Peace in Their Time*, Alfred A. Knopf, New York, 1963.

Lamont, Thomas W., *Across World Frontiers*, Privately Printed, New York, 1950.

Larson, Henrietta, Jay Cooke, *Private Banker*, Harvard University Press, Cambridge, 1936.

Latimer, Elizabeth Wormeley, *France in the Nineteenth Century, 1830–1890*, A. C. McClurg and Co., Chicago, 1894.

Lord, Walter, *The Good Years*, Harper and Bros., New York, 1960.

Loucks, H. L., *The Great Conspiracy of the House of Morgan Exposed and How to Defeat It*, Privately Printed, 1916.

Lundberg, Ferdinand, *America's Sixty Families*, The Vanguard Press, New York, 1937.

Marshall, Logan, *The Story of the Panama Canal*, no publisher, 1913.

McElroy, Robert, *Grover Cleveland, the Man and the Statesman*, Harper and Bros., 1923.

Morgan, Appleton, *The History of the Family of Morgan, 1089 to Present*, undated.

Morgan, Nathaniel H., *Morgan Genealogy, A History of James Morgan of New London, Connecticut and his Descendants from 1607 to 1869*, Case, Lockwood and Brainard, Hartford, 1869.

The Morgan Fund, *Wadsworth Athenaeum*, Hartford, Connecticut.

Morris, Richard B., *Encyclopedia of American History*, Harper and Bros., New York, 1953.

Myers, Gustavus, *History of the Great American Fortunes*, 3 volumes, Charles H. Kerr and Co., New York, 1909–1911.

Nevins, Allan, *Henry White, Thirty Years of American Diplomacy*, Harper and Bros., New York, 1930.

Nevins, Allan, editor, *Times of Trial*, Alfred A. Knopf, New York, 1958.

O'Connor, Harvey, *The Guggenheims*, Covici-Friede, New York, 1937.

Perlo, Victor, *The Empire of High Finance*, International Publishers, New York, 1957.

Pickering, William, *An Account of the Proceedings at dinner given by Mr. George Peabody to the Americans connected with the Great Exhibition at the London Coffee House, Ludgate Hill, on 27 October 1851*, Privately Printed.

Pitkin, Albert Hastings, *The Morgan Collection*, Hartford, 1918.

Representative Men of Connecticut, The Massachusetts Publishing Co., Everett, Mass., 1894.

Root, E. Merrill, *Frank Harris*, The Odyssey Press, New York, 1947.

Saarinen, Aline B., *The Proud Possessors*, Random House, Inc., New York, 1958.

Satterlee, Herbert L., *J. Pierpont Morgan, An Intimate Portrait*, The Macmillan Co., New York, 1939.

Satterlee, Herbert L., *The Life of J. Pierpont Morgan*, Privately Printed, New York, 1937.

Schlesinger, Arthur M., Jr., *The Coming of the New Deal*, Houghton Mifflin Co., Boston, 1959.

Schlesinger, Arthur M., Jr., *The Crisis of the Old Order*, Houghton Mifflin Co., Boston, 1957.

Seldes, George, *One Thousand Americans*, Boni and Gaer, New York, 1947.

Seymour, Charles, *The Intimate Papers of Colonel House*, Houghton Mifflin Co., Boston, 1926.

Smith, Arthur D. Howden, *Men Who Run America*, The Bobbs-Merrill Co., Indianapolis, 1935.

Starr, Frank Farnsworth, *The Miles Morgan Family of Springfield, Mass, in the line of Joseph Morgan of Hartford, Conn, 1780–1847*, Tuttle, Morehouse and Taylor Co., Hartford, 1904.

Tarbell, Ida M., *The Life of Elbert H. Gary*, D. Appleton-Century Co., New York, 1933.

Thayer, William Roscoe, *The Life and Letters of John Hay*, two volumes, Houghton Mifflin Co., Boston, 1908.

Wasson, R. Gordon, *The Hall Carbine Affair*, Privately Printed, New York, 1941.

Wecter, Dixon, *The Saga of American Society*, Charles Scribner's Sons, New York, 1937.

Who's Who in America, 1920–1960, A. N. Marquis Co., Chicago.

Williams, Henry Smith, *History of the World*, Outlook Co., New York, 1904.

Winkler, John K., *The First Billion, The Stillmans and the National City Bank*, The Vanguard Press, New York, 1934.

Winkler, John K., *Incredible Carnegie*, The Vanguard Press, New York, 1931.

Winkler, John K., *Morgan the Magnificent*, Garden City Publishing Co., Garden City, N. Y., 1930.

Woodward, W. E., *A New American History*, Garden City Publishing Co., Garden City, N. Y., 1938.

PAMPHLETS AND BOOKLETS

"Guide to the Loan Exhibition of the J. Pierpont Morgan Collection," 1914.

"Investigation of Financial and Monetary Conditions in the United States under House Resolutions Nos. 429 and 504 before a Subcommittee of the Committee on Banking and Currency," Government Printing Office, 1913, 62nd Congress.

"Investigation of the United States Steel Corporation under House Resolution 148," 62nd Congress.

"Morgan, J. P. and Company, Reprints of statements submitted by members of J. P. Morgan and Company to Senate Committee on Banking and Currency," 1934.

"Morgan Stanley Company, Summary of Financing," 1965.

Taylor, Francis Henry, "Pierpont Morgan as Collector and Patron, 1837–1913," Pierpont Morgan Library, 1957.

NEWSPAPERS AND MAGAZINES

American Heritage, The American Mercury, The Hartford Courant and its predecessor *The Conecticut Courant, The* London *Times, The New York Herald, The New York Times, The New York Tribune, World's Work.*

INDEX